THE MORTAL NO:

DEATH AND THE
MODERN IMAGINATION

   . . . The mortal no

Has its emptiness and tragic expirations.
The tragedy, however, may have begun,
Again, in the imagination's new beginning,
In the yes of the realist spoken because he must
Say yes, spoken because under every no
Lay a passion for yes that had never been broken.

—WALLACE STEVENS, from
Part VIII of *Esthétique du Mal*

THE MORTAL NO:

DEATH AND THE
MODERN IMAGINATION

BY

FREDERICK J. HOFFMAN

PRINCETON, NEW JERSEY
PRINCETON UNIVERSITY PRESS
1964

FREDERICK J. HOFFMAN,
presently at the University of California
at Riverside, has taught at the University of Wisconsin,
the Ohio State University, Harvard University,
and elsewhere. He has been
a Fulbright Professor in France and Italy.
The best known of his several works are *Freudianism
and the Literary Mind*, *The Twenties*,
The Little Magazine, and *The Modern Novel in America*.
In addition, he has published books
on Gertrude Stein, William Faulkner, Conrad Aiken,
and Samuel Beckett

Printed in the United States of America
by Vail-Ballou Press, Inc., Binghamton, New York

TO WARREN SUSMAN

For Many Reasons
This Book is
GRATEFULLY DEDICATED

PREFACE

THIS book studies as elaborately as possible an important series of phenomena in modern literature. They do not uniquely belong to our century, except perhaps in the pace and intensity of the circumstances in which they are developed in our time. The title should help to explain: it is from a line in Part VIII of Wallace Stevens' *Esthétique du Mal,* which opens with a familiar line, "The death of Satan was a tragedy / For the imagination. . . ." Stevens plays upon the conceit of Satan's disappearance as "A capital / Negation. . . ." The history of my subject includes an analysis of the major metaphors which helped to define the human economy and to relate it to divinity, what Stevens calls the "phantoms": a word we may perhaps characterize as suggesting the opportunities the imagination has had in the past to invent and create in terms of the central facts of man's existing in time, which "must have a stop." The "phantoms" are the metaphors that assuage death and connect it with eternity.

My introduction is sufficiently extended and detailed to provide a full explanation of my special uses of the three governing terms: *grace, violence,* and *self.* Generally, I move from the discussion of nineteenth century backgrounds into the description of twentieth century conditions. Part One opens with a long chapter on the problem of manners, historical situations, and ideologies; the chapter which follows it is concerned largely with the twentieth century consequences: the transference of terms from one category or level of beliefs to another, the paradoxes of interrelationship of the sacred and the secular levels of interpreting time and death.

Part Two is the core of the twentieth century issue. It is concerned with pace, degree, volume, distance: and also, essentially, with both moral and literary issues. That is, my contention is that the intensity of modern violence has radically disturbed and upset the interrelationship of assailant and victim. The several variants of this metaphor are analyzed in terms of the literatures related to it. For the most part, this central section is devoted to modern times and to the two major wars in our century, though I have on occasion pointed out nineteenth century parallels and precedents. Since the metaphor is largely a visual one, the literary representation of the moral nature of man and his relationship to the scene in which he lives, on which he has an influence, are strongly emphasized.

Inevitably, the themes of this study conclude with a discussion, in Part Three, of the problem of rehabilitating, of reconstituting the self. Part of this situation is concerned with the paradoxes of temporality and eternity, which are especially well manifested in the contrasting poetry of Wallace Stevens and T. S. Eliot, though there are many other illustrations of them. I try to give a full measure of attention to them in chapter 11 of this last section. Beyond that I explore the personal forms of improvisation in self-definition, the metaphors and habits of creative invention in James Joyce and D. H. Lawrence. In the last two chapters, I suggest the kinds of existential "situationality" with which so much of modern literature is concerned. It comes to the issue of willing value and meaning, and choosing the situation in which they will be enacted and dramatized.

There is much more to be said. There are many more examples in modern literature than I have used. I cannot say that an entirely different set of literatures would have served as well. I have had to limit the scope of my treatment; the alternative would have been a ten-volume work, which would have been heavily weighted with instances and not nearly so speculatively engaged as this book. There are a number of related matters that I hope to take up in future essays or books. But I feel that what follows is pertinent and rich and deep enough—'twill

PREFACE

serve. Above all, the ground has been broken; important definitions have been made and metaphors relocated and defined. I have developed an elaborate definition of what I call "thematics" in an essay in *Proceedings of the First Conference on the Teaching of Modern Literature*, published by the Michigan State University Press, spring of 1962.

There is always a risk involved in engaging with matters so large, so central, so important. All things are relevant, and the danger of disorder is great. For this reason, I have thought of a set of terms that permit a wide scope of application but also force, by necessity, a precision of limit and definition. There are qualitative differences in experience, brought about by circumstances which are related to history. The special terms according to which modern circumstances have forced us to look at the prospect of death and the relationship of time to our expectation of it are my special province in this book. I hope that the impact upon the "mortal no" will be more clearly seen, upon all of us who are engaged in finding alternative "phantoms," in filling our lives that are in danger of being deprived. In any case, the book which follows offers a set of major speculations concerning the condition of "no" and the desperate interest in the "yes" that underlies it.

FREDERICK J. HOFFMAN

Riverside, California
August 26, 1963

ACKNOWLEDGMENTS

WORK ON THIS BOOK began in the summer of 1956. In the years that followed, I have had many occasions to feel grateful to persons and universities, for financial assistance, for encouragement, and above all for the kind of sharp, discerning, and co-operative analysis of my ideas without which no set of ideas could become a book.

In the summer of beginnings, I was awarded a research grant by Dean Mark Ingraham of The College of Arts and Sciences, the University of Wisconsin. Subsequently, I was given two semesters of research leave, fall of 1958 and fall of 1959. For these I am very grateful to Professor J. H. Herriott, Associate Dean of the Graduate School, the University of Wisconsin. To Dean Herriott I owe many debts, which I can repay only in publications of this kind; I hope that this one will justify his continued confidence in me.

Since coming to the Riverside campus of the University of California, I have been given annual grants-in-aid for research assistance. While these have been used in a variety of projects, some of the assistance has been spent to produce typescripts of the several drafts this book has had. I am grateful to the Research Committee of the Academic Senate for its help, as I am to these typists who have worked so patiently on the manuscripts: Miss P. K. Brehaut, Mrs. Betty Ann Harker, Mrs. Joan Kibbe, Mrs. Donna Lippert, Mrs. Haverly Parker.

I wish to acknowledge the friendly criticism and encouragement I have had from many people over many years. Some of these people have read portions of the manuscript; others have simply talked about the ideas as they were taking shape, or reacted to essays published in journals or reviews. My dedication will underscore the name of one of my friends. Indeed, I owe him more than I do anyone else in my career, for his intelligent interest and encouragement. There are many others: Lionel Trilling, Herbert Lindenberger, Haskell Block, William Elton, Antonio Sanchez-Barbudos, Carlos Blanco y Aguinaga, and Ralph Matlaw, among them. None of them is responsible for any mistakes I may have made.

Since 1957, I have had the opportunities that my profession occasionally allows, to test my ideas before the best of all audiences, mature and intelligent faculty and graduate students. I want especially to thank the following: a seminar at the University of Washington, summer of 1957; two seminars at the University of Wisconsin, spring of 1959 and spring of 1960; and a seminar at the University of California, Riverside, spring of 1963. I have tried out some of my ideas in lectures at the following places: the University of Michigan, May 1957; Ripon College, April 1958; Duke University, December 1958; The Ohio State University and Antioch College, May 1959; the University of Wisconsin, April 1960; and the Twelfth Annual Research Lecture, the University of California, Riverside, April 1963.

I have published sections of chapters from time to time, as the several drafts of the book were in the making. I wish to thank the following journals and reviews for giving me permission to print them (in each case the work is substantially changed from its initial appearance):

The Virginia Quarterly Review, for "Grace, Violence, and Self," summer 1958, now, in revised form, the Introduction. The same magazine for "Freedom and Conscious Form: Henry James and The American Self," several pages of which (revised) are part of Part Three, chapter 10.

The Georgia Review, for "*Darkness at Noon:* The Consequences of Secular Grace," in the fall 1959 issue; a revision of it is now a part of Part One, chapter 2.

The Centennial Review, for "The Assailant and the Victim:

Some Definitions of Modern Violence," in the spring 1961 issue, for a version of Part Two, chapter 3.

Essays in Criticism, for "The Moment of Violence: Ernst Juenger and the Literary Problem of Fact," in the fall 1960 issue, for a version of Part Two, chapter 4.

Modern Fiction Studies, for two essays: "The Scene of Violence: Dostoevsky and Dreiser," in the summer 1960 issue, a version of which is in Part Two, chapter 5; and "*Howards End* and the Bogey of Progress," in the issue of fall 1961, a version of which is a part of Part One, chapter 1.

The Bucknell Review, for "Kafka's *The Trial*: The Assailant as Landscape," in the May 1960 issue, a version of which is in Part Two, chapter 9.

The Kenyon Review, for "The Authority of the Commonplace: Joyce's Bloomsday," in the spring 1960 issue, a part of which is in Part Three, chapter 12.

Criticism, for "William James and the Modern Literary Consciousness," in the issue of winter 1962, a part of which is in Part Three, chapter 10.

Wisconsin Studies in Contemporary Literature, for "Norman Mailer and the Revolt of the Ego," in the issue of January 1961 (also published in Italian translation in *Tempo di Letteratura*, Naples, Italy, number 2, 1961), a part of Part Three, chapter 14.

The Journal of Existential Psychiatry, for "The Wheel of Self," in the issue of summer 1961, a part of the end of Part Three, chapter 14.

The Chicago Review, for " 'Ecstatic Temporality': The Self in Time," in the issue of summer 1961, a part of Part Three, chapter 11.

In the new and enlightened society of the University of California, my wife, Eleanor C. Hoffman, no longer has to divide her time among garden, household, and typist duties. But the beginnings of this book antedate our residence in California; and she saw the first draft of it through, as she has faithfully lived through the history of many other manuscripts. I am deeply grateful to her once again, and to my daughter, Caroline (who has acquired wisdom and tact long before she could reasonably be expected to have them), for enduring and surviving the crises related to the publication of this book.

F.J.H.

CONTENTS

THE MORTAL NO:

DEATH AND THE
MODERN IMAGINATION

INTRODUCTION:
A LOOK AT THE TERMS

SINCE NO ONE has been known to experience death and survived to describe the experience, its actual nature (aside from physical and perhaps psychiatric notations of the degeneration of tissues) must always depend upon imaginative speculation. Mortality attracts to itself all of the major images and metaphors of any culture; they can certainly be regarded as a crucial perspective upon it. There are two principal ranges of image which seem always to attach to the phenomenon; one is thoroughly realistic, the other as thoroughly "idealistic." In the one case we have the "memento mori," the conqueror worm, and other paraphernalia of maggotry. In the other case, the imagination strives to eliminate as much as possible the evidences of physical dissolution by rearranging them in the view of eternity and regarding them as a transition to the spiritual life. We have in this second view the suggestion that death is an act of transcendence. All transcendental illusions have at their source a wish to deny the corporeal nature of man. In fact, religious energy may often be said to intensify as physical power declines.

Death has a special influence upon literary manners. The choice of image and metaphor depends upon current milieu sanctions and determinants, upon the relative ease or difficulty of belief (or, whether it is a simple or difficult matter to accept what is not absolutely known), upon the nature of man's view of his condition at any stage of his progress toward death, and upon the forcefulness of systems of eschatology. One of the most important of all elements in the literary view of mortality is the time-space relationship that at any moment helps to define human nature. This relationship is indispensably associated with eternity and its effect upon the measurement or the sensing

3

of time. One may say that if eternity is accepted without doubt, it is easier for man to make his peace with temporality. That is, a man expecting and believing in eternity will be less concerned with his temporal experiences, will see them less in depth than as a move toward eternity.

As the belief in immortality (which is that special aspect of eternity that belongs to me) becomes less and less certain, more attention is paid to time, and time achieves a spatial quality. Instants of time become spatial objects in a scheme of succession; it is their spatial quality that attracts and not their sequential nature. An age whose people are little convinced of immortality or little comforted by the hope of it is likely to produce a literature that emphasizes the spatial qualities of life. This literature is also concerned with the density of objects, with their texture, and with the specific values residing in experiences. If death is a wall and not a doorway, the pace of experience diminishes, the attention to time is translated into an absorption in space, and every detail of change is noted and treasured. Instead of a metaphysics dependent upon an infinite extension of the given, we get an ontology of objects and experiences. Death turns us toward life and forces us to admire or cherish it (even though we may despair of it as well), to begrudge the passing of time (which is signified by changes occurring in objects) and eventually to despair of conclusions.

—[ii]—

The three terms, *grace*, *violence*, and *self* are the organizing principles of this book. They form a thematic as well as a chronological order: one may say that the violent destruction of the possibilities of grace has forced upon the self the responsibility of adjustment to death. At any rate, there is some justice in assuming that the terms represent three essential phases of our thanatology. This may be thought a universal condition. I propose to examine its special twentieth century variants.

Grace is a condition of allowance. It is a way of guaranteeing immortality, however qualified by restrictions and rules. Grace requires an imaginative effort; we must believe in "miracles as things." Its effect is to aid us in distributing our native energies; they need not be expended entirely upon current demands, but can be allocated and "deposited," arranged and postponed. In the expectation or hope of grace, we do evil on an installment basis; we are always aware of the necessary compensatory forms of remorse and penance. If we believe in grace, we also believe in immortality; in short, we *believe*. Such a circumstance has a remarkable influence upon our power of metaphor. We expend as much of it upon our vision of the postmortem world as upon the description of the world as a way to death. This does not mean that the world is slighted; on the contrary, the assurance of immortality often makes sin more vividly possible; we sin not from despair but in the expectation of a saving grace. It also affects the quality of sin, and in any event makes both the commission of it and the atonement for it more specifically and concretely and vividly active in the range of self-judgment and self-criticism.

I do not suppose that there was ever a time in twentieth century life when expectations of an eternal life, with proper and discernible sanctions of conduct, were universally or even widely held. It is a matter of degrees of credibility, forms of imaginative effect, phases of partial or almost total suspension of such assurances. Most writers who have concerned themselves with the presence of grace have done so in metaphoric terms. Some have put the time of grace in the past, have borrowed the most vividly effective metaphors of grace from history and tradition. Others have conceived of grace as an almost purely personal issue: the search for a means of defining the reality of man's life demands a scope of metaphor that exists not as the sign of belief but as the area of imaginative speculation concerning mortality.

An important fact of modern attitudes is that religious metaphors and lines of thought have become secular; or they have been partially secularized, and religious and secular images are confused with one another. In one example of this process, personal immortality is dissolved into a social immortality. A state is progressively strengthened; evil is gradually purified out of it; and I as citizen, in working toward that future condition of bliss (not for myself but for my children's children), share posthumously in it. This concept of grace depends upon an almost absolute faith in futures. Only future time is important in this case; the past is valuable only in showing what we ought to avoid in the present to make the future pure. An exact and exacting discipline of *known* procedures and sound hypotheses is here mixed with an almost blind faith in the linear progress toward a condition infinitely better than the present. Disillusion comes hard in a matter such as this and is likely to lead to a change from secular to religious values out of desperation. One of the keys to emotional realization in this context is pain: in a secular crisis, aches, wounds, and welts encourage skepticism concerning ends.

It is possible of course to see immortality as a purely secular abstraction. The most materialistic of social systems often has the most purely dedicated martyrs. This kind of immortality, expected not on the other side but on this side of death, is a common enough phenomenon in a time when "the other side" is hard to realize, to imagine, or to see. It involves the most rigidly doctrinaire and rational discipline as well as the most thoroughly sentimental, even irrational, trust in futures. All of life is in this case governed by a secular monasticism. Life is first preparation, then action, then sacrifice. Death is a proper conclusion, not a beginning at all. It is a sacrifice paid to the future, and the ultimate objective becomes ever more remote as the effort to achieve it becomes more frantic.

There are resemblances between secular grace and spiritual grace: the ways in which each acts to provide sanctions and directions for behavior on this earth, the idea (rather hesitantly entertained, it is true) of a postmortem state of blessedness (for secular grace, it is "postmortem" in the sense of existing in a future beyond the deaths of those who are working for it), the sense of dedication, commitment, surrender of self. The basic difference lies in the extraordinary value put upon history in secular grace. Eliot can dramatize the situation of Thomas à Becket (in *Murder in the Cathedral*) almost as though neither he nor the situation had ever existed in history. Indeed, any historically grounded temptation offered Thomas is scornfully turned aside; only spiritual temptations really disturb him. In the best modern literature devoted to problems of secular grace the reverse is true. Rubashov's major concern (in Koestler's *Darkness at Noon*) is with history; all of his acts, selfish or self-sacrificial, are referred to history, and the question that haunts him to his death is that of the two forms of historical relevance, the humanitarian concern over persons living in the present (that is, *are* people now living a *part* of history, or do they merely antedate it?), as against the impersonal view of history that puts ends entirely in the future and thus abstracts them. Thus definitions of secular grace are constantly being modified in particulars but strengthened and hardened in generalities.

Grace may also be seen as the essence of a culture. This is another form of abstraction. At one extreme it is a kind of exalted *tourisme*. Americans are especially vulnerable; sensing that there is something "spiritual" lacking in skyscrapers, they search for it in cathedrals. The literature of the First World War (or a part of it) had many examples of this kind of grace. Here it is the architecture, the gardens, the visible forms of a cultural state that inspired. It is not easy to speculate upon the terms of immortality in these cases, but I believe that grace does successfully influence the relationship of human life to the ideal of immortality here as well. The cathedral and the abbey are symbols of tradition, forms of immortality; when they are destroyed, man is reduced to despair. The culture is linked to goodness, to virtue, to a spiritual world that is otherwise not clearly seen. When an American society wishes to "immortalize" an aspect of its culture, it does so in terms of an architecture that recalls the past.

Let me try to suggest some of the meanings of grace in modern literature. It is first of all influential in extremely naturalistic cases as a spiritual residue. Even blasphemy and profanity testify to its persistence. Some of the extreme forms of what appear to be "non-Christian" literature give evidence of its endurance. They are black masses which follow the ritual for apparently perverse aims; or, perhaps, because no other aims are present. Secondly, the presence of grace testifies to a continuity of tradition. Grace is usually held, in modern literature, to be a condition of the past. We are reminded of the past when we think of immortality. Several ambiguities appear, and they may well provide one of the clues to the meaning of modern literature. Secular conversions often have many of the characteristics of their religious counterparts. The case of Joaquín on El Sordo's hill is pertinent (Hemingway's *For Whom the Bell Tolls*); his conversion to the Communist ideal had been so thoroughly along Christian lines that in the end it changed into a Christian faith. Often modern literature follows the forms of conventional illusions of immortality while at the same time it appears to be renouncing them. The true occasions of grace in modern literature, however, are linked to the image of a past that is as much unlike the present as possible.

More specifically, immortality has a profound effect upon the description of death scenes, of dying. Consider in any number of cases the scene and what it involves. While death is linked to life as its cause (since living is a succession of devices for bringing life to a close), it is also linked to a postmortem future. The dying man is at the edge of learning the secret of that future. His body, corrupt, is to be given up, his soul to be transported into space, which is limited at the beginning but ends by being infinite. One thinks of the deathbed scene of Father Lucero in Willa Cather's *Death Comes for the Archbishop*: "Among the watchers there was always hope that the dying man might reveal something of what he alone could see; that his countenance, if not his lips, would speak, and on his features would fall some light or shadow from beyond." [1]

Most important, death is a means of purification. No immortality has been conceived which perpetuates the impurities of the body; these impurities are invariably signs of mortality. There are stages along the way, which may be compared with the religious experience of a devout worshiper. The most vivid of these experiences is the expansion of space—pure space, uninhabited and undefiled. The soul "enters into" space, no matter how constricted the actual scene of the dying may be. This is what gives much discussion of "the spirit" a sense of spaciousness. The mystic talks of the loss of material consciousness, but is ultimately interested in expansion: of space, of air, of light. Immortality begins when the soul gains space and light at the expense of life. There is also the anthropomorphic sense of the absorption of an inferior by a superior being; this is especially interesting when the superior is the invention of the inferior being. Death is thought of as a rebirth into another life, quite unlike this life but with certain metaphoric associations with it. It is also considered a "wedding" of the spirit with God. These metaphors are essentially nonspiritual in their origin, linked to the anthropomorphic aspects of belief.

Of special relevance to questions of the atmosphere of death are the spatial figurations in E. M. Forster's novel, *Howards End*. Howards End itself, presided over by Ruth Wilcox and after her death by the Schlegel sisters, is spatially related to immortality and its requisite acknowledgment of death in the

[1] New York, Knopf, 1929, p. 194. Originally published by Knopf in 1927.

9

human economy. As a country house not too far separated from the rapidly growing city, it is constantly threatened by roads, motors, industrial developments; dust, smog, smoke similarly threaten the horizon. But it is there, where one has a feeling of space, that the soul is nourished and prepared for its entrance into death. The recognition of death will save man, as against his horrifyingly naive and urgent effort to deny it.[2]

To these speculations about death much of the literary view of mortality is indebted. The basic ambiguity of the death scene lies in the struggle to the end with the devil; for death is not only a way to eternity, it is also the entrance to a place of judgment. The devil is associated throughout with the senses, with the pleasures and dissipations of the body. The dying man must therefore be purified; hence the predominating representations of whiteness, of spaciousness, of purity, of emptiness. This is a state devoutly to be desired, but it is also one much feared; and it casts a pall upon those who must calculate all offenses in terms of relative and absolute purification.

But there is another struggle, to keep Satan alive in modern moral thought. In its speculations concerning the phenomena of death, modern literature usually contrasts the images of space and congestion (uncongested space is pure, crowded space is foul). Slum death occurs with every reminder of the constrictions of the grave. The grave is a crowded place, and uncomfortable, as are a jail cell, a flophouse room, a hospital ward, a trench, a city street. None of these places is a proper one for communing with God. Many of the modern images which specify the loss of belief in immortality emphasize this kind of space-congestion: furnished rooms, gutters, passageways, subways, et cetera. They are forms of a hell on earth, a terrestrial hell. The doubter, the skeptic, the intellectual rebel go underground. Contrarily, immortality (which must save persons from these congested areas) is often thought of in terms of the most

[2] See below, Part One, chapter 1.

expansive spatial senses: ocean, sky, church (where the spatial sense moves upward, unifying ritual object with infinity), desert spaces, "wide open spaces," or "God's country." Suicides increase as space decreases, as land gives way to water.

These images are much more conventional than those which describe the hell of disbelief. There is a strong line from Whitman through modern poetry describing both death and immortality in terms of the sea (for example, Hart Crane's "Voyages," Marianne Moore's "A Grave," Eliot's "Dry Salvages"). As for desert spaces, one need only to observe the very effective imagery of retreat into death and immortality in Miss Cather's *The Professor's House,* or contrast many of the love scenes of D. H. Lawrence's *The Rainbow* and *Women in Love* with his portrayal of the soul's *mise en scène* in *St. Mawr.* Perhaps the most elaborate use of the sea symbol is found in Mann's *Death in Venice.* Premonitions of death begin with the cemetery as background; Venice and the sea are at the beginning of Aschenbach's decline (before he knows of it) framed neatly, though even then there are omens of disaster; as he falls in love with Tadzio, the sea acts as background of the "perfect form" of his beloved; eventually we see the terrifying conflict between Aschenbach's notion of "perfect form," which itself is empty, and the chaos described both in the sea and in the pestilential streets of Venice. Mann comes close to ridiculing a pretentious artist, but the horror of the plague is nevertheless pre-eminent.

The significance of grace depends upon the predictability of the relationship between the dying man and his expectation of immortality. He must know in advance that he will die, that death while inevitable is also an event for which he has the privilege of preparing. If he dies suddenly, the nature of the assailant as well as his complicity in the pattern of events leading to his death must be comprehensible. It is indispensable to him that his imagination have the privilege of reviewing the ambiguities of dying; he must understand them well enough to accept them and to know his relationship to the causes of his death. In short, he must be in command of both the space and the time in which his life reaches its conclusion.

—[iii]—

Violent death does not in itself need to involve the destruction of a belief in immortality. It is not really so much a question of violence as it is one of degree and passion of commitment. If the violence of one's death (whether he be actor or victim or both) bears a discernible relationship to passion—that is, if the circumstance of death is consistent with the energy of one's earning it—then the balance of life, death, and immortality may still be maintained. Most concrete visions of hell have some fairly intelligible design of punishment according to the quality and intensity of the deaths that have preceded it. One entertains a metaphor of punishment or purgation consistent with the nature of sin. This personal disposition toward dying is a privilege that is not easily surrendered.

There are two kinds of violence, however, in which this balance is not achieved: violence in excess of expectation ("sentimental violence"), and impersonal violence. A remarkable portrayal of "sentimental violence" is found in the behavior of Robert Cohn, in Hemingway's *The Sun Also Rises*; Cohn's skill as a boxer propels him into violence against his friends for "romantic" purposes. His romanticism (a naive failure to read human situations correctly, a literal earnestness concerning literary clichés) is powered by his skill, which had originally been acquired for unrealistic purposes.[3]

One may say that any violence is comprehensible if it is inflicted upon another by personal means within view of the victim, or at least within the range of the victim's expectation. Any violence which goes beyond these limits is not compre-

[3] See below, Part Two, chapter 3, for a full discussion of these and other matters.

ions of reason and logic (*The Tragic Sense of Life*). The
of Kierkegaardian existentialism and of the literature
calls it is abundantly supplied with issues involving the
God, belief and acceptance in the face of overwhelm-
iscouraging evidence. When once the shock of violence
counted for, unseen, unreal, and unreasonable, the self
ated from most doctrines of sufficient reason; it has to
s "separate peace." Since the self cannot be sustained
some viable code or some illusion, there are many con-
eadjustments. The search for a sustaining illusion also
to the byways of mythopoeic research and avails itself
typal resources. The modern self tries to re-read the past
s of its present situation. This is unusual only in the
y with which it is done. Revivals in literature con-
sly emphasize the heroic struggle with evil, or seize
amatizations of force in the near or remote past, or try
rm old religious orthodoxies by combining them with
s in mysticism.

ot so much that the self needs a God, but that it can-
loes not wish to stand alone. It is a comfort to know
terns of behavior, actual or imagined, are repetitions,
archetypically with the entire history of the race, are
a part of a "collective unconscious," to which each self
nd if the need occurs. This is not to defeat death but to
ind of immortality in the sharing of undying patterns.
t popular contrivance for maintaining a belief in life is
ttention to the fact that living has been going on a
e: to say, in other words, that Everyman "haveth
everywhere."

dern literature we may notice a remarkable variety of
itions. They begin with the "pure, practical" conscious-
William James, developed in a time when basic forms
liance were put seriously in doubt. The pre-eminence
or of sensitive self-awareness, could not long endure
its own scorching ironies. Shortly after the beginning

hensible, and it upsets the calculus of understanding in the matter of dying. One needs to know from what and from whom one
is dying, or he will not be able to cast up his accounts. The obvious next step leads us to a consideration of the "mechanics"
of death. The history of death moves from the circumstances
of calculated risk or predictable consequence to the condition
of the impersonal, unreasonable, unreal, and unseen assailant.
All moral and religious systems depend upon at least a core of
reality and predication in these matters. One must at least
imaginatively, if he cannot literally, accept the circumstances of
his death.

The history of our culture is quite adequately clear in these
matters. When once physical law describes the limits of our
world, our literature begins to work within these limits, to
borrow the broad, vague metaphors of fate and destiny, to invoke images of vast natural forces which overwhelm man. Naturalism so directs man away from the moral, confessional, and
willed levels of his life that events must take place in a world
and in a way that cannot be understood. As a result, naturalist
literature fumbles over the question of motivation, because
motivation is no longer clear if "forces" dictate beyond the
power of man to accept and adjust. One of the simplest examples is that of Clyde Griffiths in Dreiser's novel, *An American
Tragedy*; his failure of decision, while Dreiser tortures his text
in an effort to explain it, is a form of motiveless violence; he
allows a crime to happen (and thus distinguishes himself from
Raskolnikov of Dostoevsky's *Crime and Punishment*, who
forces it to happen), and the crime is therefore a result of
criminal indecision.[4]

Impersonal violence upsets all of the equilibrium noticeable
otherwise in the relationship of life, death, and immortality.
There is neither a cause nor a corpse; since in a great majority
of cases both are necessary to sustain a belief in immortality,
most of the sanctions which support a faith in something be-

[4] See below, Part Two, chapter 5.

yond the self are entirely lacking. Our literature therefore treats of violence in terms of the psychological equivalents of the distance between assailant and victim. There is a direct relevance in the matter of passion expended, both to deal blows and to suffer them. The intellect cannot be substituted for the passion. In fact, most of the ambiguities associated with death in modern literature arise because the intellect is accessible to almost infinite expansion, the ratio between cause and corpse becomes more and more disproportionate. The credibility and acceptability of death are both dependent upon one's knowing, suspecting, sensing, or imagining the cause. If death comes as a "surprise," it may still be understood as a consequence of one or another kind of inadequacy of body, mind, or spirit. Violent death, however, destroys all expectations, reasonable or imaginable.

The history of violence in the twentieth century (and in its literature) follows somewhat along these lines, in terms of the character of the assailant: the assailant as human being, as instrument, as machine, as landscape. In this last case, the assailant is neither human nor mechanical but the entire environment, the land itself, or the world or the solar system: whatever extent of space the instrument of the assailant has put at his disposal. Many of the literary expressions of this circumstance have been given in terms of vast landscapes of desert, or ice-bound images of terror, or mountain perspectives; they are the reverse of the spiritual metaphors I have already discussed. They have the double function of separating man from time and eliminating most associations with ordinary reality. The strategy of adjustment to this kind of violence usually takes the form of making the generalizations defending it as vast, unreal, unavailable to rational explanation as the circumstance itself. The natural reaction to them is to trust nothing that is vague, abstract, not associated with immediate experience.

Most of the poetry written about World War II considers

the landscape of violence that is the met space suspended between the past the s future to which he hopes to return. The identical and together they are antithe present. A soldier is given a number; he mous—that is, he is asked to give his that it may be regulated according to tl tary needs. Having lost or temporarily he exists in a state of unreality, of anon the circumstance of his death, should means that he must risk the chance of He is an "unknown soldier" in a vivid shock of dislocation is much more vivid First World War than it is in that of cause the violence had little or no prec fore not expected. Both the occasion a a violent separation from the reality t accustomed. Further, the occasion of had the double result of destroying p circumstances of violent tension. Mu literature of tension caused either by u the expectation of violence that does major theme of this book may be de man's attempts to account for violen to adjust to its dislocations.

—[iv]—

Our final term is *self*. The basic m phenomena of modern dying is that c of self-definition. Considered as a spe a sex, a set of qualities identifying either in "partnership" with God o denied Him or accommodated the s sociation that Unamuno, for exampl

dissua
history
that r
self an
ingly
is una
is sepa
make
withou
trived
leads i
of arch
in tern
intensi
spicuot
upon d
to reaf
resourc
It is
not or
that pa
shared
actually
may att
gain a
The mc
to call
long ti
childers
In m
self-defi
ness of
of self-r
of self,
without

hensible, and it upsets the calculus of understanding in the matter of dying. One needs to know from what and from whom one is dying, or he will not be able to cast up his accounts. The obvious next step leads us to a consideration of the "mechanics" of death. The history of death moves from the circumstances of calculated risk or predictable consequence to the condition of the impersonal, unreasonable, unreal, and unseen assailant. All moral and religious systems depend upon at least a core of reality and predication in these matters. One must at least imaginatively, if he cannot literally, accept the circumstances of his death.

The history of our culture is quite adequately clear in these matters. When once physical law describes the limits of our world, our literature begins to work within these limits, to borrow the broad, vague metaphors of fate and destiny, to invoke images of vast natural forces which overwhelm man. Naturalism so directs man away from the moral, confessional, and willed levels of his life that events must take place in a world and in a way that cannot be understood. As a result, naturalist literature fumbles over the question of motivation, because motivation is no longer clear if "forces" dictate beyond the power of man to accept and adjust. One of the simplest examples is that of Clyde Griffiths in Dreiser's novel, *An American Tragedy*; his failure of decision, while Dreiser tortures his text in an effort to explain it, is a form of motiveless violence; he allows a crime to happen (and thus distinguishes himself from Raskolnikov of Dostoevsky's *Crime and Punishment*, who forces it to happen), and the crime is therefore a result of criminal indecision.[4]

Impersonal violence upsets all of the equilibrium noticeable otherwise in the relationship of life, death, and immortality. There is neither a cause nor a corpse; since in a great majority of cases both are necessary to sustain a belief in immortality, most of the sanctions which support a faith in something be-

[4] See below, Part Two, chapter 5.

yond the self are entirely lacking. Our literature therefore treats of violence in terms of the psychological equivalents of the distance between assailant and victim. There is a direct relevance in the matter of passion expended, both to deal blows and to suffer them. The intellect cannot be substituted for the passion. In fact, most of the ambiguities associated with death in modern literature arise because the intellect is accessible to almost infinite expansion, the ratio between cause and corpse becomes more and more disproportionate. The credibility and acceptability of death are both dependent upon one's knowing, suspecting, sensing, or imagining the cause. If death comes as a "surprise," it may still be understood as a consequence of one or another kind of inadequacy of body, mind, or spirit. Violent death, however, destroys all expectations, reasonable or imaginable.

The history of violence in the twentieth century (and in its literature) follows somewhat along these lines, in terms of the character of the assailant: the assailant as human being, as instrument, as machine, as landscape. In this last case, the assailant is neither human nor mechanical but the entire environment, the land itself, or the world or the solar system: whatever extent of space the instrument of the assailant has put at his disposal. Many of the literary expressions of this circumstance have been given in terms of vast landscapes of desert, or ice-bound images of terror, or mountain perspectives; they are the reverse of the spiritual metaphors I have already discussed. They have the double function of separating man from time and eliminating most associations with ordinary reality. The strategy of adjustment to this kind of violence usually takes the form of making the generalizations defending it as vast, unreal, unavailable to rational explanation as the circumstance itself. The natural reaction to them is to trust nothing that is vague, abstract, not associated with immediate experience.

Most of the poetry written about World War II considers

the landscape of violence that is the metaphor of that war as a space suspended between the past the soldier has left and the future to which he hopes to return. The past and the future are identical and together they are antithetically opposed to the present. A soldier is given a number; he is asked to be anonymous—that is, he is asked to give his passion to the army so that it may be regulated according to the strategies of its military needs. Having lost or temporarily suspended his identity, he exists in a state of unreality, of anonymity, which constitute the circumstance of his death, should he meet it there. This means that he must risk the chance of death without identity. He is an "unknown soldier" in a vividly statistical sense. The shock of dislocation is much more vivid in the literature of the First World War than it is in that of the Second. This is because the violence had little or no precedent and it was therefore not expected. Both the occasion and the shock of it were a violent separation from the reality to which the soldier was accustomed. Further, the occasion of violence on a vast scale had the double result of destroying precedent and setting up circumstances of violent tension. Much of our literature is a literature of tension caused either by unexpected violence or by the expectation of violence that does not occur. In fact, the major theme of this book may be described as the history of man's attempts to account for violence, to anticipate it, and to adjust to its dislocations.

—[iv]—

Our final term is *self*. The basic mode of adjustment to the phenomena of modern dying is that of a search for a new basis of self-definition. Considered as a specific entity (with a name, a sex, a set of qualities identifying it), the self once existed either in "partnership" with God or with a philosophy that denied Him or accommodated the self to Him. It is this association that Unamuno, for example, insists upon, against all

15

dissuasions of reason and logic (*The Tragic Sense of Life*). The history of Kierkegaardian existentialism and of the literature that recalls it is abundantly supplied with issues involving the self and God, belief and acceptance in the face of overwhelmingly discouraging evidence. When once the shock of violence is unaccounted for, unseen, unreal, and unreasonable, the self is separated from most doctrines of sufficient reason; it has to make its "separate peace." Since the self cannot be sustained without some viable code or some illusion, there are many contrived readjustments. The search for a sustaining illusion also leads into the byways of mythopoeic research and avails itself of archetypal resources. The modern self tries to re-read the past in terms of its present situation. This is unusual only in the intensity with which it is done. Revivals in literature conspicuously emphasize the heroic struggle with evil, or seize upon dramatizations of force in the near or remote past, or try to reaffirm old religious orthodoxies by combining them with resources in mysticism.

It is not so much that the self needs a God, but that it cannot or does not wish to stand alone. It is a comfort to know that patterns of behavior, actual or imagined, are repetitions, shared archetypally with the entire history of the race, are actually a part of a "collective unconscious," to which each self may attend if the need occurs. This is not to defeat death but to gain a kind of immortality in the sharing of undying patterns. The most popular contrivance for maintaining a belief in life is to call attention to the fact that living has been going on a long time: to say, in other words, that Everyman "haveth childers everywhere."

In modern literature we may notice a remarkable variety of self-definitions. They begin with the "pure, practical" consciousness of William James, developed in a time when basic forms of self-reliance were put seriously in doubt. The pre-eminence of self, or of sensitive self-awareness, could not long endure without its own scorching ironies. Shortly after the beginning of the twentieth century the ironic modes of Laforgue, Corbière, occasionally of Rimbaud, became popular and seemed necessary. Some such form of ironic contemplation is evident in at least one phase of the work of most important writers: Eliot, Pound, Joyce, Gide, the early Faulkner. In any case, the self is separated from the "herd," the "mass," the "mostarian" by some contrivance or other, or by virtue of a powerful *non serviam* gesture, or a "separate peace" which requires redefinition of the terms of an enduring armistice. In the 1930's, when the self was not absorbed by the state, it became an isolated intelligence, looking as hopelessly upon the waste land as ever did Eliot's Tiresias, though here with even less prospect of salvation because associated with no system whatsoever of values. Religious exertions on behalf of the self are conspicuous in this and in the following decade.

The Catholic assertion in modern literature, independently avowed in the psychological circumstance of conversion, is also of great importance. This is like a re-examination of the Catholic orthodoxy done over entirely from the perspective of an ego formed from quite different sources. In the poetry of Robert Lowell, for example, the Calvinist condemns, the Catholic saves; both are indispensable, the Catholic only more so. Many of the Catholic views of the self, while they stay within the knowledge of the Catholic judgment of evil, make dramatic substance of the very real conflict between doctrine and human fallibility. Graham Greene again and again takes his characters on the most complex and tortured of journeys to an end which can be called neither salvation nor damnation but appears an intolerable mixture of both.[5]

The most important and in many ways the most scrupulous

[5] For all of its popular appeal, Greene's work does illuminate many of the pressing issues of our lives; at the same time, it continues to "entertain" the reader by assuring him that he is a participant in the decisions leading to his death. There is at least one exception: in *The Quiet American* (New York, Viking, 1955), death is presented as impersonal on one occasion.

adjustment of the self in recent years is the existentialist. Literary existentialism usually begins by denying that an appeal to religious forms can successfully explain the self; it begins with the naked fact of an isolated self. In these terms, the problem of the "absurd," which is after all what the violence of our century has given us, can be and must be considered.[6] It is related to the defeat of rationalist expectations, and it begins with the acceptance of such a defeat. In these circumstances, the entire growth of the sensibility is seen with death as a terminus. At least for the purpose of present realization, there is nothing beyond death. It is important that there be nothing, because self-awareness ought not to be mitigated by promises or prior soothing knowledges. The terror of immediate self-realization is an experience of death-in-life which, at least in some of its manifestations, is consonant with the century's violent history. In terms of it Sartre, at least, has developed a cosmogony, an eschatology, an earth and a hell (there is no heaven in Sartre's work), solely along lines of the immediate issues of existence in space and endurance in time that emerge from the abandonment of immortality. One endures, not because man is good and "will prevail," but because he exists, because he will die some time and meanwhile must live.

—[v]—

I have suggested only a fragment of the speculation necessary in any thorough study of death and modern literature. My principal objective has been to show that each of the three major terms—grace, violence, and self—has a determining influence upon the ways in which death as event is invested with image and metaphor, and that the pattern of life-death-immortality is distinct in each case. We have in the first of these cases a clearly seen development of the human consciousness; the images of death are borrowed from those of life, and there

[6] See below, Part Three, chapters 13 and 14.

is a close relationship between primary and secondary qualities (between abstractions and sensuous detail). In the second case, the ordinary expectation of immortality is violated, and the balance of assailant and victim, of cause and corpse, is upset. As a result death ranges from statistical loss to complete annihilation, but in any event the calculus of proper and responsible judgment of death as a predictable result of understandable causes no longer obtains. Finally, the various mutations of the self in the twentieth century lead us perhaps to the present and to the need to see self-identity of some kind as an irreducible starting point. This is a reconstructive beginning, perhaps; it is prefigured in a number of ways in twentieth century literature.

The subject I discuss in this book is quite simply that of a change of pace, rhythm, and purpose, and of its effect upon substantial and defining metaphors. In the literature I shall now examine, these qualities of human life are seen in many varieties of modification, as indeed are the circumstances that inspire the literature. Time and space acquire new meanings, as do their interrelationships. Heroism undergoes drastic changes. Manners of discourse and behavior suffer an almost fatal, surely a forceful, intrusion. The major threat to modern existence is that of annihilation, a state in which not only the body but the ego deteriorates or is dissolved. Desperate maneuvers are required to rescue *amour-propre* from the fear of *la mort sans cesse*; most of these produce new insights into the major figure of man's approaching death, as they suggest entirely new views of the language necessary to describe it. The facts of violence are not merely "sensational"; they are profoundly disturbing, and they deserve a serious and probing examination. I trust that I have given them just that and that, in doing so, I have offered to the twentieth century condition a new and significant interpretation.

PART ONE

GRACE

1

VIOLENCE AND DECORUM

"Aux armes!" s'écria Julien. Et il
franchit d'un saut les marches du
perron de l'hôtel.
  —STENDHAL, *Le Rouge et le noir*

—[i]—

MODERN violence is in some respects a result of calculation, of
equations which "metamorphose into use," as one poet has
described it.[1] It is a matter of pace, a genuine struggle of language and structure to enable man to comprehend radical
changes in his external, physical world. Literary forms develop
within a metaphysical context; but they lag behind actual in-
novations in social, political, and military strategies. Writers
accept established forms, work within them, occasionally allow
for disturbances and exceptions; but the fundamental irony
in literary history comes as a consequence of disturbances from
the outside, pressures put upon literary custom by events and
a breakthrough in theory.

Three major patterns define the move toward the literature
of violence in our century: the ambiguities of "reason" in its
application to social definition; the growth toward secularization of literary metaphor; and the importunate, disturbing pres-

[1] Randall Jarrell, "The Emancipators," in *Little Friend, Little Friend,*
New York, Dial, 1945, p. 14.

sure of violence upon established literary forms. Our principal concern in this chapter is to point out nineteenth century efforts to define human reality and the frequent and growing need to modify terms of definition. Almost invariably, writers of the nineteenth century had to account for a vexing disturbance in this history, a steady pressure against current uses of language and structure. The most extreme confidence in "reason" was generally discredited, but two powerfully conservative habits continued in force: the Protestant *mystique* of work and its emphasis upon social growth as a sign of religious strength; and the tradition of manners as a form of literary containment. Ironies abound in the history of both. Work was itself inevitably associated with mechanical extensions of force, which tended to reduce the strength of the self in his act of self-determination. In other words, work led to a revision of social structures and to the decline of the self's initiative in relating to them.

In many ways—some of which I explore in the pages to follow —the mechanization of industry caused explosions of force outside its limits; and these proved to have a disturbing influence upon literary conventions. The romantic hero frequently became a hero *manqué,* and the very strength of his heroic force was directed both against himself-as-hero and society-as-heroic. This phenomenon cannot satisfactorily be explained by the use of such terms as "the vanishing hero." The hero did not simply "vanish"; he blasted himself off the scene, or he committed suicide as a gesture meant to help ornament his deprivation. Nineteenth century literature portrays a complex variety of suicidal gestures. These in themselves constitute a cultural metaphor, defining forceful testimonies of the self's awareness of a closed society. The hero is conscious of a diminishing prestige; he sees that human force and energy are being used to strengthen social structures that move toward an abstract, a rigid, an impersonal condition, a stasis; he finds that the metaphors of both religion and society (often they are the same metaphors) do not explain or alleviate his concern; he ends by deliberately (and garrulously) withdrawing from the social center or violently asserting his opposition to it.

Nineteenth century writers were caught by the paradox of a manner of literary self-definition which no longer adequately defined the self precisely, or defined it at some cost of credibility. Manners retreated uneasily before the pressures of disbelief; the hero of nineteenth century literature increasingly assumed the role of self-analyst; distrust of the self's power was associated with a larger skepticism, of manners themselves. The major consequence was a basic change in self-definition, which must eventually upset both the language and the form according to which literature provided a meaningful "fiction." Important moral and social conventions and securities yielded to improvisations with social manners, with human relationships, and with sustaining cultural and religious metaphors.

From being gentle, delicate ironists or avuncular editorialists, nineteenth century writers withdrew gradually and hesitantly from the position of omniscient authority and made a new literature from the condition of withdrawal. The principal event of that literature was death; the occasion of death became a source of many literary stratagems. The manner of dying often replaced the manner of living as a crucial literary maneuver. The ways in which a man disposed of himself, or of others, or of both himself and others, are clues to the progress of literature toward the center of twentieth century violence.

But the passive role of the hero as he contemplated death is also important. The literature of the past one and a half centuries describes an immense variety of stances, from Julien Sorel's death to the slow and gradual enfeebling of Beckett's Malone. At the one extreme, the hero forces the issue of his death and dramatizes the occasion, thus forcefully calling attention to himself. At the other extreme, the self diminishes to the point of annihilation. Generally, there is also a radical change from the author's vigorous sponsorship of his hero's romantic rebellion to his "giving in" to both character and external circumstance. This latter act of submission is a final step in a sequence of moves of withdrawal, shock, disillusion— in short, a set of responses to the increase of impersonal violence in the social and human economies.

Stendhal is very much with his heroes; he narrates action and superintends appropriate discourses. His creatures are the consequences of a forceful imagination which engages speculatively and actively in intrigues and adventures. His successors are less certain of their relationship to their imaginary worlds. Analysis becomes more and more often a principal means of expending creative energies. Writers yield more and more often to the "I" of their created worlds; they create heroes, then are reluctant or unwilling to allow them to behave heroically. The outer pressure gains in power, explodes in newer and stronger expressions of force; the inner self gives in to states of shock, bewilderment, and moral ambivalence. There is a great increase in the *effort* to define the self, but the lines of definition waver, are less certain, sometimes threaten to disappear altogether.

We are witnesses to a history of deceleration, of the disintegration of heroic properties, even of the dissolution of self as consciousness and self as body. Heroic discourse is more likely to be found in documents that exist outside literature and to be borrowed from them at second hand. In a sense that will become more and more clear as this book progresses, the artist as creator tends to "commit the original sin" of creating a defective being, after which he forces his heroes to improvise means of tolerating his imperfect act of creation.

Throughout this history, the noise of violence increases in volume. Popgun gives way to cannon and to ingeniously improvised bombs; the exercise of force becomes erratic and disorganized. The romantic will of the self often changes to a will toward destruction; until we have creatures apparently acting out—or suffering and tolerating—the prophecies of Nietzsche's madman. The landscape of violence increases in space and scope. The lines defining the relationship of assailant to victim grow less and less clear, until in some cases they disappear altogether, leaving the victim to meditate over the likelihood of being his own assailant.

—[ii]—

When the King arrives at Verrières, Julien Sorel senses for the first time in his life the power of both the clergy and the military. Stendhal describes the mixture of the two in full appreciation of their bearing upon his hero:

> There were a Te Deum, clouds of incense, endless volleys of musketry and artillery; the peasants were frantic with joy and piety. Such a day undoes the work of a hundred numbers of the Jacobin papers.[2]

It is one of those occasions when contrasting yet complementary investitures of power come briefly together. The peasants, in whom the energy of humanity is ordinarily contained formally, or is expressed in brief, unconvincing practical designs, here "étaient ivres de bonheur et de piété." The most convincing of all testimonies of power and display confuse the senses. Past glory and present necessity are identified with each other.

Julien is most anxious to exploit both sources of power. He has great, naive, and unsophisticated force. He is of heroic stuff, a hero *manqué*, born twenty years too late. As a novel of force, *The Red and the Black* (1831) presents both heroic potentiality and an intricate pattern of barriers to its direct expression. Julien's disposition to power is aesthetically contained

---

[2] *The Red and the Black*, tr. C. K. Scott-Moncrieff, New York, Modern Library, n.d., p. 1, 140. All references in the text are to this edition. The text will also include page references to the best French edition (Paris, Bibliothèque de la Pléiade, 1952; indicated in the text by the abbreviation "Pl"). Scott-Moncrieff's remains the the most interesting and the most reliable translation, though there are now a half dozen others.

within three major settings: the village of Verrières, the provincial capitol of Besançon, and Paris. The intricacies of social custom in each case surround and threaten to destroy him. There is a mixture of comedy and pathos in each of the novel's dramatic crises, occasioned by Julien's naive forthrightness, contemporary circumstances, and the always half-amicable, half-disgusting tactics of the bourgeoisie.

Money is society's major strategy of containment; bourgeois manners are designed to make the man of spirit take and keep his place. These are the *longueurs* of peace. Financial disparities, more than class differences, hold the human balance in order. The peasantry are permitted to observe occasional displays of force; as for the rest, they relieve boredom with gossip and maneuvers for petty advantage.

The times are not right for Julien; there is no Napoleon, there are only crudely discreet men of small power. At one time, on his way out of the village church, "he thought he saw blood by the holy water stoup; it was some of the water that had been spilt: the light from the red curtains which draped the windows made it appear like blood (1, 38; Pl, 1, 240). The mistake is almost a sign of his vocation. He will need in his time to move in terms of a prevailing power; he must assume the cloth as the only means of asserting his superiority. "Aux armes!" The battle-cry of his old friend, the Surgeon, is now his motto in a world of boring and uneasy peace. He must conquer by means of charm and intellectual power. The first conquest is through love. The circumstances of Louise de Rênal's life offer an excellent opportunity, but her love of him is hindered by a sense of duty on her part and his. Loving Mme. de Rênal is a duty, not only to her, but especially to his "plan," his mission in this world, which is to overcome his low estate through clever and forthright planning against the barriers to his imagined status. His is the romantic's vision of power; the image of himself as hero demands determined and effective action. He is both ludicrous and pathetic, and the success which crowns his efforts is always disappointing. The formula of disenchantment is always this: "Mon Dieu! être heureux, être aimé, n'est-ce que ça?"[3] The reality falls ever short of the imagined ideal: is there no more to it than this, he asks himself. The "n'est-ce que ça," spoken so often by Stendhal's heroes, is a measure of the defeat of their sensibilities in the moment of triumph against grudging, petty circumstance.

Since eloquence and skill of intellectual performance have superseded power in action, Julien moves next to the seminary at Besançon, in his climb toward prestige. Once again the promise of conquest is signalized by a vigorous mastery of ladders and Latin. In an act of daring and courage, Julien overcomes the risks and dangers residing in a Church career, to prove himself.

> When all the pillars were hung with damask, the next thing was to go and place five enormous bunches of plumes on top of the great baldachino, over the high altar. A richly gilded wooden crown was supported on eight great twisted columns of Italian marble. But, in order to reach the centre of the baldachino, over the tabernacle, one had to step across an old wooden cornice, possibly worm eaten, and forty feet from the ground.
>
> . . . Julien took possession of the bunches of plumes, and ran up the ladder. He arranged them admirably upon the ornament in the form of a crown in the centre of the baldachino. As he stepped down from the ladder, the abbé Chas-Bernard took him in his arms.
>
> "Optime!" exclaimed the worthy priest, "I shall tell Monseigneur of this." (1, 244; Pl, 1, 397–98)

As before, Stendhal portrays Julien's slow but determined move toward success, this time in a place larger, more sophisti-

[3] Pléiade edition, 1, 299. Scott-Moncrieff translates (1, 114): "Heavens! Is to be happy, to be loved, no more than that?" The idiom is all but untranslatable; it should communicate a genuine letdown, a terribly disappointing contrast between expectations and achievement.

cated than Verrières, but like it an image of the world. As he did at Verrières, Julien "scales the walls" to signify his power, and ends in approving arms. To act in this case is to aid in ornamenting the glory of God; the risks overcome are symbolically not unlike the struggle for Seminary approval. The petty malice of Verrières bourgeoisie is replaced by the gross ambitions of a group of small-minded seminarians. Julien proves his superiority over them as well as over the barriers to a public show of religious power. Both here and in Verrières he has performed his "second-best" equivalent of the worshipful display of military power he would have wished to show, had he been born in Napoleon's world. His triumphs are petty, but they are the best that can be had.

The strategy of a novel of force is to conduct its hero through several scenes of intrigue and complication, progressively more difficult and more complicated, revealing as he moves into and through them the true dimensions of *un siècle manqué*. Julien's arrival in Paris, therefore, heralds the beginning of the final and most difficult exercise of his affecting heroics.[4] On the surface he seems least of all endowed here. This is a world of cunning as well as of power. The antagonists of naked power and ambition are truly formidable. The manners of the aristocracy are the most finely developed of all strategies of containment. In a sense, Julien had triumphed over Verrières *en plein air* (the "negotiations" for Mme. de Rênal's love had after all begun in the garden of the Mayor's country home). In Paris, he is confined to interiors: libraries, dining-rooms, and drawing-rooms. The dullness of Paris is unlike that of Verrières; it comes not from a lack but from a suppression of vigor. Julien observes himself in the act of adjusting to this final cloister of social reserve.

[4] See Martin Turnell, *The Novel in France* (New York, New Directions, n.d.): "The physical journey is at the same time *a journey to the interior of the mind. . . .* The outer world loses its importance; the 'action' shifts to the world within." (p. 150)

He would have enjoyed perfect self-possession, had the dining-room been furnished with less magnificence. It was, as a matter of fact, a pair of mirrors, each of them eight feet high, in which he caught sight now and then of his challenger as he spoke of Horace, that still continued to overawe him. (II, 29; Pl, I, 451)

The mirrors magnify the difficulty, as they dwarf the human scene reflected in them. Here the buzz and confusion of human conspiracy are reduced to a frame of calculated rules. Walls and interiors have reduced men and women to politeness bordering on passivity. The young Comte, a man of spirit, nevertheless confines his show of energy to bridle paths and ballrooms. The controlling spirit, M. de la Mole, is a master conspirator of the conventional; all of his skill, learning, and will are used to contain force within present and accepted boundaries. Because he is talented, and because he has learned the necessary subterfuges of manner, Julien is surely fated to succeed in these circumstances.

But his very superiority to the tedious generality of polite submission both takes him beyond the drawing-room and leads eventually to his undoing. Julien's exasperation over the dullness of dinner-parties and calculated circumspection attracts the attention of Mathilde de la Mole. In a library scene, not too many days after his arrival at the Hôtel de la Mole, Julien expresses his displeasure to the abbé Pirard, his protector.

"It is to me, Sir, the most tedious part of my employment. I was less bored at the Seminary. I see even Mademoiselle de la Mole yawn at times, although she must be accustomed to the pretty speeches of the friends of the family. I am afraid of falling asleep. Please be so good as to obtain leave for me to go and dine for forty sous in some obscure inn."

The abbé, a regular *parvenu*, was highly sensible of the

honour of dining with a great nobleman. While he was endeavouring to make Julien understand what he felt, a slight sound made them turn their heads. Julien saw Mademoiselle de la Mole who was listening. He blushed. She had come in search of a book and had heard everything; she felt a certain respect for Julien. "This fellow was not born on his knees," she thought, "like that old abbé. Heavens! How ugly he is." (II, 40; Pl, I, 459)

Herein are the conditions of Julien's final conquest. In the atmosphere of the library, surrounded by testimonies of privilege and power, he scorns the disguises of the nobility and the passive obedience expected of him. His attitude is noticed and approved. Both Mathilde and Julien are fated to defy the constraints; both are animated by a romantic impulse to break through them, to restore genuine human power to a world frightened off by its Napoleonic expression of some decades before. The motives differ radically. Mathilde is bored, cold, even vicious in her resentment of the family decorum. Julien's opposition is modified by his view of personal necessity; he *must* abide the tedium or lose all. Nevertheless, the two spirits of necessity come together in a love both more complicated by sophistications and more patently artificial than his love of Mme. de Rênal. The force and agony of this new love are in a sense a decadent form of the extra-marital passion of Verrières.

Mathilde's admiration of Julien develops into love as a matter of principle. Slowly and painstakingly she measures her obligation to admire this man who, quite obviously and alone, represents in male form her own spirit of opposition. Like him she resents barriers; like him she idealizes strength and power and despises all the petty forms of submission needed to survive and to remain in society's good grace. But their romantic egos are as different as their fortunes of birth can have made them. His has been nourished by the *Mémorial de Sainte-Hélène* in its active stage of wishful aspiration and by the psychologizing of

Rousseau's *Confessions*. In neither case is there more than a suggestion of manners; both Napoleon and Rousseau have succeeded through the triumph of egoism over manners.

The crucial test of romantic rebellion against the la Mole decorum is the feeling toward death. Men in the present economy, she reflects, fear death. The interior scene of the dining-room is introspective and intellectually incestuous. Wit is so inhibited by the political conscience as to be dry and dull. "The smallest living idea seemed an outrage" (ii, 38; Pl, i, 457). She is first drawn to Julien's independence, which has survived all of his strenuous ambitions. "These follies surprise you without tempting you," she says to him (ii, 78; Pl, i, 488). In the midst of a formal ball, of which she is the honored guest, she can think of nothing but the stupidity and the human deficiency of those around her. Only death survives the scramble for power, she reflects. "I can think of nothing but a sentence of death that distinguishes a man; . . . it is the only thing that is not to be bought" (ii, 80; Pl, i, 489). The death scene is the true means of discriminating between the romantic ego and its bourgeois defections. The advantages of a fortunate birth make it all but impossible for one so endowed to act in such a way as to merit a sentence of death. Only the underprivileged can so act; force is still sufficiently strong there, and ambition and resentment may direct it in acts of indecorous violence. Julien is in her eyes the only man capable of such heroism.

In her meditations upon the failure of heroism among her class, Mathilde is drawn more and more toward Julien, who stands aloof from the ball, talking earnestly and blasphemously to the Comte Altamira, an exile from Spain, another rebel against the repressive force of privilege. The Comte offers the shrewdest and the most significant of all comments upon the *status quo*:

> ". . . There are no longer any genuine passions in the nineteenth century; that is why people are so bored in

France. We commit the greatest cruelties, but without cruelty." (ΙΙ, 88; Pl, Ι, 496)[5]

Men resent and are bored, but they are not willing to take a larger risk. Once invested in an exhilarating but destructive charge (in Napoleonic times), force is now constrained beyond immediate hope of renewal. It comes through in petty niceties of manner or in nicely planned meannesses to advance the self. The aristocracy bows to inhibition, the peasantry are engaged in small stratagems, and pure force lives on only in such spirits as Julien's. The Comte's observation concerning cruelties is of the essence. Julien would be cruel to advantage; the others commit cruelties to preserve the right to commit cruelties.

Mathilde broods over this condition, which she despises as cowardice twice compounded. Her melancholy ideal is the vision of one of her ancestors who went to the guillotine for an attempt to abduct Queen Marguerite of Navarre:

> "What impresses her in this political catastrophe is that Queen Marguerite of Navarre, who had waited concealed in a house on the Place de Grève, made bold to ask the executioners for her lover's head. And the following night, at midnight, she took the head in her carriage, and went to bury it with her own hands in a chapel which stood at the foot of the hill of Montmartre." (ΙΙ, 99; Pl, Ι, 504)

On these terms the love of Julien and Mathilde grows. She dreams of him as the successor of the beheaded. Only he will ask the privilege of death, and only he is in a position (or has the vigor) to act to deserve death. But the love affair is hedged by social comedy. The merits of Julien as hero are qualified and at times almost canceled by his lack of poise. He has always been a hero who watches himself acting as he acts.

---

[5] Cf. Eliot's "Gerontion":

> . . . Think
> Neither fear nor courage saves us. Unnatural vices
> Are fathered by our heroism. Virtues
> Are forced upon us by our impudent crimes.

Il est dans l'essence de cette âme d'agir à la fois et de se regarder agir, de sentir et de se regarder sentir.[6]

The act of observing himself now takes the form of an elaborate game of *Tartufferie*. The spirit of Molière haunts and all but reduces to ridicule the young man's elaborate strategy. He is thrilled and at the same time frightened by the chance of Mathilde's submission to him. His love of the experience is never free of his pride in and fear of the achievement. She on her part wants the thrill of the "grand passion," the love that would stimulate great deeds, that would in itself be an emotion of major importance. It will be her climactic defiance of the inhibiting circumstances which have bored her so long. It is only fitting that she should offer her love to a man of no means but of much power.

Julien's difficulty comes not from his timidity but from his incredulity. He cannot believe his good fortune and suspects a trap. A series of comic episodes follows from his suspicion, with Julien acting the role of a Machiavelli turned almost into Malvolio. The torture of his love is not genuinely affecting; his lack of worldly wisdom plays him false, and he attempts to make up for it by the most extravagant of devices. This strikes one as one of Stendhal's most skillful insights; Julien's original decision is to outwit hypocrisy itself by appearing hypocritical before it. The effect is a mixture of the pathetic and the ludicrous. Mathilde's submission to it is similarly ridiculous; having earlier misread his aloofness, she is now entirely overcome by it and gives in hysterically to the vision she has had of him—a counter-vision of the boring tedium which she has so long resented in her society.

Besides the comedy of the young naif forcefully imitating the formal adventures of gentility, Stendhal intends another com-

---

[6] Quoted, in Turnell, *The Novel in France*, p. 147, from Paul Bourget, *Essais de psychologie contemporaine*, Paris, Alphonse Lemerre, 1886, Vol. I, p. 298. "It is of the essence of such a spirit to act at the same time he watches himself acting, to feel and to observe himself feeling."

edy: that of his disappointment in achievement, the "n'est-ce que ça." The milieu is after all not deserving of the grand passion. There must be a touch of the ridiculous in its occurrence, like the grand actor who accidentally sticks himself with the sword he is using in the culminating scene. The affair of Julien and Mathilde eventually becomes a tangle of household arrangements. M. de la Mole frowns paternally, is terribly but expectedly angry, settles Julien with a title and a small fortune, and is saved from compromising his principles altogether only by a note sent to him by Julien's former mistress, Mme. de Rênal.

In the concluding act of *The Red and the Black*, reality intrudes upon the romantic visions of both Julien and Mathilde. Julien hurries to Verrières, buys a brace of pistols, and enters the church. As the young acolyte rings the bell for the Elevation of the Host, Julien shoots: ". . . he fired a shot at her with one pistol and missed her, he fired a second shot; she fell" (II, 280; Pl, I, 645). A few moments later he is in prison, expecting the guillotine:

> His reasoning went no further; he felt a pain in his head as though it had been gripped with violence. He looked around to see if anyone was holding it. A few moments later, he fell into a deep slumber. (II, 281; Pl, I, 645)

In the remaining days of his life, Julien rescues himself as a hero from the excesses of the Hôtel de la Mole. At the trial he asserts his prescriptive right to the violence he has committed. He refuses to maneuver either his escape or his pardon: either would have meant submission to the pettiness of his environment. In effect, he wills his death; it is an act of suicide, an act which testifies for the first time to his moral superiority over those to whom he has abundantly already proved himself intellectually superior. He becomes a kind of bitter satirist of social pretension and worldly ambition in the hours before his death. When the guillotine finally cuts him off, Mathilde has her wish, to replay the romantic gesture of her ancestor; she buries the head of Julien separately, after undertaking her own form of death-ritual with it. In this, only Mathilde seems ludicrous. Julien has been translated beyond the bounds of his own excessive romanticism. He has, in short, had the courage to arrange his own death, and he has refused either to evade it or to consecrate it by ordinary means.

—[iii]—

The problems of violence and decorum can best be seen in the light of two stages of the human and social economy: first, the relationship of human passion to social and moral forms (the question of "manners" is of great pertinence); and, second, the interaction of human acts with ideologies. One can imagine two antithetic poles: at the one extreme "manners," at the other ideological systems. In nineteenth century literature, these two radically opposed forms of the human mind moved more and more closely together, until they came within range of each other. The result was to challenge the novelist in a curious way: he had in all conscience to produce a "novel of manners of violence"; that is, he had to account for violence in a literary form that was not prepared to accommodate it.

I do not mean to say that violence is in itself necessarily alien to manners, but rather that the pace, volume, and quality of impact of violence changed steadily. It became more impersonal, less available to the ministrations of ordinary decorum. The novelist of manners needed to assume that the relationships of his characters with one another and with social structures were credible (not necessarily "realistic," but acceptable on the level of the imagination). The increase in pace and rhythm of violence diminished the possibility of credible human relationships. Distortions of the human and social patterns increasingly troubled the best nineteenth century novelists. In some cases, these distortions were ingeniously maneuvered into fictional designs that accounted for them and yet somehow ended in a personal revelation, tragic, ironic, or pathetic. But the effort became more and more arduous, the results less and less certain.

To return to the initial subject of this chapter: Stendhal portrays his heroes performing willed acts of revolt against, or exploitations of, the existing order; but these heroes also live in a society that either is not easily maneuverable in terms of individual heroics or is indifferent to them. For the Beyliste, energy is exhausted in private wars, cloak and dagger intrigues, futile stratagems in *opéra-bouffe* little states. He lives amid the ruins of Napoleonic energy. It is not that there are no opportunities for vigorous acts, but that they do not lead to satisfactorily "heroic" results. As a result, the Stendhal novel invariably yields to comedy and irony. Intelligence, virtue, skill, manners are never really soberly exercised or observed. Fabrice of *La Chartreuse de Parme* (1839) is continually engaged in activities the futility or absurdity of which drains him of his seriousness. He is, of course, at center, "un homme serieux"; but he does not live in a serious time, or at least the kind of man he is cannot really act seriously within it.

There is another strain in nineteenth century literature, which is worth at least a brief mention; it leads to a reversal of manners and such terms as nobility and virtue belong to the commonplace, to men and women at the bottom of the economic and moral ladders. This hierarchic reversion, quite thoroughgoing and devastating, is a development parallel to the technological enhancement of violence. Ultimately it led to the Marxist dialectic, which is fundamentally secular and proletarian, and it forced a reversal of social and literary evaluations. It led also to the type of novel that uses the masses as hero, in which virtues are gleaned from commonplace acts or are rescued from the ruins of nobility, or are quite inversively judged in terms of the distortions of former heroism. Zola's *L'Assommoir* (1877) and his *Germinal* (1885) are obviously the most remarkable nineteenth century examples of this type.

Germinal is an especially fascinating example of the genre. The ancestor of the proletarian or "strike" novel of the twentieth century, it is a consequence of research energy, and of a simple and even a crude "block structure." [7] Unlike either Stendhal or James, Zola had no set of manners to use as a basis of his examination of social forces. Though the middle class was central to the cohesiveness of Second Empire society, the established manners of that class were there primarily to be abused and ridiculed; and Zola did not possess Stendhal's subtlety in the manipulating of social strategies.

He had therefore to work in terms of a balancing and counterbalancing of forces and appetites; these terms need almost to be taken literally. What makes *Germinal* interesting is that, in the absence of a respected set of manners, Zola "imported" ideologies as forms of order, definition, and even decorum. Zola visualized a social pattern of progress toward a new society and a "new man." *Germinal* is an examination of the several forms by which social forces and human appetites may be balanced. In a genuine sense, Zola tried to improvise manners to accommodate forces, while James attempted to bring forces within the patterns of convention and decorum, to assimilate violence formally and to preserve the "grand design" of manners with which he examined the intricacies of human moral exchange.

In the sense of its being constructed out of basic materials, *Germinal* is an important antecedent of the twentieth century novel of social change. There is much improvisation, much quick adjustment to the immediate exigency, and the kind of

---

[7] F. W. J. Hemmings describes the problem very appropriately as follows: "The form of *L'Assommoir* . . . could be illustrated by a curved line, rising to a zenith and then sinking again; but *Germinal* has more than one dimension: it has to be described in terms of cubic capacity, of the balance of weights and counter-weights. . . . (*Emile Zola*, Oxford, Clarendon Press, 1953, p. 179.)

alert characterization of environment and action that suggests a novelist's working "on the run," keeping pace with events and formulating their meaning as he describes them. The novel is both "scientific" and tendentious. Fortunately neither characteristic is strong here, though they are both responsible for causing damage to other Zola works. Instead, we are confronted with powerful forces driven by powerful appetites; and the novelist plays the two against each other, usually with considerable success.

There are a number of pertinent scenes in the works in which violence and decorum exist in an uneasy imbalance: Souvarine's destruction of the mines (*Germinal*), Stevie's destruction (his having been literally blown to bits) (*The Secret Agent*, 1907), the growing dominance of the abstractly materialistic symbol of the silver mine (Conrad's *Nostromo*, 1904), a variety of suicides in the novels of Dostoevsky and Turgenev, the suicide of Hyacinth Robinson (James's *The Princess Casamassima*, 1886). The truth is that violence and its ideologies gradually succeeded in pulling the novel of manners entirely out of focus; it is replaced by the novel of violence, whose angle of vision is consistently distorted, whose author first yields to the distortion and ends by creating an art from its terms. Looking at the extreme poles of this development, one may put at one the half-comic analytics of Julien Sorel's courtship of Mathilde de la Mole (it is an ironic use of "classical" literary mannerisms), and at the other, Picasso's *Guernica* painting. There are many literary expressions of that painting's techniques (war novels, portrayals of concentration camp experiences),[8] but Picasso's work has the grace and power of distortion to suggest itself as a basic text of modern violence.

The novel of manners died hard, in a sense is not dead at all, but is certainly diminished. Our concern with it here is not to describe its decline, but to examine its attempts to come to terms with violence. Everyone involved in this history begins

[8] See below, Part Two, chapters 6, 7, and 8.

with a disturbed social conscience: the novelist is sensitive to the weakening of the aristocracy, the "upper class," knows about the sporadically successful explosions of revolutionary enthusiasm. He tries to bring the facts of violence within the range of manners. His successes are always only partial; the discourse of manners becomes less and less competent to discuss violence.

Manners are at first a source of protection against violence, an attempt to contain it within social forms. To be serious about manners is to argue a moral preference for older forms but at the same time a conscientious attempt to examine them for weaknesses. The novelist asks himself: Why do they no longer account for *all* human exigencies? Why do they no longer serve to motivate all moral decisions? Why is the *direction* of social motivations changing, even reversing itself? This reversal occurs in every aspect of nineteenth century life: the shift from Hegel to Marx, the continuous failure of efforts to establish societies of "rational harmony," the shift of rhetoric from the drawing-room to the street barricades, the resistance shown by revolutionary characters to efforts to represent them as comic or absurd figures, the steady move toward the secularization of thought and life.

Henry James tried, in *The Princess Casamassima* (1886), to attend directly to these matters, more than that to contain them within the "novel of manners." "Experience, as I see it," he said in his Preface, "is our apprehension and our measure of what happens to us as social creatures. . . ." [9] His original idea was to find a hero who is somehow linked to both extremes of society, whose act of violence would therefore be an act against himself or "his own." James combined this device of a social suicide with a personal suicide; in doing so, he preserved his most cherished moral expression, that of the hero's renouncing an end or purpose to preserve the decorum of means. But he had also to "give way" in this novel to the force of violent cir-

[9] *The Princess Casamassima*, New York, Scribner's, 1908, Vol. 5, p. vii. Other references, acknowledged in the text, are to this edition.

cumstance. That is, in order to have Hyacinth "renounce" his purpose, he must have him turn the violence against himself. So there is blood after all; there is an explosion. And this suicide is different from all other deaths in James's fiction. It is, for example, the second suicide with which the Princess is associated; but Roderick Hudson's death (if indeed it is a suicide) is a romantic gesture of despair, to which no superficial social motive is attached.

Hyacinth Robinson dies of the violence of forces to which he has attached himself, for idealistic and for hereditary reasons. His mother had killed his aristocratic father for motives that are halfway class resentment, halfway partake of the full intensity of the *crime passionnel*. Neither motive suffices to force Hyacinth to repeat the violence. He remains dedicated to both extremes of the social scale; but he cannot so divide his loyalties and still escape some kind of violence. Many significant deaths in nineteenth century fiction have ideological motives of one degree or another of intensity: Julien Sorel, whose ideological struggles fail him because of an essential weakness in society, who cannot therefore avenge himself against either society or passion; Nezhdanov, of Turgenev's *Virgin Soil* (1877), who like Hyacinth finds it impossible to clarify or strengthen his loyalty to either class of society, and who must therefore die by his own hand (that is, his hand is maneuvered ideologically into the commission of suicide); Kirillov, of Dostoevsky's *The Devils* (1871), who wills his suicide in the interest of proclaiming a secular defiance of God; Decoud, of Conrad's *Nostromo*, who commits suicide because he cannot stand isolation, but fundamentally because he is possessed of no ideology that will enable him to endure it.

The force of Robinson's predicament is revealed to him early. At a very early age he is taken by Miss Pynsent to the "huge dark tomb" of Newgate prison to see his dying mother for the only time of his life. She is on the edge of death, wasted and old, and Hyacinth is overcome by distaste. She whines repeatedly, "Il a honte de moi—il a honte, Dieu le pardonne!" (v, 53.) Eventually Hyacinth agrees to an embrace, but the experience stuns him into a moody silence: ". . . he sat looking out of the window in silence till they reentered Lomax Place" (v, 56). The dreadful experience of ugliness and age, so frequently a crucial event in modern literature, is here given a special Jamesian "turn."

The full force of this scene is revealed only gradually: Hyacinth looks at death in a prison hospital; he defines himself in terms of the scene, as a member of the disinherited, disenchanted, "illegitimate" class. He is a "bastard" and "of the left." There are many reasons why he will not be able to forget these origins. A child of bad fortune, he will grow to something resembling manhood (though in one sense he simply moves from one mother to the next), and the taint of his illegitimacy combines with the political fact of his mother's French ancestry.

It is not surprising that the major effects of *The Princess Casamassima* should be achieved through a succession of misesen-scène, but it is unusual that one of them should be the London streets: The "feeling and smell of the carboniferous London damp; the way the winter fog blurred and suffused the whole place . . ." (v, 82). In fact, James's novel is in this respect a "manners" version of Dostoevsky's use of St. Petersburg.[10] But for James the street scene communicates a social disturbance; it is not a projection of Robinson's conscience, as St. Petersburg is of Raskolnikov's. Instead, the details of London stand in clear distinction from the décor of the Princess' town and country homes. The Jamesian line goes all the way down, from the drawing-room to the slum and prison.

From the London streets James selects social and socialist types. He is not interested in making them doctrinally precise and would regard ideological niceties as unnecessary distractions. Eustache Poupin is characterized as "an aggressive socialist," all "humanitary and idealistic" (v, 93). Socialist slogans

[10] See below, Part Two, chapter 5.

came easily to him and he is accustomed to violence, but ultimately the slogans do not triumph over personal commitments; Poupin and Robinson are in the same corner at the end, and the old man despairs over the criminal necessities that have emerged from his political training.

The pivotal word for the Poupins, as it is for the Princess, is *they*. The word has directly opposite meanings: "they" are the aristocrats and owners to Poupin, anarchists and socialists to the Princess. But "they," in Poupin's phraseology, "was a comprehensive allusion to everyone in the world but the people— though who, exactly, in their length and breadth, the people were was less definitely established" (v, 107). Here James touches lightly upon an aspect of the clash between ideology and manners: the difficulty in ascertaining the human condition within a frame of ideological reference.

Hyacinth is alone to resolve the ambiguity. Both of the "they's" ultimately define themselves to him: the people have a democratic energy; the aristocracy seems to him largely necessary to art. But this is an "old-fashioned" realization. It does not prevent Hyacinth's suicide, as its kind did not prevent the destruction of churches in the Spanish Civil War. The disparity between the two extremes is too obvious and is forced too passionately for art or the love of tradition to forestall disaster. In this sense, there is a direct line of descent from Robinson's suicide to Picasso's *Guernica*; both are the consequence of violent distortions of what Hannah Arendt has called "the miracle of being." [11]

But M. Poupin has after all a great respect for "conscientious craftsmanship," and in the business of book-binding there is a chance that art may survive. Robinson thinks at one time that he will go beyond binding books, to writing one, but this is a slender line of resolve, as against the crude power of print in doctrinary pamphlets and leftist newspapers. *The Princess is*

[11] *The Origins of Totalitarianism* (1951), New York, Meridian Books, 1958, p. 469.

The Princess Casamassima is a strangely rich, varied, and confused book. The superficial line of meaning is clear enough: Hyacinth, a bastard product of the aristocracy and the proletariat, has first to confirm himself in his role of proletarian "questing knight"; then, because of his having seen other worlds, his education progresses antithetically to his resolve. He must therefore, as a noble young man, fulfill his pledge, which is to help destroy the nobility. That is, he must acquit himself honorably and to do so requires the use of violence against a world of manners. But he can no longer serve this role, and must therefore set himself up as the "nobility" he will destroy.

The suicide is James's way of resolving the tensions caused by a conflict of violence and manners. It is a neat, a "clever" device; but the wonder is if James truly means it. For, in terms of the novel of manners, of the aesthetic maneuvering of moral conventions, the suicide restricts and limits violence, sets it aside and leaves its major concerns unresolved and inoperative. In a sense, the novel of manners retreats from the implications of violence, while at the same time it tries to "personalize" it, to remove it to the introspective singularity of a man who (by birth, degrees of education, consciousness) is both, and inextricably, assailant and victim.

But, as the character of the conspirators is mysterious beyond necessity, the progression of events leading to Hyacinth's suicide is arbitrary and unconvincing. At best, it testifies to a few simple truths: that James was aware of imbalances in society that were too serious to be ignored; that he knew of the sporadic explosions of violence, the social earthquakes of 1848, 1871, and others;[13] finally, that he could not give up the one principle that dominated both his life and his fiction: that the moral conflicts could and would be represented in the relationships

[13] For a detailed examination of these matters, see W. H. Tilley's *The Background of the Princess Casamassima*, Gainesville, University of Florida Monographs, number 5, fall 1960.

nevertheless one of a few James novels in which a commercial enterprise is not only respected but admired. Most of James's Americans produce obscure and vulgar "things" which they sell in huge quantities, as a result of which they are able to travel to Europe to see and even to buy "real things." It is ironic that Hyacinth, when once he knows the Princess, can think of nothing better to do for her than to give her books beautiful bindings; the tribute merely bores her. Since the craft of bookbinding is halfway a trade and halfway an art, it is very appropriate that it should provide Robinson a livelihood. The Princess's scorn of his gift is an expression of her apparently uncompromising rejection of the Prince's world of *bibelots* and *objets d'art*.

The closest James came to an accurate representation of a leftist functionary is the figure of Paul Muniment: ". . . he probably indeed had a large easy brain quite as some people had big strong fists . . ." (v, 114). Muniment does represent the bureaucracy of violence, the orderly and efficient leftist stance which made Hyacinth think of "a rank of bristling bayonets . . ." (v, 119). He is the only character of the novel, in fact, who seems consistently and casually impersonal. There are slogans and there are personal idealisms which yield a harvest of abstractions; but only in Muniment do the ideological lines seem to harden into an *abstract* person. Everyone else is in at least some respect vagrantly human and "inefficiently" humane. It is true that Paul seems at times to love his crippled sister, but she is proved in the end to be an unattractive person, on precisely the same level—the ideological—on which he is proved to be less than personally real. Rosy Muniment's illness is hopeless, and she should therefore expect sympathy, but her bright cheerful indulgence is willful.

The only person among Hyacinth Robinson's generation who is miraculously free of ideological encumbrances is Millicent Henning, a middle-class professional woman by virtue of a hard, sure determination, who had come as far as her type could. She had absolutely no sense of the "masses," except that she "simply loathed them, for being so dirty . . ." (v, 163). Millicent is significantly the only person who offers Hyacinth sexual love; but she is entirely and arbitrarily amoral, and when he seeks her out before his suicide, hoping to escape into her arms, she has already taken up the mediocre playboy, Captain Sholto. Sex is scarcely ever an important resort for James's heroes, but here he brings to it a value that it does not elsewhere have—the value that Winston and Julia found in it, in Orwell's 1984. But Millicent is a shameless and unsentimental Philistine, whose most "artistic" ambition is for "a front garden with rock-work . . ." (v, 164). She is a heroine of another revolution, the unideological one of middle-class raisings—as distinguished from Communist or Fascist "risings."

In a very real sense, *The Princess Casamassima* is a novel of manners that criticizes manners. It does more than offer a genteel satire of aberrant or ridiculous types within a social structure; James honestly tries to come to grips with the evil that has come to threaten society. In the end he is a conservative, for he could be no other; and Hyacinth's long letter to the Princess from Venice is written more by his creator than by him. The center of James's criticism is the Princess herself. Women are always the focus of his moral criticism. The Princess "sins" at both extremes of the social spectrum. When she marries the Prince, at the urging of her mother (*Roderick Hudson*, 1876), she denies everything she might independently have believed to be valuable; and she forces the death of Roderick Hudson, an artist. There is something dreadfully serious about James's interest in monuments, the arts, scenes, which Christina Light has defied and defiled in her marriage.

The punishment is boredom. The Princess' weariness over the dull Prince and his world is James's symbol of nineteenth century *acedia*. At one extreme we have the Princess living in a world of precious and dull objects (Hyacinth, in his first visit to the Princess, sinks into "a seat covered with rose-coloured

brocade and of which the legs and frame appeared of pure gold") (v, 284). At the other extreme, resentment of the world's harsh inequities variously seeks articulation. The Princess suffers the illusion (it is the form taken by her sense of atonement) that "they" at the other extreme are more "exciting," more purposeful, more courageous and noble. As James says of her, she belongs to the class who "could be put on a tolerable footing only by a revolution" (v, 293). She wants to avenge herself upon the Prince's class because she has also been exploited by it.[12]

She does not succeed in doing much more than merely demean herself, and in being one of the instruments (Miss Pynsent and Mr. Vetch are the others) of the education of Hyacinth, which leads to his suicide. As the Princess descends, she moves from one kind of décor to another, and ends in a "vulgar little house" in Madeira Crescent. James's description of the place is rich in the several ironies at his disposal. His interest in the relation of scene to human motive is nowhere more clearly relevant. It was obviously, he says, "her theory that the right way to acquaint one's self with the sensations of the wretched was to suffer the anguish of exasperated taste . . ." (VI, 182). It is not the place that is important, but her reasons for choosing it. She is not the repentant sinner choosing a life of remorse, but a would-be conspirator. And she is left at the end with the realization that neither charm nor conviction interests the conspiratorial group at the "mysterious, revolutionary center." As Paul Muniment tells her, the movement is interested only in her (or the Prince's) money; it is her so "value."

[12] It must be admitted that most of the Princess' motives for her acts come from her hatred and scorn of the Prince and his world, and especially from her resentment over having been "caught" in a form of *mariage convenance*. In this sense, she is James's instrument for dramatizing a sense of distress, even horror, over the decline of the aristocracy, and its venality and mediocrity. The energy of the Princess' attachment to "a cause" is not easy to analyze; the least one may say of it, however, is that it is *not* motivated by any ideological interest in history.

nevertheless one of a few James novels in which a commercial enterprise is not only respected but admired. Most of James's Americans produce obscure and vulgar "things" which they sell in huge quantities, as a result of which they are able to travel to Europe to see and even to buy "real things." It is ironic that Hyacinth, when once he knows the Princess, can think of nothing better to do for her than to give her books beautiful bindings; the tribute merely bores her. Since the craft of bookbinding is halfway a trade and halfway an art, it is very appropriate that it should provide Robinson a livelihood. The Princess's scorn of his gift is an expression of her apparently uncompromising rejection of the Prince's world of *bibelots* and *objets d'art.*

The closest James came to an accurate representation of a leftist functionary is the figure of Paul Muniment: ". . . he probably indeed had a large easy brain quite as some people had big strong fists . . ." (v, 114). Muniment does represent the bureaucracy of violence, the orderly and efficient leftist stance which made Hyacinth think of "a rank of bristling bayonets . . ." (v, 119). He is the only character of the novel, in fact, who seems consistently and casually impersonal. There are slogans and there are personal idealisms which yield a harvest of abstractions; but only in Muniment do the ideological lines seem to harden into an *abstract* person. Everyone else is in at least some respect vagrantly human and "inefficiently" humane. It is true that Paul seems at times to love his crippled sister, but she is proved in the end to be an unattractive person, on precisely the same level—the ideological—on which he is proved to be less than personally real. Rosy Muniment's illness is hopeless, and she should therefore expect sympathy, but her bright cheerful indulgence is willful.

The only person among Hyacinth Robinson's generation who is miraculously free of ideological encumbrances is Millicent Henning, a middle-class professional woman by virtue of a hard, sure determination, who had come as far as her type could. She had absolutely no sense of the "masses," except that she "simply loathed them, for being so dirty . . ." (v, 163). Millicent is significantly the only person who offers Hyacinth sexual love; but she is entirely and arbitrarily amoral, and when he seeks her out before his suicide, hoping to escape into her arms, she has already taken up the mediocre playboy, Captain Sholto. Sex is scarcely ever an important resort for James's heroes, but here he brings to it a value that it does not elsewhere have—the value that Winston and Julia found in it, in Orwell's 1984. But Millicent is a shameless and unsentimental Philistine, whose most "artistic" ambition is for "a front garden with rock-work . . ." (v, 164). She is a heroine of another revolution, the unideological one of middle-class raisings—as distinguished from Communist or Fascist "risings."

In a very real sense, *The Princess Casamassima* is a novel of manners that criticizes manners. It does more than offer a genteel satire of aberrant or ridiculous types within a social structure; James honestly tries to come to grips with the evil that has come to threaten society. In the end he is a conservative, for he could be no other; and Hyacinth's long letter to the Princess from Venice is written more by his creator than by him. The center of James's criticism is the Princess herself. Women are always the focus of his moral criticism. The Princess "sins" at both extremes of the social spectrum. When she marries the Prince, at the urging of her mother (*Roderick Hudson*, 1876), she denies everything she might independently have believed to be valuable; and she forces the death of Roderick Hudson, an artist. There is something dreadfully serious about James's interest in monuments, the arts, scenes, which Christina Light has defied and defiled in her marriage.

The punishment is boredom. The Princess' weariness over the dull Prince and his world is James's symbol of nineteenth century *acedia*. At one extreme we have the Princess living in a world of precious and dull objects (Hyacinth, in his first visit to the Princess, sinks into "a seat covered with rose-coloured brocade and of which the legs and frame appeared of pure gold") (v, 284). At the other extreme, resentment of the world's harsh inequities variously seeks articulation. The Princess suffers the illusion (it is the form taken by her sense of atonement) that "they" at the other extreme are more "exciting," more purposeful, more courageous and noble. As James says of her, she belongs to the class who "could be put on a tolerable footing only by a revolution" (v, 293). She wants to avenge herself upon the Prince's class because she has also been exploited by it.[12]

She does not succeed in doing much more than merely demean herself, and in being one of the instruments (Miss Pynsent and Mr. Vetch are the others) of the education of Hyacinth, which leads to his suicide. As the Princess descends, she moves from one kind of décor to another, and ends in a "vulgar little house" in Madeira Crescent. James's description of the place is rich in the several ironies at his disposal. His interest in the relation of scene to human motive is nowhere more clearly relevant. It was obviously, he says, "her theory that the right way to acquaint one's self with the sensations of the wretched was to suffer the anguish of exasperated taste . . ." (vi, 182). It is not the place that is important, but her reasons for choosing it. She is not the repentant sinner choosing a life of remorse, but a would-be conspirator. And she is left at the end with the realization that neither charm nor conviction interests the conspiratorial group at the "mysterious, revolutionary center." As Paul Muniment tells her, the movement is interested only in her (or the Prince's) money; it is her sole "value."

---

[12] It must be admitted that most of the Princess' motives for her acts come from her hatred and scorn of the Prince and his world, and especially from her resentment over having been "caught" in a form of *mariage de convenance*. In this sense, she is James's instrument for dramatizing his sense of distress, even horror, over the decline of the aristocracy, and its venality and mediocrity. The energy of the Princess' attachment to "the cause" is not easy to analyze; the least one may say of it, however, is that it is *not* motivated by any ideological interest in history.

The Princess Casamassima is a strangely rich, varied, and confused book. The superficial line of meaning is clear enough: Hyacinth, a bastard product of the aristocracy and the proletariat, has first to confirm himself in his role of proletarian "questing knight"; then, because of his having seen other worlds, his education progresses antithetically to his resolve. He must therefore, as a noble young man, fulfill his pledge, which is to help destroy the nobility. That is, he must acquit himself honorably and to do so requires the use of violence against a world of manners. But he can no longer serve this role, and must therefore set himself up as the "nobility" he will destroy.

The suicide is James's way of resolving the tensions caused by a conflict of violence and manners. It is a neat, a "clever" device; but the wonder is if James truly means it. For, in terms of the novel of manners, of the aesthetic maneuvering of moral conventions, the suicide restricts and limits violence, sets it aside and leaves its major concerns unresolved and inoperative. In a sense, the novel of manners retreats from the implications of violence, while at the same time it tries to "personalize" it, to remove it to the introspective singularity of a man who (by birth, degrees of education, consciousness) is both, and inextricably, assailant and victim.

But, as the character of the conspirators is mysterious beyond necessity, the progression of events leading to Hyacinth's suicide is arbitrary and unconvincing. At best, it testifies to a few simple truths: that James was aware of imbalances in society that were too serious to be ignored; that he knew of the sporadic explosions of violence, the social earthquakes of 1848, 1871, and others; [13] finally, that he could not give up the one principle that dominated both his life and his fiction: that the moral conflicts could and would be represented in the relationships

[13] For a detailed examination of these matters, see W. H. Tilley's *The Background of the Princess Casamassima*, Gainesville, University of Florida Monographs, number 5, fall 1960.

of consciousnesses to each other, no matter how violent these conflicts might be.

James sacrificed his "son" to preserve this principle, to give it a fund of "grace" from which it might subsequently draw. *The Princess Casamassima* is substantially different from other James novels. For one time, evil (which is always present in one form or another in the other novels) is here for a while externalized, brought out into the open, dissociated at times from the systole and diastole of the human conscience, made "a public thing." But it does not long remain so extrusive. James "accommodates himself" to the violence, which is a natural consequence of moral extraversion. With the Princess and a minor functionary of the "movement" looking on, the "thing" that was Hyacinth Robinson becomes mute testimony of a violence finally captured and turned against itself: "Hyacinth lay there as if asleep, but there was a horrible thing, a mess of blood, on the counterpane, in his side, in his heart" (vi, 430).

—[iv]—

The "horrible thing" that testifies to the suicide of Hyacinth nevertheless is still "of a piece." Brutality spent, the idea of an intelligence superintending the moral conventions is saved. Partly this is because the violence is still triggered by a personality, against another or against itself. We do not know what dark plots have initiated or will survive Hyacinth's act. Julien Sorel and Hyacinth Robinson have comparable instruments of destruction at their disposal. Not long before their time, men of violence hacked at each other with swords, or tortured each other with primitive (though sometimes very ingenious) instruments. Both James and Stendhal are concerned to "personalize" ideological tensions; both succeed only partially in doing so.

However inadequately explained the suicide of Hyacinth is, as an act of violence it differs radically from Sorel's attack upon

Mme. Rênal. Both sources of the tensions that cause the suicide are impersonal. They have to do with class differences, with classes formulating them, with leaders announcing the necessity of acts. *The Princess Casamassima* is not a novel of "class warfare," but it is one of a few nineteenth century novels which identify the possibilities of such warfare and try to range the classes against one another.

The major conflict in the "great tradition" of nineteenth century fiction is that between manners and ideologies. The latter term undergoes important changes; the most important of these is the change from an implicit set of beliefs to one that is forcefully, creatively explicit. An explicit ideology begins as a theory of history, and it proceeds in the direction of "proving" the future in terms of a "proven" past. This kind of ideology generates several types of personality that are marginal to it. One of the most interesting of these is the skeptic. Others are the opportunist, the "bushwacking" secret agent; the *isolé* whose moral conscience is almost entirely engaged in coming to terms with itself outside of or beyond established society (Africa and Asia, "dark" or "mysterious" continents both serve as the locale of such retreats); and finally, the victim per se, who suffers violence after having achieved only a rudimentary sense of the "bad, bad" world.

Conrad's *The Secret Agent* gives us a startling glimpse of the second and the last of these. It is a remarkable demonstration of a distasteful task nobly and even heroically acquitted. "It is one of the minor satisfactions of my writing life," Conrad said retrospectively in 1920, "that having taken that resolve [to treat the subject ironically] I did manage, it seems to me, to carry it through to the end." [14] As an example of defensive irony, *The Secret Agent* is a significant novel; but it is much

[14] "Author's Note," *The Secret Agent*, New York, Doubleday, Page, 1926, Vol. xiii, p. xiii. Other page references to the novel are to be found in my text and are to this uniform edition, known as the Kent Edition.

more than that. Conrad goes far beyond James in meeting major issues of the twentieth century.

In many respects, *The Secret Agent* is our first novel of violence. While the anarchists are characteristically, like James's, of the nineteenth, the implications go far ahead. The basic organization of his idea is simple: the middle class, the marginal world, and the law; or, sentiment, violence, and legality. It is the function of the law to preserve freedom, while at the same time it protects the citizenry from violence. Adolf Verloc attempts to maneuver within all three spheres: he tries to keep the law from closing in, he is of the middle class and avails himself of its comforts, and he is responsible for all of the kinds of violence of which the novel treats. He is also the object of Conrad's most withering contempt.

Two scenes provide us with extreme illustrations of the novel's antitheses: the "Professor's" first talk with Comrade Ossipon, and the voyage of three Verlocs to a charity cottage. The first of these is from all standards of aesthetic judgment an extreme and an imperfect characterization. The Professor is not a character at all, but an abstraction scarcely blooded. He is concerned almost exclusively with the task of perfecting a bomb with a flawless detonator. He wears the explosive on his person and promises to use it as an assertion of his superiority over "people," who otherwise make him feel small and insignificant.

> ". . . I walk always with my left hand closed round the india-rubber ball which I have in my trouser pocket. The pressing of this ball actuates a detonator inside the flask I carry in my pocket. It's the principle of the pneumatic instantaneous shutter for a camera lens. The tube leads up. . . ." (66)

The Professor also has his theoretic views of mankind, but these are either pure abstraction or meanly motivated. Revolution and legality, he says, are "counter moves in the same game; forms of idleness at bottom identical . . ." (69). Since "idleness" is one of Conrad's major concerns, the Professor's statement bears some examination. We have a vision of an elaborately peaceful social structure, which is illusory because both the police and the anarchists maneuver within it for advantage. Idleness is apathy, ignorance, fear; it is also a disease of the moral will, which impedes self-analysis.

The delusive calm is susceptible at any time of explosive interruption. The Professor, a caricature of the scientist's view of social energy, is centrally concerned to provide the opportunity for such explosions. Conrad wishes us to take him seriously at least in this respect. The irony of his description is in deadly earnest.

> . . . The extreme, almost ascetic purity of his thought, combined with an astounding ignorance of worldly conditions, had set before him a goal of power and prestige to be attained without the medium of arts, graces, tact, wealth—by sheer weight of merit alone. . . . (80)

The key phrases are "ascetic purity," "astounding ignorance of worldly conditions," and "sheer weight of merit." They damn the Professor definitively, and they point to the menace of undisciplined violence. Conrad's view of anarchism condemns its irresponsibility, the "ignorance" and narrowness of its dedication, the idleness which is at the heart of its danger.[15] The

[15] Conrad disowned any knowledge of or interest in anarchists or revolutionaries, a disclaimer that seems odd in view of the fact that *Under Western Eyes* (1911) is a direct use of their Russian and Continental confederates. ". . . I don't think I've been satirizing the revolutionary world," he wrote R. Cunninghame-Graham on October 7, 1907. "All these people are not revolutionaries—they are shams. And as regards the Professor, I did not intend to make him despicable. He is incorruptible at any rate. . . . At the worst he is a megalomaniac of an extreme type. And every extremist is respectable." (G. Jean-Aubry, *Joseph Conrad: Life and Letters*. Garden City, New York, Doubleday, Page, 1927, Vol. II, p. 60.) Whether Conrad's purpose is to treat directly of the pre-World War I revolutionary situation is perhaps an academic question. It is true, however, that in *The Secret Agent* anarchists, nihilists, or reasonably satirical

Professor is a dedicated "saint" of the new religion of indiscriminate violence, the very symbol of a naked power, the formula of which he follows with a "pedantic fanaticism" (81). He *believes* in destruction, and sees himself as its agent:

> Lost in the crowd, miserable and undersized, he meditated confidently on his power, keeping his hand in the left pocket of his trousers, grasping lightly the india-rubber ball, the supreme guarantee of his sinister freedom; but after a while he became disagreeably affected by the sight of the roadway thronged with vehicles and of the pavement crowded with men and women. He was in a long, straight street, peopled by a mere fraction of an immense multitude; but all round him, on and on, even to the limits of the horizon hidden by the enormous piles of bricks, he felt the mass of mankind mighty in its numbers . . . (81–82)

He fears and hates the people, but fears most of all their chances of surviving his act of "ascetic purity." Should he press the bulb, express his power, would not "the people" survive? But, who are "the people"? We are offered a few privileged glimpses of the wealthy and the poor; but mostly the human spectacle remains lost in a maze of speculation and rhetoric. We see them only as an object of the law's protective concern or of marginal abuse. Where is the human reference in *The Secret Agent*? It exists in the very trap set for it by amoral opportunists and hateful anarchists.

---

facsimiles of them are at the center of the novel's thematic development. And the *agent provocateur*, Adolf Verloc, is a masterpiece of ironic characterization. Leo Gurko's study (*Joseph Conrad: Giant in Exile*, New York, Macmillan, 1962) accepts the revolutionaries as an "analogue" of the novel's main theme, the *isolé* in the great city: "The total split that exists between the anarchists and the society they seek to overthrow is matched by the split that exists within the lives of the individual characters. In the structure of the novel the great, teeming, grimy city is the appropriate format for this incohesiveness and the image which supplies it with an ultimate source of reference!" (p. 173)

The human condition is here cast almost entirely in the role of victim. Conrad's desire to point up the danger, and the mockery, of a dislocated marginal superiority forces him to reduce "the people" to the scope of three members of Verloc's family: Winnie, her mother, and Stevie. They are either passionately or nervously "good." They are, in any case, almost as "astoundingly ignorant" of "world conditions" as is the Professor; but they exist, nevertheless, in protest against the lack of love and the failure of moral precision that exist around them.

Chapter eight offers as full an analysis of the sentimental victim as we have. Winnie's mother decides to leave the Verloc ménage, to retire to a charity cottage. Her reasons are warmly sentimental; she does not know that she is the only member of the family who will die naturally. The cottage is intimately associated with that kind of death.

> In the privacy of a four-wheeler, on her way to a charity cottage (one of a row) which by the exiguity of its dimensions and the simplicity of its accommodation, might well have been devised in kindness as a place of training for the still more straitened circumstances of the grave, she was forced to hide from her own child a blush of remorse and shame. (160)

As for the others, they are to die violent deaths, all of them triggered by the "scientific," the "intelligent" explosive of the Professor. Stevie is deliberately muted. He is the privileged idiot, the blessed, *selig* fool, whose simplicity allows him to react with extreme pain or extreme trust to a variety of human aberrations. To him *any* cruelty is entirely bad, *any* superficial sign of affection entirely good. Pain or images of pain distress him absolutely. The measure of his failure to sense the "worldly condition" is taken many times. On the way to the charity cottage, the cabman tries to defend his whipping of the horse ("the steed of apocalyptic misery") on domestic grounds: he has "my missus and four kids at 'ome."

> The cabman grunted, then added in his mysterious whisper:
> "This ain't an easy world."
> Stevie's face had been twitching for some time and at last his feelings burst out in their usual concise form.
> "Bad! Bad!"
> His gaze remained fixed on the ribs of the horse, self-conscious and sombre, as though he were afraid to look about him at the badness of the world . . . (167)

Stevie is the absolutely "committed" victim, as the Professor is the dedicated menace, of a world of violence. It is quite impossible for Stevie to penetrate the surface of the world, or to analyze the rhetoric of its pundits. He can only retreat into abstract positions: a total distress over pain or the threat of pain, or a feverish concentration upon the drawing of circles at the kitchen table.[16] He is therefore, in his failures to detect the nuances of either mercy or villainy, apparently an absolutely "safe" assistant in the accomplishment of Verloc's designs. He is destroyed absolutely, as well, blown to bits and fragments.

> They had to gather him up with the shovel. Trembling all over with irrepressible shudders, [Winnie] saw before her

[16] The circles of course have a supra-rational meaning which Stevie can no more articulate than Faulkner's Benjy can articulate the symbolic meanings of his world of flowers, spaces, and smells. Conrad comes closest to defining Stevie's act in relation to brutality and pain in chapter 3: ". . . Mr. Verloc, getting off the sofa with ponderous reluctance, opened the door leading into the kitchen to get more air, and thus disclosed an innocent Stevie, seated very good and quiet at a deal table, drawing circles, circles, circles; innumerable circles, concentric, eccentric; a coruscating whirl of circles that by their tangled multitude of repeated curves, uniformity of form, and confusion of intersecting lines suggested a rendering of cosmic chaos, the symbolism of a mad art attempting the inconceivable. . . ." (45)

the very implement with its ghastly load scraped up from the ground. Mrs. Verloc closed her eyes desperately, throwing upon that vision the night of her eyelids, where after a rainlike fall of mangled limbs the decapitated head of Stevie lingered suspended alone, and fading out slowly like the last star of a pyrotechnic display. . . . (260)

To this vision of a total, a "pure" destruction of a "pure" victim, Winnie Verloc now addresses all of her passionate energy. Abstract violence in this case generates personal violence. The opportunity still exists to turn impersonal violence into a crime of passion. Winnie destroys her husband in an amazing scene, one of the most startling of all *crimes passionnels* in all fiction. Its appropriateness to its object all but justifies Conrad's heavy emphasis upon ironic representation in this novel. Adolf Verloc has profited from, indulged in, and almost entirely abused the virtues of the domestic scene. Domesticity has enclosed him, and protected him in his idleness. Ultimately, however, domesticity becomes a weapon. The kitchen knife, which he has just used in preparing his supper, now becomes the instrument of his death.

> . . . He saw partly on the ceiling and partly on the wall the moving shadow of an arm with a clenched hand holding a carving knife. It flickered up and down. Its movements were leisurely. They were leisurely enough for Mr. Verloc to recognize the limb and the weapon.
> . . . But they were not leisurely enough to allow Mr. Verloc the time to move either hand or foot. The knife was already planted in his breast. It met no resistance on its way. . . . Mr. Verloc, the Secret Agent, turning slightly on his side with the force of the blow, expired without stirring a limb, in the muttered sound of the word "Don't" by way of protest. (262–63)

Verloc's death, and Winnie's suicide which follows upon it, are openly, personally motivated. They fit into the pattern of the *crime passionnel,* to which even the most savage butchery in traditional literature belongs. But Stevie's death is entirely irrational: irrationally "bad," as Stevie is himself irrationally "good." The two kinds of death, and the contrasts so easily seen between the two, are the major contribution of *The Secret Agent* to a study of modern violence. In his very simplicity, Stevie signifies the modern victim; in his "ascetic purity," the Professor symbolizes the sources and character of the modern assailant. Adolf Verloc, a paragon of irresponsible idleness, is a middle man, both a symbol of the moral failure Conrad so vehemently condemns and an agent of the undisciplined destructiveness sponsored by the Professor's pseudo-science.

There is no extenuation in this novel of the irrational ghastliness of violence; in this lack *The Secret Agent* significantly differs from *The Princess Casamassima.* Manners exist only in the ironic effects Conrad is able to give to his open expressions of anger and pity. The violence is not contained within a suicidal resolution of tensions; Winnie's suicide is out of fear and despair, and it is quite unsubtle. In this one case at least, we may say that manners give way altogether to violence.

—[v]—

In the scope of *Nostromo* (1904),[17] in the depth of its analysis, in the intricacies of its perspective, the problem of violence is much more subtly examined. Conrad offers us a geography, an anthropology, even a geo-metaphysics of violence. The San Tomé silver mine is at once a natural resource, a "buried treasure," and the focus of political and economic organization. Men and women are what and where they are because of the mine. The novel examines many significant truths, not the least of which is the relationship of force (energy, nat-

[17] Edition used: Garden City, New York, Doubleday, Page, 1926. References to this edition (the "Kent Edition," Vol. IX) will be found in the text.

PART ONE: GRACE

ural powers) to the moral economy. Consider the mine as a focal center of the technological genius and political fallibilities of man. It exists in a Latin American state, and as if inevitably it attracts men to it, makes them behave specifically in several ways because it is a resource to be mined, moulded, shipped.

The boldest and most obvious antithesis is the contrast of Charles and Emilia Gould in their responses to its challenge. Emilia, who has been won over to the romantic excitement of Charles' inherited adventure, remains throughout a patroness of the finer distinctions and graces; as Charles moves further and further away from her, she remains wedded to the human condition of the scene. Gradually it develops that the mine is an object of scientific exploitation, of "engineering," and Emilia's emotions and interests abandon it. Her "conquest" of the community is a feminine achievement, similar to those of Jane Austen's and Henry James's women. In defeat, she grows morally, in the power of defining the limits and the excesses of man. She remains a goddess of "manners," taking measure of the excesses, absurdities, and violences of law, order, engineering, and revolution.

"What is wanted here is law, good faith, order, security," Charles tells her. "Anyone can declaim about these things, but I pin my faith to material interests . . ." (84). No matter what the momentary brutality, the outbursts of violence, these are in the end justified by the focal and disciplinary functions of these "virtues." Gould, in short, becomes an inflexible technological materialist whose rationality is rhetorically supported by an idealism of ends. As Decoud says of him, he "cannot exist without idealizing every simple feeling, desire, or achievement . . ." (214–15). The master of the treasure and of its expropriation, Gould is at the same time its slave; in the end he is as much the guardian of "progress" as his wife is its critic.

The mine is also a moral focus; it draws from men their best and their worst. Conrad's point is that men do not honestly or adequately act until or unless they have morally come to terms with their conscience. He provides us with three characters who are engaged in such a struggle: Emilia Gould, whose senses are consistently trained upon the object at hand; Decoud, a skeptic who fights cynicism because he cannot bear what it does to him; and the supremely natural man, Nostromo, who performs deeds of valor and nobility in the interests of his emotional status. All three of these are engaged in the act of self-definition. Only Mrs. Gould achieves it. Decoud is guilty of intellectual pride, fights his way out of that position, reluctantly assumes the role of a political man, engages in acts and adventures for specific reasons, then is finally thrown back upon his own resources. In the end he is an *isolé*, unable to tolerate the moral emptiness his skeptical view engenders; and he commits suicide because he can no longer endure himself.

Decoud's tragedy comes from his mistrusting words, those used by others to defend what they have done, and, in the end, his own. Since he can penetrate to the falsity of all rational formulas, he is left with a talent which does not serve him in isolation. All around him there are people who make words, from the stately prose of Avellanos, father of his fiancée, to the irrational pretentiousness of revolutionary leaders. Nostromo, on the other hand, is a romantic of deeds. Like Decoud, he does not trust improvised ideological formulas. He does not believe in a future, or in immortality, and cannot spare the time from his adventures to bring a priest for the last rites of Teresa Viola. In the words once again of Decoud, Nostromo is "a man for whom the value of life seems to consist in personal prestige" (248). But this "natural man" is as inadequate to himself as are Charles Gould and Decoud to themselves. His natural talents do not save him, and he is rightly portrayed in the end as corruptible, shot and killed by mistake as he is making his way to the silver hoard he has so successfully hidden from everyone.

There are no anarchists in this novel, for the scene is an isolated, supra-historical image. A revolution does occur, and a counter-revolution; but they are scattered and fragmentary events, or at least they are represented in this complex narrative as fragmentary. The truth is that the political development of this country is very close to being identical with its physical development and with the progress of its "manners." None of these can be trusted; revolutionaries are children playing a game of democracy and dictatorship. The only reality is the San Tomé mine, which attracts efficient exploiters who have the words and weapons needed to define and defend themselves if they are called upon to do so.

The country of Costaguana is represented as a transcendent, paradigmatic world. The very atmosphere—its calmness, its difficulty of access which for so many years has prevented its political growth, the alternation of geographical grandeur with human meanness—contributes to the sense of its being a world in and of itself. Conrad maneuvers the vision of it, in the beginning, in from the sea, about the Isabel Islands, until its seaport appears to the eye as a surprise:

> From that low end of the Great Isabel the eye plunges through an opening two miles away, as abrupt as if chopped with an axe out of the regular sweep of the coast, right into the harbor of Sulaco. It is an oblong, lake-like piece of water. On one side the short wooded spurs and valleys of the Cordillera come down at right angles to the very strand; on the other the open view of the great Sulaco plain passes into the opal mystery of great distances overhung by dry haze. The town of Sulaco itself—tops of walls, a great cupola, gleams of white miradors in a vast grove of orange trees—lies between the mountains and the plain, at some little distance from its harbor and out of the direct line of sight from the sea. (7–8)

There is a quality of gem and setting. For a moment, one does not feel that people are necessary to it. But the silence is broken; the line of vision changes to a café on the approaches to the town, the Albergo d'Italia Una, managed by Giorgio Viola, an old "Garibaldino," who was once devoted servant of the master himself. This image of a classic example of revolutionary force alternates with the scene of sporadic fighting— shots heard intermittently, shouts, the sight of horses moving quickly across the plain. "Bursts of great shouting rose and died away, like wild gusts of wind on the plain round the barricaded house; the fitful popping of shots grew louder above the yelling. Sometimes there were intervals of unaccountable stillness outside, and nothing could have been more gayly peaceful than the narrow bright lines of sunlight from the cracks in the shutters, ruled straight across the café over the disarranged chairs and tables to the wall opposite . . ." (18).

The noises of revolution violate the air in an act of deep imposition. Yet the shots are as certainly and as accurately an accounting of force as the sounds of Hyacinth Robinson's suicide and of the explosion that scatters Stevie over the landscape. *Nostromo* is, after all, a novel of violence. What distinguishes it from others is its isolation from specific historical reality. It is an imaginary country, but it has real revolutionaries in it. The narrative becomes an elaborate speculative game of moral perspectives; its major effect is that of the physical resource and the words that are used to define human relationships to it.

Conrad presents us with an intricate intellectual puzzle. In this country of vast topographical contrasts—mountains and plain and water located in an order grotesquely intimate—there is a natural resource, which can be left as it is, can remain unexploited. But the silver is after all a valuable metal, and it is difficult of access; it therefore needs technology, power, speed, efficiency to extract it, law and order to guard it and to guide its transport. The mine attracts to itself all of these, and an infinite number of variants of revolutionary and executive rhetoric and manners besides. Costaguana is an almost perfect symbol of the way in which nature and man both attract and need ideological definition.

Only the man who has himself come to know with what he in all conscience believes is right can remain faithful and trustworthy, or so Conrad seems to say. But where is there such a man? Charles Gould comes to believe in the verbal formulas he has invented, but these are easily seen for what they are. Decoud cannot bring himself to trust any formulas at all. Nostromo is handsome and compelling and courageous, but he is an empty adventurer, corruptible because his naïveté leaves him susceptible to disillusion. An "adventurer," Conrad says through his characterization, has nothing left when no one praises him. His acts are performed to gain a hero's rating. The alternative is to "get rich slowly." Dr. Monygham, tortured into giving away important information in an earlier revolution, lives in bitter and shameful memory of his disgrace. Viola is a revolutionary of the old, the European school, but he has many times the opportunity to see that revolutions can be as corrupt as their causes.

Nostromo moves rapidly to a "happy" climax. The revolution is defeated, order is restored, progress has come again. But there is no assurance that this state of affairs will continue. The silver now moves out of the country, without hindrance. There is some sophistication in Sulaco. Is this a justification of the process of law and order? Temporarily, it is. Conrad, however, is nonsocial; or, rather, he knows that the social order has been preceded by aberrant disorders. The great variety of minor insights into human corruption—Sotillo, The Montero brothers, the miserable Hirsch, and many others—live at the edges of seemly progress. Above all, the history of Costaguana has been a succession of irrational acts—aimless heroism and pointless brutality—to bring about the apparent triumph of Charles Gould's orderly universe. In the end, no one is unscarred, except perhaps the imperceptive English manager, Captain Mitchell, who does not count except as a mockery.

Above all, *Nostromo* is an analysis of the relationship of rhetorics to forces. A score of rhetorical systems or improvisations are invoked by as many persons or groups to explain, define, or exact approval of political and moral positions. At the two extremes are Charles Gould's "ascetic" missionary zeal for material interests and the self-ending skepticism which ultimately leads to Decoud's suicide. Because Gould's mission has practical results and forces even to practical devices, it becomes an activist and—for the time at least—a successful organizational stratagem. But it often takes on the character of a monastic discipline; Emilia's is an "immaculate conception" of "the first spongy lump of silver yielded to the hazards of the world by the dark depths of the Gould Concession . . ." (107). In the end she is resigned to the life that follows, with a man ascetically devoted to the mine, the Protestant ethic which provides him (and perhaps her) with limited rewards, and a half dozen of abstract virtues. But she cannot overcome her feeling that "there was something inherent in the necessities of successful action which carried with it the moral degradation of the idea." *She* sees the menace of the San Tomé mine, but she also sees that Charles cannot see it:

> He could not see it. It was not his fault. He was perfect, perfect; but she would never have him to herself. . . . With a prophetic vision she saw herself surviving alone the degradation of her young ideal of life, of love, of work—all alone in the Treasure House of the World. The profound, blind, suffering expression of a painful dream settled on her face with its closed eyes. In the indistinct voice of an unlucky sleeper, lying passive in the grip of a merciless nightmare, she stammered out aimlessly the words—"Material interest." (521–22)

More clearly than *The Secret Agent*, *Nostromo* is a record of the conflict of violence with forms of decorum, manners, moral convention. Its portrayal of expedient ideological maneuvers is a prescriptive analysis. As in *The Princess Casassima* and *The Secret Agent*, intelligence and sentiment lead to suicide. Violent death of some sort is a constant reminder in most nineteenth century fiction of the inadequacy of both reason and sentiment to the growing depersonalization of force. The forms which explain, fulfill, and contain man's irrational impulses are adequate only in a world in which a *status quo* is assured. Violence can be tolerated if it is seen in a humanly limited context.

Beginning with Stendhal's novels, this context is seen breaking apart. Romantic force leads only to crimes, seen and comprehended and punished within social limits. But gradually explosions of force yield less and less gracefully to explanation. Ideological maneuvers are taken out of the hands of amateurs and made a driving importunate historical force. This is the "lesson" of the deaths of both Decoud and Nostromo: neither a penetrating skepticism nor a naive gestural romanticism is adequate to explain or settle the issue. Emilia Gould remains, but she is after all "widowed" and has lost her husband to the mines. Her "graces" have become an empty ritual, a pathological washing of hands.

—[vi]—

You, "to excess," simplify, said Henry James, by way of acknowledging one of H. G. Wells's books. But he granted that the social prophet must work superficially: ". . . I can't imagine a subtilizing prophet." James would, however, like to know, "where is *life* in all this, life as I feel it and know it?" Where, too, is fineness of distinction? "There are for instance more kinds of people, I think, in the world—more irreducible kinds —than your characters meet." [18] Wells's utopianism did stimulate James's admiration—the "cheek" of it, the bold, unswerving unsubtlety of it:

[18] Leon Edel and Gordon M. Ray, eds., *Henry James and H. G. Wells*, Urbana, University of Illinois Press, 1958, p. 76.

... As in everything you do (and especially in these three last Social Imaginations [*Anticipations, Mankind in the Making, A Modern Utopia*] it is the quality of your intellect that primarily (in the Utopia) obsesses me and reduces me—to that degree that even the colossal dimensions of your Cheek (pardon the term that I don't in the least invidiously apply,) fails to break the spell. Indeed your cheek is positively the very sign and stamp of your genius ... I hold, with you, that it is only by our each contributing Utopias (the cheekier the better,) that anything will come, and I think that there is nothing in the book truer and happier than your speaking of this struggle and of the rare yearning individual toward that suggestion as one of the certain assistances of the future. . . . (103–104)

This strange friendship of two men who saw life from radically different points of vantage serves to underscore still another set of nineteenth century polarities. To accept science without qualification, to insist upon immutable law as a guarantee of social survival, is at the least to risk setting aside "nuances" in the interests of "cheek." Both extremes begin in respect for reason. The difference between them is largely in the matter of scope and range of conviction. To have lived so much of one's life—as Wells did his—insisting that large assumptions will grow in effectiveness through repetition is almost automatically to forego intellectual responsibilities. In his insistence upon the strong moral generalization, Leslie Stephen encouraged many a man like Wells. Setting aside much of the forensic daring and the love of melodrama that were part of Wells's stock in trade, Stephen performed many of the same acts of rational independence and asserted some of the same kinds of liberal necessity in the interests of progress. Stephen was also an analyst of human motives; he restricted his analysis to those motives that were assumed to have a rational origin. He wished, in short, to "do good" and, as well, to find out the root sources of what prompted men either to do good or to refrain from doing it. Wells is an extreme example of what one of his meditations upon human society might have helped to produce.

Leslie Stephen's convictions regarding the religious power of secular law required above all the sanction of obligatory right reason: the belief that "there exist universally and eternally certain moral truths obligatory upon all men to follow, which are directly intuited by right Reason, as it operates in all normal men." [19] But at the same time that scientific speculation attacked religious ontologies, it was itself being disabused of its confidence. David Hume's analysis of the relations of mind to objects and actions was a continuing demurrer. If the "laws" of morality can actually be proved to be predications of relationship, at best they can be said to be generally true or frequently observed as occurring. They are not therefore immutable or constant laws; moral discriminations return to the quality of the mind which relates to the quality of objects, and finally to a cluster of qualities, of mind, object, and relationship.

There are two major lines of development in the history of this attempt to triumph over both superstition and mortality. The one, emerging from the analysis of Hume, moves at times wearily through utilitarian bogs, is redefined and renewed in the Cambridge colloquies of G. E. Moore, and (in terms of literary history, at least) moves to the Bloomsbury of Virginia Woolf, Roger Fry, Clive Bell, John Maynard Keynes, and Forster. The other, its source in the eighteenth century complexes of rationalism and rationalization, pursues its way through Victorian adaptations of science to morality, becomes involved in the melodramatic schemata of Herbert Spencer, and leads to the wildly and weirdly volatile speculations of H. G. Wells. In the one case, Hume's "relations" become Forster's

[19] R. V. Sampson, *Progress in the Age of Reason*, Cambridge, Harvard University Press, 1956, p. 150.

"personal relationships"; in the other, scientifically verifiable moral law comes eventually to be administered by the "voluntary nobility" of Wells's *Samurai*. The approach to death widely differs: the one ignores it, at least as a challenge to social enthusiasm, and concentrates upon the cultivation of "states of mind" and the appreciation of objects; the other works hard to conquer death, through prolonging life, eliminating disease, perhaps hopefully speculating upon the time when death is altogether forestalled. In any event, enthusiasts of Progress settled for a second best kind of immortality, the immortality of a species steadily improving, moving toward a conscious being of the race's excellence and its approach to perfection.

The human mind resolutely and with integrity willed progress, or willed organizations of society which made for progress. Mill had talked of the mind of "normal" man; Leslie Stephen spoke of the disinterested man possessed of a strong, unselfish will; eventually, in the utopian fantasies of H. G. Wells, it was the mind of a "voluntary nobility" that saw the law and willed its effective operation in the progressive state. But beyond this development of moral heroism, there was in almost all variants of progress theory the belief in change as morally good: scientists, in addition to their responsibility to laws, effect changes in society, both material and moral; men change their beliefs, to accommodate these alterations of welfare; and this process is continuous. It is biologically necessary that man continue to evolve; it is socially necessary that his moral evolution not be impeded by intolerance or superstition.

While brutality and "unreasonable conduct" existed, they were seen as aberrations, abnormalities, and described as exceptions rather than threats to the norm. Popular science extracted evil from the world's body, or promised its elimination. A simple and understandable confusion existed in the popular mind: evil, rarely if ever associated with the psychology of man, was regarded as almost exclusively a discernible and accessible part of external society or of the human body; it was equated with disease, or with bad drains, or in extreme cases with bad manners. The optimistic denial of evil reached some kind of progressive height in this passage, which concludes Winwood Reade's *The Martyrdom of Man* (1872):

> The God of Light, the Spirit of knowledge, the Divine Intellect, is gradually spreading over the planet and upward to the skies. . . .

> Satan will be overcome; Virtue will descend from heaven, surrounded by her angels, and reign over the hearts of men. Earth, which is now a purgatory, will be made a paradise . . .

> Hunger and starvation will then be unknown, and the best part of the human life will no longer be wasted in the tedious process of cultivating the fields. . . .

> Disease will be extirpated; the cause of decay will be removed; immortality will be invented. . . .[20]

Since the guarantee of immortality is one of the distinguishing functions of gods, Reade's prognostics conclude with this statement: "Men then will be perfect; he will then be a Creator; he will therefore be what the vulgar worship as a God" (Houghton, 36). There is a direct relationship between the stages of bodily corruption and the time of dying, and progress in the elimination of disease and the halting of decay necessarily suggested longevity; the margin of difference between a very long life and immortality was a relative matter. Richard Gerber says of modern utopian fiction that "Individual immortality is one of the attributes of the perfect superman, and extremely long individual life is a characteristic feature of all the utopian

[20] Quoted in W. E. Houghton, *The Victorian Frame of Mind, 1830–1870.* New Haven, Yale University Press, 1957, pp. 35–36. That the "invention of immortality" is not a wish peculiar to nineteenth century Britain is testified to in a Reuters dispatch to the New York *Times* from Lahore, Pakistan (December 27, 1960): "Prof. V. Koranov . . . has told doctors here that it may be possible in the future to 'banish death altogether' by means of the transplantation of animal organs." (p. 3)

dreams covering a greater time-span." [21] More soberly restrained prophets of progress were inclined to be satisfied that immortality was more an evolutionary metaphor than a valid promise. T. H. Huxley and Leslie Stephen both reflected upon the loss of loved ones as necessary sacrifices. Wells spoke, in *First and Last Things* (1908), of himself as "not a continuing thing" and suggested that a personal God, "who is always going about with me," would make him uncomfortable.[22] The next best thing, and the conviction that sustained most of those who had abandoned Christian hopes, was the immortality of generations, the thought that goodness in the present led to increased health in the future. Nevertheless, longevity is a natural and expected consequence of medical progress.

In the absence of theological sanction, the driving moral obligation was to illuminate the pages of history by working hard. Since the theory of progress (perhaps inevitably) had also to deny the Christian sanction of *good* works, the incentive had to come somehow from within the character of the work itself and its social effects. But suppose one were to doubt the value of work, to question the validity of this secular incentive? *Ennui* without God is vastly more devastating than fear of Him. We fall back upon such honorable secular terms as sincerity, integrity, honor, and courage. But individual expressions of these after all need some form of generalized incentive and supports; too often they are mocked in the quality and setting of their achievement. In consequence of the double peril, of loneliness and *ennui*, critics of progress were often led to some variant of this gloomy summary: man has lost the privacy which he needs to sustain himself as an individual; he is cut off from any real communication with his fellows by the annihilating work of progress; and, whether events have convinced him or he has unaided begun to doubt his goals, he suffers from an all but complete failure of incentive.

[21] *Utopian Fantasy*. London, Routledge and Kegan Paul, 1955, p. 27.
[22] New York, Putnam's, 1908, p. 110.

There is a pattern of tensions between work ("good works") and death in nineteenth century literature. In German literature these tensions are summed up in a great novel (Thomas Mann's *Buddenbrooks*, 1901) and a distinguished work of sociology (Max Weber's *The Protestant Ethic and the Spirit of Capitalism*, 1904–1905). Both of these are thorough retrospective analyses of the development of the nineteenth century German bourgeoisie, and each in its own way treats of the problems of adjusting work, business, and the accumulation of exterior distinction to the Christian—more precisely, the Protestant—ethic.

Buddenbrooks describes four generations of a distinguished burgher family of Lübeck. They are, with variations of degree and intensity, driven by a religiously motivated activism, the proof of whose value lies in accumulations of money and space. In Mann's tale of the patricians of Lübeck, aestheticism (latent in some Buddenbrooks, pathologically open in others) is at war with the Calvinist principle of moral exertion. Ennui, tedium, a lack of drive or of interest: these are the signs of the bourgeois illness. On the other hand, mental and physical exertion in response to duty is a virtuous exercise which has, in addition to obvious external blessings, an intrinsically valuable reward. The virtuously busy man follows a rational plan which has its own dogmatics. When a Buddenbrook begins to doubt the inevitability of the plan, or to lose the incentive to follow it, the suggestion is that he is acting irrationally, or at least "irresponsibly."

The decline of the Buddenbrooks—first shown explicitly in the "reign" of Thomas (the fourth generation)—runs parallel with the growth of aestheticism in the family. When the Frau Consul (Thomas' aunt) dies, the Buddenbrook world ceases being a locus of religious and business exertions; and Thomas' own death comes after he has sought a romantic explanation of mortality, in Schopenhauer's *World as Will and Idea* (1819), as against the pietistic or rational view upheld in the

Protestant ethic. A succession of events proves that the decline is associated with aesthetic, nonmaterial interests: Thomas' marriage to the alien Gerda, who is sensitive, frail, and sophisticated; the last, weak bough of the family tree, Hanno, who prefers music to mathematics, and chooses dissonance to symbolize his inner distrust and fear of the outer world; finally, and crucially, Thomas' loss of interest, of initiative and drive, and the growth of weariness and of doubt concerning his "consequence" as a man of competence and distinction.

In both the German and the English developments of this theme, death plays an important admonitory role. Mann's descriptions of deaths are often ironic: they come from an overindulgence in the sweet rewards of labor and have much to do with eating and the digestive processes (one of the burghers literally eats himself to death, many of them die of coronaries brought on by over-indulgence). But there is a great difference between the burgher who dies at his desk (who literally works as well as eats himself to death) and the deaths of Thomas and his son Hanno: in both cases, the sensibility has been eroded by a loss of confidence, a growth of romantic pessimism, and the weakening of will power. For Mann, the break seems irreparable between the aesthetic sensibility and the Protestant "work" ethic; his characters reflect again and again on their desire to heal the wounds caused by their separation. But what has begun in *Buddenbrooks* culminates in *The Magic Mountain* (1924). The education of the "new man," Hans Castorp, is undertaken in the special circumstances of the *isolé*, separated from the activity of the lowlands, and it encompasses every variety of contradictory theory and advice. Most pathetic of all is the loss of religious sanctions for personal initiative, which is in any case scarcely ever an initiative in the old Buddenbrook sense.

The great, popular British enthusiast of progress was H. G. Wells. Early in his life he declared his independence of Protestant theology. From an underprivileged, overspiritualized lower-middle-class home, he managed to escape on his own initiative; the pattern of this gesture is repeated many times in his fiction. He seems to have had a personal grudge against the God to whom his mother so often referred his complaints about the poverty and dullness of his youth. In consequence, his major hero is the scientist, objective, dedicated, indifferent for the most part to personal glory or wealth, the nobleman and knight-errant of modern life. Since he had neither the sensitivity of Leslie Stephen nor his education, Wells thought matters out more or less on his own, with a degree of simplicity that made him a literary hero and a bumbling intellectual. There were superstitions, which he thought of as rather elaborate subter-fuges; there was science, neat and circumspect and honest; there was, finally, the "Rational Word," which it was his duty to de-liver to his people. To the time of the First World War he had things pretty well his own way. His scientific romances (fore-runners of many later utopias which alternately thrilled and chilled his readers) played about skillfully with current scientific ideas and prospective realities. He was not above suggesting that evil motives might damage or destroy the bright promise of his world; such a fate was (in *The Island of Dr. Moreau* and elsewhere) an inversion of the Apocalypse as he saw it: the scientific Christ destroys himself and the "good" all but goes under with him.

Wells's world of futures is essentially static; it is also grossly over-simplified. He took a reasonable facsimile of the laboratory situation, noted the kinds of patience and objectivity and de-tachment necessary to make an experiment succeed. He then set up the "scientific man" as the hero of the actual world. In his view, this man is not only desirable but also realizable, and in sufficient quantity somehow to make the world of the future a macrocosm of the laboratory. For the mechanics of history he had access to a very few simple devices: all evidences of calami-tous unreason are not signs of the collapse of hope but inter-ferences, evidences of "waste," shocking but necessarily tolerable. Looking at them in that way, he could neither make them function dialectically, as Marx tried to do, nor entirely protect his progressive view from their recurrence. Entirely without safeguards against the irrational, he assumed first that passion is evil and patience is good, next that reasonable men will deal with evil because they must, and finally that the survival of civilization depends upon a desperate victory of the good man over evil forces.

The paradoxes of nineteenth century speculations upon progress bring Wells, Stephen, G. E. Moore, and Forster within range of one another. Somehow, secular manners borrowed from Protestant morality, scientific optimism, post-utilitarian meditations upon "the good," and aesthetic discourse. The manners that were Bloomsbury's special concern were a part of the literary and philosophical tradition that included Jane Austen, David Hume, and Henry James. In each of these cases, an irreducible minimum of analysis was assumed; the literary and philosophical investigation of human states was primarily an exhaustive consideration of man's reasons for moral choice, whether these were explicitly moral, or generally institutional, or precisely epistemological. To point up the link of Bloomsbury with this tradition of manners, it is useful to think of the common interest in G. E. Moore's *Principia Ethica*, and especially in chapters one and six of that work.[23]

To begin, Moore defined the good as one of those "ultimate terms by reference to which whatever *is* capable of definition must be defined" (10). It is, therefore, an intrinsic value; that which is good may be defined in terms of its possessing or leading to the possession of this value. That is, "good things" are not in themselves referable to a state *for which* they may be said to "be good" (such as a political state, or a moral principle), but rather are good *in themselves*. Beyond this mini-

---

[23] Published 1903. Edition used: Cambridge University Press, 1956. This, the seventh printing, does not differ (except for a 1922 correction of misprints) from the first edition.

mum, Moore holds that states of "the good" are often "highly complex wholes," in which the mind, the object it contemplates, and the relationship we call contemplation, all exist in an organic whole. This suggests a complete analytic freedom with respect to what is good.

> . . . "What things have intrinsic value, and in what degrees?" . . . In order to arrive at a correct decision on the first part of this question, it is necessary to consider what things are such that, if they existed *by themselves*, in absolute isolation, we should yet judge their existence to be good; and in order to decide upon the relative *degrees* of value of different things, we must similarly consider what comparative value seems to attach to the isolated experience of each. . . . (187)

This closely woven analysis involves one in the question of what roles reason and intuition might have. Reason is the methodological instrument according to which we will approach the good (a man under irrational influences will apparently not be in a position to devise such methods); but since good is an intrinsic value, it is up to intuition to recognize goodness when it exists in isolation. To avoid the danger that the intuition might erratically choose external objects that are not good in themselves, Moore asserts that "By far the most valuable things, which we know or can imagine, are certain states of consciousness, which may be roughly described as the pleasures of human intercourse and the enjoyment of beautiful objects" (188). That is, not the objects themselves, or the relationships themselves, but "certain states of consciousness" are of the highest value. It is inevitable that such states are organic complexes, the intrinsic values of which are immediately intuited as the *effects* of an experience of the highest quality. There need be no effort of the imagination to suggest that intuition and taste come to mean the same thing, that they are interchangeable, and that

74

they in no way depend upon custom or present condition or institutional evaluation of moral states.[24]

Since these states of consciousness are intrinsically valuable, they are "the *raison d'être* of virtue," and "it is they—these complex wholes *themselves*, and not any constituent or characteristic of them—that form the rational ultimate end of human action and the sole criterion of social progress . . ." (189). If this is true, then taste is absolutely important and its cultivation (or, if it is the equivalent of intuition, its progressive improvement) is of the essence. An error in taste is a moral error; to improve morality requires initiation into taste, which is something quite different from period courses in literature or "art appreciation." The important aspect of this assertion is not only that the state of consciousness is an ultimate value (that is, intrinsic, a thing-in-itself), but also that in order to communicate it accurately, precise language is necessary, language that is not loaded with emotional pressures or sentimentality or forms of distractions, but rather precisely relevant, nothing more nor less than the thing itself.

The state of mind, which is a form of *the good*, is made up of a complex variety of conditions. That which is beautiful is not a "good in itself" but is good only in the sense that it is related to the act of appreciating and responding to it and to the act of relating the act of appreciating it to the act of another's appreciating it.[25] This leads Moore to assert that personal af-

[24] This is undoubtedly the reason why such a man as Clive Bell is able to say (in *Civilization*, 1928) that men of taste exist in *any* civilization, and that our social concern is simply over the conditions that suppress them or allow them to flourish.

[25] This analysis of taste and its relationship to the consciousness of "the good" bears a superficial resemblance to Henry James's concern over the development of consciousness in his crucial "personages"; but James's vision of the human consciousness is much more in the nature of an invented or imagined "felicity of the soul," and the exploration of its career bears moral implications closely related to the personal interchange of the drawing-room. In a general respect, James and Moore are agreed: that the contemplation of the good by both A and B is a form of enhancing

75

fection is another intrinsic good. In a limited sense this good consists in the sharing of states of consciousness, in augmenting the one with the other. This is not sufficient; or, at any rate, each consciousness must be of the highest good in itself; in the quality of the relationship the good of the whole is enhanced. One is tempted to suggest here that a communication of minds is superior to an isolated consciousness; and Moore admits to that much:

> Though, therefore, we may admit that the appreciation of a person's attitude towards other persons, or, to take one instance, the love of love, is far the most valuable good we know, and far more valuable than the mere love of beauty, yet we can only admit this if the first be understood to *include* the latter, in various degrees of directness. (204)

This is a crucial, though an obvious enough, addition. It suggests not only that personal relationships are valuable, but that the mere desire for personal relationships is not enough; their quality will depend upon the initial state of mind according to which they are set up. The entire range of the literature of manners abundantly documents the varieties of good, evil, beauty, ugliness, distress, and tragedy that result from the challenge of personal relationships. Moore is saying that the motivation for wishing to transcend an isolated appreciation of beauty must in itself be beautiful; that, in the sharing of beauty, the consciousnesses of those sharing affect the quality of the beautiful object, as they in turn affect each other, and thus finally the total economy of "the good" that is the consciousness.

interaction between A and B as much as it is a relationship of A or B to the object of the good. Communication with respect to a defined and an intuited "good" is indispensable to moral growth. Those writers who seem to have taken most from Moore are particularly interested in pairings and groupings of consciousnesses, as we see in the famous dinner scene of Virginia Woolf's *To the Lighthouse* (1927).

The personal relationship so finely wrought in Moore's analysis of it, must be blessed with qualities of intelligence and mutually recognized interests. A successful union of this sort is perhaps the happiest gift of social community. To miss such an opportunity, or obstinately to deny it to oneself, in the interests of adherence to some dogmatic "general good" is a tragedy: one just barely averted, for example, in Forster's novel, *A Room with a View* (1908). But the talent of precisely identifying and yielding to such an opportunity is rare indeed. Insofar as Bloomsbury followed Moore's lead in these matters, they were concerned to identify intelligences, to test them against rather severely held ideas of taste, and (in the person of Roger Fry at least) to educate as a means of bringing latent taste to the surface or increasing the opportunities of exercising what taste did exist.

The final state of the development of rationalism should now be available to some kind of definition. In elevating the value of "states of mind," in shifting ground from sociology to art, Bloomsbury radically changed the perspective upon mortality, from futuristic extensions and utopian anticipations to a limited analysis of forms and values inhering in objects and states of consciousness. The two perspectives come at least in part from the same recognition of mortality per se, without the aid of religious myth or dogma. For the most part utopianism is motivated by a hatred of the world of the present and not especially concerned to study the value of objects existing in that world. The other approach to mortality is not to despise the world but to uncover it, or to *re*cover it. This involves the need to delimit the act of the mind, almost to the point of saying that its sole or proper function is to contemplate itself and the form it creates. This perspective upon our world, unencumbered by reference to another and superior one, brings one to the proper definition of essentials—not essential goals, which are the concern of utopian adventurers, but essential existences. These are only a few, but they are intrinsic values and, as we have seen, their nature grows as they become more revealingly complex. In this latter sense, we do not try to remake the world, nor do we allow formulas of patriotism or religious dogma to interfere with our attention to objects and experiences.

In any really exhaustive attention to intellectual history, these two outgrowths of rationalism will have to be seen, if not in conflict with each other, then in a state of tension which threatens at any moment to become what Forster calls a "muddle." In the circumstances of the "muddle" reside the chances of terror and destruction; but the terror is most often a result of the failure of human beings to see what is at hand or to avail themselves of the opportunities life presents. It may also come from a lack of *sufficient* awareness, or from apathy, which nourishes ignorance and encourages its continuance. The *fact* of death therefore assumes a renewed importance, in any genuine survey of this early century reaction against progress. It has a threefold bearing upon the problem of progress: in fear of it, men push ahead with materialistic projects, thinking to deny its case by forgetting it; it is linked closely with progress, as man becomes a victim of progress and deaths increase instead of being shut off; finally, death is a reminder of life, associated as it is terminally with biological history. Rejecting all extreme forms of ideology, Forster returned simply to the minimum of cant-free personal relationships, the values of which are forever brought back to consciousness by the incidence of death.

No one has so precisely or so aptly defined the role of death in man's affairs. He saw that the fear of death was a major barrier to a full commitment in secular affairs. In several ways, secularized man attempted to exclude death from consideration, and each attempt required, as it led to, forms of social and intellectual abstraction. Forster says that man survives his own enormities of behavior and planning *in spite* of this tendency toward abstraction; at any rate, he has survived so far. Force and violence are a consequence of intellectual cleverness isolated from and denying human sensitivity. This latter is indispensable; it is all that gives us the hope of surviving as human beings. "What is good in people—and consequently in the world—is their insistence on creation, their belief in friendship and loyalty for their own sakes; and though Violence remains and is, indeed, the major partner in this muddled establishment, I believe that creativeness remains too, and will always assume direction when violence sleeps."[26]

These specifically human and humane values are not to be thought as merely surface mannerisms. "Personal relationships" are again and again differentiated in his fiction from social habitude. They are, above all, closely related to a core of human experience, whose movement from birth to death is scrupulously attended to in all of its particulars by the Forster hero and heroine. Moreover, the worth of personal relationships is made secure by another conviction which in isolation from life becomes a monstrosity but in tune with life lends them dignity and value. "The people I respect most," he says, "behave as if they were immortal and as if society was eternal. Both assumptions are false: both of them must be accepted as true if we are to go on eating and working and loving, and are to keep open a few breathing holes for the human spirit." (*Two Cheers*, 71.)

Howards End (1910) is the the most thorough, as it is the most subtle, of Forster's explorations of these human frailties. Here he does not oversimplify the human alternatives. The rhythm of the novel is a movement back and forth between them, with some suggestion that they are coming closer to a resolution each time. Nor does he hedge in the matter of the seriousness of human separations. They lead to violence, but pathetic and not heroic violence, which comes from misunderstanding rather than from passion.

The absolutes are themselves evils, as Forster sees them, because they force the human being into acts of melodramatic

[26] *Two Cheers for Democracy*, New York, Harcourt, Brace, 1951, p. 72.

self-vindication, and are otherwise destructive of human balances. The only acceptable and feasible absolute is the center of the human consciousness of self, in relation to other selves and in full and clear recognition of its association with natural and biological existence. Crime against human nature comes from a distortion of that relation, stemming mostly from either a basic misunderstanding of the relation itself or a deliberate movement (however motivated) away from the center of fusion. In this sense, Forster is "anti-intellectual," but he is also "anti-passional," if either of these states be caught in isolation from its necessary opposite. The "ideal character" is one who has found or will find a balance and who will, moreover, quite unselfconsciously act out the balance in all details of human relationship.

This is one of the reasons why Forster's novels have so uncertain a progress. They are actually very skillfully written, and the surface appearance of casual incoherence is a testimony of his moving quite certainly in terms of extremes seeking resolution. *Howards End,* for example, begins with Helen Schlegel's visit to the Wilcox country home; her impressions are given in letters to her sister Margaret. The scene is itself the important fact: Howards End is a lovely home inhabited ambiguously by Wilcoxes who understand it only as the place Ruth Wilcox cherishes. In a few pages, the "prose and the passion" that are so disastrously far apart in Forster's view of human pathos are specified for us. Helen Schlegel, herself given to passionate distortions of half-understood generalities, reacts to Howards End with enthusiasm, then mistakenly assumes that all of the people who live in it must be worthy of it, and ends in arbitrarily renouncing all Wilcoxes but one. At this point the extremes are far apart indeed.

Throughout, the consequences of Wilcox manliness are seen in the disasters of dust and motion. The dust mingles with the sunset, to obscure the London atmosphere, until, on several occasions, the London scene suggests the wasteland character of Eliot's London and Baudelaire's "brouillard sale et jaune." The dust becomes smoke, fog, a choking off of light, and it hangs over most of the novel's London scenes: "One visualizes it as a tract of quivering grey, intelligent without purpose, and excitable without love; . . . as a heart that certainly beats, but with no pulsation of humanity. . . ." [27]

The imagery of motion is a supplementary Wilcox decor. Forster suggests that we ideally move in accordance with natural rhythms; at any rate, the rapid movement of Charles Wilcox's "throbbing, stinking" car destroys these rhythms, as it ignores them. The vulgarity of the Wilcox children, as well as their colossal failure of perception, is a human aspect of this accelerated motion. Occasionally, and briefly, one has glimpses of the Wilcox tribe that grimly remind us of one or another of the Darwinian fantasies of Forster's time. They have children with astonishing and "efficient" regularity, but they give little promise of producing persons. The Wilcox view of the future is that of a straight line of inhuman efficiency, which is progress, "good for" the human race, to which humans as individuals must bow in submission. The line of this progress is a straight one, the straighter and the faster the better. It demands not only efficiency but speed, and the speed endangers the chance of human association.

Like the Wilcoxes, the Schlegel sisters suffer from a kind of incompleteness. They are all library and books and cloistered intellectual sufficiency; they also have "good will," an untutored sympathy and a strong desire to believe that people are good: "they desired that public life should mirror whatever is good in the life within" (25). The "life within" is the intellectual life motivated by idealistic good will as yet not tested in the life of action and therefore inclined to fall short of necessary

[27] *Howards End*, London, Edward Arnold, 1910, p. 105. Other references to this edition are in the text.

81

keenness of practical perception. The brother "Tibby" goes the long way toward complete scorn of persons, and is largely useless in the struggle. The suggestion is that Wilcox and Schlegel need each other, have something to give each other. But how bring them together? How "connect"? They arouse disgust and suspicion each time they are brought together.

The means of "connecting" is Mrs. Wilcox, who is substantially of the earth, and not long after the novel opens returns to it. Ruth Wilcox and Howards End are the centers of balance. She is never happy away from Howards End, which she regards as a preserver of balance. Here life goes on and Wilcoxes are somehow prevented from destroying each other and the world. But the condition is precarious indeed, and one is not at all sure that she is not fighting a losing battle. A garage has been built; Charles' car stirs up the dust; and Howards End is itself in danger of being absorbed by anonymous suburbia. She must communicate her mission in life to Margaret Schlegel, must will it and Howards End to her, in the hope that Margaret can educate herself in the role of human mediator. The life of Ruth Wilcox has barely enough minutes left to enable her to find and designate her successor. Almost the selection fails to take place; but Margaret shows adequately enough her sensitivity to the delicacy of human relationships before Mrs. Wilcox dies, to guarantee the choice.

Her death is an event of paramount importance. In terms of the novel's plot, it is necessary as a means of initiating the major action of the novel, the move of Schlegel and Wilcox toward the Howards End center. The death is also a symbolic act, connected with the earth and its continuance. The funeral is a slow, deliberate ritual, which says each moment to those who will have the patience to hear that this is what we have instead of progress. We die. It is a difficult fact to comprehend. One of the truly important differences between the two Schlegel sisters lies in their quite different understanding of it:

[Margaret] had not realized the accessories of death, which are in a sense more memorable than death itself. The atmosphere of precautions and recriminations, and in the midst a human body growing more vivid because it was in pain; the end of that body in Hilton churchyard; the survival of something that suggested hope, vivid in its turn against life's workaday cheerfulness;—all these were lost to Helen, who only felt that a pleasant lady could now be pleasant no longer . . . (101) ·

They are not lost to Margaret, and it is her sense of the intimate value of experience (the need delicately to balance cruelty against fright, to penetrate misunderstanding and to make what can be made of imperfections) that attracts her to Ruth Wilcox and makes of her, her successor.

"Oh, to acquire culture! Oh, to pronounce foreign names correctly! Oh, to be well informed, discoursing at ease on every subject that a lady started!" (37) This earnest Victorian, Ruskinian wish is identified with Leonard Bast; by accident, he comes within the world of both Wilcoxes and Schlegels, and each group contributes to his undoing. For Margaret and Helen, Leonard *is* "The people" with whom they have been told in many books and many conversations they must identify. In their own ways, through their cleverness, they are accused, or accuse themselves, of *gaucheries* in their treatment of him. But their worst mistake is their taking him as the illustration of an ideal line of moral idealism, no less wide of the mark than Henry Wilcox's dismissal of him as a member of the lower classes who should keep his place.

As the novel proceeds, Leonard Bast becomes what each Schlegel and each Wilcox will make of him. He also becomes, against almost impossible odds, a plausible human being. As the problem of Leonard grows, the Schlegels grow further apart: Helen's enthusiasm carries her further and further away from center; Margaret, pledged to marry Henry, must remain closer to center. On one calamitous occasion, Helen condemns Henry Wilcox as the arch-demon of modern progressive villainy. Here is one intellectual extreme crying out against the other:

> "But he must be one of those men who have reconciled science with religion," said Helen slowly. "I don't like those men. They are scientific themselves, and talk of the survival of the fittest, and cut down the salaries of their clerks, and stunt the independence of all who may menace their comfort, but yet they believe that somehow good— it is always that sloppy 'somehow'—will be the outcome, and that in some mystical way the Mr. Basts of the future will benefit because the Mr. Basts of to-day are in pain." (189)

This is a parody of one form of nineteenth century moral earnestness—of the "practical" line of progressive thinking. But since it is spoken by a person who has quite thoroughly if momentarily taken leave of her good sense in the interests of her good will, it is in effect a parody of a parody. There is truth in it, but the elements of confusion and emotional distortion tend to warp it beyond recognition. The consequences can only be disastrous for poor Leonard Bast. Margaret Schlegel, on the other hand, has quite abandoned her too literally smug interest in ideals, to turn to the task of making the reality of the world more bearable. "Mature as Henry was, she might yet be able to help him to the building of the rainbow bridge that should connect the prose in us with the passion. . . . Only connect! That was the whole of her sermon. Only connect the prose and the passion, and both will be exalted, and human love will be seen at its height. Live in fragments no longer . . ." (183–84).

Calamities result from misunderstandings, from distortions, inherently willed or consciously maneuvered, of the delicate and precarious truth. Helen, in her excess of humanitarian zeal for her prize specimen of mistreated souls, eagerly submits to Leonard and encourages his love; after which she retires to Germany, to await results. The illness of Aunt Julia brings her back to England before the child has been born. After a series of incidents, both comical and somber, Helen and Margaret find themselves again at Howards End, to which a repentant Leonard comes, to beg Helen's forgiveness for the "sexual crime." The motive for confession is not far from the Wilcoxes' own for condemning Helen. Leonard contrives in his death, with the Wilcoxes as champions of the "moral right." The scene is an affecting illustration of Forster's sense of climax:

> He entered a garden, steadied himself against a motor-car that he found in it [Charles's car, the vehicle of righteous triumph], found a door open and entered a house. Yes, it would be very easy. From a room to the left he heard voices, Margaret's amongst them. His own name was called aloud, and a man whom he had never seen said, "Oh, is he there? I am not surprised. I now thrash him within an inch of his life."
>
> "Mrs. Wilcox," said Leonard, "I have done wrong."
>
> The man took him by the collar and cried, "Bring me a stick." Women were screaming. A stick, very bright, descended. It hurt him, not where it descended, but in the heart. Books fell over him in a shower. Nothing had sense.
> (324)

This passage sums up the novel, as its opening scene anticipates it. The comedy and pathos of human failure are completed. Consider the style of the passage. Leonard entered "a" garden and steadied himself against "a" motor-car, which belonged to "a man whom he had never seen." The violence done to Leonard is unexpected and strange; "nothing had sense." These details suggest Forster's interpretation of the calamitous anonymities into which men of good will and men of determination have forced him. Leonard is to become, posthumously, the father of the heir to Howards End, a place from which he as personal type should never originally have been removed. He will share parenthood with a woman whose extravagant and sentimental sponsorship of the "public good" has precipitated unreason. Charles Wilcox, a most inflexible and inhumane sponsor of Wilcox standards, delivers the blows, with the flat of a decorative sword that had formerly graced the Schlegel library. Finally, Leonard feels the hurt not where the blow descended, "but in the heart." The melancholy fate of Leonard Bast is proved finally to have been a blow at the heart, because the "passion" (uninstructed and insensitive force, in this case, of Charles's inheritance from the Wilcox manner) has not "connected" with the "prose."

One is reminded of the early scenes of this novel, and especially that in which Charles Wilcox, standing in his "throbbing, stinking car," calls out to his brother Paul for plain answers to plain questions. His mother, who knows better, says that one doesn't ask plain questions because "there aren't such things," and turns "away from him towards her flowers" (19–20). Charles's education never reveals the slightest evidence of her influence. Leonard Bast, among the crowds of people she had seen in London but not known, falls victim to Charles's final demand for "plain answers." The context in which these demands for plain answers to plain questions are made, in defiance of the fact that "There aren't such things," may be considered a fine, subtle, pertinent reflection upon the vagaries of separation and isolation which are the consequence of a restless search for the definition of human progress. The Wilcoxes instinctively deny much that exists in the human economy. Helen Schlegel is confused over much else. Only Margaret heroically (though not unerringly) assumes the almost hopeless but somehow worthwhile task of bringing the "prose and the passion" within "connecting" distance of each other.

Howards End offers an admonitory glance at both the principles and the scene of progress. Its sights, smells, noise, and confusion are all critical of a view of human destiny that almost excludes persons from definitions of people. It is most strikingly a novel of contrasting rhythms and paces: the car speeds along the road and threatens to annihilate living things; the air is saturated with its dust; there is a frenetic quality in Charles's commitment to duty. But the novel restrains all of these, slowing them down if need be. The voice of Margaret, superintended by the spirit of Ruth Wilcox, corrects the haste of Helen's anxious tirades. In the end, only Leonard Bast dies as the victim of a world in which "Nothing had sense." Forster tries to save as much as he can of "the good"—which is to say, what is negotiable in G. E. Moore's "states of mind," as they contemplate the "beautiful" and enhance each other in the act. He is aware of the limitations inherent in the mediating act; Margaret Schlegel is never entirely in charge of the situation. But he also feels that the human sensibility must take as much profit as it can from the intervals of quiet that succeed violent eruptions of passion.

—[vii]—

It is possible to see most of the literary scenes presented above as ingratiations of violence, or rationalizations of it. But there is also a hard, relentless, irresistible drive toward the literature of violence of the twentieth century. Either violence is an expression of force freed almost altogether from the formal means of restricting it, or it "explodes" in a condition of easy or strict controls. Julien Sorel, a man of almost pure, uninhibited energy, tries to express himself by overcoming obstacles, though he tries also to resist the temptations of overt rebellion. He plans to express his force within the very circumstances of containment. This he succeeds in doing through most of his life. His access to violence is a blind fury of resentment against the woman who (he thinks) has, unaided, attempted to prevent his final social triumph.

Literature is a noble enterprise, whose aim is to sustain humanity. But it also strives to keep pace with social and mechanical growth in modern times by virtue of its portrayals of the major tensions between force and the circumstances of its containment. Romanticism invests all aspects of the human will, including the will to die, with an extravagance of sentiment and emotion. The history of the nineteenth century novel shows it moving from the extreme of romanticism to an extreme of naturalist passivity. At the one extreme (of which Melville's *Moby Dick* is an eloquent example) the extravagances of the will lead to a dénouement that is significantly tragic. This sense of human tragedy requires a full respect for both person and circumstance. In the eyes of Captain Starbuck, Ahab is a grotesque menace to the peaceful economic purpose of the *Pequod's* voyage. The success of *Moby Dick* as a tragic conception involves the destruction of Starbuck as well as of Ahab. Above all, it involves the destruction of Starbuck's point of view, as of little consequence in eternity.

Stendhal believed, with many of his contemporaries, that the French Revolution was the last full expression of human power. After that, Napoleon afforded many young men the chance to act decisively, heroically, and unconventionally, to move quickly either to great heroic prestige or to death. Waterloo, Stendhal said, was the death blow to heroic opportunity. From that time forward, the hero is no longer a means of dramatizing force; nor is he ever again pure hero. His position is ambiguous: he is both of and not of his world, both disdains it and assumes many of its characteristics. Describing a few of the heroes of Stendhal, Balzac, and Flaubert, Raymond Giraud says:

> All creatures of a bourgeois age, these heroes are expressions of the growing sentiment among anti-bourgeois writers that they could feel more sympathetic toward a

solitary, sensitive and inactive hero than toward one who had innocently and whole-heartedly made his pact with contemporary society.[28]

The literature of violence in our time is part of a very significant historical design, to which both social condition and technology have made important contributions. One begins by arguing an amount of energy or force, which exists in relation to the devices and forms needed for containing it. The manner of containing this force has a vital connection with the current development of technological means. Raw, unmechanized force is used in a limited way, and the psychological techniques for maintaining social balance are limited and even naive. Organization of humanity as instrument and the perfection of techniques of exploitation immensely complicate the issue.

Above all, the forms in which force is contained need to appeal both to the emotions and to the will of those who are governed by them. Both Stevie's circles and the silver mine of *Nostromo* suggest that human analogy with cosmic force is not only useful but indispensable to an understanding of violence. Hyacinth Robinson speaks several times of the "admirable energy" of a democracy. Human force consists mainly in the disposition of men to act passionately, or to act with a strength that exceeds necessity. For the most part human history has alternated periods of tedium with times of violence. Violence suggests a radical change, or at any rate the desire for one. In the earlier stages of the history of violence, expressions of it are almost invariably personally motivated. An act of violence in these circumstances suggests both an overwhelming desire to exert force and a victim (who in one way or another deserves his fate) upon whom this excessive force is destructively impressed. This is the form of the *crime passionel*, an assertion beyond accepted limits of the human will. It is an *explosion* of force beyond the power of the forms of society to contain it.

[28] *The Unheroic Hero*, New Brunswick, Rutgers University Press, 1957, p. 51.

Force is therefore subject to forms of containment, which are violated when and if men accepting their demands neither are overtly disturbed by them nor will a change in their formal arrangement. When human motives allow these forms to absorb force in small details, in fragments neatly put together in the daily economy, the result is tedium but safety. In these circumstances (bourgeois circumstances in nineteenth century society), men of spirit and/or sensitivity grow ashamed or irritated or bored. They resort to satire, or withdrawal, occasionally to personal excesses (which are a form of hastening death and therefore a culturally induced suicide), finally to rebellion. This is to say that a placid, complacent, quotidian grinding down of human force makes for a society outwardly prosperous and happy, inwardly restless and ashamed.

There is another instrumentation of force, however, the growth of which in the last half century has thrown the human economy entirely off balance. In the first chapter of *The Red and the Black* the smell of incense competes for attention with the sound of artillery. At the novel's end, Julien Sorel attempts to kill Mme. de Rênal with a brace of pistols. The two sounds are expressions of technological force. In 1831 these sounds were still noticeably within the control of the persons responsible for making them. The history of violence marks a steady growth in the mechanical extensions of force, which threatened to increase impossibly the distance between assailant and victim. The major distinction is this: between force as an expression of the human will with respect to a discernible and visible object, with the emotional tone of the forceful act fully preserved in its particulars; and force *in itself* (as we have seen in *The Secret Agent*), independent of either agent or victim, with neither logical nor emotional connection sustaining the two. This quality of change is also to be seen in the development of personal relationships. The same kind of depersonalizing effect is noticeable in the loss of clear lines of demarcation between individual and mass. A similar economy of ratio can be worked out to demonstrate the destructive effects of this tendency. The hero in modern literature suffers from both the increase in power mechanisms and the quantitative increase in public human demonstrations of standard similarities.

Julien Sorel's life and death are an expression of human force intervening against the power of social containment. His resolution of the problems created by that power makes him one of the last truly aggressive romantic heroes, if by that term one means a person who acts "singularly" from personal motives. Madame Bovary is similarly bored and acts violently to escape boredom, even to the point of personally willing her death; but she is scarcely of Julien's caliber, and her motives are tainted by the limitations of her own sensibility. She has been trapped by her own romanticism, and she consumes her force, first in self-indulgence, then in self-destruction. Other great nineteenth century heroes and heroines are less bold and less strongly motivated to act. They are so involved (or their authors are) in the circumstances to which they object that their acts of aggression are almost invariably vitiated by a sense of guilty participation or a feeling of embarrassment. They are bourgeois Hamlets. Dostoevsky's heroes save themselves ultimately in their acknowledgment of sin and their commitment to the necessities of atonement. Even so, they engage for a time, for a significant part of their careers, in acts of willed violence: that is to say, they aggressively, forcefully resent the forms of containment and commit violence against them. This is true of *Crime and Punishment*, whose resolution is a truly masterful irony. For much of its progress, Dostoevsky's *The Devils* is a profound investigation of the psychology of willed rebellion. Violence committed against others and against the self is a major subject of that powerful novel.

In twentieth century naturalism the power of the will all but disappears, because force has been incorporated into the laws by which its containment is understood. Even Frank Norris' muscular heroes do not will their violent acts but for the most part act violently out of deference to Norris's assumption that the universe is violent. Clyde Griffiths, who in a few particulars resembles Julien Sorel (there are two women, his social success is being threatened by the interference of one of them, and he is therefore exasperated into wishing her violent removal), is otherwise altogether different from him. It is only when the human will is freed from its prison of *a priori* theory that men of the twentieth century are able once again to act forcefully. Camus' Meursault in this respect comes closest to resembling Julien Sorel. Once he has become fully aware of the circumstances of containment (for most of the novel he cares too little for them to see them clearly), he acts with full command of will and accepts the violence contemplated on his person as an act of violence upon his assailants. The milieux of the two novels are vastly different, as are the ideologies assumed in them; but the comparison is at least worth a brief glance.[29]

I have been mainly concerned to determine the growth of violence as an intrusive—and, eventually, an overwhelming—force. In order to see this history more clearly, I have tried to explore selected illustrations of it in nineteenth century fiction. The novel of that century—whether "realistic" or "naturalistic"—is largely a register of the career of social manners. But, since manners depend upon a closed society, or are in any case best exploited in one, the novelist of manners is uneasy about the necessity to accommodate external, inexplicable force, which intrudes upon manners and the contemplation of them.

The dominating literature of violence in the twentieth century describes the gradual encroachment upon the human will of technological extensions of power. Technology has radically altered the relationship of assailant to victim, and has quite thoroughly upset the moral and social forces according to which

[29] See Everett Knight, *The Objective Society* (New York, Braziller, 1960): "Julien Sorel and the Meursault of Camus' *L'Étranger* were executed for what was, fundamentally, the same crime—the refusal to feign an identity which society sought to impose but which subjectivity could not confirm." (p. 83)

man decides to commit violence or prepares to suffer it. In the fiction I have described in this chapter, there is some investiture of power in a "hero," or at least a calculable set of human circumstances in relation to forces. But the development from Stendhal to James to Conrad clearly suggests that the distribution of responsibilities and incentives becomes more and more difficult—until the time arrives, as I shall explain, when language and literature have to yield more than they would seem able to afford. The novel of manners becomes vestigial. The new literature is a composite of new stratagems for enclosing and containing new situations. These include growth in the impact of "facticity," a failure of eloquence, and a radical need for new arrangements of language and "scenic meditation."

2

THE CONSEQUENCES OF
SECULAR GRACE

L's M

a rigid pyramidal composition of blocks; an
impurely mathematical game of edges: not quite
cruelly a cubic cerebration—equally glamourless
and emphatic, withal childish . . . perhaps the
architectural equivalent for "boo!—I scared
you that time!" (hard by are buried martyrs)

—E. E. CUMMINGS, *Eimi*

—[i]—

IN A MOCK ceremony, rich in irony and in meaning, one of Pietro
Spina's friends (Nunzio Sacca) invests him with clerical garments, which are to serve Spina as a disguise in his return to
Italy. Spina is himself hidden out in a stable; his retreats are
usually of that sort; he is "like the Child in the Manger." [1] The
choice of a priest's vestments is a practical one for both Spina
and his author; Spina's career enforces the analogy here first
pointed out by Nunzio Sacca:

"These vestments," he said, "are descended from the primitive mystery religions, from the priests of Isis and Serapis,

[1] Ignazio Silone, *Bread and Wine*, tr. Gwenda David and Eric Mos-
bacher, New York, Harper's, 1937, p. 33. Other references to this edition

94

as, of course, you know. . . . And now, here you are, a man dedicated to the new revolutionary mysteries, to the mysteries of revolutionary materialism, donning the dark vestments that have been symbols of sacrifice and supernatural inspiration for thousands of years." (36–37)

The strategy of the disguise serves more than a practical purpose. Spina, become Don Paolo Spada, lives and moves in terms of two versions of an institutional metaphor: the Party leader and the priest are similarly dedicated; each in his purest sense is a living symbol of an elaborate organizational effort to codify man's life in time and his expectation of eternity. They are also widely different; the differences come essentially from the relationship of each to history and to eternity.

Given Silone's revolutionary perspective, it is natural enough to suppose that Spina's adventures among his Italian friends have the rough grain of his peasant origins; the peasantry in revolutions have a decelerating effect upon the line of their progress. They are inclined to examine miracle as plausible fact; they hold tenaciously to superstitions; and they remain on the lower strata of revolutionary and religious symbolism. To the farmers and villagers of Spina's Abruzzi, he is a saint walking the surface of a privileged earth, but he is also possibly a Christ visitation. So close to reality is the peasant's vision of the miraculous that the possibility cannot be dismissed. But it is not so much the question of who he is that matters, as that of his purpose, his special interpretation of the social and economic conditions he examines. Silone's review of that purpose is highlighted several times in *Bread and Wine* and in its successor, *The Seed Beneath the Snow* (1942). The Party and the Church are analyzed intimately, the one in terms of a future, the other in the light of a present that reflects eternity fitfully:

are in the text. This novel was first published in a German version in 1936. The original Italian version and the English translation appeared in the same year.

"Have you never thought of justice as an ideal capable of being realized in this world, among men?" he asked.

"Our Kingdom is not of this world," Cristina replied.

"But the land behind the stable is of this world. Why is it refused to people who would be safer on it than beside the stream?"

"God made rich and poor," answered Cristina. "Every man is answerable to God for what he has received. One must be content with one's lot."

"I do not understand," said Don Paolo. "You wish to enter a convent and renounce the world, but you are unwilling to renounce the land behind the stable."

"I personally renounce everything," said Cristina. "But my family has a rank which it must maintain." (*Bread and Wine*, 104-105)

This dialogue is characteristic of Silone's habitual exercise in literary dialectic. The common matter of Party and Church concerns brings them together repeatedly. Their basic differences in both strategy and metaphysics provide the dramatic tension that gives his novels mobility within historical circumstances. Above all, the priestly disguise and its suggested analogy make vivid enough an important, even a crucial, issue in twentieth century history. Within the milieu chosen by Silone for his novels, a major Christian symbol is revived and becomes actively engaged. Stated simply, it is the fact or the miracle of the Incarnation, of the divine made secular, yielding as it does the mysteries and paradoxes of eternity imbedded in time. Much of the social revolution of our age has been an attempt to secularize the system and to redefine the advantages, even the metaphysics, of Christian grace. Silone's novels repeatedly describe the corruption of the divine by the secular, the channeling of absolutistic energies into secular ways, finally the startling conjunctions of secular aspirations and spiritual yearnings. The peculiarities of the Incarnation involve us in a study of both the risks that divinity takes in becoming human and the human drive toward a transcendent security against the corrupting tendencies of the body and the earth. The miracle of the Logos involves God in history, man in eternity. "As God has entered history and has accomplished a divine intention," says Martin D'Arcy, "history cannot possibly be unaffected by such an event. The act of God, which is in our human calendars begun and finished within a small, definite number of years, has a transcendent power and quality which, so to speak, makes it at home in any period of history." [2]

The Christian story of Grace is at first glance remarkably simple and ultimately very complex. Man, a creature of God, is dependent upon Him: striving to act independently of Him, he falls from grace and incurs the historical burden of original sin. To restore the balance of man's dependence and his hope of transcending his limited nature, the act of Incarnation is introduced into human history. Thus man is universally accountable to God, and history becomes a temporal image of God's consequent adjustment to the gap opened between humanity and divinity. Christopher Dawson has outlined the pattern in this way:

> The dynamic force of both the individual and the society is found in the will, and the object of their will determines the moral character of their life. And as the corruption of the will by original sin in Adam becomes a social evil by an hereditary transmission through the flesh which unites fallen humanity in the common slavery of concupiscence, so too the restoration of the will by grace in Christ is a social good which is transmitted sacramentally by the ac-

[2] *Communism and Christianity*, New York, Devin-Adair, 1957, pp. 100–101.

tion of the Spirit and united regenerate humanity in a
free spiritual society under the law of charity.[3]

The rival claims of secular and religious grace, when examined in terms of their literary representation of modern
perspectives upon death, yield their most complex values in the
field of eschatology. Is it possible to think of human history as
self-contained and independent of divine grace? Can society be
explained, defined, and "saved" solely in terms of the history
of man's relationship to nature? In the effort to prove secularism equal to the task of an independent human history, Marx
and his interpreters have had to give materiality to many of the
images characteristically ascribed to the spiritual state. Secular
order begins with the assumption that morality is completely
and infallibly understood in the forms of adjustment man
makes to nature's requirements. Nature defines, as it had in a
pre-theistic philosophy, the boundaries of right and wrong. As
society moves to levels of complication, these natural boundaries
are translated into economic relationships: man orders nature,
and he must thenceforth order himself. Spiritual resources are
an outgrowth of superstitions, of the sense of human limitation,
and most significantly of man's fear of death. Religion, says
Ernst Cassirer, develops from the failure of man to understand
his death; since religions almost invariably describe some form
of immortality, religion is itself introduced to allay that fear.[4]
Much of modern ideological history is taken up with the effort
to secularize that fear and to realign the hope of immortality.
The need for a City of Man to replace Augustine's City of God
combines the history of man's disappointment in the Church
as institution with his desire for absolutes.

The most significant aspect of this secular history is its ac-
celerating effect upon the movement in time. While Christ

[3] In M. C. D'Arcy, *et al.*, *A Monument to Saint Augustine*, New York,
Dial, 1930, p. 75.
[4] *The Myth of the State*, New Haven, Yale University Press, 1946, pp.
48–49.

exists in history and the Logos is a constant reminder of His humanity, the nature of His presence in history is static. While the biography of Christ exists in history, the fact of Him need not. At best one may say that the earthly state either antedates the heavenly or proves slowly to progress toward suggesting it. The Logos is therefore a static symbol; it exists in time but independently of it, and its real value lies in eternity, to which man aspires to translate his own absorption in time. The secular modifications of the Logos invariably require a nonstatic move from present into future. According to them, man does not simply assume a spiritual status as a consequence of death; he is moving toward a state of perfection in history itself. The hope of immortality is thus revised, to become a movement toward future secular states—or, in any ultimate definition of these expectations, toward an "ideal state," which is for the most part described in negative terms: class*less*, its people *no* longer exploited, economic *im*balances removed, etc. As man was spiritually moved to prefer the City of God to his temporal state, in secular terms he exists in history, and acts in it, for the sake of eliminating present imperfections and realizing the perfect human condition.

Eternity must therefore become absorbed in a temporal, natural, and historical sequence. If the ideal classless society is to exist on this earth, it must exist in the future. History therefore becomes the story of man's movement from an imperfect past toward a perfect future, an attempt to place heaven in time. What one does in the present is judged good or bad as it encourages or impedes this movement. Secular monastics are therefore constantly in the act of scrutinizing time as present in terms of its status as a point in the evolution toward a point in the future. The quality of the present is judged impure insofar as it lacks the status of that future. Evil existing or committed in the present is considered good if it can be explained as a means toward the achievement of that future. Sentimentality, pity, "bourgeois good," are considered distractions, flaws in the means toward an end. The secular order has its quality of the eternal only in the way in which any vision of the future society is postponed or seen as remote in time. Secular saints have always to resist the temptation to think the present good or the future accomplished. This earnest and continuous analysis of the present in the light of its relationship to a future not accomplished tends more and more to become abstract, even nonhuman. A human being who is the agent of human futures is liable in the present to act as an abstraction, serving the interests of abstractions. He exists in history for the sake of purifying it, and can therefore not yield to the temptation to idealize his present state. He is a martyr only if he transcends his person, if he acts impersonally.

If it is defined as a linear development from past to future, history thus becomes, in this reading of it, a tyrant over human society. The present must be seen in the light of its progressing toward the future. In secular terms, the human self, hungering for the perfection of his nature, is moved to act within his brief temporal span to facilitate the progress of time toward a splendid and majestic future. This intense desire for an absolutely determined future eventually, in its extreme forms, ruins the character of time present altogether. Present fact is "erased" from history, as are present persons if they do not serve it without qualification; a present lie becomes truth if it fits into the system of truth according to which the future is ideally seen. The true pathos of this disposition toward time (ironically much more severely dislocating than the Christian perspective of eternity) is given in Orwell's 1984 (O'Brien is speaking):

> ". . . We are the dead. Our only true life is in the future. We shall take part in it as handfuls of dust and splinters of bone. But how far away that future may be, there is no knowing. It might be a thousand years. . . ." [5]

[5] 1984, New York, Harcourt, Brace, 1949, p. 177. The irony of this situation needs to be emphasized, for O'Brien speaks from a fixed position

There are many suggestions of this pathos in modern literature; not the least of these is the spectacle of the man who, having lost the sense of his link to eternity, cannot abide the thought of his death. Combined with this feeling of loss is the sense of the disappearance of social or cultural continuity. George Bowling's comment on the disappearance of common securities underscores this kind of pathos (Orwell's *Coming Up for Air*):

> Whatever might happen to themselves, things would go on as they'd known them. I don't believe it made very much difference that what's called religious belief was still prevalent in those days. It's true that nearly everyone went to church, at any rate in the country . . . and if you asked people whether they believed in a life after death they generally answered that they did. But I've never met anyone who gave me the impression of really believing in a future life. . . . It's easy enough to die if the things you care about are going to survive. . . . Individually they were finished, but their way of life would continue. Their good and evil would remain good and evil.[6]

Perhaps worse than this feeling of Bowling's loss is the agony suffered by the thoroughly secularized hero who, having succeeded in transforming his desire for immortality into a temporally limited expectation, ends by finding even that expectation implausible. The disaffected revolutionary is perhaps the most pitiful specimen of the modern antihero. While Orwell's heroes mourn the loss of decencies, Koestler's are tangled in a net of revolutionary and counter-revolutionary ambiguities. It is one of the great ironies of the Russian Revolution and of the consequent growth of a gigantic bureaucracy that the ideal society, dimly seen as "Over There," was actually becoming a

and has already denied the past. What he says here traps Winston Smith because of its insincerity.

  [6] *Coming Up for Air* (1939), New York, Harcourt, Brace, 1950, pp. 125–26.

complex Hell of institutional and impersonal abstraction. It is
as though a Christian, having practiced the good all his life,
had discovered that after all the consequence of the good was
Hell rather than heaven. The man who suffers the concentration camp and is rewarded by the state prison can scarcely be
said to have any logical sense of direction from means to end.[7]

—[ii]—

However otherwise they may differ, both secular and spiritual
expectations are similarly motivated by a strong desire for absolute fulfilment. One of the consequences of secularization is
that a static vision of eternity becomes involved in a powerful
secular drive toward perfection in history. Both are absolutes.
The energy as well as the pathos of secular hopes is quite
effectively described in Koestler's autobiographical explorations
of the secular infinite. When he was twenty-five, Koestler says,
"Marxist theory and Soviet practice were the admirable and
ultimate fulfilment of the nineteenth century's ideal of Progress,
to which I owed allegiance. The greatest electric power dam in
the world must surely bring the greatest happiness to the
greatest number." [8] This sense of an absolute necessity to fulfill
oneself was basically the same as animated saints in earlier
times. "In other ages aspirations of this kind found their
natural fulfilment in God" (51). God symbolizes a transcendent
perfection whose ideal merit may be either accepted irrationally
or rationally proved. The pattern of Incarnation made belief
both provable and plausible. Since the eighteenth century,
Koestler maintains, "the place of God has been vacant in our
civilization; but during the ensuing century and a half so many
exciting things were happening that people were not aware of

[7] See the figure of "Rip Van Winkle," *Darkness at Noon*, tr. Daphne
Hardy, New York, Macmillan, 1941, pp. 123–24.
[8] *The Arrow in the Blue*, New York, Macmillan, 1941, p. 279.

it" (51–52). Scientists worked with a monastic dedication and an emotional commitment. The secular design of progress toward perfection in the twentieth century assumed the qualities of nineteenth century absolutism.

This astonishing strength of single-minded purpose is featured in many literary portraits of the secular hero. Almost every proletarian hero of our century must have had, at one time or another, some sense of the progressive movement toward an ideal alleviation of distress, an ideal achievement of the abstract good. The elder Gisors of Malraux's *Man's Fate* had once thought of the revolution as a stage of progress very similar to the stages of spiritual history:

> "A civilization becomes transformed, you see, when its most oppressed element—the humiliation of the slave, the work of the modern worker—suddenly becomes a *value*, when the oppressed ceases to attempt to escape this humiliation, and seeks his salvation in it, when the worker ceases to escape this work, and seeks in it his reason for being. The factory, which is still only a kind of church of the catacombs, must become what the cathedral was, and men just see in it, instead of gods, human power struggling against the Earth. . . ." [9]

There is a passion for infinity in the modern secular hero that is as strong as that which motivates religious martyrdom. The context changes, but the desire remains intrinsically powerful. Silone's heroes especially seem to have been educated in their

[9] *Man's Fate*, tr. Haakon M. Chevalier, New York, Smith and Haas, 1934, pp. 352–53. Originally published by Gallimard, Paris, as *La Condition Humaine* (1933). Gisors is incapable of sustaining this vision. The very abstractness of its phrasing (it was a quotation from one of his early lectures) must have seemed to him, in the light of the confusions experienced in the Chinese Civil War, to be not only untrue, but dangerous. Nevertheless, the acts of heroism performed by his son and other revolutionaries are emotionally qualified by such a belief in secular progress as this suggests.

youth in a sense of ideal righteousness which, when they mature, is devoted to the revolutionary cause.

> Revolutionary action had always seemed to be demanded of [Pietro Spina] by the collective good. The ideal of the collective good had been inculcated into him from his earliest years by his Christian education. His subsequent intellectual development had modified the premises on which his original adherence to Socialism had been based, but he had not been able to modify the internal structure of his mind. (*Bread and Wine,* 129)

"I lost my faith in God many years ago," he says to the saintly Don Bernedetto. "It was a religious impulse that led me into the revolutionary movement. . . . Perhaps it was the religious education I received as a boy that made me a bad revolutionary, a revolutionary full of fears, uncertainties, complexities. On the other hand, should I ever have become a revolutionary without it? Should I ever have taken life seriously?" (241) The tragic circumstance of Spina's life, as of that of most secular heroes, lies in the demand for action; the contemplative life is inadequate, and it may even be condemned as evasive. But a life of action always risks ceasing to be a life of principle; the pressure of the need to act in a state of continuous emergency tends to widen the gap between abstract principle and immediate moral practice. Ideology without intimate perception becomes a void, into which the selfless energy of the secular spirit rushes. Another Silone hero represents perhaps even more vividly the consequences of this secularization:

> "Rocco was born with an evident vocation for religious life. He was the object of the clearest call from God that I have ever witnessed. That he did not follow it is one of the mysteries that only God can explain and judge. But although he did not obey his vocation he has constantly demanded from secular life the absolute quality that he could have found only in a monastery. For this reason he

is in a tragic, absurd situation, much harder to solve than any living in sin." [10]

For Silone the issue is more simply resolved than in most cases. This is because his heroes, while they are endowed with an extraordinary moral energy, are never pushed entirely out of the range of quotidian morality and superstition. Spina, when he does go to his death, does so for no grandiose ideological purpose but to save a ragged deaf-mute who is "blessed in his simplicities." Rocco becomes involved in a native struggle which preserves him from committing an ideological folly. And Andrea Cipriani (*The Secret of Luca*, 1958), recently returned from Partisan triumphs in the war, busies himself with the altogether human complications of a friend. None of these suffers the indignities of ideological suicide. Silone's novels remain perhaps the most restrained analyses of the career of secular grace in our century.

—[iii]—

The similarities of the spiritual and secular patterns of grace should now be sufficiently familiar. Historically the change from the one to the other follows along the lines of the history of man's powers of visualization. It is based on the narrow range of man's concrete, practical life experience. As Bronislaw Malinowski has put it, "Death as the extinction of one's own personality, or the disappearance of those who are near, who are loved, is a fact which will always baffle human understanding and fundamentally upset the emotional constitution of man. . . . And here religious revelation steps in and affirms life after death, the immortality of the spirit, the possibilities of communion between living and dead." [11] The need of grace

[10] *A Handful of Blackberries*, tr. Darina Silone, New York, Harper's, 1953, p. 84.
[11] B. Malinowski, *The Foundations of Faith and Morals*, London, Oxford University Press, 1936, p. 27.

begins with the discovery of the fact of death. Since man is inadequate to himself (that is, he grows old and feeble, and dies), he needs assurances of a complementary power which, while it does not radically alter the condition of the real, nevertheless acts to transcend its limitations. Immortality is itself an extension of the real in time. The Christian tendency is to make a postmortem future similar to a temporal present, perhaps to purify the circumstances of eternity a bit but always to retain the personal value of the extension. Once his initial inadequacy is realized (that is, the imperfections leading to the death of the body), man recognizes himself as an incomplete and imperfect being. The myth of grace thereafter is a story of the movement of an imperfect spirit toward perfection, of the spirit's arduous labor to perfect itself and to make itself immortal—in other words, to defeat death, initially and always the most formidable of all threats to his security.

To triumph over death, man must speculate upon the possibility of immortal being. The more intense his creative act becomes, the more formidably isolated from him is the God who fills the need. If divinity is all that we are not, then we are not divine, or we risk losing the hope of becoming so. The initial sense of inadequacy is first morally extended, then institutionally enlarged and ordered. The metaphor of original sin is at once a sign of man's defiance of God and a reminder of his dependence. The vision of Eden is a static one; existence in and movement through time signalize corruption. Disasters are signs of God's anger; He will prove man's mortality by destroying his life. Before the gates of Eden, Adam is immortal; beyond them, he is engaged in mortal strife and suffers the anguish of a recurring sense of death.

The metaphor of grace supplements the metaphor of original sin, in fact saves us from it. Christ suffers our humanity to His death, but His divinity mitigates our own death. We have willed to sin, but we also will to save ourselves. In some such way as this, man compensates for the discovery that he is mortal, that he lacks the physical power to continue and to perpetuate himself. The fact that God is what he is not has its attendant risks. God must both be superior to man (otherwise it would be futile to imagine Him) and available to him. Some variant of the metaphor of the Incarnation is therefore crucial to the history of man from the very moment he recognizes that he will not live forever.

From these beginnings there are many developments in both secular and spiritual history; two of them can be conveniently generalized. One moves toward the denial of the flesh, renunciation of earthly pleasure, purification of the soul; it involves the paradox of action and passion, of existing within time but in the recognition of eternity:

. . . Neither does the actor suffer
Nor the patient act. But both are fixed
In an eternal action, an eternal patience
To which all must consent that it may be willed
And which all must suffer that they may will it,
That the pattern may subsist, for the pattern is the action
And the suffering, that the wheel may turn and still
Be forever still.[12]

The human soul so fully inducted in the demands of eternity will act in time as a patient martyr to its demands; he will both recognize and endure the felicities of historical temptation, but for him they are impurities, signs of a recurrent and constant state of imperfection.

There is a time of transition from this view of eternity to the other. Within it, man becomes confident of the power of his reason. The ingenuity and complexity of his mind persuade him momentarily that he is after all without flaw. One version of this brief, illusory state involves the belief that it is not man

---

[12] T. S. Eliot, *Murder in the Cathedral*, New York, Harcourt, Brace, 1935, p. 21. Other references to this edition are in the text. Originally produced, Canterbury, June 1935.

but society that is imperfect. Some small remnant of this belief remains in all Utopian inspirations. But if mortality is the major flaw, then man must see himself as immortal in order to approach perfection. There is a haunting suggestion of this extraordinary ambition in all actuarial estimates and predictions, but only in satirical Utopias is it contemplated at all seriously. It is more feasible to perfect the state and then immortalize it. In this, the most common of all modern variations upon the myth of grace, man attempts to secularize immortality; that is, he tries to put heaven in time. He abjures the present, not because it is earthly but because it is not earthly enough. The present contains a mixture of social evil (that is, all that is not perfect is evil) and partial good. The present is a stage in the evolution toward the future; and, since we *are* evolving, the passage of time leads inevitably to a future state where perfection is. While perfection is by definition a static end, its position is indeterminate; hence the movement toward it is always dynamically concerned with "rational planning" and emotional justifications.

Since both the instrumental power of reason and the vision of an ideal society depend upon movement in time, this second version of the myth of grace, secular grace, is linked irrevocably to history. Marx vacillated between an objective view of history as happening and the ambition to accelerate its pace. The "dialectic" of history can presumably be merely contemplated, without one's interfering with it; but apparently also, knowledge of dialectic process, political shrewdness and opportunism, and a ruthless and selfless dedication to the future can combine to facilitate its progress. Ironically, a strenuous effort to hasten the processes of history seems to have the effect of prolonging the conclusion toward which it is or should be proceeding. The ideal state (the vision of secular immortality) seems gradually to have assumed qualities of remoteness, inaccessibility, unreality, that have characterized the goal of spiritual grace from the beginning. The systems of secular and spiritual grace do seem in many cases to have much in common, but there is this essential difference: on the secular level, immortality is visualized in time, and it is expected that man will achieve it in time. It is one of the greatest risks ever assumed in human history: man somehow hopes to overcome the fear of death by thinking that immortality is available to him from an act of will, rationally disposed. Since he is not satisfied that it should exist beyond the grave but insists that it be available on this side, he must himself confront the fact of death in the expectation of a movement in time toward secular perfection.

—[iv]—

The major challenge to the revolutionary is that he be able to die independently of the assurances of spiritual grace. The condition of a martyr's death is a crucial test of secularization. Eliot's Becket, four days before his martyrdom, offers his congregation a spiritual interpretation of death in its purest form. The martyr, Becket says, does not will his death as a means of securing his spiritual glory, but submits to God's will:

> A martyrdom is never the design of man; for the true martyr is he who has become the instrument of God, who has lost his will in the will of God, not lost it but found it, for he has found freedom in submission to God. The martyr no longer desires anything for himself, not even the glory of martyrdom. (49–50)

To deserve saintliness, one must not will it; since willing for oneself what only God can will for you is an act of arrogance, or at the least of selfishness. Submission to God is the necessary means to a triumph over both life and death. Eliot's principal image for the place of God in the world is that of the still point of the turning world; the metaphor suggests also that God is both in history and not of it. "Little Gidding" defines the paradox of time and eternity to which this situation refers:

PART ONE: GRACE

If you came this way,
Taking any route, starting from anywhere,
At any time or at any season,
It would always be the same: you would have to put off
Sense and notion. You are not here to verify,
Instruct yourself, or inform curiosity
Or carry report. You are here to kneel
Where prayer has been valid. And prayer is more
Than an order of words, the conscious occupation
Of the praying mind, or the sound of the voice praying.
And what the dead had no speech for, when living,
They can tell you, being dead: the communication
Of the dead is tongued with fire beyond the language of the
    living.
Here, the intersection of the timeless moment
Is England and nowhere. Never and always.[13]

The purest martyrdom is endured beyond self and beyond time. Yet the religious martyr can scarcely be said to have submitted to his death without some lingering assurance such as is suggested in the Christian formula of losing oneself in order to gain oneself. It is necessary to "care" only in spiritual terms, not to "want" in a material sense. But the saint does not face annihilation; Christian grace has taught him to believe that in dying he is eliminating the lesser self, to gain the greater; in other words, to become absorbed in the will of God. The martyrdom of Thomas was surely a triumph not only over time but over his political enemies, the King, and worldly temptation. Eliot has tried to purify Thomas' act out of the world, but it remains within the world as a moment of history, "never and always," a "lesson" to those more selfishly motivated, and especially to the expedient strategists of the state. Dr. K. R. Eissler, in the only extended psychiatric account of the expe-

[13] From "Little Gidding," in *Four Quartets*, copyright, 1943, by T. S. Eliot. Reprinted by permission of Harcourt, Brace and World, Inc.

rience of dying (*The Psychiatrist and the Dying Patient*), speaks of the martyr's death as a form of "narcissistic gratification," a "highly active process leading to the victory of the Church over the evil of paganism." [14] It is obvious that Eliot wishes his Becket to move to higher ground than that; the words of the Fourth Tempter contain a reminder of the final danger: one may unselfishly submit to death in order selfishly to gain the role of martyrdom and sainthood; this is to set oneself apart from God.

On the level of secular grace, of revolutionary martyrdom, the God to whom one submits can variously be called the "cause," the "future," or simply "time." The most common form of literary representation of this attitude toward death is the "strike novel," which faces directly the issue of time moving toward a secular future. In one sense at least the proletarian martyr takes a greater risk than does Becket; he is willing to die with no expectation of rebirth.[15] This is one of the consequences of having placed heaven in history; it is forever linked to time, which moves forward and presumably is animated by a form of secular, mystic power, but it is not divine or eternal. The death of a secular martyr is therefore never either "never" or "always"; it is always "here" and "now." Within the limits of time, however, a secular sacrifice must certainly be accompanied by some of the same temptations or "narcissistic gratifications" as was that of Eliot's hero. Secular heroes die for various reasons in modern literature. Silone's heroes assume for themselves a form of Kantian wager: to die disinterestedly is

[14] New York, International Universities Press, 1955, p. 150. Since the publication of this volume, a collection of essays has appeared, edited by Herman Feifel, and called *The Meaning of Death*, New York, McGraw-Hill, 1959.

[15] When it was suggested to Stalin that Pope Pius XII be represented at discussions concerning the future of Catholic Poland, Stalin is supposed to have answered by demanding "How many divisions does he have?" The Pope, hearing this report, said, "Tell my son Joseph that my divisions are in heaven." The incident suggests a "militant" approach to the conflict between spiritual and secular objectives.

an act of essential proof that man is capable of disinterested-
ness. The paradox of willing selflessness in the interest of self-
gratification exists in both theological and secular heroism.
Often the hero wills his death as an active and violent proof of
man's triumph over the threat of death. Many cases of secular
martyrdom are versions of the motives laboriously explained by
Dostoevsky's Kirillov (*The Possessed*); he had planned his
suicide as a proof of man's power over death. Such a death is
annihilation; it means changing a life for a corpse, not a life
for a life. If the imagination which motivates the act and sustains it ceases in the death of the hero, the result is a melancholy
and an uncertain act of martyrdom.

The challenge to martyrdom on the secular level has nowhere been analyzed so exhaustively as in Malraux's novels. The
revolutionary power gained by the dying hero who accepts his
death as a change to "nothingness" is crucial to the movement
toward secular objectives. Malraux's heroes are in many ways
adventurers in secular grace; they have the added advantage of
Malraux's own religious perspective. He dramatizes the crucial
developments in modern secular history, but his sensitivity to
Catholic criticisms of materialism acts as a precaution. His
heroes are therefore never free to die for blindly secular motives; their primary motive is to restore or to continue the recognition of human dignity. Communism is simply an historical
form which may be useful temporarily as a means to destroy
forms of oppression; through it man may recapture the dignity
of his life.

> "I think that Communism will make dignity possible for
> those with whom I am fighting," Kyo says to his inquisitor.
> "What is against it, at any rate, forces them to have none,
> unless they possess a wisdom as rare among them as among
> the others—more perhaps, for the very reason that they
> are poor, and that their work separates them from their
> lives. . . ." (*Man's Fate*, 306)

Whatever the objective—and it is here really to "improve the human circumstances," to make *la condition humaine* possible —the secular hero must learn to die, which is to say that he must be able to die in full knowledge that he will not exist after his death. The details of putrescence have horrified and fascinated the modern observer, so that annihilation is by no means an abstract term but a disgustingly real physical condition. When a secular hero "triumphs over death," therefore, he does so in the expectation that death is undignified, vulgar, maggotty, and grimly final; he is fortified by the knowledge or the hope that life might in general improve (in the restoration of human dignity or in the clarification of the state), as a consequence of his willing or accepting death. He submits to a hope whose temporal direction can only be the future. One of Malraux's earliest revolutionary heroes, Garine, puts it most succinctly:

> "With the new idea of a death which involves nothing, neither compensation nor atonement, has been born the idea that every man has it in his power to overcome the collective life of suffering and to attain to that individual, independent life, which is in some way regarded as the greatest treasure of the rich. . . ." [16]

Unlike many of his contemporaries, Malraux does not think in terms of a change from one absolute to another. The hero faces the prospect that the Christian absolute will decline, and he is not altogether sure of its surrogate. He is in the position of being an existential person willing a change from one absolute to another; he is uncertain of the validity of either. But Malraux's men often die believing that they have sacrificed themselves to some kind of universal objective. [17] They explore

[16] *The Conquerors*, tr. W. S. Whale, New York, Random House, 1929, p. 144. French edition in André Malraux, *Romans*, Paris, Bibliothèque de la Pléiade (Gallimard), 1947, p. 81.
[17] See Murray Krieger's brilliant analysis of *Man's Fate*, in *The Tragic Vision* (New York, Holt, Rinehart, and Winston, 1960): "Needless to

death with the same intense and active analysis that most men apply to life. The moment of dying, the psychological qualia of the experience, becomes the essential; and it is different from the dying of either the religious or the secular martyr.

The experience of dying-as-annihilation is obsessively central in Malraux's fiction; the career of Ch'en (of *Man's Fate*) elaborately analyzes an extreme case. In dying Ch'en loses all touch with discipline and extracentric order; and death becomes a thing in itself, a fate without external attachment. He dies selfishly in the sense that his death contains its own meaning and relevance. He had received his education in religion from a Lutheran pastor, a "consumptive intellectual . . . who was struggling patiently at the age of fifty to overcome, by charity, an intense religious anxiety" (67); from him he had learned the agony of contemplating man's general depravity. The pastor had taught Ch'en of Christ and of hell, but had said little of God or of heaven; he had warned against the striving for God or for heaven. In this way, Ch'en had lost all sense of the Christian doctrine of grace for which was substituted a "limitless love or terror"; it is as though Christ had died to show man the way to a deserved perdition. The revolutionary condition as Ch'en saw it was therefore remarkably distorted. It was impossible for him to see his life in ideological terms. The revolution is an opportunity for his violently acquitting himself of his fear of hell and willing his own terror. Ch'en's acts are planned and consummated in a scene of men dying and giving death; they are reflections of himself, their acts duplications of his own. Violent action is his only choice; it is a form of contemplation, and the moment of his death is an eternity; these are Ch'en's ways of embracing the absolute. The sensation of death is close to resembling the mystic's experience of religious ecstasy. But this

say, the existential sense that gives the novel its deepest life frequently has the Marxist sense intruded upon it . . ." (p. 69). See also Victor Brombert's precise summary of basic attitudes, in *The Intellectual Hero: Studies in the French Novel, 1880–1955*, Philadelphia, Lippincott, 1961, p. 154.

is a perversion of the revolutionary's faith, according to which one should die for others, not for himself nor entirely for the experience of dying.

"You want to make a kind of religion of terrorism?"

Ch'en's exaltation was growing. All words were hollow, absurd, too feeble to express what he wanted of them.

"Not a religion. The meaning of life. The . . ."

His hand made the convulsive gesture of molding something, and his idea seemed to pulsate.

". . . the complete possession of oneself. Total. To know. Not to be looking, looking, always, for ideas, for duties. . . ." (196)

The death of Ch'en is a somber parody of the circumstances of secular martyrdom. Malraux's other heroes view death in less obsessive ways; the expectation of dying is linked with a futuristic imagining of the lives of others. Kyo's move toward death is a gradual induction into the meaning of others; the specific carries its small reminder of the universal. No doubt, says his father, he wants to die "on the highest possible plane" (65). That is, his death must have a meaning beyond the experiencing of it and beyond the merely narcissistic satisfaction of political martyrs.

. . . The heroic sense had given him a kind of discipline, not a kind of justification of life. He was not restless. His life had a meaning, and he knew what it was: to give to each of these men whom famine, at this very moment, was killing off like a slow plague, the sense of his own dignity. . . . "There is no possible dignity, no real life for a man who works twelve hours a day without knowing why he works." That work would have to take on a meaning, become a faith. . . . (70)

While Ch'en wished to experience the absolute personally, to "taste it," Kyo saw it in terms of a life stream contained within the banks of human social organization. Since death is inevitable, it is unwise to try to arrange its terms as though a man were setting a stage for a melodrama, with himself as sole actor. In any case, the act of dying is decisive, whether it be a Christian meeting his God or a revolutionary participating in the drama of secular time. Kyo, on his way to a meeting, which as it turns out leads to his death, pauses on the threshold of his father's home:

> . . . Before opening he stopped, overwhelmed by the brotherhood of death, discovering how derisive the flesh appeared before this communion, in spite of its urgent appeal. He understood now that the willingness to lead the being one loves to death itself is perhaps the complete expression of love, that which cannot be surpassed. (216)

Throughout this characterization of Kyo, Malraux traces the delicate lines of a secular hero's awareness of human dignity in the revolutionary situation. Even so, it is not an easy experience. Ideology seems forever to draw blood from human relationships and to make them cold and abstract. Kyo never wholly triumphs over this condition, but is awkward and embarrassed before his father. "Whenever Kyo came into [his father's] presence, his own will to action was transformed into intelligence . . . he became interested in individuals instead of being interested in forces" (45). Kyo sees agents as persons, and like his author notes the special conditions each sets down for maintaining dignity: Ch'en's ecstatic experience with his own exploding flesh, König's ruthless search for revenge on those who had earlier humiliated him, even the warder of the prison, who seemed to have nothing of humanity to observe. When Kyo goes to his own death, he has resolved in his mind the ambiguities of revolutionary dying:

> . . . It was in this yard, separated from everyone by the machineguns, that the Revolution, no matter what its fate or the place of its resurrection, was receiving its death-

stroke; wherever men labor in pain, in absurdity, in humiliation, they were thinking of doomed men like these,
as believers pray. . . . In all of the earth that this last
night covered over, this place of agony was no doubt the
most weighted with virile love. . . . (322)

His death is not an agony or an obsessive ecstasy or a conscious
martyrdom; it is meaningful because the circumstances of the
life leading to it have shown its meaning. There is one last
worry: the moment of death itself disturbs him, for what it
might do in violently erasing his sense of identity:

He had opened the buckle of his belt and was holding
the cyanide in his hand. He had often wondered if he
would die easily. He knew that if he made up his mind
to kill himself, he would kill himself; but knowing the
savage indifference with which life unmasks us to ourselves,
he had not been without anxiety about the moment when
death would crush his mind with its whole weight and
finality. (323)

Even more than the Chinese, the Spanish Civil War was
an exercise of meaningful dying for Malraux. Man's Hope
(L'Espoir) shows as much advance in the search for secular
meaning as the word hope is an advance upon the word fate.
In an almost literally simple sense, the activity of defense
against falangist rebellion is equated with the struggles of early
Christians, the "dark, underground communion that Christianity had once provided, that today the Revolution gave
them; . . ." [18] The overwhelming impression the novel gives
is that of men associated vitally and fatally with each other
—not in any sentimentally patriotic sense, but rather in a
psychological absorption in the details of union, of "fraternity."
In scenes so slightly described that their meaning almost es-

[18] Tr. Stuart Gilbert and Alastair Macdonald, New York, Random
House, 1938. Originally published as L'Espoir, 1937. Other references to
this edition are in the text.

capes, Malraux suggests the union of rotting flesh and trans-mortem values: "The stench of rotting flesh seemed to be flood-ing his senses wave on wave, and throbbing with the beating of his heart under the dazzling effulgence that merged living and dead together in a holocaust of light . . ." (129). The imagery of light and shadow, violently intermingled, has a primary im-portance, even though it is no more than a nuance of the total portrait. One has more of a sense, in this novel, of the action's being only a moment in the eternity of God's willing man's fate; moments of violent death are frequently succeeded by moments of peace, and God seems eternally willing to "wait patiently" the resolution of this human conflict. This is not the arbitrary, explosive violence of Picasso's *Guernica*, so emotionally charged as to become at once a physical and a metaphysical absolute.

Man's Hope once more puts the issue of death for "a cause." The complex of revolution-death-annihilation is ever-present in the minds of Loyalist leaders. "A man can put up with every-thing," says one of them. "What he can't bear is to feel certain that after being knocked about and trampled on, he's going to be killed. And that after that there's—nothing!" (227) This is precisely what the revolutionary must accept; in place of the Christian evaluation of the soul, he must consider an equation of flesh and time: so many corpses per inch of progress. Malraux analyzes the issue scrupulously. The décor of death is often suggestive of Christian martyrdom; even the images of Christian immortality are present in revolutionary disarray (in-evitably a Civil War in Spain must involve some destruction of churches), and secular heroes often spend hours in medita-tion upon the worth and purpose of their sacrifices. The history of modern executions begins with Dostoevsky's narrow escape in Petrograd (April 1849); since then the blank wall, the cer-emony of arranging martyrs, the open pit dug by victims, has often appeared as a necessary part of secular martyrology. "The principal thing about death," says Moreno, one of Malraux's heroes, "is that it makes all that has preceded it irremediable, eternally beyond redress. Torture and brutality *followed by* death—these are the really terrible things . . ." (*Man's Hope*, 251). Hernandez submits to death, in a scene which admirably illustrates the manners of secular martyrdom. Preparations for his death assume ceremonial properties almost as if by accident. The men go halfway toward their tormentors; they are not cattle waiting passively for slaughter, but men actively engaged in putting the stamp of their vitality upon the act of their dying. About them is a landscape that suggests eternity; it is not an eternity such as may be glimpsed by the spiritual martyr, but one marked by buildings made by men, and by black-clothed women ready to join the ranks of widowhood.

> They were getting into the routine; those on the right— of killing, those on the left—of being killed. Three more lined up on the ridge where the others had stood. The drab expanse of ruined mansions and closed factories was taking on an aspect of eternity, the agelessness of graveyards: as if up to the crack of doom in never-ending sequence, groups of three men would take their stand there, waiting to be killed. (258–59)

Above all, Malraux's novel is an exhaustive exploration of its title: what is "hope," and how are its psychological origins linked to its metaphysical ends? In the secular pattern the metaphysics of hope is realized in action: "Among other functions, the revolution plays a part that an 'eternal life' used formerly to play; . ." (323). It is in a sense a hope of eternal bliss, but it has to become depersonalized; circumstances too often make it impossible to link person to future. The revolutionary scene is all but impossible as a setting for a personally achieved "grace." Thomas à Becket died in "his" cathedral: the threat, the menace, the pain, the fear had all been previously absorbed in meditation upon the theological ground of sacrifice. No such decorum is observed in Malraux's Madrid; here, secular grace assumes a surrealistic quality. Incendiary bombs cast a perverse glow upon the setting, a profanation of the Church's purple of twilight and quiet mourning. In the foreground are carts of refugees, piled high with the remnants of civil life.

> . . . A building was burning, from top to bottom, a moving-picture conflagration. Behind an elaborately ornamental façade, as yet intact, the gaping, shattered windows on every floor were lurid with the flames within, as if the house were inhabited by elemental Fire. Farther along, at a street corner, a bus stood waiting. Suddenly Lopez stopped, breathless for the first time since he had come out. He started frantically gesticulating— . . . he shouted. "Get down!" . . . There was an explosion. The bus went up in flame.
>
> When Lopez got to his feet again, blood was streaming down the walls. Among the dead stripped by the explosion, a whiskered gentleman, naked but unhurt, picked himself up, screaming. The shelling, still pounding the vicinity of the telephone building, grew more intense. (374)

In circumstances like these, irrational violence seems to have taken over altogether. The scene is grotesque; nothing is certain except the instinct of survival and the quick and active assumption of some form of secular grace. Malraux leads us to no foreshortened conclusions. His view is contained within the destructive scene. Hope remains within the very images of dislocation:

> With their quilts, alarm-clocks, canary cages and pet cats in their arms, all were streaming out—why they knew not —towards the richer quarters, unflurried, stolid as the poor are stolid. (346)

. . .

The slums of Cuatro Caminos were as full of poultry as any country village, and with the crashes of the first bombs cocks had started crowing by the thousand; . . . furiously, frantically, all crowing together, they blared a shrill chorus, brazen with rage, the battle hymn of poverty, towards the menace of the sky. (347)

—[v]—

One of Malraux's most effective scenes is that of the church bombed, the fragments of spiritual order mingled with evidences of secular heroism. It is inevitable that the two kinds of milieux should frequently show points of suggestive likeness. Secular grace has its heaven, its purgatory, its hell. Its heroes move steadily in time, surrounded by objects, the atmosphere suffused with a secular haze. Malraux's Spaniards move in such an atmosphere, as do Silone's Italians. There are secular catacombs, monasteries, chapels, processions of the faithful, relics and ikons. This unity of man's secular imagination suggests not so much its poverty as its sense of the profoundly and shockingly appropriate. Even Trotsky appreciated the strength of religious image within secular crisis when he quoted with obvious approval a journalist's account of a workers' demonstration of April 1917:

> "About a hundred armed men marched in front; after them solid phalanxes of unarmed men and women, a thousand strong. Living chains on both sides. Songs. Their faces amazed me. All these thousands had but one face, the stunned ecstatic face of the early Christian monks. Implacable, pitiless, ready for murder, inquisition, and death." [19]

The concentration camp and the prison cell alternate as hell and purgatory. Hell is also seen as a slum, a human setting without hope of rescue. Orwell's portrayal of down-and-outers in London and Paris sometimes touches upon this suggestion of hellishness. The time sequence of hell is different in secular

[19] *The History of the Russian Revolution* (1932), tr. Max Eastman, Ann Arbor, University of Michigan Press, n.d., p. 345.

terms from its position in the Christian scheme. Hell exists in the past; it is imposed upon men before the move toward heaven begins, and men do penance not for themselves but for history. Above all, in the images of hell which secular literature offers, the infernal quality of the scene has always some suggestion of unreality, as of a man placed alive in a tomb. Most of the Russian saints served their apprenticeship in such a hell. The concentration camps of World War II are an extension of it.

The unreal has a quality of absence, emptiness, constriction. Here man, confined when he would be active, alternately blinded by naked light and thrust into unmitigated gloom, fights the menace of his insanity, of his loss of temporal and spatial links to the belief in reality he must preserve, if he expects to recover sanity. The risk of losing it is brought powerfully to his attention in moments of physical torture:

> The blow of a fist in the stomach doubled him over as though he had suddenly caved in; and the moment his face dropped, another blow to the chin threw him violently backward; his ribs met simultaneously the hard resistance of the cement floor and the boots which began to kick at him. . . .

. . .

> When the door of his cell again closed, his first sensation was one of comfort. This door whose crushing weight hung over him protected him from the abjectness and the absurdity outside; and at the same time the solitude, the bareness, and the end of unconsciousness brought him back that dim sense of being enclosed which he had experienced in childhood when he played Indian under the tables. . . .[20]

[20] Malraux, *Days of Wrath,* tr. Haakon M. Chevalier, New York, Random House, 1936, pp. 33, 34. Originally published in Paris by Gallimard (1935), as *Le Temps du Mépris.*

His act of suffering pain is at least a testimony of his commitment. Hell is confinement or torture without purpose. The hero must, actually or in imagination, survive as an active person meaningfully existing in time, since time is of the secular essence. If he does survive, he can be said to have suffered the equivalent of purgatory.

Heaven is in a majority of instances visualized as a practical achievement on earth. There are accretions of Eden, Five-Year Plans, and dams. The principal irony of secular grace is that the line of development toward a practical, earthly paradise is always threatened by lifeless abstractions. Arthur Koestler describes his first impression of the Dnieper dam: "In the shrill light of the August morning the white semicircular dam offers a supernatural sight. . . . Vibrating high-tension wires of altogether six hundred miles' length convey the stream of electrones, fed with energy from the stream of water drops, to the new giants of industry which will transform the rural Ukraine into an industrial base of the Red Continent, second only in importance to the Urals." [21] Each accomplished image of progress is a stage on the way toward "a universe in our own image, without weakness, a universe in which man, rid of the old rages of Christianity, will attain his cosmic grandeur in the supreme culmination of the species . . ." (155–56). Of course this prospect is often the victim not only of historical fact but also of anti-utopian satire. But it was nevertheless a sustaining vision, of the perfection of useful and grandiosely serviceable objects.

The Communists, says Koestler, "like Catholics, live in a constant awareness of original sin." [22] The sense of original sin

[21] *The Invisible Writing*, New York, Macmillan, 1954, p. 67.

[22] *The Invisible Writing*, p. 33. The original sin of the secular theology is associated with human deviations from an organizational absolute—symbolized by the toothache (Rubashov, *Darkness at Noon*), a fear of rats (Winston Smith, *1984*), etc. When pain is associated with personal as contrasted to large social objectives, it is an expression of weakness, not a sign of the secular purgatory. A variant of this matter is suggested in Martin Turnell's analysis of Zola in *The Art of French Fiction* (New

in the secular economy is a complex of misunderstanding, surrender to bourgeois taste and morality, the too frequent communication with the individual "I" as opposed to the metaphysical "we." In many cases, original sin first becomes obvious in a secular hero when he has passed the time of youth, when he pauses too often on the straight line he must take to the future. An awareness of human depravity, a central experience in the spiritual discipline, becomes in itself the sin.

Silone's work touches frequently upon the parallels of saint and secular leader. Pietro Spina of *Bread and Wine* is after all both; he wears the priest's garments as he looks at his Italy through the eyes of the member of a secular order. The details of a parallel sometimes are ludicrously evident—as in the case of the Party secretary of *A Handful of Blackberries*:

> She was one of the most fanatical comrades. She neglected her family in order to attend all ceremonies of both Church and Party. And in spite of it all, she showed no signs of strain from the simultaneous practice of these two highly exacting forms of worship. Indeed, her liturgical needs seemed insatiable, and her capacity for belief bottomless. The innumerable discrepancies between the mysteries of the Party and those of the Church were consumed, leaving no trace, in the flame of her faith.[23]

She had once had a dream of the Divine Saviour, who "had appeared to her clad in a red robe. He did not utter a word, but He showed her His heart, on which the new symbols of

York, New Directions, 1959), in which he maintains that the Rougon-Macquart novels are a secular rewriting of *Genesis* (p. 134). The *lésion organique* transmitted by Tante Didi is the equivalent of original sin. It proliferates in Zola's novels, as signs of physical weakness parallel evidences of social corruption. But Zola's use of inherited "taints" is complicated by a vision of progress as well; his "illuminism" suggests that science will effect a new world condition, into which the "new man" will enter. The picture is confusing; there are no guarantees concerning the analogue, nor is one sure that the "new man" enters Eden in a state of knowledge or a condition of innocence.

[23] *A Handful of Blackberries*, p. 225.

the hammer and sickle were engraved in gold" (226). To the simple-hearted peasant, both Christ and Marx might be expected to act the role of the holy mediator, to alleviate poverty or to suggest a way to heaven.

For similar reasons, "deviationists" were hunted out and persecuted as heretics. Party members, according to Koestler, lived in the "insurmountable horror of excommunication" (*The Invisible Writing*, 245). As saints were made, so were heretics burned. Silone inserts a brilliantly suggestive parable in *The Seed Beneath the Snow*; it is applicable to both the Christian and the secular worlds. Donna Carolina, sister to the priest, busies herself with exterminating the church mice:

> "[They are] sprayed with kerosene and burned alive. . . . Every morning, outside the sacristy, there is a crowd of boys enjoying the sight. . . . Sometimes, on Sundays, it's hard to tell the smell of incense from that of the burning mice. . . . Donna Carolina says that if the church is to be entirely rid of mice, an example must be made of the offenders and the smell of the burning must serve as a warning to the rest. . . ." [24]

This small detail says as much about the parallel as any of the explicit discussions of heresy, of which there are many in modern literature.

It is no marvel that these parallels should occur. Marx both feared and abominated the Gods, as having captured the mass imagination and thus endangered history's dialectic. But when one attempts to secularize the entire life of man, the images that have given texture to that life will remain. The Church, a stronghold of reaction, is also an enduring monument of man's conquest of death; the secular drive to change the nature and setting of that triumph encounters many images of the spiritual past. The secular discipline proposes a strength of renunciation; the hero has no right to a private life. He exists in a Party

[24] Tr. Frances Frenaye, New York, Harper's, 1942, p. 186.

"cell"; he must forswear the temptations of wealth and become a mendicant; his gestures of obeisance to the secular god are not less ambitious or energetic than the rituals of Christian worship. The ultimate state resembles in many ways a divinely abstract synthesis of human aspirations.

—[vi]—

At four a.m. Rubashov is arrested. No reasons are given for his arrest, and none are needed. He moves from the still vivid world of the real to the angular unreality of his cell. "The courtyard was still; the sentry was just turning; above the machine-gun tower he saw a streak of the Milky Way." [25]

Koestler's hero is the most sharply delineated portrait of the tarnished secular martyr. One of the "old revolutionaries," zealous in his youth, marked by the scars of apocalyptic struggle, he is now among the last of a diminishing generation: a "defective saint," both scapegoat and Christ. The full meaning of secular grace, and of its divergencies from spiritual design, may be read in his history.

The span of his revolutionary career includes two distinct versions of secular grace. In the beginning he had been an agent of revolutionary progress: ". . . we had descended into the depths, into the formless, anonymous masses, which at times constituted the substance of history; and we were the first to discover her laws of motion. . . . We dug in the primeval mud of history and there we found her laws. We knew more than ever men have known about mankind; that is why our revolution succeeded . . ." (82–83). The basic ambiguity of the revolution is that of the nature of time and its absorption in eternity. This ambiguity is not clearly seen in the revolution's first stages, when any energetic and orderly effort seems happily to contribute to its success. In these first stages Rubashov en-

[25] *Darkness at Noon*, tr. from the French by Daphne Hardy, New York, Macmillan, 1941. The French title was *Le Zéro et l'infini*.

joyed the exaltation of success. As a revolution stabilizes, it becomes rigid and inflexible, to prevent its dynamic power from destroying it. Its leaders no longer need to hide in the catacombs; but there is no easeful time for discussion of principles: "Revolutionary theory had frozen to a dogmatic cult, with a simplified, easily graspable catechism, and with No. 1 as the high priest celebrating the Mass . . ." (176–77).

Darkness at Noon describes the trials (there are three, two private and one public), the temptations, the agony and passion, and the death of its secular hero; its outlines are a secular parallel of the theological passion of Thomas à Becket in Eliot's *Murder in the Cathedral*. These two works are a literary realization of the Christian and the secular struggles to define and conquer the problem of human mortality. Ivanov, Rubashov's first inquisitor, significantly marks the limits of the contrast:

> "There are only two conceptions of human ethics, and they are at opposite poles. One of them is Christian and humane, declares the individual to be sacrosanct, and asserts that the rules of arithmetic are not to be applied to human units. The other starts from the basic principle that a collective aim justifies all means, and not only allows, but demands, that the individual should in every way be subordinated and sacrificed to the community—which may dispose of it as an experimentation rabbit or a sacrificial lamb. . . ." (157)

In the background of the two struggles are the masses. Eliot's chorus of Canterbury women passively endure the consequences of their cathedral without its leader, and they grow spiritually as their master triumphs over a succession of theological temptations. Koestler's chorus is less prominent; a note here, a look of understanding there testify only to its probability. The masses are otherwise numb or uninterested. Eliot's women eventually overcome the feeling of earthly indignity, and in a real sense—on the level of physical drama at least—move from ignorance to an awe-inspiring recognition of their hero's saintliness:

The horror of the effortless journey, to the empty land
Which is no land, only emptiness, absence, the Void,
Where those who were men can no longer turn the mind
To distraction, delusion, escape into dream, pretence,
Where the soul is no longer deceived, for there are no objects,
    no tones,
No colours, no forms to distract, to divert the soul
From seeing itself, foully united forever, nothing with nothing,
Not what we call death, but what beyond death is not death,
We fear, we fear. . . .[26]

The chorus moves slowly but steadily toward a renunciation of worldly distractions, fearing only death without God, a void first sensed, at the beginning of religions, in man's mortality, and compensated for by the metaphor of grace, of the Incarnation. Thomas must move securely away from the seductions and pleasures of the earth. He must similarly reject the promise of earthly power and the satisfaction of spiritual power personally desired and shrewdly grasped. He must die entirely in humble submission to the will of God so that the power of God's grace will remain unharmed on the earth. To have done that—and Eliot wishes us to assume that he has done that—is to return the gift of Incarnation by rejoining the human to the divine. Spiritual grace becomes, in this play, a complex ceremony of the Incarnation and its effects in human circumstances. No act of Thomas has value without its reference to divinity: Thomas' sainthood clarifies only as his humanity is progressively cleansed and the motive for his acts is seen more and more clearly to have come from the will of God.

Darkness at Noon shows the career of grace in a time-bounded system of values. The end in each case is death. Rubashov is at the last conscious of a violent blow, and then another:

---

[26] *Murder in the Cathedral*, p. 69.

"A wave slowly lifted him up. It came from afar and travelled sedately on, a shrug of eternity" (267). As Thomas dies, the chorus cries out against the foulness of the air and the drouth of spiritual crisis. Rubashov and Thomas are both uncertain of the meaning of their death for the eternity that yawns after: the one because he must think only of history as legitimizing his "martyrdom," the other because eternity is contained within God's will, which is timeless and beyond human understanding.

Koestler defines the quality of history as a record of the movement of secular grace, by setting up two distinctly different kinds of inquisitor. The first, Ivanov, is in a sense Rubashov's double (it is significant that he too is executed): of the early generation, logical, reasonable, even sentimentally attached to the values of old-fashioned heroism. His treatment of Rubashov is cynically kind; Rubashov is permitted indulgences, and he is in a sense seduced to confession by Mephistophelean means. Ivanov tells him that there is no real point in resisting the need to lie, since he has already lied, and often; at any rate, truth is the expedient character of present means. There is a final truth to which all temporary lies are sacrificed. The passion of the secular hero is to endure (while committing) the expedient sin until the movement of history has finally reached the absolving truth. The impurity of the means does not in any way defile the end. In cynical mockery, Ivanov sketches the irony of Rubashov's temptation to act with Christ-like gestures:

". . . I would like to write a passion play in which God and the Devil dispute for the soul of Saint Rubashov. After a life of sin, he has turned to God—to a God with the double chin of industrial liberalism and the charity of the Salvation Army soups. Satan, on the contrary, is thin, ascetic and a fanatical devotee of logic. He reads Machiavelli, Ignatius of Loyola, Marx and Hegel; he is cold and unmerciful to mankind, out of a kind of mathematical mercifulness. He is damned always to do that which is most repugnant to him: to become a slaughterer, in order to abolish slaughtering, to sacrifice lambs so that no more lambs may be slaughtered, to whip people with knouts so that they may learn not to let themselves be whipped, to strip himself of every scruple in the name of the higher scrupulousness, and to challenge the hatred of mankind because of his love for it—an abstract and geometric love. . . ." (149-50)

Ivanov wishes only that Rubashov acknowledge the figure of the Devil in these terms. Only from the Christian point of view can he be seen as a devil. A Christian conscience in the revolution is as useless and menacing as a cancer. Scruple opens the eyes where they should be blind. Rubashov has belatedly become aware of himself as a creature of pain, regret, and scruple. He has yielded to temptations similar to those Thomas à Becket rejected; for remorse suffered because of sin recognized may be an extension of the sin, the sin in another guise.

Rubashov's second tormentor, Gletkin, is another type altogether; he belongs to another generation. He is of the crowd "born without umbilical cord, without frivolity, without melancholy" (228). The circumstances of this second inquisition are entirely different. He is roused at night, staggers to Gletkin's office, is forced to stand under a harsh, glaring light, which is modified and softened only as Gletkin gets the confessions and signatures he wants. He not only wishes Rubashov's death but wants Rubashov to want it and to state publicly good Party reasons for wanting it. In these terms Rubashov's trial and death are a part of the strategic, historical moment in time. The significance of Gletkin lies in his fundamental inhumanity: there are no shades or soft lines to mitigate the geometric hardness, the coarse-grained brutality of his presence. He is like the brutal simplicity of his setting. The light in the corridors is harsh and unrelieved (either jaundice-yellow or remorseless white); the design of cell, office, and exercise yard is similarly unrelieved by variation in angle or plane. Gletkin bears a scar on the top of his head, a memento of his suffering in the Civil War; but it suggests not suffering but impersonality, like the socket for an electric light. He asks Rubashov to exert himself emotionally at the trial, but only in the attitude of abject, lying humility before the inhuman, abstract policy of his secular leaders—after which, he will be asked to die, but with no consciousness of heroic sacrifice. His death is a "liquidation" (as in the world of Orwell's 1984 it was a "vaporisation"):

> It was a logical consequence, a factor with which one reckoned and which bore rather an abstract character. Also death was rarely spoken of, and the word "execution" was hardly ever used; the customary expression was "physical liquidation." The words "physical liquidation" again evoked only one concrete idea: The cessation of political activity. The act of dying in itself was a technical detail, with no claim to interest; death as a factor in a logical equation had lost any intimate bodily feature. (136)

From the wreckage of his revolutionary hopes, Rubashov rescues a conscience—a quality, as Ivanov had reminded him, as useful to the revolution as a double chin. The drama of his trial and death (The "Passion of Saint Rubashov") is explicitly given in terms of a conflict between the abstract "We" and what, embarrassed as a trained revolutionary may be, he can only call "the grammatical fiction." The "I" according to which a person notes himself as self is signified by the liking for a sketch of the *Pietà* in an art museum (he had visited it really on Party business, but the image had survived the plot), by the specific values of his secretary as body (her skin, her eyes, her desire to be "of service"), by the temptation to feel romantically sorrowful and to pity, finally and above all by the toothache. This last is a physical index of pain, a reminder of his duty to conscience and scruple. It is a degrading reminder of the corruption of the flesh, and communicates to him at crucial moments his past denials of his own humanity.[27] The toothache is a testimony of the "I," which is finally his only companion in the hours preceding death. "He had followed every thought to its last conclusion and acted in accordance with it to the very end; the hours which remained to him belonged to that silent partner, whose realm started just where logical thought ended . . ." (254). Rubashov must finally be pained into recognizing not only himself as body but the bodily fact of those whom he has tortured in the interests of Party.

The toothache as sensual experience serves the same role in Rubashov's life as the scent of brown hair and the music of the flute in the lives of Eliot's protagonists. With this difference: that Rubashov needs to be reminded of pain rather than pleasure, and he is therefore brought back to the center of life by a sensation that images that of his victims. Pain is the physical pathway to a final consideration of the ambiguities of secular grace. If the objective of Party activity is the elimination of human suffering, and if the present stage requires that many more people suffer than would ordinarily, then the question the toothache asks is:

> Was such an operation justified? Obviously it was, if one spoke in the abstract of "mankind"; but, applied to "man" in the singular, to the cipher 2—4, the real human being of bone and flesh and blood and skin, the principle led to absurdity. (255)

The flaw in this laborious effort to stimulate and accelerate progress was the monstrous increase in what he called "senseless suffering." It led to a sense of hopelessness and dread in the people, and to their giving in to mechanical and unthinking obedience to a system they did not understand, but were too frightened to question. This is not the agony of Eliot's chorus,

[27] Compare the pain suffered by the chief of police in Graham Greene's *The Power and the Glory* (1940); it provides an ironic commentary upon the priest's death, and is in fact an illustration of one of the points made in the "debates" which precede it.

but the numbness of masses of people caught in the brutal and inevitable movement in history toward an end no longer clearly seen or actually trusted. Rubashov goes to his death not knowing why. He surely cannot say that he is grateful for having finally served the Party, for he does not trust the Party. Looking at his death another way, perhaps he may say that it is "a mistake in the system"; or, he might understand it as an inevitable result of his having participated willingly in the "running amuck" of the revolution. "We have thrown overboard all our conventions," he had once written in his diary; "our sole guiding principle is that of consequent logic; we are sailing without ethical ballast" (260).

As protagonists in the drama of grace, Eliot's Becket and Koestler's Rubashov point up the deficiencies and underscore the pathos of man's most daring imaginative creation, the metaphor of the Incarnation. Becket moves away from, Rubashov toward, the human. Becket, having fully understood the limitations of the human will, submits humbly to the divine; Rubashov, having lived in the fullest sense a life of dedication to a nonhuman objective, submits finally to it, and may be said therefore to be scheduled for canonization as saint-scapegoat of the secular faith, though he dies finally in recognition of the moral "mistake" his life has been. Becket's four tempters are the equivalent of Rubashov's two inquisitors; but Eliot's epilogue is a post-dramatic examination of an expedient milieu. The four knights of Eliot's play, who appeal to their contemporary English audience are in the background of Rubashov's trial paralleled by the press, the judicial mechanisms, all of the vehicles for explaining a death in expedient terms. Eliot writes with the confidence that the purpose of Becket's martyrdom is fixed and that, in terms of the role of grace in history, it may be defined as "natural," even determined. Koestler would have us believe, however, that the path of secular grace has been perverted, perhaps even seriously distorted.

Rubashov dies in the awareness that the men he had killed

are men (and that he too is being killed as a man); Orwell's Winston Smith (1984), having rebelled in a situation in which rebellion is fantastically difficult, lives out his days in the cage of his fears. That men are decent and deserve a better fate than either Koestler's or Orwell's vision will permit them is a kind of truth rescued from the rubble of their novels. Against them, the conclusions of Silone and Malraux are modest to the point of self-effacement. Pietro Spina becomes Don Paolo Spada; man's hope is seen in the inviolate energy of human and domestic objects scattered in the debris of Madrid. All of these novelists seem to point to the dangers of trying to take part in propelling society toward an absolute end. The values that risk extinction by such a move are the tangible and sensible ones that in the end survive human efforts to transcend them.

By contrast, Eliot's archbishop will not be frightened by formidable transcendent values and symbols—perhaps because they *are* transcendent. The weaknesses of secular movements toward grace result finally from man's wish to defy mortality purely within mortal limits; that is, without an appeal to God. A quantity of "senseless suffering" eventually overrules the purpose of suffering altogether, unless the objective transcends the nature of the victim. But it is very difficult for man to tolerate the thought of this transcendence. It is exasperatingly slow of visualization, and it is marked by slow, painful agonies of the spirit:

> Every horror had its definition,
> Every sorrow had a kind of end:
> In life there is not time to grieve long.
> But this, this is out of life, this is out of time,
> An instant eternity of evil and wrong.
>
> (*Murder in the Cathedral,* 75)

So speak Eliot's chorus when they are faced with the necessity of suffering a spiritual agony. Koestler, Malraux, and Silone have shown that the attempt to secularize the processes of grace in history leads to similarly ambiguous agonies, which are perhaps even more agonizing because their ends are not hidden in eternity.

While all of the heroes described in this chapter consider absolutes and are even sometimes close to grasping them, the circumstances of grace are regarded almost invariably from a personal center. The scenes are violent, and the prospects of death imminent. In the novels of Silone, Malraux, and Koestler, violent death is a major risk; and each hero must decide how he will kill or be killed. The paradoxes of secular grace are the subject of an elaborate personal meditation: on the metaphysics of secular history, on personal involvement in directing or contributing to that history, on the universal need to rescue man from the negative absolute of annihilation (which they define as death to no end or purpose). These are in a sense still meditations within a world of possibilities, a world in which violence has not yet destroyed all personal initiative. Nevertheless, violent explosions of impersonal force grow in frequency and intensity. We have examined the problems of violence in its relation to manners and to rational orders, and have tried to suggest some of the ambiguities resulting from the translation of grace from spiritual to secular levels. The acceleration of force to its twentieth century levels of power and menace ought now to be examined. What are the limits of force beyond which language and form as we know them become inoperative? How does literature adjust to force at any level or in any dimension? What reforms are necessary in the moral disposition of man toward a violence that is beyond his powers personally to comprehend? In what ways does the self attempt to will survival in a condition of extreme violence? These questions have a major and an importunate claim upon our attention. We shall need to examine them from every conceivable point of view in the following chapters.

PART TWO

VIOLENCE

3

THE ASSAILANT AND
THE VICTIM: SOME DEFINITIONS
OF MODERN VIOLENCE

On fait les plus grands cruautés, mais sans
cruauté.

—STENDHAL, *Le Rouge et le Noir*

—[i]—

IN A BRILLIANT and suggestive essay in revaluation of *The Iliad*,
Simone Weil says that the ultimate objective of force is to reduce men to things. The horrifying fact is that the real *materiel*
in warfare is the human personality, "fallen to the level either
of inert matter, which is all passivity, or to the level of blind
forces, which are all momentum. . . ." The primary means of
a successful war is the reduction of men to the condition of
beasts: ". . . the veritable object of the art of war is no less
than the souls of the combatants." [1]

The two major wars of our century are the focus of any discussion of modern violence. From every point of view, sociologi-
cal, psychological, and aesthetic, they have helped severely to
dislocate the forms according to which force in the past was
contained. Miss Weil defines force as "that which makes a

[1] "The 'Iliad,' Poem of Might," in *Intimations of Christianity*, tr. Elizabeth C. Geissbuhler, Boston, Beacon Press, 1958, p. 45.

thing of anybody who comes under its sway. When exercised to the full, it makes a thing of man in the most literal sense, for it makes him a corpse" (24). The concentration of force upon a single area may also reduce survivors to the level of soulless victims who expect such treatment and live in the expectation of it.

The crucial result of the modern maneuvering of force has been the loss of human power to think, plan, and act in terms of the metaphors of his cultural inheritance. These metaphors have survived only peripherally; they are no longer at the center of human schemes. They have always depended upon the belief in a transcendent power, and they work out from such a central metaphor. Put simply, and perhaps superficially, the power of nature has in the past either been incorporated into or equalized by the power of gods. From this central idea the language of belief, ceremony, and ritual assumed its character. Basic to this arrangement is the belief that the power of the gods is sufficient to provide a ritual haven from human death and corruption. The secret of classical tragedy—of its effect— lies not only in the fact that the hero's death is an active resolution of the moral and spiritual disturbances caused by his life; it depends also upon the conviction that the hero's role will persist in a postmortem, retrospective consideration of these disturbances. Almost invariably tragedy requires a controlled view and estimate of corpses. It also demands a clear line of progress in the analysis of events leading to death. Death as total surprise loses much of its tragic value. Reflection upon causes is difficult in these circumstances. The character and number of corpses resulting from the action must in some way or other be deducible from the quality of mind and spirit responsible for them.

Tradition in literature has always relied upon some such conviction regarding the rhythm of causes in life and results in death. The earliest literary representation of the ways in which this rhythm is violated was the metamorphic tradition. Metamorphosis is necessary to a successful comprehension of a religion in which the divine and the human are closely related. The gods are an enabling cause of metamorphosis in human dramas which involve violent extremes of conduct. They protect, punish, and correct the affairs of men. Metamorphosis is an instrument of divine intervention, in the interests of preserving the belief in a balance of divine and human natures. But the word may also simply mean *change*, and in this sense it may suggest reduction rather than transcendence. The balance of natural and transcendent powers requires that force be contained: that it be understood as metaphorically and ritually accessible to human comprehension. Men are held accountable for their persons and their acts at each point in the progress. Their power should submit at each point to the systems and rituals of containment. The principal instrument of that slow and gradual process is form, a product both of man's mind and of his imagination. Man is above all a formalizing creature, and his sanity and balance depend upon the success of his comprehending experience formally.

One important description of violence is that it serves to threaten the balance of forms. Since forms are a result of the mental and imaginative functions, violence frequently comes from a distortion of one or the other, which throws the formal economy into imbalance. The important requisite of forms is that man should *intend* them, and that, intending them, he should believe in them as more than adequately constructive explanations of his condition and its prospects of continuity. One may explain modern culture by saying that the relationship between the two functions responsible for forms has broken down, that as a result of this failure of balance it has become extremely difficult to comprehend life and death formally. The forms no longer contain the force; the force is unleashed; it is perhaps at the disposal of the intellect, but not reliably of the imagination. Man has arrived at the point in his history where he regards force as an autonomous evil, available only occasionally and not predictably to human controls.

Several important formal agents of balance are therefore

menaced. For it is indispensable to morality that the objects involved in human relationships be *visible* both to the mind and to the imagination. This concept of visibility is crucial to the problem of containment. Emotions expressed outwardly assume a comprehensible interaction of agent and object. Love necessitates both lover and beloved; they are necessarily visible to each other. Hatred likewise suggests an agent who expresses hostility and a victim who receives and in some way deserves it.

Visibility suggests measurable distances. A relationship that is forcefully expressed is no longer formally contained if the distance between the motivated agent and his object is too great to be comprehended. The moral problem of the twentieth century begins at the point at which the distance between agent and object is lost to the mind and to the imagination. It can no longer be formally contained; or, at any rate, the forms used to comprehend it no longer serve the purpose adequately.

Both the morality and the literature of our time are irresolute in their search for forms to explain present dispositions of force. Extremely weird phenomena result. Innocence and ignorance combine with a narrowly specialized training to the achievement of motiveless and apparently blameless mass murder. Exorbitantly forceful heroism is hurriedly mobilized to save men from the consequences of "impudent crimes." Man lives in danger not only of death but of extinction. The vision of death in these circumstances is no longer of a conclusion to an orderly rhythm of the life process. The dignity of dying is continuously and shamelessly insulted. The most insufferable characteristic of modern calamities is their casual suddenness, their informality; this lack of formal relationship disperses man's power to anticipate, expect, prepare, and comprehend. Simone Weil has described this condition with great pertinence:

> . . . That men should have death for their future is a denial of nature. As soon as the practice of war has revealed the fact that each moment holds the possibility of death,

> the mind becomes incapable of moving from one day to the next without passing through the spectre of death. . . . That soul daily suffers violence which every morning must mutilate its aspirations because the mind cannot move about in a time without passing through death. In this way war wipes out every conception of a goal, even all thoughts concerning the goals of war . . . (41)

A constant threat of death and the absence of any formal means of expecting and adjusting to it serve to destroy man's power to live meaningfully. Modern wars have therefore thrown the moral and literary economy very much off balance. Our literature abounds in illustrations of men submitting blindly to a condition of overwhelming force, supported indifferently or inexpertly by abstract substitutes for individual motive. The individual detail of this landscape of violence testifies again and again to the serious dislocation of result from motive. Distances all but exclude the chance of determining the assailant or making the necessary adjustment to him as an agent expressing hostility for an object. In any really meaningful sense, both the agent and the object of this relationship have disappeared from the scene; and since they have, the individual is left, as Miss Weil has said, with the immediate and continuous prospect of death as extinction.

Modern literature has acted in various ways to describe this emergency. In the First World War, certain writers invoked large abstractions from the past as a talismanic substitute for motive, or (as in the case of H. G. Wells) invented abstractions pointing to an imagined postwar future. According to these, we endured the prospect of sudden death in order to preserve a tradition. This is not the same as fighting *for* tradition; it is rather as though a religious war were fought solely to enable God to survive His enemies. Neither tradition nor God is in this case a viable force in determining the motive for combat. For the majority of war novelists, poets, and dramatists, the literary portrayal of the new violence was one of two kinds: either the artist focused upon the factuality of circumstance or he portrayed the physiological and psychological changes occurring in the hero as he shifted from an abstract to an explicit understanding of his status.

There have been many variations in this literature, but perhaps the major development from World War I to World War II is that the literary analysis of the assailant-victim relationship has increased in subtlety. The human circumstance of World War I permitted fairly easy and simple ironies, both those caused by an obvious disparity between promised objective and actual reality and those implicit in the miscarriages of justice that attend a condition of extraordinary violence. In other words, the violence of the first war was still new and the shock of dislocation fresh. Men were angry, but they were still not willing to surrender the privilege of being angry over a specific cause. War literature of this kind tends to rely upon a certain strength of romantic emotion; even the sense of horror is influenced by sentimental survivals of meaning which attach to the victims of the horror. That is, men are angry but still fairly sure of the sources of their anger; or they are horrified in the sense that they still remember what it meant not to feel horror.

The literature of the second war is at once more fully committed to scatologies of violence and more subtly analytic of the individual's ambiguous role in the drama of violence. This does not necessarily mean that it is a superior literature. In some respects it is much more remote from the human possibilities of maintaining a formal balance. It is only that the artist is not satisfied to suggest either irony or horror in its simple or pure form. The literature of violence has moved away from social satire to an analysis of the forms of "metaphysical conceit" available in present circumstances. These "conceits" have largely to do with the dissolution of corpses or their dismemberment, or with the phenomena of masses of men dead from an assailant so far removed as to be entirely invisible, or with the totally irrational situation of a village of smiling citizens scrupulously ignoring a nearby "experiment" in mass extermination. These are aberrational instances of the new violence. The moral questions they raise cannot be discussed according to any simple equations, but must be considered in terms of the most complex of Kafkan ambiguities. As a reminder of death, the "bracelet of bright hair about the bone" is superseded by the tangle of bodies in a denatured landscape.[2]

The strangeness of the war situation is testified to, and analyzed, again and again in J. Glenn Gray's *The Warriors* (1959). The commentary alternates with selections from his World War II journal. The details are not unlike those of Ernst Juenger's reports of the First World War,[3] but Gray's position is not that of a professional soldier but of a philosopher temporarily engaged in battle. Though there is much here that goes beyond the actual circumstances of conflict, his description of the soldier as a *homo furens* offers additional evidence of the human changes that occur at the center of violence.

> . . . the soldier who has yielded himself to the fortunes of war, has sought to kill and to escape being killed, or who has even lived long enough in the disordered landscape of battle, is no longer what he was. . . . His moods and disposition are affected by the presence of others and the encompassing environment of threat and fear . . .[4]

Gray speaks of the "lust of the eye," which may become an aesthetic pleasure in the war as spectacle; this effect diminishes

[2] There *is* a group of war novels that are "ideologically" motivated and directed (see below, Part Two, chapter 7). Frequently this type of novel comes from the ideological impulses of the 1930's, which were badly damaged by the Loyalist loss in the Spanish Civil War; but a few examples (Irwin Shaw's *The Young Lions*; Stefan Heym's *The Crusaders*) retain the dramatic formulas of the democratic man-turned-soldier fighting the Nazi in the world and in himself. These formulas are what we have instead of romanticism in the literature of World War II.

[3] See below, Part Two, chapter 4: "The Moment of Violence."

[4] *The Warriors*, New York, Harcourt, Brace, 1959, p. 27. Other references to this edition are in the text.

as war is mechanized, though in air warfare it remains and is even increased: "Because these powerful new weapons usually remove those who use them further from the gruesome consequences of their firing, they afford more opportunity for aesthetic satisfaction (32). In these circumstances, the self is detached at least momentarily from the scene; it is difficult to maintain a normally critical view of the situation; and even after it is over, a return to civilian status is not invariably accompanied by the recapture of prior moral standards. The soldier has been infected by violence, and is psychologically changed.

Gray's analysis includes the phenomenon of the soldier's "delight in destruction," the line that separates self-defense from fighting for its own sake (52–53).

> Unlike other delights, it becomes, relatively soon in most men, a consuming lust which swallows up other pleasures. It tends to turn men inward upon themselves and make them inaccessible to more normal satisfactions. Because they rarely can feel remorse, they experience no purgation and cannot grow . . . (57)

The psychology of soldiers is closely related to the question of abstractness or impersonality. Those who "hate impersonally" and without awareness of the enemy as human make viciously efficient soldiers; they fight to destroy not human foes but "embodiments of undifferentiated evil" (140). The question of guilt is difficult to comprehend, particularly as the efficiency and power of guns serve to remove the soldier further and further away from his target.

> I realize that thousands of soldiers fired incessantly in recent wars without once seeing their targets, and bombardiers destroyed uncounted lives with no conception of the manner of people who were cowering under the falling bombs . . .(136)

This image of the enemy as subhuman is given regularly in recent war literature; he is scarcely if ever seen, and is imagined as a stereotyped figure, more beast or devil than man. The kind of reductiveness involved in it is closely associated with the emotion of guilt, a dreadful issue which many soldiers try to avoid, in favor of the less complex one of the lust for indiscriminate killing. As the soldier diminishes as a human being in the mind of his enemy, so his enemy yields to simple and brutal passions, and both are reduced to a level of dreadful and powerful simplicity. In these circumstances, the soldier serves no moral end, nor even an organizational purpose, but a machine whose strategic role in the total pattern of war is scarcely ever seen.

> The automatism of military life has been immeasurably increased by the perfection and intricacy of instruments and weapons, and it is certain that the human beings who serve them are actually influenced by their automatic character . . . (179)

Impersonality thus has two effects: in the one case, a stereotype of the enemy arouses passions but does not explain them; in the other, the impersonality caused by distance from the target gives no immediate sense of moral involvement with the victim and makes a mechanical game of killing. The great difficulty in modern wars is not so much in performing one's task as in *seeing* it: that is, examining it morally, in terms of one's moral and emotional commitment to it. The question of guilt is of course related to that of moral sensitivity; the emotional engagement may be suppressed, or it may be concealed by the more obvious passion to serve one ideal and to destroy its opposite. Nevertheless, the human sensibility only infrequently endures the spectacle of destruction caused by soldiers and civilians alike, without eventually cracking under the strain or at the least surviving the experience with some sort or other of psychological damage.[5]

—[ii]—

The usual description of a nonviolent death and its relationship to life is that the two exist in a formal pattern; in this case, man lives according to the formal rhythm of his expectation of death. Violent death results from a concentration of force which disrupts these patterns. There are kinds of violence that are still comprehensible in terms of them. A criminal who kills another man may express himself violently, but in this case the cause of the crime is discernible, can be described and indeed is analyzed according to all of the means at our disposal for understanding his violent act.[6] Further, the victim of the crime shares implication in the cause; the victim as object collaborates with the assailant as agent, to the extent at least of being somehow and to some degree involved in the act as cause. An adulterer, surprised by a woman's husband or lover, has in the few seconds before he dies a chance to consider the nature of his deserving the violence. Violence of this kind is contained within the formal possibilities governing the move from birth to death.

There are two kinds of violence which do not submit to such formal explanation: sentimental violence and impersonal vio-

[5] Cf. Jean Paul Sartre's play, *Les Séquestrés d'Altona* (performed 1959; translated as *The Condemned of Altona* and published in 1961 by Knopf), which treats ostensibly with Nazi guilt but is equally applicable to the French experience in North Africa. Specific atrocities, Sartre maintains, have both a past and a future; and the soldier who commits them must eventually identify himself morally with both: he must recognize his toleration of the forces in the past which have led to them, and he must atone for them.

[6] See Porfiry's superbly subtle insights into Raskolnikov's mind in *Crime and Punishment*. His is not a legalistic nor a sleuthing, but a moral intelligence; he is therefore eminently more effective in drawing out Raskolnikov's confession because the latter desperately needs a moral context for his post-criminal feelings.

lence. The first is a violence committed in excess of all possible degrees of expectation, or violence "in excess of the occasion." The second is violence committed in the absence of an agent, a condition in which an agent cannot be logically or reasonably or even metaphorically determined. A *cause* can be found, of course, but it is not contained within any set of motivations belonging to an agent. When Randall Jarrell says, of scientific discoveries, that "The equations metamorphose into use" ("The Emancipators"), he suggests an extreme case of impersonal or agentless violence. The equations are abstract, or if based on concrete instances have no necessary connection with them or with instances of them, in perpetuity. Similarly, "use" means result and is not emotionally or responsibly identifiable with a specific person in the act of using. In an act of impersonal violence, the agent no longer serves the object; his mind, imagination, and skill serve the cause instead. Knowledge of or acquaintance with the object, if it ever exists, is accidental, and may even be forbidden. In another poem, Jarrell describes this situation and provides an illustration of it:

. . .

It is unnecessary to understand; if you are still
In this year of our warfare, indispensable
In general, and in particular dispensable
As a cartridge, a life—it is only to enter
So many knots in a window, so many feet;
To switch on for an instant the steel that understands
Do as they said; as they said, there is always a reason—
Though neither for you nor for the fatal
Knower of wind, speed, pressure; the unvalued facts.[7]

. . .

These two types of violence between them account for most of the ambiguities residing in modern literature. Each has an

[7] "Siegfried," in *Little Friend, Little Friend*, New York, Dial, 1945, p. 19. "The Emancipators" is in *ibid.*, p. 14.

almost endless range of variation. Sentimental violence occurs when the agent distorts his responsibility to the object; he exercises pure force but is guided by an impure motive. Nevertheless, he still functions as a person, though his grasp of what a personality is is often vague, clouded, aberrant. Robert Cohn of *The Sun Also Rises* is such an agent. He does not exist within the "code" of explicitly understood limits that govern or should govern the intimate friends of Jake Barnes; he acts in terms of another group altogether, and each of the persons with whom he associates has an isolated meaning for him. The power he exercises is his skill in boxing. With it, he serves the role of single-minded romantic, against images of supposed opposition. In a sense, Cohn's blows are struck for purity against impurities and as such are an additional commentary upon the pathos of Jake's contemporaries. But the occasion does not call for violence of the kind he exerts; the violence is directed not in understanding but in willful distortion of its object.

Sentimental violence can also be seen in its relation to impersonal violence. Whenever an agent acts sentimentally against a victim in such a way as to include in the resulting disaster persons not in any way associated in the role of victim with him, sentimental violence becomes impersonal. The change is almost entirely a matter of instrumentation; the agent chooses both weapon and circumstance that involve persons who are not designated victims. Had Cohn used a machine gun and shot at Pedro Romero in a crowd, the two kinds of violence would have combined. Or, if a man who wished to avenge himself upon another should place a bomb in a plane and destroy him as well as thirty-five other passengers, he would be guilty of both kinds of violence. He is the agent of one death, the cause of the other thirty-five.

Impersonal violence occurs when instruments of force are so powerful and so intricately developed that the agent of destruction can and does cancel himself as a person motivated to do violence upon another. In some respects, many acts of abnormal violence committed in concentration camps are a mixture of sentimental and impersonal violence: as in the case reported in Ernst Wiechert's novel, *Missa Sine Nomine*. The hero's memory of his concentration camp experience includes the dreadful image of the torturer who smiled as he tortured.

> "I could have shot him through the heart, but I shot into his face. Perhaps I thought that with a heart-shot he might get up again, because there was a vacuum in his body where we have a heart. Nothing but an empty space. His life was only in his face which we had seen smiling. Many, many times. And I shot into this smile." [8]

This man's smile was a violation of his role as minister to an impersonal assailant. It either betrayed an extraordinary sadistic pleasure in what he was doing or was a form of decadent commentary upon the disruption of human values that characterized the scene. There is no question that the hero's act of violence (for which he atones, that he may once again live at peace in the world) was neither sentimental nor impersonal, but a *crime passionnel* of an exceptional kind.

Conditions of extreme impersonal violence, as for example those of our two World Wars, are followed by times of great tension. Attempts to restore forms that have been respected before a time of great violence almost invariably fail. The most eloquent defense of these forms proves inadequate, because each violation of the rhythm of life-death expectancy upsets the formal capacity for acceptance. Men live in a state of tension, which is a minor peacetime legacy of violence. In a sense also, the experiencing of violence stimulates the demand for its repetition, if only for the purpose of challenging and testing man's ability to raise the forms to a new level and to accommodate the new violence within them.

A great many phenomena in literature can be explained if we

[8] Tr. Marie Heynemann and M. B. Ledward, London, Nevill, 1953, p. 36.

accept this fact. Eliot's interest in the metaphysical poets comes not only from the conviction that feeling and thought are inseparable, but also from the realization that the present feeling, with which thought needs to be fused, is of a different kind and force. The fascination with Donne is explainable in part in terms of his skill in combining "metaphysically" the emotion of love with the thought of death. There is a nostalgic value involved in Eliot's admiration; the metaphoric study of death involved in the several "conceits" attributed to it suggests above all that death is comprehensible as an event and does not merely mean the annihilation of the body. In the years between the wars, the interest in Dante's *Inferno* greatly exceeded that in the other two books of the *Comedy*, because the *Inferno* provides concrete images of punishment for documented crimes, but mostly because the details of the punishment expanded by eternity become absorbing extensions of the real. Donne's paradoxes concerning the body in death and the transcendent spirit served the same role (as a means of comprehending the tension) as did the bullfight in Hemingway's case. They were extraordinarily different ways of containing the violence, but each in its own selective way was an experiment in adjustment.[9]

Tension may be defined as the emotional and psychological disposition of the victim toward the assailant. This condition persists beyond the assailant's tenure. Indeed, the quality of tension experienced at any time is influenced by the violence that has preceded it. In a time of war, men become accustomed to a certain accelerated form of expectation. This tension remains when the conditions causing it have been removed. As a result, they attempt various kinds of improvisation. The change

[9] Another illustration of postwar tensions in literature is the sexual paradox, the presence of which suggests social tension or a resistance to normalities. Both Hemingway and Fitzgerald become "sentimental" over such abnormalities in the fiction of the 1920's. There is a direct relationship between the "biological trap" Lieutenant Henry speaks of in *A Farewell to Arms* (1929) and Brett Ashley's society of "queers" in *The Sun Also Rises* (1926).

from war to peace is too difficult for any survivor to assume that prewar moral forms will suffice. Hemingway's story, "Soldier's Home," has many interesting contemporary variants. After each of the two war experiences, there has been a redisposition and revaluation of peacetime forms, to account for and, if possible, to adjust to the new accesses of violence. The new, peacetime equivalent of forms must somehow suggest the recently quieted violence. In every case, the most difficult of the tasks of adjustment comes in the attempt to restore the experience to familiar, comprehensible terms. Tension is the way one has of reconciling himself to the violence, of bringing it back to the level of personal event over which he has a chance at least of personal control. There can be little doubt that the violence in Hemingway's novels is a compulsive repetition of his own experience of it. In this respect, the exploration of forms of accommodation in *A Farewell to Arms,* and of their failure, is motivated by a restless desire to adjust formally to violence; other works are concerned to treat the postwar tensions caused by the imbalance of violence and form described in it.

Paul-Louis Landsberg describes the bullfight as one of the forms in which violence and death are contained in dramatic retrospect and thus the human condition restored to an acceptable balance:

> In the bull ring the bull takes the place of man and man plays the role of the archangel or demon. He revenges himself for being in the grip of fate by taking on the role of fate towards another. For once it is *man* who knows and foresees what he will accomplish. Thus for two hours he can forget his own inevitable death by becoming master of the death of a substitute . . .[10]

It is not only that a man can temporarily reverse his roles. Primarily the appeal of the bullfight for Hemingway, who most

[10] *The Experience of Death: The Moral Problem of Suicide* (1951), tr. Cynthia Rowland, New York, Philosophical Library, 1953, p. 49.

successfully defined postwar tension, is that it was a violent sport and—more important—that it involved not only the element of risk of violence but the possibility of controlling it. Hemingway turned precisely to the condition which was most often lacking in the war situation, the condition of forces opposing each other in such a formalized way that grace and courage could triumph over the assailant. As the source of the violence, the bull offered neither sentimental nor impersonal violence, but a formally contained, traditionally and dramatically developed experience of antagonism. *The Sun Also Rises* is a major literary testimony to the postwar act of adjusting to the tensions created by the experience of World War I.

The full range of modern violence may be comprehended in terms of the metaphor of assailant and victim. I have already described several aspects of the relationship. The assailant as person in the comprehensible relationship of the *crime passionnel* is the most conventional and the most traditional of these literary situations. One may include certain types of suicide in this formula: as for example, Anna Karenina's killing herself, in which she acts both as agent and as victim. Emma Bovary may be said to have committed sentimental violence upon herself; that is, the initial impulse was sentimental, though the agony of dying itself was a prolonged "punishment" dealt her by her author for romantic indulgence. A more frequent modern pattern is that seen in the figure of the assailant as an ideological instrument. Here the assailant is an idea, or a system of ideas, to which one becomes attached at various times as agent, perhaps only once as victim. This formula frequently issues in impersonal violence, and much of the surface irony of modern literature is concerned with man's efforts to preserve the personal relationship of agent to object, in the face of very strong pressures toward impersonality. Perhaps Dostoevsky was the shrewdest of all commentators upon this irony. Raskolnikov, who strives to commit a murder on ideological grounds, ends by atoning for the crime of violently despising humanity. The murder of Shatov in *The Devils* is an elaborate expression of this formula. Surely the twentieth century examples of it are abundant, in the novels of Malraux, Silone, Koestler, and Orwell, and in scores of lesser works.[11]

A variant of these first two forms is that of the assailant as mob. The mob is still personal, in the sense that human passions of specific kinds discernible to the victim are the motivation of the violence. But it is also and more powerfully impersonal in the sense that a mob is many persons and no one person. The assailant is in this case a mass emotion or an expression of mass power against a victim, coming from a distortedly narrow and a morally ambiguous source. In Faulkner's *Intruder in the Dust* (1948) the mob appears to young Chick Mallison as "The Face," suggesting a composite which is not a personality, but the dehumanized expression of partial motivations. It is interesting to see also that in this novel Faulkner sets "The Man" against "The Face," and in that sense suggests that only a precisely understood relation between a personal assailant and a personal victim can be justifiable.[12]

The next level, the assailant as machine, comprehends a wide variety of dislocations in the relationship. An instrument in the hands of the agent acts immediately to pervert the relationship. Guns, artillery, planes, tanks, are all mechanical extensions of force; in use against a victim, they increase the distance between him and the assailant to the point of rendering the situation impersonal and fortuitous. The continuing increase in mechanization of the instrument, while it does not rule out courage in fighting, acts radically to alter the nature and the prerequisites of courage. As Lewis Mumford has said, "The difference between the Athenians with their swords and shields fighting on the fields

[11] See above, Part One, chapter 2, "The Consequences of Secular Grace," where I have discussed the ambiguities of this relationship of agent to victim in terms of important changes of vocabulary and metaphor.

[12] Examples of this type of assailant occur frequently in literature. Faulkner provides several others ("Dry September," "Pantaloon in Black," *Light in August* among them); the classic "Western" demonstration of it is Walter Van Tilburg Clark's *The Ox-Bow Incident* (1940).

of Marathon, and the soldiers who faced each other with tanks, guns, flame-throwers, poison gases, and hand-grenades on the Western Front, is the difference between the ritual of the dance and the routine of the slaughter house." [13] The important distinction is that of a decreasing power of personal evaluation; the assailant begins by having a mechanical advantage over the victim. In the end, the assailant is the machine itself, and whatever of the person remains has itself become mechanical. The ethics of power are indistinguishable from technics. We can discuss the rightness or evil of an act of mechanical destruction only after it has been accomplished. These machines of destruction produce quantities of victims, and their effectiveness increases as the distance grows between them and the victims. Eventually they produce death of several kinds; they destroy not only persons but the scene itself which is the ground of the action. They create waste lands and prepare the way for the final type of assailant-victim relationship, the assailant as landscape.

One might also call this last the assailant as space. It is a special kind and quality of space, combining monotony of surfaces with dehumanization. The metaphor of the landscape as assailant suggests the total withdrawal of human familiarity from both assailant and victim. Literature describing this kind of assailant is necessarily full of spatial images, whose qualities are repetitious and lifeless. They are externalizations of fear, horror, despair. They frequently suggest death or an eternity of dehumanized landscape. Their primary modern image is the concentration camp, though there are many other investments of them. The phrase "assailant as landscape" suggests either a narrow constriction of space or an immense expansion of waste. Its primary psychological characteristic is fear or doubt of "the enemy"; ultimately, the enemy proves to be one's self,

---

[13] *Technics and Civilization*, New York, Harcourt, Brace, 1934, p. 310. Time and again, we see in the literature reflecting upon World War II, situations in which force or power makes the emotional disposition of one person to another (if indeed such a disposition exists) so one-sided as to suggest "no contest" from the beginning.

and the landscape of evil is a spatial projection of indeterminate guilt. The phrase suggests this kind of elaboration: we are all criminals *in intent*, but most of us are not legally so; we are guilty of "homicidal neglect" (that is, we do nothing to deter crime in history, or to arrest developments toward it); we may (and do, in times of war) actively participate in crime, and we lay waste to the human landscape on one or another pretense of saving or glorifying it; ultimately, the landscape is a projection of ourselves (it is the "assailant as landscape").[14]

[14] See below, Part Two, chapter 9, on Kafka's *The Trial*.

4

THE MOMENT OF VIOLENCE:
ERNST JUENGER AND THE LITERARY
PROBLEM OF FACT

—[i]—

THE PRIMARY impact of modern war literature is to make the reader aware of war's unreasonableness, whether with the object of forcing him to accept it as unreasonable or with the aim of setting in motion the means of checking its unreason. More indirectly than not, the war situation also forces the necessity of a style equal in character and intensity to it. To say that something is unreasonable is only in a limited sense to describe it, as a datum unacceptable to current standards of rational appraisal.

The progress of literary style in time can usefully be seen in terms of a scale of tensions between fact and eloquence. Fact calls attention to itself; eloquence, to the meaning of fact. Eloquence is that use of language which exceeds the minima needed to define fact. The purpose of eloquence is to direct the reader's attention away from fact, or to link fact with one or several of the systems of larger meaning which in any period circumscribe fact. Eloquence also acts to slow the rhythm of factual succession. In key passages of classical drama, sequences of minor facts lead to a major fact; this latter requires a pause, for in the very announcement of major fact is suggested the necessity of some kind of meditation. The language of the drama at that point is designed to encourage, perhaps to require, a meditative pause. The more intensely violent fact becomes, the more solicitous is eloquence to mitigate its intensity. The occasion of violence is of itself instantaneous; eloquence devises rhetorical associations of the instant to cause and occasion.

The complex systems of rhetorical ceremony—religious, doctrinal, and aesthetic—are elaborate patterns of mitigation. They say in effect that man is more than any given fact, however intensely a part of his experience that fact may be. A rudimentary "scientific" fact exists within a chain or sequence of facts but owns its value primarily because of its answering to the requirements of factuality. That is, it is not distinctively one in a chain but rather one in itself, for the moment that it is. In an extremely literal sense, a "factual style" is one that excludes as much as is linguistically possible (which is to say, culturally possible) of the mitigating circumstances of eloquence. Eloquence fights against the isolated factuality of fact, and struggles to enable cultural implications to establish themselves, to distract the mind from the factual center, in short to allow the mind the chance to move away from the fact into the area of associative rhetoric.[1]

Eloquence moves toward the area of structure; fact is at the core of texture. Architectonics suggest a complex mesh of interrelations, which are created, controlled, and expanded by the imagination. One basic problem of the literature of violence is to find an adequate means of recording fact independently of structural subterfuges. Violence tends to destroy structures, to isolate experiences, to force them away from containing forms. The style developed along these lines comprehends these essentials, in a descending order of their relevance to a factual center: nouns (as spatial integers); verbs (as signs of physical motion or energy);[2] noun/verb fusions (to suggest the point

[1] See chart on next page.
[2] Forms of the verb *to be* indicate the *location*, either of an object or of a state of mind.

A Chart Illustrating the Relationship
of Fact to Rhetoric

C. Level of religious,
doctrinal, aesthetic
systems of mitigation

B. Forms of eloquence
which slow pace of fact,
require meditation

A. Level of fact_____   XXXXX_____

1. A situation of violence accelerates pace of facts, frustrates attempts to alleviate or mitigate.

2. Tropes require at least a minimal pause for language to move beyond factual level.

3. Arrangement of fact sequences may communicate profound meanings without intrusive eloquence (Kafka).

4. Metaphors may remain close to factual level, but there is a dividing line between the metaphor which *enforces* factuality (Hemingway) and one which attempts to mitigate it (Faulkner).

in time and space at which violence occurs); adjective/adverb fusions (to define and describe the qualities of the moment of violence); finally, figurative language, the precision of which comes from the moment of violence and not from related contexts. T. E. Hulme has offered an image which may help the discussion:

You know what I call architect's curves—flat pieces of wood with all different kinds of curvature. By a suitable selection from these you can draw approximately any curve you like. The artist I take to be the man who simply can't bear the idea of that "approximately." He will get the exact curve of what he sees whether it be an object or an idea in the mind. I shall here have to change my metaphor a little to get the process in the mind. Suppose that instead of your curved pieces of wood you have a springy piece of steel of the same types of curvature as the wood. Now the state of tension or concentration of mind, if he is doing anything really good in this struggle against the ingrained habit of the technique, may be represented by a man employing all his fingers to bend the steel out of its own curve and into the exact curve which you want. Something different to what it would assume naturally.[3]

While this statement relates to a quite different type of literary problem, there are several important suggestions in it: the metaphor is after all visual (it is basically concerned with a visual experience); it pays almost no attention to temporal sequences, but is rather a way of fastening to the quality of an instant; it suggests the closest kind of integrity of relationship of artist to instant; the "tension" of which Hulme speaks is caused by the mind's reaction to the object. In this last case, the power of tension may depend upon two circumstances: the nature of the object itself and the degree of uninhibited and undistracted attention the artist pays to it. In conditions of extreme violence, as we know from psychiatry, the tendency is to turn away from conditions which cause extraordinary pain, in the same sense as a man turns from an intense light to which his eyes cannot adjust. A frequent detail in war literature is that of the living soldier who can easily accommodate himself to the sight of a corpse, since inanimate nature does not *physically* challenge the nerves, but cannot bear the sight of a wounded man, because pain is psychologically infectious.

A related problem is that of the pace of experience. Eloquence functions to moderate the pace, by interjecting matters that are only relatively pertinent to fact. This function is most

[3] *Speculations*, ed. Herbert Read, London, Kegan Paul, 1924, pp. 132–33. The essay from which the above passage is taken was written ca. 1913–1914.

successful in circumstances that are not in themselves shocking, though they may be profoundly disturbing. In an important sense, the effectiveness of the function depends upon
the degree of intensity of the fact.[4] A serious traffic accident,
which suddenly translates a peaceful scene into a landscape
littered with corpses, can permit little if any eloquence. Even
in retrospect its meaning is communicated factually, or in terms
of the most unadorned kind of symbolic reminders: say, a
photograph of the scene itself, in which case the fact is repeated
in replica; or a statistic added to a cumulation, in which case
the fact is abstracted and the task of reinstating its factuality
is left to the reader; or, a skull and crossbones combined with
statistics.

The irony of statistics is that they cannot function except in
terms of unembellished fact: as when Hemingway says that the
cholera "was checked and in the end only seven thousand died
of it in the army" (A *Farewell to Arms*); or when Jarrell speaks
of dead airmen as "losses," or casualties, or "scores."[5] The impact of a statistic of this sort is that it forces a man to return

[4] A significant treatment of this problem is James Agee's A *Death in
the Family* (1956). The death is sudden, and the forms of mitigation
are successively proved inadequate. The family shock comes from a failure
of ceremony; the hero does not die ritually, but violently.

[5] In the poem "Losses," *Little Friend, Little Friend*, pp. 15–16. The
young aviators of Jarrell's poem wake up "One morning, over England,
operational." The transition is abrupt from bombing "games" to the real
thing; yet there is little discernible difference in practice or psychological
bearing.

. . .

> It wasn't different: but if we died
> It was not an accident but a mistake
> (But an easy one for anyone to make).
> We read our mail and counted up our missions—
> In bombers named for girls, we burned
> The cities we had learned about in school—
> Till our lives wore out; our bodies lay among
> The people we had killed and never seen.
> When we lasted long enough they gave us medals;
> When we died they said, "Our casualties were low." (p. 15)

. . .

to the helplessness and horror of which it is a sign. Eloquence, on the other hand, strives to prevent the corporeality of fact from communicating with a too intense directness: as when Antony attempts to persuade his audience that the body of Caesar is not a corpse violently subtracted from the affairs of men but a hero to whom all retrospective honor and tender devotion are due. But Caesar's corpse was after all (in this representation of it at least) but one body, and the circumstances leading to his death allowed for much rhetorical maneuvering of it into mitigating areas of conventional ceremony. One of the most difficult problems of modern literature is to locate the hero. He is either on the periphery of the action (as a man not capable of directing it or altering its course); or, if he is at the center, he is dead before we can get to him with the rites of living.[6] Sudden death is often vulgar and grotesque; eloquence may easily be (and usually is) perverted in this circumstance into macabre humor, of the sort we often expect in surrealist works. Paul Elmer More inadvertently contributed to a statement of the problem when he indignantly reviewed Dos Passos' *Manhattan Transfer* as "an explosion in a cesspool." [7]

[6] A note on the excitement over the centenary of the American Civil War: it is essentially a sentimental desire to comprehend war in "tragic" terms no longer available to literature that treats of twentieth century horror and violence. Like most civil wars, the American permitted much access to rhetorical mitigation, to melodrama and sentimentality; even the most intense fighting and the most confused battle scenes allowed for emotional intimacy in which the assailant and victim were aware of each other. But this war was also a landmark in the nineteenth century history of violence.

[7] In *The Demon of the Absolute*, Vol. 1 of New Shelburne Essays, Princeton University Press, 1928, p. 63. Harry Levin has recently explored the literary implications of the fatal reduction of humanity to things. When facts are more graphically impressive than fiction, reportage is likely to take over. "The merest newspaper holds the advantage of authority over the novel of reportage, which combines watered-down fact with water-logged fiction. A first-hand reminiscence of concentration camps, such as David Rousset's, is bound to be far more impressive than any fictitious approximation" (*The Gates of Horn*, New York, Oxford University Press, 1963, p. 459). One way out of this impasse is to treat commonplace fact with superb artistry, as did Flaubert in *Madame Bovary* and

—[ii]—

It is commonplace enough to talk about "the new style" and to trace its origins in critical dissatisfaction with the old. Much of this kind of discussion is valuable enough; it is ground well and necessarily covered. Very little has been done, however, by way of analyzing not only the style itself but some of the cogencies determining it. Because the First World War provided so many of the explosive circumstances that determined literary change, an effort to adjust the language to the fact of them is of enormous importance to an understanding of modern literature. The most profitable of such studies is that of the style used by Ernst Juenger to record his experiences in the first war. It is precisely because his work is so limited, so conscientiously dedicated to the instant, that it is valuable and useful.

Juenger had two important preoccupations in his lifetime, violent warfare and nature-study. The first gave him the peculiar circumstances representative of modern violence; the second provided a range of discrete metaphor, or a variety of references that might enforce factuality without "eloquently distracting" from it. The field of violence is remarkably foreshortened, bounded, and restricted; within an area so circumscribed, action takes place that is limited almost always to the form of acceleration and declaration of force. The human reactions are similarly reduced; so far as possible ironies and rhetoric attaching to the nonviolent or less violent periphery are ignored. The interest in nature (plant life and animal) is used as a resource of accessory image.[8] These are perhaps not unusual qualities in war literature; the concentration upon them, to the exclusion of almost all other matters, surely is.

Joyce in *Ulysses:* "Like his master, Flaubert, [Joyce] would construct a monument to banality by utilizing the utmost resources of artistry." (p. 456)

[8] For an American analogue, see John Steinbeck and Ed. Ricketts, *The Sea of Cortez* (1941), and its significance for Steinbeck's fiction. A naturalist image permits the observer to consider violence disinterestedly.

The Storm of Steel is not a novel, but is rather made up of excerpts from a diary; it is fitting that it should be so, for to write a novel in this case would require violating the stringent factuality the style demands. War novels are made novelistic by means of a studied though limited eloquence that takes the reader from the fact to the narrative of which the fact remains the cause. Novelistic techniques involve the passions and the distracting intellect.

Juenger attends at first to the landscape of violence, with an obsessively diligent attention to descriptive minima:

> . . . The waste and overgrown fields, with great cloud shadows flitting over them, checkered and crossed the network of trenches with yellow lines. Only here and there the smoke of a shell wavered up, as though propelled by a ghostly hand, and fluttered loose in the air; or the ball of a shrapnel hovered over the desert land like a great flock of wool and slowly dissolved away. The face of the earth was dark and fabulous, for the war had expunged the pleasant features of the countryside and engraved there its own iron lines that in a lonely hour made the spectator shudder.[9]

This passage is relatively unconcentrated, but it is so because the scene is prelude rather than the action itself; it is intermediate between moments of action, the past showing in its effects ("waste," "desert land"), the future in simple descriptions of expectation ("ghostly hand," "shudder"). Something of this quality is seen in a passage near the beginning of Book Three (Caporetto) of *A Farewell to Arms*:

> It stormed all that day. The wind drove down the rain and everywhere there was standing water and mud. The plaster

---

[9] Tr. Basil Creighton, New York, Doubleday, Doran, 1929, p. 33. Other references to this edition are in the text. *Copse 125: A Chronicle from the French Warfare of 1918* (London, Chatto and Windus, 1930) is a continuation of Juenger's report.

of the broken houses was gray and wet. . . . There were many Austrian guns in the woods on that ridge but only a few fired. I watched the sudden round puffs of shrapnel smoke in the sky above a broken farmhouse near where the line was; soft puffs with a yellow white flash in the center. You saw the flash, then heard the crack, then saw the smoke ball distort and thin in the wind.[10]

The opening paragraph of Stephen Crane's *The Red Badge of Courage* (1895) shows an intermediate stage in the factual record of war scenes; the perspective is different and suggests a separation from its subject not noticeable either in Hemingway or Juenger. The fact that the American Civil War is the scene also permits impressionistic effects; while this war is a step on the way to the modern "war of attrition," tragic action involving personal commitments is still possible.

The cold passed reluctantly from the earth, and the retiring fogs revealed an army stretched out on the hills, resting. As the landscape changed from brown to green, the army awakened, and began to tremble with eagerness at the noise of rumors. It cast its eyes upon the roads, which were growing from long troughs of liquid mud to proper thoroughfares. A river, amber-tinted in the shadow of its banks, purled at the army's feet; and at night, when the stream had become of a sorrowful blackness, one could see across it the red, eyelike gleam of hostile camp-fires set in the low brows of distant hills.[11]

The conspicuous feature of these passages is the degree of attention paid the functional relationship of fact and descriptive embellishment. The purpose is of course the same: to establish a scene from which one can infer precisely action past and to come. Juenger's vision slowly shifts from skyline and

[10] New York, Scribner's, 1929, pp. 196–97.
[11] (1895) In *The Work of Stephen Crane*, ed. Wilson Follett, New York, Knopf, 1925, Vol. I, p. 21.

landscape to details of devastation: "Torn packs, broken rifles, pieces of equipment, and among them, in grim contrast, a child's plaything; . . ." (34) Consider briefly the idea of a "grim contrast"; it is based above all on a factual inventory of desolation, and whatever appeal it may momentarily have to sentiment is rudely (that is to say, factually) brushed aside. At the other extreme in literature is the use of the child to enforce an opposition to the scene itself, as in this poem of Muriel Rukeyser:

> M-Day's child is fair of face,
> Drill-day's child is full of grace,
> Gun-day's child is breastless and blind,
> Shell-day's child is out of its mind,
> Bomb-day's child will always be dumb,
> Cannon-day's child can never quite come,
> but the child that's born on the Battle-day
> is blithe and bonny and rotted away.[12]

There is of course a wide range of values to be considered. Surely the words "grim contrast" are not especially effective; but the risk of distraction is relatively limited. Miss Rukeyser appeals to a vast area of linked emotions, social, religious, political, and otherwise; she is ironically perverting Christ's invitation, to make it read "Suffer the little children to suffer and die."

Three ranges of style are suggested here: pure factuality, sentimentality, and rhetoric forced upon a passage because of ideological pressures. Miss Rukeyser's poem is obviously influenced by the second and the third. An important aspect of modern style is the use of eloquence by association, as in this passage from Hemingway's *For Whom the Bell Tolls* (1941). Robert Jordan is considering his dedication to a hero's task,

---

[12] "M-Day's Child Is Fair of Face," *A Turning Wind*, New York, Viking, 1939, p. 84.

his selfless loyalty to a cause he finds it difficult to explain adequately:

> At either of those places [Gaylord's, or the headquarters of the Fifth Regiment, Madrid] you felt that you were taking part in a crusade. That was the only word for it although it was a word that had been so worn and abused that it no longer gave its true meaning. You felt, in spite of all bureaucracy and inefficiency and party strife something that was like the feeling you expected to have and did not have when you made your first communion. It was a feeling of consecration to a duty toward all of the oppressed of the world which would be as difficult and embarrassing to speak about as religious experience and yet it was authentic as the feeling you had when you heard Bach, or stood in Chartres Cathedral or the Cathedral at León and saw the light coming through the great windows; or when you saw Mantegna and Greco and Brueghel in the Prado . . .[13]

Juenger's deadly inventory continues: "shell fuses, deep shell holes, water bottles, torn books, broken utensils, holes whose mysterious darkness suggests a cellar in which, perhaps, the bones of the unfortunate tenant have been gnawed clean by the never idle swarms of rats . . ." (34). This is a relatively simple assortment. Juenger restrains his desire to invest the details with any but the most elementary power. In a later passage the landscape of violence is more crucially given, because it is a scene of greater and more immediate disaster:

> The sunken road now appeared as nothing but a series of enormous shell-holes filled with pieces of uniform, weapons, and dead bodies. The ground all round, as far as the eye could see, was plowed by shells. You could search in vain for one wretched blade of grass. This churned-up battlefield was ghastly. Among the living lay the dead. As we

[13] New York, Scribner's, 1940, p. 235.

dug ourselves in we found them in layers stacked one upon the top of another. One company after another had been shoved into the drum fire and steadily annihilated. The corpses were covered with the masses of soil turned up by the shells, and the next company advanced in the place of the fallen. (90)

Juenger is again interested primarily in a descriptive catalogue. There is almost no supporting adjective or adverb that might have helped to provide a description in depth. He is in a sense assuming the role of guide, and communicates not so much the terror as its results in a disorder of things. The basic device is the stress on familiar objects in unfamiliar disorder. The key to much of the effect in war literature is this relationship of the familiar to sudden disruptions. A significant line of Hemingway's disposition can be found in the minor details he offers when he describes refugee carts, in the "Introduction" of *In Our Time*, in *A Farewell to Arms*, and in his long reportage of the Spanish Civil War in London's *Fact* magazine (July 1938). The same management of detail is found in Malraux's *Man's Hope* and Silone's *Fontamara*. In all of these cases the pressure of fact in a literature of violence depends not only upon its pointing up the unfamiliar but eventually upon its convincing one that it is to be expected. The roles of the familiar and the unfamiliar are in this way reversed. This is of the greatest importance in our understanding of postwar dislocations. The fact is that the dislocation begins in the details found (in their purest form) in Juenger's landscapes. The soldier is shocked to the point of his becoming used to shock, and subsequently what he had earlier been used to shocks him when he moves away from violence.

In a very real sense, this inversion of values comes from the efficiency of the machine as assailant. Other wars had left their desolation, but the First World War was conspicuous in its spreading of desolation with efficient and repetitious regularity.

So that we have such a comment as this from Juenger: "Thus all the frightfulness that the mind of man could devise was brought into the field; and there, where lately had been the idyllic picture of rural peace, there was as faithful a picture of the soul of scientific war." He is concerned also to point out that the energy of desolation is also noticeable in the soldier's face: "And it seemed that man, on this landscape he had himself created, became different, more mysterious and hardy and callous than in any previous battle" (99).

Most novelists present this effect quite radically differently. The excess of violence softens rather than hardens, causes what Andreas Latzko calls "a paradoxical softness born of a surfeit of brutality. . . ." [14] The clue to the preservation of heroism in a literature of violence is this "paradoxical softness." It is especially conspicuous in the American novels of World War II: violence in these cases purges the soldier of accidental hardnesses, and the passions are carefully allocated to both present and future needs. But Juenger's purpose is accurately to portray a mutual influence of machine and victim. In that limited sense (perhaps it is a nonliterary sense), the observation is astute and true. To survive the experience, one must become more and more like the experience. In these circumstances the soldier either goes shriekingly off from the center of action and, sobbing, renounces it; or he acquires a second self, suspending the first for the duration of need.

> The soldier who after such a sight goes back under fire with ardor unquenched has indeed withstood a test of nerve; for every fresh and terrible impression claws itself into the brain and is added to the prostrating complex of imaginings that make the moment between the rush and the burst of a shell ever more frightful. (106)

Such an adjustment is at once a testimony of endurance and a commentary upon the fact of man's somehow mediating the

[14] *Men in War*, New York, Boni and Liveright, 1918, p. 24.

most violent of psychological extremes. In another but quite validly related sense, Hemingway's heroes accustom themselves to the shock. They are first of all impelled to flee the violence —not so much its force as its unreasonableness. But the extreme of escape is suicide, and fortitude returns to the Hemingway hero, in *For Whom the Bell Tolls,* in a studied determination to resist the temptation of suicide. None of Hemingway's heroes is ever entirely reshaped by the ordeal of violence. The Hemingway warrior abides tensions, and seeks to re-dramatize scenes of violence; he is not himself a creature of violence, but is rather a victim adjusting to its consequent stresses.

Juenger offers many illustrations of the moment of violent experience. It is here that his notations are of the greatest value. On the one hand he is concerned with the scatology of war, an important part of the atmosphere of violence in literature. The worst indignity is that a man should look grotesque at the time of his death, a moment when dignity is indispensable, whether to his vision of immortality or to what he wishes the memory of him to be in the minds of survivors. Whatever frustrates this wish is extremely grotesque and cruel. The bitterest denunciations of war in literature are accompanied by catalogues of the details of anonymity; and the unknown soldier is a culmination of indecencies.[15] Juenger's matter-of-fact descriptions of fragmented bodies force the attention upon this worst of all effects of modern violence. This example is pertinent:

> . . . Jumping out of the trench in the early morning mist, I found myself in front of a huddled-up corpse, a Frenchman. The putrid flesh, like the flesh of fishes, gleamed greenish white through the rents in the uniform. I turned away and then started back in horror: close to me a figure cowered beside a tree. It wore the shining straps and belt of the French, and high upon its back there was still the loaded pack, crowned with a round cooking utensil. (20)

[15] See John Dos Passos, "The Body of an American," the final passage of *1919*, New York, Harcourt, Brace, 1932.

The moment of death itself does not horrify so much as the agonizing time of an insufferable wound before death, or the spectacle (so often evident in modern warfare) of bodies left unburied, so that the processes of decay which should be private (as should all awkward and grotesque bodily functions) have obscenely been left to public gaze and smell. The landscape of sudden ruin offers a distortion of images. Looking at the scene (of which he is both observer and object), Juenger remarks what a "breathless sight it was to see how small parties and dispatch carriers chased over the shelled area, often throwing themselves flat, while the ground was flung up on every side of them" (121). In every case there is the spectacle of men dying suddenly, or in haste, or slowly but without recourse either to medical help or to accesses of dignity: "The sallowness of death was already on his face. He did not seem to like our looking at him. With a listless movement he drew his cloak over his head and lay still" (19). In every case the dead are seen in macabre and obscene visions:

> One had the head struck off, and the neck on the trunk was like a great sponge of blood. From the arm stumps of another the broken bones projected, and the uniform was saturated by a large wound in the chest. The entrails of the third poured out from a wound in the belly. (123)

Not only the frequency and the indecency of the dead, but the atmosphere of haze, mist, smoke, and fire communicates the impression of a terrestrial hell. The fire and smoke make vision difficult; groups of soldiers appear and disappear in the mist. "We were everywhere pressing on the heels of death. It was almost as though not one living soul were to be found in this desolation" (192). From such an experience comes the character of the modern man of violence. Shock is followed by paralysis of the will, which in turn is superseded by an entirely new disposition toward violence. "Everyone was mad and beyond reckoning; we had gone over the edge of the world into superhuman perspectives." The will to preserve oneself is perverted into the will to destroy: "The tremendous force of destruction that bent over the field of battle was concentrated in our brains" (229). In the end, one becomes indifferent to death and views the processes of destruction with curiosity and indifference: "You are a world in yourself, and the dark and horrible atmosphere that broods over the waste land has sucked you in utterly to itself." (64) [16]

The man who survives such a sequence of horrors as this is obviously not so much hero as antihero. A most important change has taken place: man begins by struggling against the assailant; he is shocked both by the force and by the willful trickery of the assailant; he adjusts, however he may, to its devices; and he ends by assuming many of its peculiarities. He is thus a hero who has turned upon himself, the victim twisted to the shape of the assailant. The vision of character which Juenger leaves us is that of a "functional" hero, a man sufficient to the violent needs of the occasion. While such a conclusion is most unpleasant, it is an honest statement of what occurs, within the limitations of its area and range of discourse.

Juenger scarcely offers a very useful sourcebook for the literature of violence. What he does is in many respects anti-literary. But in accepting the fact of unacceptable, even loathsome experiences, he sets the minimal limits according to which modern violence must be accounted for. He says in effect that emotive and connotative excursions in modern literature must begin at this irreducible point of modern fact. Systems of explanation must take it into account. The vision of corpses in disarray, unburied and uncalled for, humankind reduced to matter, the privacies put publicly on display: these need to be included among the hazards of the modern sensibility. Violence

---

[16] The distribution of pronouns in war literature is also of great interest. The "I" of Hemingway in the 1920's becomes the "you" of Robert Jordan's inner debates. Elsewhere the lower-case decapitates the "I"; or it is reduced to a literal "eye," a helpless observer (as in Dos Passos' trilogy, USA, 1923–1936).

calls attention to itself in the sense that it defines fact in terms of exploded fragments of reality. The human sensibility is not necessarily exploded beyond recognition as a consequence. But as Juenger's soldiers end in a very close, a necessarily close, rapprochement with the assailant that would have destroyed them, the modern hero performs in an altered role. He remains a self-conscious hero; he observes himself as in a distorted mirror of the world's making, and from what he sees there makes his decisions as to how he will act.

Juenger has above all pointed up the enormous difficulty of sustaining a moderate rhythm of life expectation. Not only is the career of the victim uncertain, in times of peace as well as of war; the behavior of the assailant becomes more and more unpredictable, as his power increases. It becomes a hazard to attempt a style most suitable to the truth. The most one may be expected to do is to risk in style a definition of the object as it exists in relation to a present scale of event and motion. War literature does exactly that. It strives for a practicality of fact, but there is no certainty otherwise as to the meaning of fact beyond its discrete context. Juenger offers no solution to the problem of structure; his account is crudely held together by indifferent movement from one scene of crisis to another. The movement itself is of no help in answering the question of the value of the moments of crisis. A common enough reaction is to say that these moments are unbeautiful and that they have sources in the ugly history of man. The question remains unanswered. In fact, it becomes more and more difficult to answer it without risking a formula whose very inadequacy to the occasion makes it sentimental, no matter how strong the integrity of its incentive.

—[iii]—

Reviewing John Hersey's *Hiroshima* (1946), in itself a document of some relevance, Dwight Macdonald raises several questions of interest:

The "little people" of Hiroshima whose sufferings Hersey records in antiseptic *New Yorker* prose might just as well be white mice, for all the pity, horror or indignation the reader—or at least this reader—is made to feel for them. And yet Hersey's intention, which apparently was successfully communicated to many thousands of other readers, was to convey precisely such emotions. It is puzzling. Perhaps my feeling is simply that naturalism is no longer adequate, either esthetically or morally, to cope with the modern horrors.[17]

The truth is that pity and horror and indignation do not suffice precisely because they are human reactions to an inhuman situation. Setting aside the question of responsibility in this case —whether it be Truman's or Churchill's or Hirohito's or Fermi's —the event goes beyond the saturation point of human pity, horror, and indignation. This is why modern violence poses a problem that traditional standards of criticism cannot cope with. Modern violence presents a situation that is serious, fragmentary in itself, and of an incredibly devastating magnitude; so that language is inadequate to the double task of remaining clearly faithful to its circumstance and at the same time arousing pity and fear in such a way as to effect a purging of these emotions. The participants in this situation protect themselves by absorbing enough of the energy of the assailant to avoid being destroyed by it.

Any discussion of war literature must account for its several characteristics, leading from the need to adjust to what from any reasonable point of view is an intolerable situation. There is first of all a discussion of style; and the norms of competence in this matter have long since been established. But this matter of style is after all equivalent to only a small part of the whole. One reason for Macdonald's objection to Hersey's book is that the event itself is so enormous that neither Hersey nor Macdonald can do it justice.

[17] *Memoirs of a Revolutionist*, New York, Farrar, Straus, Cudahy, 1957, p. 180.

Beyond the matter of style, there is the "frame of the event" —that is, the move to and from it into the lives of the characters. As we know, the fiction of both wars varies from the most stringent economy to the most elaborate exploitations of naturalistic devices. Some measure of pity, horror, and indignation might be extracted from this maneuvering in time and space; but one is more than likely to examine, not the relation of the frame to the event, but the frame and the event separately; and in any case, whatever the frame, the event remains definitely, shockingly, and irrevocably there. Only if a corpse has resulted from a series of actions visibly and emotionally known as leading logically to it is it possible to produce adequate reactions to the process. But corpses are rarely made according to such an orderly process; a prevailing image of violent death is surprise and resentment over the victimization. The bodies of Hiroshima *were* in this sense "white mice." Since they were not understood as persons before they became corpses, they cannot challenge an immediacy of sympathetic reaction such as Macdonald wished to find.[18]

The final judgment of war literature must have to do with "interpretation." The range here is from books with no interpretation at all (beyond whatever the facts themselves offer) to the most elaborate of ideological melodramas. Again, there is no necessary connection between the event and the interpretation. The interpretation is strictly a pattern of meaning which is affected by the event, but does not in itself alter the event. The deaths of Noah Ackerman and Christian Diestl of Irwin Shaw's *The Young Lions* (1948) are possible, but they are not

[18] Of course, they have been examined as persons *since* the event: which means that they have become persons restrospectively and penitentially. The conscience of an assailant in a situation like this begins to function only after he has been able to look back upon what he has done. A curious psychological penalty is paid by an assailant in this case: he asks himself, not what shall I do, but what have I done? There is a strange embarrassment over these inquests, a great difficulty in determining moral reasons for something that has been done several or many years ago. It is a very different kind of reminiscence from that which was taken down in the years following the American Civil War.

probable, and in any case their literary integrity would require a high degree of probability indeed. Similarly, both John Andrews of *Three Soldiers* and Lieutenant Henry of A *Farewell to Arms* enjoy privileged reactions to the violence at the core of their novels. They do not alter the event, but merely take a stand with respect to their personal involvement in it. Surely there is much to be said for the criticism of the specifics of their wars; and in a sense their acts of desertion are as close to being a part of the pattern of violence as any can be.

There are two other conceivable perspectives upon the violence. One is the framework of acceptance involved in Billy Budd's attitude toward his death. The motives for killing him are mixed, and in a limited sense his own inadequacy is a part of the chain of responsibility leading to his death. The reaction of Melville's Billy Budd is repeated in corrupted form again and again in modern war literature. Ordinarily the Captain is not admirable, nor is his cause discernibly just (that is, the modern soldier does not die *for* Captain Vere, but only because of him). The death of Melville's hero left a glow of self-sufficiency, an aura of acceptance, as legacy to the crew. Some war novelists have tried to recapture that glow: noticeably, Colin McDougall of *Execution* (1958) and, in a very different way, Willi Heinrich of *Cross of Iron* (1956). The position is nevertheless very shaky. The evidence given by Juenger's reports of World War I experience suggests that. The victim enjoys no intricate relations of trust, loyalty, or love to either the assailant or any of his several agents on a field of battle. Billy Budd's descendants merely offer an additional interpretation of the violence, which differs from the others in perhaps being rather less improbable than most.

Finally, there is the analytic self, who questions his motives for everything he does. Not only does he question them, but he addresses his analysis to himself as victim in a complex web of circumstance involving every shade and nuance of adversity. This hero is much more involved in the villainy that brings him to his death than his stammering involves Billy Budd in his. His very innocence contributes to the likelihood of death. His protests against the unreasonableness, the unfairness, the extraordinary circumstances into which he is being led are all in some very important sense a part of the tissue of culpability. He is right to protest; he is wrong if he thinks protesting will do any good. For, whatever his disposition to the maze of violence to which he has been introduced, he becomes both a creature and a creator of the violence. He wills the death of others, as they will his death. He behaves irrationally at the same time as he protests the irrationality of the scheme of things.

Perhaps the phenomenon of the concentration camp is the end result of the modern experience; through its constant pressure of irrational violence, it succeeds in reducing its victims to the level where they participate in it. It is to this fantastic pattern that Juenger's factuality leads. The fact remains and the fact destroys. As Simone Weil has said, force is "that which makes a thing of anybody who comes under its sway. When exercised to the full, it makes a thing of man in the most literal sense, for it makes him a corpse." [19] No literature of violence can possibly disturb the factuality or change it basically. Literature may only present it and make some effort to see the individual involved in it as a man both pathetically doomed as victim and privately, ambiguously, even conspiratorially involved in it as a form of assailant. Franz Kafka makes us uncomfortably aware that in mysterious ways we urgently will our doom and act in a something more than passive way as victims of it. Joseph K. of *The Trial* and the Corporal of Faulkner's *A Fable* (1954) are at the introvertive and extravertive poles of the modern tragicomedy of violence. In the one, the facts are brilliantly clear, the meaning deliberately and extraordinarily ambiguous. In the other, rhetoric dominates, the style is exhaustive and exhausting, and the facts are obscured by both.

[19] Simone Weil, *op. cit.*, p. 24.

5

THE SCENE OF VIOLENCE:
DOSTOEVSKY AND DREISER

Je suis la plaie et le couteau!
Je suis le soufflet et la joue!
Je suis les membres et la roue,
Et la victime et le bourreau!
—BAUDELAIRE, "L'Héautontimorouménos," stanza 6

—[i]—

DOSTOEVSKY AND DREISER stand in extreme opposition as sources
of the literary comprehension of modern violence. There are,
of course, many issues involved in any critical discussion of
literature along these lines. A major problem requires bringing
the external facts of violence into some integral relationship to
the conditions of the creative intelligence. I should suggest that
two areas of metaphor are necessary in this connection: the
first ought to bring to the history of violence a set of terms that
makes it available to critical discussion; the other should consider the severe threats to the creative consciousness caused by
the acceleration of destructive means in the twentieth century.
I shall want briefly to outline the scope of each of these.

One way of comprehending the first is to think of the history
of violence in terms of a basic relational metaphor, that of the

assailant and the victim.[1] If looked at closely, this ratio offers a complex variety of interactions. One of the issues raised in a comparison of Dostoevsky and Dreiser is that of the loss of willed control by the naturalist hero. At no time should the victim be entirely passive in the relation; he is concerned, even in the most traumatic of sudden encounters, with the question of guilt, of his deserving the blows he has received. In short, the victim's role in the metaphor is the moral one of understanding the phenomena of violence in terms of his own abilities to avoid, return, or react to them. The central crisis in modern violence is the point at which it ceases being accessible to personal moral and emotional economies. When it does so, the effect is either to make the victim meditate upon his wound in metaphysical rather than in personal terms or to cause him to withdraw almost entirely from the center of action.

As I have pointed out, there are at least five major stages in the modern history of this ratio. The first is the commonplace one in which the assailant is visible as a person—in other words, the relationship seen in examples of the *crime passionnel.* Modern variations of this provide a transition from the earlier literature of violence. The relationship is more complex at the level where the assailant is seen in terms of some pattern or other of ideological instrument. A crime committed "for the good of a cause," or for "the security of the state," may retain many of the conspiratorial aspects of the *crime passionnel;* but the question of motive in this case leads steadily away from human passion to the level of the motive as idea or the motive as a system of ideas. Rubashov's death (at the end of Koestler's *Darkness at Noon*) is a testimony of the rich complexity available at this point in the history of the ratio.[2]

A variant of the first two is that of the assailant as mob. A mob is still discernibly "personal" (in a way in which a missile or even a shell is not); yet it is after all personal in only a

---

[1] See above, Part Two, chapter 3.
[2] See above, Part One, chapter 2.

limited sense. Beyond this level, the move toward impersonality is rapid and frightening. The metaphor of assailant as machine comprehends a wide variety of dislocations in the relationship of assailant and victim. The assailant as a personality diminishes; we may almost say that he disappears, or at any rate that he is replaced by an *instrument* or an *agent* of the violence. It is not only that the victim does not understand what or who is responsible; the assailant does not understand either, or understands in only a very limited sense. There is no genuine scale of human emotional or moral terms for comprehending the acts of violence at this level.

I have called the final stage "the assailant as landscape." This metaphor suggests a total withdrawal of the humanly familiar from both the assailant and the victim. Moreover, the assailant and the victim are both a *part of* the landscape. One way of seeing this condition might be imagined if we included in Picasso's Guernica panel fragments of the airplane (and of the pilot) responsible for the chaos and suffering described in it.[3] The important facts of this level are that both assailant and victim suffer dislocation, and that the ratio as imagined at the four other levels has disappeared.

This disastrous circumstance raises a major question in the criticism of modern literature. One way of putting it is to ask if such extremes of violence are not after all beyond the power of literature to comprehend or to represent. Irving Howe's discussion of Orwell's 1984 [4] would seem to imply so desperate a conclusion. A more useful suggestion is to think of the landscape of violence as, in one or another of an almost infinite variety of ways, a projection of the mind of the hero, or victim,

[3] Cf. these concluding lines of Randall Jarrell's poem, "Losses":
> It was not dying—no, not ever dying;
> But the night I died I dreamed that I was dead,
> And the cities said to me: "Why are you dying?
> We are satisfied, if you are; but why did I die?"

[4] In *Politics and the Novel*, New York, Meridian Books, 1957, pp. 235–51.

or protagonist. Surely one of the major contributions of nineteenth century realism and naturalism has been the growing importance of *scene* as a literary focus of what an artist wishes us to accept as a *state of mind*. The value of scene in this case comes primarily from its function in defining and describing the moral and psychological condition of the protagonist.[5] In this sense (and in many others) the poles of Dostoevsky and Dreiser serve admirably as examples of literary comprehension. Both novelists are concerned to show themselves as omniscient, but the omniscience of the one contrasts markedly with the omniscience of the other.

—[ii]—

A full understanding of this metaphor, however, requires some additional comments on the relationship of landscape to protagonist. The arrangement of objects in space suggests man's regard for himself, the rule of law and the power of the spirit, the status of *amour-propre*. Spatial relationships in a landscape are signs of the degree of intelligence, faith, trust, and confidence marking the relationship of peoples inhabiting space. The natural scene has often been at the basis of an illusion that nature and man can live closely and in harmony if he is not inhibited by artificial social pressures. Much of John Steinbeck's fiction develops his analysis of man in terms of his inhabiting space and identifying himself normatively and symbolically with it. The land challenges man, and man's aberrant treatment of it results in making it uninhabitable. Throughout this fiction, the abstract lines of human development clash with the image of a plot of ground—indispensable to the needs for sustaining man. There is a formula, represented in a variety of ways, of

[5] The images of punishment relate to "states of mind" in a way that is the reverse of conditions of "the good" as seen by Henry James and G. E. Moore. See above, Part One, chapter 1, and below, Part Three, chapter 10.

this analogy of man with the power and spirit of the land. Loss of contact with the land is most often represented in images of drouth: the land is barren, the dead tree gives no shelter, and spirits of the living dead describe abstract lines of motion (the circle, the straight line, the repetitious movement of a hand, etc.) to indicate their loss of significant relationship.

Violation of the minimal needs to sustain a peaceful landscape is imaged in several ways. In Eliot's *Waste Land* the prevailing landscape is the desert, which suggests fear and loss as consequences of the disappearance of a vitally confident and a passionately felt trust. A visual projection of *The Waste Land* will define this loss admirably well. The desert is in the city, the city in the desert. In the city itself the decor suggests again and again the disappearance not only of significant action but of meaningful spatial relationships. Persons do not recognize each other, since they are not aware of the commitment necessary to spiritual relationship. This failure of recognition involves the use of the mask in modern literature, whether to conceal or to display madness.[6]

Eliot employs spatial extensions and spatial constrictions with equal facility. The major desert imagery with which the landscape begins and ends establishes the terms according to which the poem is to be seen. In the structure of the poem there are also many images of limited space, in which the arrangement of objects directly signifies the state of the spirit. Generally, a state of spiritual disorder is suggested by the pressure of objects upon a narrow and constricted space. An extraordinarily limited space may indicate the pressure of the unknown and the feared world beyond man's power to understand; or it may reveal a spiritual vulgarity. In either case there is a decline of values, of the means that men have to communicate with one another, with respect to their claims to dignity. Similarly, the quality

[6] The talk of impersonality in both poetry and criticism (see Eliot's *The Sacred Wood*, 1920) and the distrust of romanticism are undoubtedly related to the loss of respect for rhetorical celebrations of the self consequent upon the increase of violence.

of objects combines with their disposition in space to define a
condition. The opening lines of Part Three are an example:

The river bears no empty bottles, sandwich papers,
Silk handkerchiefs, cardboard boxes, cigarette ends
Or other testimony of summer nights. The nymphs are departed.
(*Complete Poems and Plays*, 42)

In the seduction scene of the typist and the "young man
carbuncular," the irony of reductive objects combines with the
restricted space of an "efficiency apartment" to define the
terms of the scene and the conditions of the act. The entire
atmosphere of the affair is one of negation—as indeed is that
of all the sex relationships of the poem. Negation in terms of
objects indifferently disposed leads ultimately to the capital
negation of the desert scene, at the beginning of Part 5, in
which once again negatives dominate the quality of the syntax.
The negation is both aesthetic and moral.

The important fact concerning these aspects of *The Waste
Land* is what they have to say about the effect of landscape
upon persons, or the function of objects distributed in a landscape to reveal the spiritual condition of persons. The several
features of the scene strongly connote hostility, a primary
characteristic of the landscape as assailant. A person survives in
this climate (in the sense that a soldier on a battlefield does
not), but he is not well. Baudelaire's *Tableaux Parisiens* closely
resemble Eliot's images of constricted and hostile space. "Le
Cygne" quite literally stresses the oppressive effect of space
upon the spiritual aspirations of those forced to occupy it:

. . .

Je pense à la négresse, amaigrie et phthisique,
Piétinant dans la boue, et cherchant, l'oeil hagard,

Les cocotiers absents de la superbe Afrique
Derrière la muraille immense du brouillard.[7]

. . .

In many respects Baudelaire's vision of the city is of human
life reduced to the status of a terrestrial hell; specific images
from an urban landscape are brought into an infernal context.
"Les Sept Vieillards" offers the city of Paris as a secular imaging
of hell. It is in many respects one of the most profound early
contributions to the literature describing the assailant as landscape:

Fourmillante cité, cité pleine de rêves,
Où le spectre en plein jour raccroche le passant!
Les mystères partout coulent comme des sèves
Dans les canaux étroits du colosse puissant.

Un matin, cependant que dans la triste rue
Les maisons, dont la brume allongeait la hauteur,
Simulaient les deux quais d'une rivière accrue,
Et que, décor, semblable à l'âme de l'acteur,

Un brouillard sale et jaune inondait tout l'espace,
Je suivais, roidissant mes nerfs comme un héros
Et discutant avec mon âme déjà lasse,
Le faubourg secoué par les lourds tombereaux.[8]

. . .

Not only the atmosphere itself, but the features of its inhabitants ("du même enfer venus") signify the hostility of the

[7]   I think of the negress, thin and phthisical,
          tramping through filth, seeking with haggard eyes
          behind the heavy fog's unending wall
          the absent palms of Africa's proud skies;

                    . . .

Tr. C. F. MacIntyre, in *Les Fleurs du mal*, Berkeley, University Press,
1947, p. 188.
[8]   Ant-heap city, city filled with dreams,
          where specters in broad day grab him who passes!

landscape, its devastating effect upon the human condition. Important to this scene also is the suggestion throughout that the desolation does not exist merely objectively but is in large part a projection of the human soul. The ego of the poem actually projects the scene it inhabits. Quite aside from the sadness to which the decor contributes, there is the over-whelming impression of a congestion of space ("Fourmillante cité . . ."), of persons who merely repeat themselves in ex-ternal mass and who crowd the space, so that one has the impression of walking down a narrow corridor, past an infinite repetition of identical caricatures of the self.

> Son pareil le suivait: barbe, oeil, dos, bâton, loques,
> Nul trait ne distinguait, du même enfer venu,
> Ce jumeau centenaire, et ces spectres baroques
> Marchaient du même pas vers un but inconnu.[9]

Several images here belong to the modern vision of the land-scape as assailant: the succession of grotesque figures, the im-pression of hell (which the dirty, yellow fog that floods the space enforces), the absence of specific purpose or aim ("vers un but inconnu"), above all the collapse of healthy spatial relationships among the persons inhabiting a "fourmillante cité."

> Everywhere like sap the mysteries stream
> through the narrow arteries of the vast colossus.
>
> It happened one morning in a sorry quarter
> where the fog had made the houses tall,
> resembling the two quays by a shrunken river—
> thus the setting matched the actor's soul,—
>
> space was flooded by the yellow dreary
> mist, as I walked on, tightening my nerves,
> like a hero arguing with my weary
> soul, and the heavy carts shook the suburbs.
> (MacIntyre tr., *ibid.*, 191)

[9] His likeness followed: beard, eyes, back, rags, stick, they differed in nothing, come from the same hell; these centenarian twins, specters baroque, walked with a like step toward an unknown goal.
(MacIntyre tr., *ibid.*, 192)

There are two primary extremes of space imagery; Eliot's use of them in *The Waste Land* is superbly appropriate. One is the image of a narrow, constricted space, in which there are too many objects for clear definition of their value. The other is the impression of vast spaces indifferently inhabited, from which life has all but disappeared and in which an "enemy" or an evil is suggested merely by the range and scope of desolation apprehended.[10] The hostility suggested in either landscape is a feeling shared both by the landscape itself and by the victim of its frightening aspect. In each case the pressure upon the victim comes from an atmosphere he has—quite probably unwittingly—helped to create. The most specifically successful of these literary efforts to determine the landscape of violence have been a part of the urban landscape. The city seems to modern writers most directly and most sharply to reveal the moral impact of hostility, crime, and violence.

—[iii]—

At the end of Dostoevsky's *Crime and Punishment*, Raskolnikov, in the first of his eight years of imprisonment, falls victim to a truly horrifying nightmare:

> He dreamt that the whole world was ravaged by an unknown and terrible plague that had spread across Europe from the depths of Asia. All except a few chosen ones were doomed to perish. New kinds of germs—microscopic crea-

[10] In many of Auden's early poems, and especially in the play, *The Ascent of F6* (1936; done with Christopher Isherwood) this psychological extension of landscape as "enemy" is used. There is a startling change from the great confidence in spaces expressed, for example, in Willa Cather's fiction (see especially, *The Professor's House*, 1925; *Death Comes for the Archbishop*, 1927) and these latter-day uses of them. An interesting study may someday be made of the symbolic mountain in modern literature, beginning with Leslie Stephen's acts of "dutiful heroics" in climbing Alps, moving to the kind of rhetoric typical of Ibsen (*When We Dead Awaken*, 1899), and ending in the imagery of nameless fear and doubtful heroism in Auden's poetry and plays.

tures which lodged in the bodies of men—made their appearance. But these creatures were spirits endowed with reason and will. People who became infected with them at once became mad and violent. But never had people considered themselves as wise and as strong in their pursuit of truth as these plague-ridden people. Never had they thought their decisions, their scientific conclusions, and their moral convictions so unshakable or so incontestably right.

This is surely more Dostoevsky's dream than Raskolnikov's. Yet it contains in a very real sense the meaning of *Crime and Punishment*. Most effective in the report of the dream is the vision of persons fanatically destroying the landscape and distorting relationships possible within it. Lines of understood relationship are twisted and distorted; people turn against each other, insanely move from place to place with no clear line or purpose: "Here and there people gathered in crowds, adopted some decision and vowed not to part, but they immediately started doing something else, something quite different from what they had decided. And they began to accuse each other, fought and killed each other." [11]

Dostoevsky's novel meditates throughout upon the possibilities of this disorder, and not the least on Raskolnikov's crime itself. The motive of the crime is most complex, and more than half the time disease or insanity is suggested as an acceptable explanation. The important problem Dostoevsky sets forth concerns the set of mind, the studied and intense vision of the narrow self, which causes violence. Like Ivan Karamazov, Raskolnikov is the victim of a "theory," which is imperfectly understood and is not at all fortunate in its consequences. Misfortune and evil are not exclusively the result of distorted power in the service of an unrestrained ego. Evil exists in every man, and sometimes—as in the case of the Marmeladov family—it

[11] Tr. David Magarshack, Harmondsworth, England, Penguin Books, 1951, p. 555. Other references to this edition are in the text.

has no clearly discernible source, except in the overwhelmingly general disposition of the race to suffer.

The major vision is of the crime itself. Raskolnikov had brooded many days over the question of his criminal privilege. To assume it, he has not only to affirm moral superiority and immunity as an especially endowed person; he has brutally to deny that all of God's creatures have at least a minimum right to exist, however barren and pitiful their claims to deserving it may be. Raskolnikov refers to his victim as a "louse," and thus quite arrogantly denies her the privilege of personality. This is the first of the confusions wrought by evil, of which Raskolnikov's concluding nightmare is a large-scale elaboration. He wills disparity so that he may act on privilege. The crime is extraordinarily brutal. Raskolnikov uses a hatchet as the instrument of force; both contempt and fear move him to bring it down upon his victim:

> . . . Being a small woman, the blow fell straight across the crown of her head. She uttered a cry, though a very faint one, and suddenly dropped to the floor . . . It was then that he struck her again with all his strength, and then again, every time with the back of the hatchet and across the crown of the head. Blood gushed out as from an overturned tumbler, and she fell straight on her back . . . (96)

The extra blows are an expression not only of his strength but of both fear and contempt, of the act and its victim.[12] Still another crime, an unexpected one, follows. The simple and

[12] In a dream, Raskolnikov re-enacts the crime, but this time the victim refuses to die; instead she "was convulsed with noiseless laughter, doing all she could, it seemed, to prevent him from hearing her" (294). The question of the "gratuitous extra blow(s)" or shot(s), as extensions or repetitions of the *crime passionnel*, has an interesting association with both man's guilt and his energy. It is the beginning of impersonal violence, yet it is also an expression of superfluous passion. Indeed, the morality of violence might be calculated in terms of the excess volume or force expended beyond the requirements of passion or military necessity.

quite innocently good Lisaveta arrives unexpectedly upon the scene, and Raskolnikov must destroy her as well.

> And so simple, crushed, and cowed was this unhappy Lisaveta that she did not even lift her hands to protect her face, though that was the most natural and inevitable gesture at that moment, for the hatchet was now raised straight over her face . . . The blow fell straight across her skull. She was hit with the blade of the hatchet, which split the top of her forehead open, penetrating almost to the crown of her head. (99)

The carnage thus completed reveals a scene vulgar and filthy with the effects of violence complexly motivated. Raskolnikov has thought carefully through to his right to the first murder, but the second disgusts him with its surprise, the victim's entire failure to deserve it, and the attitude of passive fear displayed by her in the act. For a few minutes the novel pauses to contemplate a scene of violence. The young man, confirmed in his assumption of the privileges of self, employs force to prove his superior right, and is himself drawn into the web of criminal force so that he must do more than he had wished.

From this time on, Raskolnikov must consider the nature and meaning of his crime. He is of course frightened at the prospect of being discovered, but the long days and nights that conclude in his confession are concerned not so much with the legality as with the morality of his position. As a man self-avowedly devoted to the privileges of a rational superiority, he has committed a crime that from any point of view must be considered an aesthetic failure. He cannot really maintain his self-respect after the fiasco of the murders. Surely the motive must have been other than he had thought. Perhaps the real crime lay in the brutality of all men; if so, he cannot claim that it demonstrates his immunity of will.

An earlier dream, which had at that time reminded him once more of his plans to kill the old pawnbroker, stresses this fact of shared brutality of will: he had dreamed of a peasant's beating an old horse to death, from no other motive than pleasure in the brutality; when the horse is all but dead, others take up the game:

> A few young men, also red-faced and drunk, seized whatever they could lay their hands on—whips, sticks, the shaft—and ran to the dying mare. Mikolka stood on one side and started raining blows across her back with the iron bar without bothering to see where the blows were falling. The mare stretched out her head, heaved a deep sigh, and died. (77)

The little boy of the dream tries desperately to find the reason for the brutality; but it is nothing, says his father: the man was drunk, and besides it is none of our business. "He put his arms round his father, but his chest tightened and he felt choked. He tried to draw a breath, to cry out and—woke up" (78).

This dream and that at the novel's end combine with the scene of the crime itself to describe the limits of the violence the novel comprehends. It is important to see that *Crime and Punishment* is a meditation upon violence, with the terms according to which it may be morally as well as legalistically contained. The landscape of violence is very much in evidence, and there are many hints of unmotivated and incomprehensible evil. But each time the novel begins to resemble even in minor details the forms of meditation seen in Kafka's novels, it is pulled back to a frame of sharply outlined moral certitudes. We are, in other words, still within a world governed by a solicitous omniscience. *Crime and Punishment* explores Raskolnikov's disturbances of mind and spirit with a clear sense of what motives are dangerously inadequate and what the circumstances of criminality are that threaten to destroy the effectiveness of spiritual restraints.

Nevertheless, *Crime and Punishment* offers many insights

into the manner in which a landscape images violence. There is no question that the landscape of Petrograd is an "assailant," in the sense that it scenically and atmospherically invites suspicion of its force. Raskolnikov's journeys through its streets are scenically a projection of his mind and heart. Wild suspicion alternates with sentimental affection. At times, he comes briefly in contact with persons who avoid him as though they see in him the very spirit of evil. He stares, and is stared at. Persons vacillate between cold contempt of him and a Dickensian exaggeration of unmotivated sentiment. At one point, a woman, staring blankly beyond him, plunges into the Neva in a suicide attempt.

Rooms are also images of the uncertainty and the implicit violence of the total scene. His own is small, filthy, deathly, shaped rather like a coffin. At the police station, he walks down a narrow corridor as in a passageway to a prison or to his tomb. In a very profound sense, the city is an extension of his crime. The disposition of objects within it signifies the disorder of his mind as he fights through to a recognition of his deed. Dislocation threatens insistently. Gestures of kindness lead comically and even ludicrously to disorders. Raskolnikov's loyal companion is herself a "criminal," obliged to sell her body to support her mother and family. These are all signs of the great complication of evil with the landscape of Raskolnikov's violence.

In the end, however, the confusion and incipient horror of the situation are redeemed; the primary agent of redemption is Porfiry, the police superintendent. His insights into Raskolnikov are not only admirable sleuthing; they probe deeply the mind and soul of the criminal. Porfiry leads him on, invites him to confess, finally communicates his belief in Raskolnikov's guilt, then awaits his free decision to confirm it. He talks at great length of disease, exhaustion, fatigue, malnutrition, and of the poverty that he suspects is a conditioning factor. These are mitigating circumstances in Raskolnikov's case, and they among others lead to a reduced sentence. Projected into the scene itself, however, into the city and its people, they are both comically and grotesquely a feature of Dostoevsky's Petrograd as a landscape of implicit violence.

The true crime is of course one of pride. To exercise pride is to register contempt for those who are thought to be inferior. Raskolnikov reasons his crime in the most thorough and complex of ratiocinations. In this sense, he is not just victim of the scene but a sponsor of his own victimization. He wills both his act of violence and his submission to punishment. *Crime and Punishment* is therefore a considered examination of the will in its relationship as shaping force of the agent of its punishment. Its hero is not a passive victim but an active agent of the circumstances leading to his downfall. The complex landscape of the novel is the product of the hero's mind. Not only does he suffer it; he causes it—and himself—to suffer.

Modern literature is much concerned with the economy of violence and with the spatial figurations it causes. Not only does force alter space—as in the extreme examples of modern war—but space assumes the character and the decor required by both assailant and victim. One of the most baffling of all literary exercises of scene is the naturalistic. In naturalist fiction, the landscape constantly threatens to destroy, but is almost invariably thwarted because the victim, in any true sense of a person accepting violence, does not actually exist. This is because the tedious conscientiousness of naturalists leads to the establishment of violent conclusions before the literature has even been established. From the beginning the cosmic landscape is defined as arbitrarily and conclusively violent—that is, indifferent to the human will. Determinist presuppositions allow the conclusions to be placed before the premises; and if the premises involve human relationships, they are doomed from the start to forfeit their role in the human comedy. Omniscient sympathy, which in Dostoevsky's case allowed Raskolnikov's problem to reveal itself and to be solved gradually and in a full measure gracefully, becomes mere helpless pity in the naturalist novel. This is perhaps to say that a naturalist novel is not literature; but the pretenses to literature remain; and in the fact that naturalist theory is more often neglected than honored in the literature, such a novel frequently persists in spite of the motive for writing it.[13]

—[iv]—

The surface similarities of *Crime and Punishment* and Dreiser's *An American Tragedy* are many, and they may help to document the radical changes in the literature of violence since Dostoevsky's time. It is necessary to point up the similarities of landscape. Dreiser's principal figures are social, in the sense that he allows scenes to image forth the inconsistencies of the human will. In fact, his most effective formal devices are these contrasts of scene; they provide a scenic grammar of the novel. Like Dostoevsky, Dreiser is anxious to explore the extent to which the will of man has isolated itself from spiritual sanctions. The Dreiser hero wishes rather than wills, but insofar as his wishes project into the world of objects they create or help to make possible elaborate Aladdin displays of vulgar luxuries. One such display is the lobby of the Green-Davidson Hotel, in Kansas City.

> (Clyde Griffiths) went direct to a green-marbled doorway which opened from the rear of this drugstore into the lobby of the hotel. Once through it, he beheld a lobby, the like of which, for all his years but because of the timorous poverty that had restrained him from exploring such a world, was more arresting, quite, than anything he had

[13] The question of will dominates naturalist fiction. The difficulty with much of it is that what happens to a character is pathetic rather than tragic, simply because the initiative of willing does not reside in him. Even in the "strong characters" of Frank Norris and of Dreiser, the author takes away far more than he gives, and the strength is just another aspect of an external will acting through the instrument of character.

seen before. It was all so lavish. Under his feet was a
checkered black-and-white marble floor. Above him a cop-
pered and stained and gilded ceiling. And supporting this
a veritable forest of black marble columns as highly polished as the floor—glassy smooth. And between the columns . . . were lamps, statuary, rugs, palms, chairs, di-
vans, tête-à-têtes—a prodigal display . . .[14]

This assortment of property effects, designed as Dreiser says
to give the masses a feeling of luxury, acts immediately to soften
Clyde's will. He is at the moment an observer of the scene.
Ultimately he will become its victim. The scenes of the ensuing pages contrast vividly with the nightmarish disarray of
Raskolnikov's culminating hallucination. As bellhop in the
Green-Davidson hotel, Clyde is privileged to look into one
after another of the most causal of human indulgences. He is
throughout a passive servant, even of the least ingratiating of
these pleasures. The bellhop's uniform stamps him as a flunkey.
He never decisively initiates either pleasure or crime. Nor can he
be said to be in any sense a "meditative man." He is overawed
by the hotel, bored and embarrassed by his family (who wander
the streets as evangelists), resentful of his status, surprised into
gratitude for the notice of his betters, and eventually invited
passively to withdraw from the crime his victim has all but
suicidally collaborated with him in committing.

Perhaps the most vivid of contrasts can be seen in Clyde's
first walk along the street of Lycurgus' privileged upper-class
area.

He found himself ambling on and on until suddenly he
was out of the business district again and in touch with a
wide and tree-shaded thoroughfare of residences, the houses
of which, each and every one, appeared to possess more
room space, lawn space, general ease and repose and

[14] *An American Tragedy*, New York, Boni and Liveright, 1925, Vol. I, p.
29. Other references to this edition are in the text.

dignity even than any with which he had ever been in contact. . . . So many imposing wrought-iron fences, flower-bordered walks, grouped trees and bushes, expensive and handsome automobiles either beneath porte-cochères within or speeding along the broad thoroughfares without . . . (I, 183)

The truth of this landscape that Clyde never really discovers is its unreality. It is a deliberately placid, smoothly peaceful but nonexistent world. It lies at one pole of the two unrealities Clyde endures. The other is the grim and dismal street-world where his mother and father attempt to preach the word of God.

The two extremes are in effect the principal patterns of scene in the landscape which will eventually lead to Clyde's death. Remembering the "easy life" of the Green-Davidson Hotel, he wishes somehow to make it his permanent privilege. When the opportunity does come, he is already involved with a daughter of the depressed classes. Roberta Alden is, in terms of any effective comparison with *Crime and Punishment*, the counterpart of the pawnbroker whom Raskolnikov murders. In the one case she is "in the way"; in the other, she is a "first step," whose death is the one evil a superior man is permitted that he may perform a thousand good acts. Miss Alden, pregnant and adamantly insistent upon marriage, is on the way to destroying Clyde's prospects of reaching that easy, quiet, and inaccessible world he had seen in the hotel, and in his first days in Lycurgus.

At this point, *An American Tragedy* becomes abjectly itself, bows before the necessities of the naturalist disposition toward violence. Naturalism begins by saying that the universe has a specific character and as such is indifferent to the will of man—not that it is hostile, but simply that it is indifferent. Clyde Griffiths does not will the destruction of Roberta; he merely wishes it, and she obliges him. The affair presents almost no hard core of specificity to contemplate, and the speculations over Clyde's "crime" are therefore innately ambiguous. The ambiguities do not result from any violent struggle of the hero to define his meaning to himself, but instead are a consequence of the act's not being in any way firm enough to submit to probing.

This maze of uncertainty is vividly revealed in Dreiser's style, at the crucial moment of his attempt to sum up Clyde. He has brought Roberta all the way to a deserted lake in upstate New York, on the pretense of their having a premarital honeymoon. He had begun by vaguely planning a crime, but the force of will needed did not initially exist and he is merely imitating a suggestion the world outside had offered him. When the awful moment arrives, he suffers the agonies of a will-less will in a position where action is both indispensable and impossible.

> At this cataclysmic moment, and in the face of the utmost, the most urgent need of action, a sudden palsy of the will —of courage—of hate or rage sufficient; and with Roberta from her seat in the stern of the boat gazing at his troubled and then suddenly distorted, and fulgurous, yet weak and even unbalanced face—a face of a sudden, instead of angry, ferocious, demoniac—confused and all but meaningless in its registration of a balanced combat between fear (a chemic revulsion against death or murderous brutality that would bring death) and a harried and restless and yet self-repressed desire to do—to do—to do—yet temporarily unbreakable here and now—a static between a powerful compulsion to do and yet not to do. (II, 76–77)

The very language chokes itself off. It is a rhetorical imitation of a state of absolute indecision. Since Clyde suffers this state, the death of Roberta cannot really be explained. Was it an act of "moral cowardice," or was there "some anger in the blow"? The novel, in its entirety but particularly in this its crucial scene, suggests a few comments on the history of force in modern literature. The force manipulated by Julien Sorel in his own interests exists within range of his sensibility and will, and he is capable of acting decisively to avail himself of it. But already much of the force is in the hands of the peasantry and the townspeople, who have made of it a form of calculation and exchange. Business principles and "deals" occupy an astonishing percentage of the space in nineteenth century novels —to the extent that there is almost nothing of any consequence left outside them. The revulsion against commercial uses of force took the form either of extending the range of the language to a point so remote from reality that it no longer sufficed to identify its enemy (*symbolisme*), or of describing the pathos, filth, disorder, and calamity of its effect upon the landscape (Zola). The objects selected to enforce this grim portraiture were arranged in a sordid light or in a semi-surrealistic disarray. Since naturalism was in literary terms at any rate an extension of realism, the naturalist landscape incorporated not only the sordid detail used for a very much more complex purpose by Baudelaire, Eliot, and their contemporaries, but the scene itself in which social disparities could easily be imaged. Dreiser's concern with cities, hotels, clothes, and interiors helped to identify this landscape as a social record of moral deficiencies. But the landscape did not record merely despair over the disabilities of the modern world; it was asked as well to express externally the inner dispositions of its heroes.

The milieu all but swallows and destroys the hero. Clyde moves from one scene to another; in each case the scene says all that can be said about the hero. Every event of Clyde's life is determined by its locale. If there is any complication of will in Clyde's life, it is represented by a suddenly visualized contrast of scenes: as when Clyde, in the company of his newly found wealthy friends, accidentally comes upon the dilapidated farmhouse of Roberta's parents: ". . . the mere identification of this lorn, dilapidated realm with Roberta and hence himself, was sufficient to cause him to wish to turn and run" (II, 11).

There is no real chance of differentiation in circumstances of this sort.

When the death of Roberta is traced to Clyde and the trial begins, the scene shifts from one pole to the other. The upper class all but disappears; Sondra Finchley is referred to as a "Miss X" during the trial; Clyde is forced to stand before a jury and a courtroom audience made up entirely of Roberta's class of people. The visionary, unreal character of the Lycurgus landscape, which Clyde had observed when he first walked there, is confirmed in its disappearance. From this time forward the dregs of Kansas City and the factory district of Lycurgus take over. This is not a balanced representation of Clyde's worlds at all. He is doomed to die without any real exploration in depth of the terms of his having been victimized. The Reverend Duncan Macmillan strives mightily to bring him to God before he dies; but God is the streets of Kansas City, and the Alden farmhouse, and while Macmillan might bring Clyde to some kind of a psychological insight into his role in Roberta's death, he cannot effectively make him accept a religious definition of the act.

The tragedy of Dreiser's hero is singularly weak in the matter of effectively ranging his will against the scene. He is taken for a long ride, but he is never at the wheel. This absence of willed participation in his hero's role makes him so exclusively the victim as to bring seriously into question his meriting any role at all. There is no way in which the several scenes of *An American Tragedy* may be said to define a pattern of assailant-victim relationship. If we say that Clyde is entirely victim, we are faced with the question, victim of what? Raskolnikov participates actively in both crime and punishment; he not only wills the crime but goes more than halfway to accept Porfiry's invitation to confess it. Clyde does neither of these things. He is at every turn of events a passive observer of the scenes in which the terms of his crime and his punishment are being agreed upon.

Yet, in a very real sense *An American Tragedy* comes closer than *Crime and Punishment* to expressing the terms of the assailant as landscape in the modern literature of violence. Whatever the aberrations of metaphysics which led Dreiser to his concept of victimization, he presents in Clyde Griffiths a victim almost totally bound to the circumstances of the controlling scenes. He does not provide on his own initiative any means of understanding this situation; nor does he actively or entirely accept any explanation offered by anyone else. He is in neither sense an effective modern hero, but only a form of illustration of one stage on the way to modern heroism.

There is a crucial passage in E. A. Robinson's long meditative poem, "The Man Against the Sky," in which—after he has outlined five ways in which man might go to his death—he asks the question that all naturalists must and do ask, of themselves and of their creatures:

. . .

> Are we no greater than the noise we make
> Along one blind atomic pilgrimage
> Whereon by crass chance billeted we go
> Because our brains and bones and cartilage
> Will have it so?
> If this we say, then let us all be still
> About our share in it, and live and die
> More quietly thereby.[15]

Why not make an end of life, Robinson asks, if there is no more than death in view.

> If after all that we have lived and thought,
> All comes to Nought,—
> If there be nothing after Now,
> And we be nothing anyhow,
> And we know that—why live? (148)

[15] *The Man Against the Sky*, New York, Macmillan, 1916, p. 143.

The proper answer is that we do live, and that for most of us the urge to stay alive is sufficient to account for our doing so. This sentiment suggests another stage in the history of the hero's role in a literary landscape. Man lives in the security of immortality, or he is bound by an inner drive to raise his condition of life to an acceptable moral level. If the circumstances of living are not intolerable, he will merely live because he does. If, as is the case of Clyde Griffiths, he lives and acts because he sees a more attractive way of living than he presently enjoys, he will passively submit to events leading inevitably to violence and death.

There are suggestions in *An American Tragedy* of intolerable scenes; they are intolerable only because others are more attractive, but they are so intolerable that Clyde will not prevent a crime from happening in order to accept them and abide by them. This is certainly a very mild example of the assailant as landscape. The wars themselves provided more shocking and unendurable occasions. The landscape becomes an assailant when it forces the hero in literature into the role of victim. There are examples in modern literature of its forcing the individual to destroy in himself all vestiges of will, to become a victim collaborating in the crime that is his own death. Neither this extreme nor the spectacle of a hero's death like that of Noah Ackerman (Shaw's *The Young Lions*) can properly be called a culmination of the literature of violence. But the way to an understanding of it is opened when we are presented with a hero who understands neither what is being done to him nor why he is doing it.

6

THE IMAGERY OF CATASTROPHE

Fortinbras: Let four captains
Bear Hamlet like a soldier to the stage;
For he was likely, had he been put on,
To have prov'd most royally; and for his passage
The soldiers' music and the rites of war
Speak loudly for him.
Take up the bodies. Such a sight as this
Becomes the field, but here shows much amiss.
Go, bid the soldiers shoot.
      Exeunt marching; after which a peal of ordi-
      nance are shot off.

—*Hamlet*, v, ii, 407–414

—[i]—

"ONE OF THE THINGS," says Dwight Macdonald, "which make it possible for a modern civilian to participate in war without more psychological resistance than he has is the fact that the murderous aspect of war is depersonalized." [1] Macdonald suggests a direct ratio of power to impersonality: ". . . the more powerful the weapons the greater the slaughter and the less the killer's consciousness of it." Hand-to-hand fighting, with whatever weapons in aid, still requires skill, agility, a desire to kill.[2]

[1] *Memoirs of a Revolutionist*, p. 79.
[2] Macdonald cites a manual by Major Rex Applegate, *Kill—or Get*

Soldiers are to be trained in hating; but they must always learn to hate the enemy; they may lose their inhibitions and use their newly acquired skills against the drill-sergeant. Drill manuals of World War II specify precautions against this danger.

The training of the soldier stressed efficiency in methods of destruction. "The object of all this cooperation, skill, and unselfish, even heroic behavior was to blow to pieces other human beings and their homes . . ." (89). The element of self-preservation remains in close combat. It is still there as well in air combat, but there are few if any marks of identification with the enemy, in fact little suggestion that the airman knows the enemy.

The history of wars is significantly a history of the ratio of power and space. Liddell Hart suggests two important changes in modern warfare: the increase of firing power and the spread of the actual fighting, to include the civilian population. The code of war formulated in the eighteenth century, according to which rules were set up to limit the exercise of force, broke down during the French Revolution:

> The moderation that is based on far-sighted realism is at a discount in times of violence, but so also is the more usual and superficial kind that merely reposes on well-meaning sentiments. The men of good intentions who pitch expectations too high are commonly swept on by the wave they have raised, and then swept away by men more reckless and more ruthless.[3]

In the American Civil War, the idea of a "war of attrition," involving pressures upon civilian populations, was first applied on a significant scale. The two wars of our century were significantly moves toward the concept of total war, which meant

Killed, which describes the best and most efficient methods. "Ruthlessness is what we seek to achieve. It is best defined in two words: speed and brutality . . ." (83)
[3] *The Revolution in Warfare,* London, Faber and Faber, 1946, p. 46.

not only maximum pressures of force but maximum distributions of it. Wars are no longer either polite or honorable; armies aim at total destruction of the enemy, preservation of themselves.

Armies are now more and more fully prepared to exert maximum force.[4] The first impression of the result is that they annihilate a landscape before they are willing or able to occupy it. Friedrich Juenger describes his impressions of some battlefields of the First World War. He was shocked, "not so much by the spectacle of death and destruction, as by the man-made transformations of whole landscapes."[5] At Flanders, for example, "The artillery barrages which had hailed down for weeks had turned this theater of war into a sort of moonscape covered with craters." (118) Not only men but man-made objects were hopelessly tangled and twisted beyond recognition. Such violence is an expression of a pure intensity of force; there is no respecting the dignity or design of either machinery or man. Man "is not even cut up like an animal that is taken to the butcher, nor neatly carved and disjointed like a chicken; he is blown to pieces, crushed, torn to shreds" (122).

This absolute loss of decorum marks a conspicuous turning point in the literary treatment of violence. In almost all of the work which reflects the experience of World War I, the mockery of man's pretense to dignity plays a large role. The theme

[4] It is also a question of "weapons revolution." Since World War II, three of these have occurred (the atom bomb, the hydrogen bomb, the missile), and a fourth is imminent. It is conceivable that in some future time weapons will take over from men altogether. In view of this possibility of automated killing, the term "over-kill" is of some interest. It means the amount of destructive power *beyond* the number of people in the world. The United States, for example, has a power ratio of more than 100 "over-kill." A number of books debate the implications of all of these changes. See, for example: Robert Jungk, *Brighter than a Thousand Suns*, tr. James Cleugh, New York, Harcourt, Brace, and World, 1958; originally in German, Bern, 1956; Ralph E. Lapp, *Kill and Overkill*, New York, Basic Books, 1962.

[5] *The Failure of Technology*, tr. Friedrich Wilhelmson, Chicago, Regnery, 1956, p. 117. Other references to this edition are in the text.

is powerfully emphasized in Ezra Pound's bitterly ironic play upon the Horatian line, "Dulce et decorum est pro patria mori."

. . .

> Died some, pro patria,
>   non "dulce" non "et decor" . . .
> walked eye-deep in hell
> believing in old men's lies, then unbelieving
> came home, home to a lie,
> home to many deceits,
> home to old lies and new infamy;
> usury age-old and age-thick
> and liars in public places.[6]

. . .

The shock here reported is largely a disappointment in expectations: one expects that he will remain integrally whole, and his body is an outward sign of this integrity. But it is also a question of what Pound calls "wastage as never before." One of the overwhelming shocks of World War I is a consequence of attrition: not only tangled and dismembered bodies, but the treatment of men as *matériel*, so that they are so many tons of flesh, good only for what they can do to destroy the enemy's *matériel*.

Freud put the matter simply and cogently. All men instinctively desire to act violently, but it is only in a time of war that this desire is released and "used." "The warring state permits itself every such misdeed, every such act of violence, as would disgrace the individual man." [7] Civilization is based upon the renunciation of instinctual satisfactions. War sets back the progress of society, "strips us of the later accretions of civilisation, and lays bare the primal man in each of us" (24). These

[6] Poem IV of *Hugh Selwyn Mauberley*, London, Ovid Press, 1920. Copyright 1926, 1954, by Ezra Pound.
[7] (1915), in *Civilization, War, and Death*, ed. John Rickman, London, Hogarth, 1953, p. 5. Other references to this edition are in the text.

remarks (written in the first year of World War I) argue a relatively simple moral economy and suggest an individual of com-
parative innocence. Freud sees him in possession of a limited
instinctual power which in peacetime is more or less successfully contained by the discretions and formalities of a rational
civilization and in a time of war is set loose as so much energy
to be used and distributed by the state.[8]

Not only are the limits of this charge of energy, sponsored
as it is by our "instinctual love of violence," violated by technical and instrumental accelerations; the limits of man's capacity to absorb and consciously to distribute violent energy
are also exceeded. The modern man of violence is more the
victim than he is the assailant. War begins as a maneuvering
of force, together with statistical studies of available manpower.
Manpower does not long remain a form of power as such, but
becomes an accessory of the assailant as machine. Hence, the
landscape described by Friedrich Juenger discriminates only
incidentally between machines and men. A mature estimate of
this problem is given by Liddell Hart:

> The multiplication of machinery has sterilized the romance
> of war, by diminishing the value of human qualities.
> Courage and skill are of little avail against a superiority
> of machinery. The bomber has extended the de-human-
> izing effect of artillery; the flying bomb and the rocket
> bomb carry it a stage further. These automatic weapons
> make nonsense of the soldierly idea that success in war is
> a proof of a people's virility and virtue . . .[9]

—[ii]—

The psychology of man has of course had to be radically
altered, to account for this acceleration of force beyond his

[8] See Brigid Brophy's *Black Ship to Hell* (New York, Harcourt, Brace,
and World, 1962), an elaborate Freudian explanation of the instinct for
self-destruction.
[9] *The Revolution in Warfare*, pp. 81–82.

ability either to endure or (integrally as a *person*) to direct it. War literature has conspicuously many incidents of heroism on a small scale and in a quiet manner, but it is also abundantly suggestive of the experiences of shock, disgust, anger, and submission to the unknown. One of the most important protective reactions is the abandonment by the ego of his personal attachment to causes, ideals, principles. While there is always a minority of literary reactions which suggest that these ideals brightly survive the horror, the overwhelming majority correctly insist that they are at best suspended. Not only are they suspended; the consciousness is itself split. We become aware of ourselves *as objects*. It is a protective device, and, practiced over a long period of time, it permits an almost unlimited opportunity to survive, not as person but as objective consciousness. But the process is in itself outrageous. It denies the value of the self, and quite surely of the means of valuing the self. This adjustment to violence is one of the most distinctive characteristics of modern literature. It does not exist in the great realist literature of the nineteenth century, for there the self observes his actions consciously but not objectively. Stendhal's Julien Sorel is an analyst of his own behavior, but also a judge of every stage of it. Even Zola's characters, however overwhelmed they are by "scientific" detail, are analysts and conscious evaluators of their works and merits.

The process begins in a rejection of principles and ideals, and a close look at words that are supposed to inspire heroic action. The best known formula of this modern nominalism is Lieutenant Henry's "I was always embarrassed by the words sacred, glorious, and sacrifice and the expression in vain." [10] Words, linked vaguely to ideals, are checked against things, and things and specific labels are the only trustworthy facts: "Abstract words such as glory, honor, courage, or hallow were obscene beside the concrete names of villages, the numbers of roads, the

[10] A *Farewell to Arms*, New York, Scribner's, 1929, p. 196. Other references to this edition are in the text.

names of rivers, the numbers of regiments and the dates." But this is a far cry from the self's observation of itself *as thing*. It is fundamentally a romantic view of the self, which tries to protect itself against violation by adhering to the real. A *Farewell to Arms* is, after all, a work of "romantic naturalism"; it develops its romanticism in terms of the reality of things and experiences and the absolute unreliability of motivational generalities. Lieutenant Henry reflects here that he cannot experience value in the honored association of ideals with things; he will therefore have to abandon the horrible farce that is the war, which violates every expectation of integrity. But this disposition toward values and ideals goes beyond the renunciation of war as a maneuver of force in the interest of ideals. Hemingway is equally indisposed to the alternative Lieutenant Henry has chosen for himself. The deaths of Catherine and of their child strike a blow against the second major sentimentality, that of the lovers against the world. The primary stance of this kind of romantic hero is that of absolute isolation seen in the novel's last sentence (355) and a major characteristic of Jake Barnes of *The Sun Also Rises* (1926) and of most of Hemingway's heroes in the fiction of the 1920's.

Some of the implications of this attitude deserve exploration. It is closely linked to the gradual shift of a person away from those details of his living which identify him with a community. Even Henry in his new life can claim community only with one other person, and that person is shortly to be removed by death. There is no real sense of responsible association with "home"; in fact, throughout the details of "home" are pushed aside, replaced by war equivalents. Henry's love of Catherine Barkley is a move away from the brothel, but it is still doomed to remain an isolated union: "We could feel alone when we were together, alone against the others" (266). The suggestion is that home is a static affair, while the war scene is dynamically destructive. Soldier's home is a place where principles still functionally exist, where human relationships are still contained within a neat framework of manners, conventions, and mannerisms. Basically the distinction is one of force. The war's effect is to blow apart the bonds of personal, intramural respect and dignity.

Perhaps the most devastating literary expression of this dislocation is a poem of World War II, Howard Nemerov's "The Hero Comes Home in His Hamper, and Is Exhibited at the World's Fair":

> I exhibit here the well-known failure of
> Communication, nerve and power of love.
> A miracle of godly medicine,
> I am without facilities for sin,
> Being a lump of undistinguished skin
> Sans this and that after the mine went off,
> Beneath my feet, with an unhealthy cough.[11]

Compared to this "basket case," Hemingway's Krebs is an old grad returned to a campus reunion. The "Soldier's Home" theme in war literature is, however, an important step in the description of the depersonalizing of the hero's consciousness. The damaged hero returns, to use his newly acquired skill (with gun and bayonet) to destroy a civilian rival (Andreas Latzko, *Men in War*; Thomas Boyd, *Points of Honor*); or his experience in the medical corps has so overwhelmed him that he can no longer think of persons as valid beings (William Hoffman, *The Trumpet Unblown*); the civilian world seems reduced, unreal, even petty and mean (in poems of Eve Merriam, Nemerov, Lawrence Spingarn).

A rather important exception to this theme ought to be noticed. In much World War II literature, the war is itself considered an interruption, a present suspended between a domestic past and future. The strength of love and the power

---

[11] From "The Hero Comes Home in His Hamper," by Howard Nemerov. Copyright 1950 by Howard Nemerov. Reprinted from *Guide to the Ruins*, by Howard Nemerov, by permission of Random House, Inc.

of familiar association give the soldier a sustaining image of his identity as a person in a setting which is largely designed to deny the fact of his personality. Any link to home is an assertion, not necessarily of human values but of personal identity, and thus a blow against a threatened anonymity. This simple statement, for example, in Jarrell's poem "Mail Call," stresses the importance of the image:

. . .

> Surely the past from which the letters rise
> Is waiting in the future, past the graves?
> The soldiers are all haunted by their lives.
>
> Their claims upon their kind are paid in paper
> That establishes a presence, like a smell.
> In letters and in dreams they see the world.
> They are waiting: and the years contract
> To an empty hand, to one unuttered sound—
>
> The soldier simply wishes for his name.[12]

This sentiment testifies, for one thing, to a different disposition toward the war.[13] For one thing, it suggests an anticipation of what the war will be, based on a knowledge of what it has been; this knowledge is of course lacking in the soldier of World War I. But the attitude also reveals an awareness on the part of the soldier of the war's maximum destructive power

[12] *Little Friend, Little Friend*, p. 35. For discussions of Jarrell as a poet of war, see essays by Glauco Cambon and Richard Fein, in *Analects*, 1 (spring 1961), pp. 11–23.

[13] See also Charles H. Butler, *Cut Is the Branch*, 1945, p. 46; Bernard Spencer, *Aegean Island*, 1948, p. 20; Arnold Stein, *Perilous Balance*, 1945, p. 20; Alan Swallow, *The Nameless Sight*, 1956, p. 45; Peter Bowman, *Beach Red*, 1945, p. 12; and two poems by Karl Shapiro, V-*Letter*, 1944, pp. 3–4 and 62–63. Several World War II novels, conspicuously Mailer's *The Naked and the Dead* (1948) and Shaw's *The Young Lions* (1948), make a rather elaborate use of home either as the source of personal weaknesses and strengths at the front or as a civilian point of evaluating war arms and purposes. See below, Part Two, chapter 7, for further discussion of these matters.

—so that he is in a sense on guard against his own destruction and places himself, as self, in a temporal box of past and future, from which he acts as spectator of his present self in battle. Again and again, the literature of World War II portrays the soldier estimating his luck, his chance of escaping the final anonymity to which his position may draw him.[14]

—[iii]—

The literature of force and violence makes a radical shift of emphasis precisely at that point where force overwhelms personality. The initial adjustment to that fact is a romantic and profane denial of the rationality of the war. No fact stands out more clearly than the total collapse of the causal link of human will to event. Soldiers are surprised, outraged, and finally terrified that this should be true. Since men function usually in terms of some such causal association, the shock to the sensibility almost literally destroys the rational sense of responsible being. The trenches of World War I, as they are described, for example, in Erich Remarque's *All Quiet on the Western Front* (1929) compel the soldier to improvise for the sake of his safety and survival. Having at least temporarily abandoned any devotion to principle, he turns next to the matter of preserving himself as thing—as body. He observes himself as body in a variety of defensive postures: he hugs the earth and seeks low ground; he watches the skyline, and learns to distinguish one sound from another, in terms of their relationship to his survival. In short, to save himself, he literally observes himself as object, analyzes objectively and unemotionally, coldly, his capacity to stay alive, and otherwise resigns from the organization of thinking and emotionally recognizable persons.

This is a fundamental reconstitution of the ego; and while it may be called merely an emergency reaction, the existence in

[14] See Shapiro, "Troop Train," in *V-Letter and Other Poems*, New York, Reynal and Hitchcock, 1944, pp. 8–9.

the world of such potential force as was demonstrated in World War I makes it likely that it will be a recurrent one. The fundamentals of survival are not the same as those characterizing prestige or self-esteem. An extreme version of this kind of revaluation is to be found in the work of Ernst Juenger, who suggests that violence and war have now forced man to substitute pain for value as the essential criterion of his worth. Erich Kahler has summed up the meaning of this revised standard of self-judgment:

> Hence the criterion of worthiness is transferred from value to pain, or rather to the measure of self-mortification of which a man is capable. But under present conditions such self-mortification again represents an extreme formalization, mechanization of the psychic process. In extreme situations, such as in concentration camps, and from a position of faith, it is very possible to mortify one's sensory being without eradicating human feeling altogether. But it is impossible to objectify, to mortify one's self habitually and from a position in a blank void, in a nowhere, without killing not only sensation or sentimentality but the psychic roots of sentiment altogether.[15]

In an extreme case, the individual suffers successive retreats from his status as personality, as he experiences violence. Both Hemingway's Lieutenant Henry and Dos Passos' John Andrews desert the cause and source of this depersonalization. The one is left entirely alone at the end, the other is forcibly returned to the scene of his desertion. The withdrawal into things is itself illusory, and of short duration. For the things are blasted beyond recognition and the sentiments of trust and simple faith they encourage are unhinged. Signs of abnormality are numerous: the bombed cemetery, with bodies blasted from the ground, to return to a second burial; the ruins of houses and churches; pitifully grotesque signs of natural quietude in the

[15] *The Tower and the Abyss*, New York, Braziller, 1957, pp. 89–90.

midst of violence. Above all, there is the obscenity of the war: the grotesque disfigurement of the human body, its dismemberment, a variety of freakish accidents, the look of surprise on the face of the suddenly punctured soldier. In a short time, evaluations of the human spirit are reduced to estimates concerning the survival value of organs and parts, and fears of fleshly vulnerability.

These physical dislocations lead shortly to dislocations of style. Nothing was so effective in undercutting the carefully constructed and soberly balanced style of the Victorians than the explosion of raw force on the battlefield. There are lingering Georgian echoes and flavors in the style of Edmund Blunden's *Undertones of War*; such a passage as this is extremely rare in the literature of World War I:

> . . . we enter Mailly, and turn at the church, still neatly jacketed with straw, but with a new hole or two in it, along a leafy side-road; another turn, and we are between excellent meadow-grounds, which lack only a few fat sheep, an old mole-catcher, and some crows. Groups of shell-holes, however, restrain the fancy from useless excursions, and, sitting under some tall slender elms on a convenient bank for a few minutes' rest, we keep our ears eastwardly attentive.[16]

This is so exceptional as to suggest a different war altogether. Like the war of Rupert Brooke's poetry, it plays upon the sentiment of *lacking* hedgerows and white teacups, more than upon destruction itself. In contrast, the prevailing idiom and syntax of war prose are spare, unadorned, limited in metaphoric and intellectual range, based on a factuality that suffices unto itself and produces its own irony and implicit floridity. This is the style of almost all twentieth century war novels: a factuality that reports the terror and at the same time suffers it. Much is

[16] *Undertones of War* (1928), New York, Oxford University Press, 1956, pp. 124–25.

made of the ambiguities suffered by a language until now dedicated to the description of relatively static social situations and to the narration of movement within and about them. Nowhere are the ambiguities more in evidence than in the descriptions of sudden death, especially in view of the helplessness of survivors to pay any ceremonial attention to the corpse. A selection of sentences from this literature will help to communicate its quality:

Things were getting all mixed up in his mind. It seemed to be filled with flesh, cloyed with the sweetish smell of flesh that is torn open and over which blood is pouring. (Humphrey Cobb, *Paths of Glory*, 1935, 31)

The dark goes mad. It heaves and raves. Darknesses blacker than the night rush on us with giant strides, over us and away. The flames of the explosion light up the graveyard. (Erich Remarque. *All Quiet on the Western Front*, 1929, 43)

Odors, foul and fragrant, were borne upon the night wind, and formless patches of blackness deepened the brooding twilight all about them; the slanting moonlight filled the shellholes with lights and shadows. (Arnold Zweig, *Education Before Verdun*, 1936, 82)

And while we were standing there, he about to show me the picture, a twenty-eighter struck quite a distance away from us, a good two-hundred yards. We didn't even look that way. Then all of a sudden I saw something black come flying through the air—and Dill fell over with his dashing wife's picture in his hand and a boot, a leg, a boot with the leg of a baggage soldier sticking in his head . . . (Andreas Latzko, *Men in War*, 1918, 36)

. . . a rat climbed noiselessly up the jamb of the gallery entrance and watched Paolacci for a while, then it stepped onto the lieutenant's chest and squatted there. It looked to the right and to the left, two or three times, then lowered its head and began to eat Paolacci's under lip. (*Paths of Glory*, 48)

. . . The first German I saw climbed up over the garden wall. We waited till he got one leg over and then potted him. He had so much equipment on and looked awfully surprised and fell down into the garden. Then three more came over further down the wall. We shot them. They all came just like that. (Hemingway, *In Our Time*, 1925, "Chapter" III)

. . . He was quite small and his arms were by his side, his puttee-wrapped legs and muddy boots together, his cap over his face. He looked very dead. It was raining. I had liked him as well as any one I ever knew. I had his papers in my pocket and would write to his family. Ahead across the fields was a farmhouse . . . (Hemingway, *A Farewell to Arms*, 1929, 229)

The common quality of these passages is their abject factuality. Nothing suggests the exceptional. There are a few traces of irony, in an occasional word choice and perhaps sometimes in the extreme nature of the circumstance, but for the most part the style adheres to sensory and situational minima. It would be foolish to suggest that the war novelists do not object to the enormities described in them. But they do not shriek complaints about their existence. They give a factual record, reportage, of a fantastically distorted, an unrecognizable world. Each passage describes in miniature a distortion of the rhythms of life and death: the stench of death, an upheaval in a cemetery, the effect of moonlight upon a wasteland, a scene of two grotesquely accidental deaths, the macabre delicacy of a rat beginning his meal, a Chaplinesque farce of sudden death, a body left behind in the confusion of retreat.

The rhetoric and rhythm of the second Hemingway passage are especially skilled. Aymo has been killed, as it happens, by a bullet from his own army. Lieutenant Henry can do nothing but say he liked him as a person, that he will send his papers back home; and then he must go on: "Ahead across the fields was a farmhouse." The passages all do violence to their human subjects, by neglecting their humanity, or purposely ignoring it; in doing so, they simply report the violence done them by the war. These are separate incidents; they link to other separate incidents, and the whole is made up of fragments simply organized in terms of movement in space. Only *Paths of Glory* and *A Farewell to Arms* have sustaining narratives that go beyond the exigencies of the scene. For the most part the meaning of the war is the scene itself. The consciousness of the author is divided into the man who observes himself and the scene he observes, of which he is a part. Erich Kahler calls the first of these selves "the non-personal hyperobjective second consciousness," and goes on to describe what he calls the "Neue Sachlichkeit" (New Factuality) in literature:

> Factuality is handled so pointedly that it becomes symbolic; abruptness produces compression. Indeed, this peculiar factuality radiates an atmosphere which reflects the overstrained neutrality of the author—a neutrality that appears like an inversion of all the bitter experiences and disillusionments of the generation. The detachment and self-restraint of the author weighs upon the story like a tense aura, like a ghostly presence of fate. One never has that feeling with naturalistic works where everything is told neatly and elaborately.[17]

Factuality is for Hemingway a type of absolute literary responsibility, as it is for his contemporaries working in the same genre. One sees the consistency with which Hemingway maintained this sense of obligation: in Lieutenant Henry's withering analysis of the battle-police's cynically pragmatic use of high-sounding abstractions, in Jake Barnes's estimate of Cohn's

[17] *The Tower and the Abyss*, pp. 96, 99.

meandering romanticism, in the pauses in *Death in the After-noon* for discussions of literature, in his remarks there about "faking" and honesty—in general, in his emphasis upon the job that needs to be done, to communicate "the sequence of motion and fact which made the emotion." [18] As a critical statement, this has validity enough. But the important step toward a critical estimate is to ask the question concerning the causes and effects of the style in a modern literature of violence. Is there a relationship between the style and the subject? Does the matter force the style? In Hemingway's case, there is much to suggest that he consciously and deliberately sought a style that would be peculiarly modern. Even so, there remains the problem of what makes it "peculiarly modern," and why a modern style should be peculiarly different from what preceded it.

The most obvious answer is that the situation of modern violence required a full measure of "Sachlichkeit." That is, Lieutenant Henry was patently right in his suspicion of words which came from the past and led nowhere. The central ambiguities of the postwar situation were rhetorical equivalents of the fragments of body and machine strewn about the landscape. These ambiguities were caused by dislocations of bodies separated from souls and by the constant pressure of the risk of sudden death upon the observer of the modern scene. There is no doubt that ritualistic expositions of meaning require a slow, deliberate rhythm, with many meditative pauses and

---

[18] *Death in the Afternoon*, New York, Scribner's, 1932. The full meaning of this passage requires a further look into Hemingway's feeling, as he describes it here, immediately after the war: he seems dominated by a compulsion to repeat a violent experience in all its purity: "I was trying to write then and I found the greatest difficulty, aside from knowing truly what you really felt, rather than what you were supposed to feel, and had been taught to feel, was to put down what really happened in action; what the actual things were which produced the emotion that you experienced. . . ." It is important also to note that he was in search not merely of action, but of violent action: "The only place where you could see life and death, i.e., violent death now that the wars were over, was in the bull ring and I wanted very much to go to Spain where I could study it. . . ." (All quotations are from page 2.)

much suggestion of the quality of both noun and verb. Hemingway developed his style with close attention to the scene. The scene itself was disjunct, and its design was a ghastly and deadly but calculated disarray, directly related to the expenditure of mechanized force within an area. So the irony of grotesque events, the overturning of graves, the spectacle of decapitated bodies and the grey or yellow stench of death, all demanded a scrupulously honest, heavily weighted, unembellished, syntactically even, and unintrusive style.

A passage like the following is in a sense a testimony of the literary minima allowed such a setting and such events. The hero of the story "A Way You'll Never Be," Nick Adams, arrives at an Italian battle station near a town recently attacked. The dead are strewn about, and there are affecting reminders of their very recent association with the living. Corporeal deterioration is already beginning, and the grim and constant challenge that death makes to the senses is very much in evidence:

> They lay alone or in clumps in the high grass of the field and along the road, their pockets out, and over them were flies and around each body or group of bodies were the scattered papers.
>
> . . .
>
> These were the dead and no one had bothered with anything but their pockets. Our own dead, or what he thought of, still, as our own dead, were surprisingly few, Nick noticed. Their coats had been opened too and their pockets were out, and they showed, by their positions, the manner and skill of the attack. The hot weather had swollen them all alike regardless of nationality.[19]

Death has become a matter of the most meticulously routine reportage. This is to suggest not simply that death happens often in a time of war, but that it is not of much consequence,

[19] *The Fifth Column and the First Forty-Nine Stories*, New York, Scribner's, 1938, pp. 500, 501.

except as it may offer clues to the precise nature of the violence. Killing is an activity of incredible and frightening casualness:

> . . . life is simply one continual watch against the menace of death;—it has transformed us into unthinking animals in order to give us the weapon of instinct—it has reinforced us with dullness, so that we do not go to pieces before the horror . . . it has lent us the indifference of wild creatures, so that in spite of all we perceive the positive in every moment, and store it up as a reserve against the onslaught of nothingness. Thus we live a closed, hard existence of the utmost superficiality, and rarely does an incident strike out a spark.[20]

—[iv]—

It is natural enough that men should expect death, that the risk of it be ever-present, and that corpses should become commonplace on the field of battle. Nevertheless, men cringe before it, become creatures especially adapted to using all resources to avoid it, and are depressed, frightened, grim servants of the experience they most dread. "Death stands before us as the day of execution before the condemned man. We live, and live not. Two days, three weeks, perhaps half a year more." [21] Though they must of necessity accept death as imminent and immediately possible, they cannot entirely submit to it; to do so would be to deny themselves all human dignity. The image of death is variously defined. Langlois of *Paths of Glory* speaks of "The brutality of death—sudden incommunicability" (200). For Arnold Zweig's chaplain, "death was like an idiot, who split a violin for firewood and used it to heat the stove" (*Education Before Verdun*, 398). Dos Passos' Martin Howe resents the

[20] Erich Remarque, *All Quiet on the Western Front*, tr. A. N. Wheen, Boston, Little, Brown, 1929, pp. 270–71.
[21] Fritz von Unruh, *The Way of Sacrifice* (1925), tr. C. A. Macartney, New York, Knopf, 1928, p. 11.

trivial indignity of the prospect: "What right had a nasty little piece of tinware to go tearing through his rich, feeling flesh . . . ?" [22]

The disposition toward deadly circumstance otherwise assumes two principal lines: the soldiers' resentment that they should be so young as to die before their having experienced life (Remarque), and a tendency to stress analogies between the present carnage and the collapse of the tradition (Richard Aldington, *Death of a Hero*; Ford Madox Ford, *Parade's End*). Since the war is a grim joke, an absurdity, the shock of its impact in some cases provokes loud protests against it, as "hideously stupid," or as absurd, "like Alice in Wonderland."

Religious imagery is often introduced to present the soldier's ironic separation from his past. One of the more elaborate examples occurs in Unruh's *Way of Sacrifice*: soldiers billeted in a church see one of their fellows climb a pulpit and hold out a crown of thorns:

> "Look here, you sane people. I cut the barbed wire off the Saviour! What? Who's that grumbling? Wasn't I right to do it? Look! I cut this barbed wire off his brow. You sane people, why do you put up with it so long?" (176)

In most cases, the common soldier-victim is identified with the Christ figure. He is the mute, defenseless, pitiful specter of defeat, who is killed again and again, suffering the agonies of a million haphazard acts of violence. He is, in short, the scapegoat of modern violence.[23] The visions we have of him in this literature in no way remind us of Christian grace, but only of the annihilation of his people. For E. E. Cummings, he

---

[22] *One Man's Initiation*, New York, Harcourt, Brace, 1919, p. 133.

[23] Compare this statement, by Hannah Arendt, *On Revolution* (New York, Viking, 1963): "More importantly even, the terrifying question of good and evil could not even be posed, at least not in the framework of Western traditions, without taking into account the only completely valid, completely convincing experience Western mankind ever had with active love of goodness as the inspiring principle of all actions, that is, without consideration of the person of Jesus of Nazareth. . . ." (pp. 76–77)

serves another role, this a reinstatement of his Christly role but for a selected group of Cummings' depressed and deprived outcasts. Walking the last miles to his prison, the narrator of *The Enormous Room* comes upon a wooden statue, "a little wooden man hanging all by itself in a grove of low trees."

—The wooden body, clumsy with pain, burst into fragile legs with absurdly large feet and funny writhing toes; its little stiff arms made abrupt cruel equal angles with the road. About its stunted loins clung a ponderous and jocular fragment of drapery. On one terribly brittle shoulder the droll lump of its neckless head ridiculously lived. There was in this complete silent doll a gruesome truth of instinct, a success of uncanny poignancy, an unearthly ferocity of rectangular emotion.[24]

This is a strikingly pathetic reminder of the loss suffered by Christian values. Tradition and Christianity alike were victimized by the force of pain; and here, as in the image of Dos Passos' disintegrating abbey, the woe of all man's history seems to have been concentrated. An echo of this World War I sentiment—of art's share in suffering the pain of violence—is found in a poem from the second war, again concerned with the Christ image whose sculptured detail symbolically reveals an aspect of human suffering:

．．．

Where is the cup in which the blood was light
(With vinegar and sweat the natural part)?
And when the Germans bled the babies white
Where was the *skepsis* of the sculptor's art?
The question is of science not to doubt
The point of faith is that you sweat it out.[25]

[24] *The Enormous Room*, New York, Boni and Liveright, 1922, pp. 51–52.
[25] From "Sonnet," by Howard Nemerov. Copyright 1950 by Howard Nemerov. Reprinted from *Guide to the Ruins*, by Howard Nemerov, by permission of Random House, Inc.

The last two lines suggest some reinstatement of Christ's value in the human economy; we may note some evidence of this revival in the second war, in spite of an equally strong attention to the pressures of violent force in that war. If the war was not itself very often better clarified than was the first (there is much the same desolation), the enemy was clearly specified as evil and the war was often seen as a necessary act of human survival. Faulkner's *A Fable* is a culminating example of the Christ figure in war literature. Its setting is World War I, its meaning that of World War II. There is a direct line from Unruh's common soldier to Faulkner's Corporal. In every case, the Christ is the commonplace human victim of the satanic assailant, whether on a cross crazily atilt in No Man's Land or a clumsy wooden man hanging, stiff with pain, in a grove of trees. Cummings' man testifies to the shared pathos of a common victim; Nemerov's, to the grim necessity of absorbing and enduring the ordeal. Faulkner's soldier-Christ, elaborately identified with the Christ story, ends by separating from its divinity and by affirming humanity. These images are never supernatural. The Christ of war literature is forever of the earth of man. This is a form of primitive Christianity, designed to keep the Christian story with rigid fidelity along the lines of integration with a pattern of man-made, technologically accelerated violence.

In several instances of war literature, the Christ figure descends not to the level of man in the mass but to that of the clown, an outcast from the mass. In modern literature there is a sharp division between Father and Son: often the Son has all but deserted His divinity and taken up permanent tenure on earth. The reduction of Christ to the level of victim leaves God the Father in the role of the assailant. While this change in the figure of the Incarnation is merely suggested here and there, in many ways it suits more adequately the human condition in the scene of modern violence. If destruction is total, if men are totally dehumanized, they also lose their power of assimilating grace to themselves. But the Christ, though in this sense He becomes all but exclusively a man, is a special kind of man, a figure like Hart Crane's Chaplin ("Chaplinesque") or Picasso's *saltimbanque*, or Cummings' Him. As any of these, he shares the world's sorrow and bewilderment over an incredible extension of raw power.[26]

[26] In another book, *Samuel Beckett: The Language of Self* (Carbondale, Southern Illinois University Press, 1962; paperback edition, E. P. Dutton, 1964), I discuss other aspects of the Christ figure. See especially Chapter 1, pp. 3–55. See also Edwin M. Moseley, *Pseudonyms of Christ in the Modern Novel* (University of Pittsburgh Press, 1962), which is wide-ranging and inclined to view Christ more as an archetype than a figure to be presented with doctrinal precision.

7

"TERROR'S UNIQUE ENIGMA":
THE LITERATURE OF WORLD WAR II

Soldier, there is a war between the mind
And sky, between the thought and day and night. It is
For that the poet is always in the sun,

Patches the moon together in his room
To his Virgilian cadences, up down
Up down. It is a war that never ends.

. . .

Monsieur and comrade,
The soldier is poor without the poet's lines,

His petty syllabi, the sounds that stick,
Inevitably modulating, in the blood.
And war for war, each has its gallant kind.

How simply the fictive hero becomes the real;
How gladly with proper words the soldier dies,
If he must, or lives on the bread of faithful speech.

—WALLACE STEVENS, "Epilogue," *Notes Toward a Supreme Fiction*

—[i]—

THE PHENOMENA of reactions to the second great war of our
century continue to grow in number and complexity. They do,
however, lend themselves rather strikingly to a pattern of ex-

planation that allows for a fair degree of explicitness in explaining and defining them. It is not unlike the design I have already discussed, of tension between "violence and decorum," or of the pull and tug of new variants of force affected by ideological stresses and strains.[1] There are, of course, new distributions of the metaphoric meanings these terms have. The "decorum" is a complex of liberal and leftist "manners," of a type like those so shrewdly examined by Lionel Trilling in his novel, *The Middle of the Journey* (1947).

A number of facts, events, and strategies have influenced our perspective upon World War II. The ideological meaning comes out of the 1930's; aside from the many variants of social definition and positioning characteristic of that decade, there is the overwhelming fact that the war was an emotionally sustained attempt to destroy one ideology and to reinstate another. The greatest emotional pressures were exerted in the effort to expand and extend the definitions of evil, to find a new *esthétique du mal*, and particularly to make a start in an activity that grows steadily more complex: that of establishing the symbology of Nazism as a present discourse of evil, a newly available set of metaphors of Satan.

It is, of course, not nearly so simple as these remarks might suggest. Ideological exercises tend to become adulterated, and melodrama often invades the major centers of ideological heroism. The examples of genuinely successful literature from an ideological source are rare indeed. Definitions tend to thin out, to break or crack, and to affect characterizations and the vantage points of moral judgment. The counter-stress in this war literature is the violence itself. In terms I have already discussed,[2] the increase of force and the growing distance between assailant and victim had a number of consequences. For one thing, they made it difficult to maintain a clear line of heroic

---

[1] See above, Part One, chapter 1, where these terms are first used in a nineteenth century context, and their importance noted.
[2] See above, Part Two, chapters 3 and 4.

action: the words used to explain and to justify action gradually lost the effectiveness in face of the extravagant and irrational demonstrations of pure force. The *Guernica* of Pablo Picasso is a transitional gesture, as the Spanish Civil War provides the transition from the tendentious 1930's to the retrospection of postwar judgments of full-scale violence.

Of course, almost all literature asks the questions that try to define involvement, implication, relation. Sometimes there are answers; these are largely out of the liberal variants upon the leftist tactics of the 1930's. They are often interesting enough. But even negative responses to these questions show signs of responding in one of two ways: the "metaphysical" or the "nihilistic." The first of these comes from the effort to find a satisfactory metaphor of evil that will enable the soldier to meditate upon his wound. The second is an extension of the decision to present the war with no compromises, no cheap falsifications; it often leads to an examination of neurosis, of hysteria, and of the most ruthless kinds of brutality.

In the first of these two situations, the soldier of World War II examines his wound in a manner rather like Donne's meditations upon his love. Ben Belitt's poem, "The Casualty," one of many such meditations, is a study of the soldier's relation to his wound. The element of surprise is there—of "bad luck" and reluctantly accepted pain; but the soldier also tries to understand the wound as he receives it, ". . . out of the instinct's need / To render its terror tangible." While he "bent to the bullet a consented will," he strived as well to "force an unspeakable image from the maze." This reflection shows the soldier sensitively alert to the meaning—not merely of the war, but of the wound itself.

. . .

Infantryman falling, falling always: the fall is forever.
Fall to your certainty, no longer compelled and alone,
Yielding the gunstock to the compassionate image.

Turn from the bomb-burst by the powerless river
Forfeit in crossfire, on inadmissive ground—
Who have become that Host the nightmarch sought;
Terror's unique enigma, the time-serving will,
The shield whereon Medusa's manifest gaze
Glows like a boss and confronts its deliverer
In the bottomless pit and beast's face of the wound.[3]

The lines sum up much of the quality of World War II literature. The poet or the novelist wishes to discover the source of
the enigma, to bring it within range of understanding; he is
also aware of the "time-serving will," and above all he wants to
force an image from the situation, to find an appropriate rhetoric, so that he might tolerate it. In the years succeeding the
first war the shock of that experience had subsided; it became
an accepted prerequisite of modern feeling. The literature of
the 1920's offered many large-scaled rebellions against the
wound; it was in both its limited and its more ample sense,
"unreasonable."

In its explicit sense, the memory of violence was a part of
the motive for studying Webster and his seventeenth century
contemporaries. The paradoxes of blood and faith, and the
sharply focused image of beauty and death comprehended together, of Donne's poetry were objects of intensive scrutiny.
So too were other products of a literary past: Baudelaire's insights into evil, Dante's concrete imagery of a hell specifically
systematized according to forms and incentives of evil, the
abundant testimony (of which Yeats was the most eloquent
analyst) of a rationalized society nourishing its own destruction. Not only did the minutiae of the wound experience gain
admission to the mind; the years between the wars also saw a
lively examination of causes. It is natural that the literature of
World War II should reflect the intellectual turmoil of the
1930's. In many ways, the second war is the Spanish Civil War

[3] *Wilderness Stair*, New York, Grove, 1955, p. 61.

writ large, partly because, in W. H. Auden's words, in that war "Our fever's menacing shapes are precise and alive." [4]

Writers of this disposition tried to protect themselves against total absorption in the violence. More than the most energetic of planning generals, they maneuvered the war into corners of the whole. With the skill and competence learned from their immediate predecessors, they sketched in the pattern of the war, so that it was always there, in the background, then pinpointed "terror's unique enigma" for scrutiny's sake. From the work of the 1920's we get a sense of the total shock; even such work as A *Farewell to Arms*, while limited in its scope, gives us a sense of the generalities needed to discuss violence in scale. From the 1930's the literature of the second war took two important elements: violence seen in terms of those who blindly and dumbly participated in it (Dos Passos); and the line of semi-liberal, semi-leftist analysis which is seen throughout the decade and reaches a vivid crisis in the Spanish Civil War. The presiding image of this kind of soldier is suggested in Karl Shapiro's introduction to *V-Letter*: "We learn that war is an affection of the human spirit, without any particular reference to 'values.' In the totality of striving and suffering we come to see the great configuration abstractly, with oneself at the center reduced in size but not in meaning, like a V-letter." [5] A number of interesting ideas are suggested here, but the important one is that of the intellectual and aesthetic effort to understand, to articulate, and to come to terms with a violence, to make it a part of the soldier's conception of evil, so that he may accept it.

The influence of the Spanish Civil War upon the conduct of writers in World War II is hard to estimate, but several

[4] "Spain, 1937," in *The Collected Poetry of W. H. Auden*, New York: Random House, 1945, pp. 181–85. The quoted line is from Stanza 17, p. 184. This poem was printed in the important anthology, *Poems for Spain*, ed. Stephen Spender and John Lehmann, London, Hogarth, 1939, pp. 55–58.

[5] *V-Letter and Other Poems*, New York, Reynal and Hitchcock, 1944, p. vi.

reliable generalities are possible: it attracted the attention of many writers outside of Spain; it was a culmination of many ideological conflicts of the 1930's; it was the first occasion outside of Russia when ideologically motivated personal dedications were tested substantially by violence; in many cases, the defeat of the Loyalists meant at least a temporary deterioration of ideological confidence. Power politics, in the guise of "assistance" on either side, were generally successful in destroying that confidence. Most of all, as George Orwell proves with eminent success in *Homage to Catalonia* (1938), the specific circumstances of violence, the confusion of loyalties, and the collapse of doctrinal unities into scores of splinter groups, were responsible for severe disillusion at the end of the decade. As Hemingway's Robert Jordan says on several occasions: we must win to maintain our convictions; without victory, we cannot really persist in them.[6] The truth is that the effect of the Spanish War was to reduce the power of ideological explanation in World War II, or at least to disperse it and make it less certain.

As John Muste has said, "Spain provided an opportunity to study at first hand a violent situation in which, according to Marx and Lenin and their disciples, the forces of history were working to produce the dictatorship of the proletariat which was to be the first stage of the evolution of the workers' paradise. . . ." In consequence of their disillusion, almost invariably "once the ideology had been abandoned, political thinking was abandoned too; . . ." [7] In a sense, the defeat of the government forces was also a severe shock to political conviction in the literature of the next decade. The Spanish Civil War was a crisis of politics in literature; its violence was too overwhelming for ideological convictions to be sustained in the midst of it. Significantly, the bright stars of 1930's literature

[6] *For Whom the Bell Tolls*, New York, Scribner's, 1940.
[7] *The Spanish Civil War in the Literature of the United States and Great Britain*, unpublished Ph.D. Dissertation, University of Wisconsin, 1960, p. 365.

retired from political into moral realities in the next decade. Those who, like George Orwell, persisted in giving their work a political context generally made that context a fantasy of proletarian and democratic failures.

Above all, the failure of the loyalists in the Civil War forced writers into several kinds of meditation, which have crucially affected subsequent attempts to offer a moral and aesthetic perspective upon World War II. Two of these are of major importance. As I have already tried to show, there was a loosening of ideological lines and a growing tendency for the writer-soldier to offer his own private meditative and metaphoric illumination; this led to improvisation, but the literary quality of it was affected by critical and literary preoccupations in the two decades "de l'entre-deux-guerres." [8] The second reaction came from the shock of discovering that men, however nobly inspired or deeply committed, cannot fight machines.[9]

As Allen Guttmann has testified, this second is a pervasive feeling. Perhaps it comes in part from a too great naïveté, which permitted men of liberal and leftist good will to become angry without adequate means of directing and exploiting their anger, with the result that it turned to frustration. The following statement of Ernest Hemingway is one of hundreds which define the emotion:

> There is nothing so terrible and sinister as the track of a tank in action. The track of a tropical hurricane leaves a capricious swath of complete destruction, but the two par-

---

[8] See T. S. Eliot's *East Coker* (*Four Quartets*, 1943; *East Coker* first printed, 1940), which was written at the very end of "the years of *l'entre deux guerres*":

> . . . And so each venture
> Is a new beginning, a raid on the inarticulate
> With shabby equipment always deteriorating
> In the general mess of imprecision of feeling,
> Undisciplined squads of emotion. . . .
>   (*The Complete Poems and Plays*, p. 128)

[9] See Allen Guttmann, *The Wound in the Heart: America and the Spanish Civil War*, Glencoe, Illinois, Free Press, 1962, p. 168.

allel grooves the tank leaves in the red mud lead to scenes of planned death worse than any the hurricane leaves.[10]

Hemingway's major contribution to the Civil War literature, *For Whom the Bell Tolls,* has an abundance of testimonies to this feeling. The central situation is itself urgently typical: "Roberto" Jordan, an instructor in the Spanish language in the United States, goes from a hyper-organizational Madrid to a spot in the mountains where the Spaniards are engaged in guerrilla warfare. From the beginning, it becomes a war of men and horses against machines and airplanes. El Sordo's band uses dead horses to protect them against bullets; they are successful until the dive bombers come, after which all courage and conviction fail to keep them or their corner of the Spanish reality alive. And Anselmo is Hemingway's most affecting contribution to a gallery of men fighting the "vulgarity" of machines but proving again and again the practical futility of "strong" character without mechanical power. He says to Fernando: " 'We must teach them. We must take away their planes, their automatic weapons, their artillery and teach them dignity.' " [11]

Other examples prove Guttmann's thesis again and again. The major threat was that of violence provoked by machinery. Morally, power was symbolized as an infinite extension of the "original sin," and it led to the bemusement of the pure spirit. In the Spanish Civil War, it was a matter of the heavy weight of violence coming from the great symbol of evil itself. The trick was to develop enough power in the cause of the "right," to more than right the balance against evil. But the implications of this change were not lost upon many writers. Compulsive brutality and violence are central effects in World War II literature (they are "the Nazi in us"); and it becomes difficult to justify too simple a division of good and evil after Hiroshima.

[10] *New Republic,* 90 (May 5, 1937), p. 377. Quoted in Guttmann, p. 170. The image of the tank is not unlike that of the tractor at the beginning of John Steinbeck's *The Grapes of Wrath* (1939).
[11] *For Whom the Bell Tolls,* p. 328.

After two decades, the question of complicity becomes less easy to answer. But at the end of the 1930's there was an intrinsically evil menace in the image of the bomber; this image persisted in many visions of World War II. Here are stanzas from two poems of the late 1930's, one from an American, the other from a British poet:

> What was a civil war this year but strangers
> Overhead, guns at sea, and foreign guns
> And foreign squadrons in the plundered town?
> A Spaniard learnt that any time is time
> For German or Italian doom.
>
> (John Berryman, "1938," St. 5) [12]

. . .

> Black as vermin, crawling in echelon
> Beneath the cloud-floor, the bombers come:
> The heavy angels, carrying harm in
> Their wombs that ache to be rid of death.
>
> This is the seed that grows for ruin,
> The iron embryo conceived in fear.
> Soon or late its need must be answered
> In fear delivered and screeching fire.
>
> (C. Day Lewis, "Bombers," Sts. 4–5) [13]

The naïveté of these sentiments is a sign of their having been freshly indulged. It is the shock of suddenly realizing that innocence, good will, wholesome anger or sympathy, call it what you will, needs to be revised, subtilized, and elaborately reconstituted in order adequately to provide a rhetoric that will comprehend the raw violence.[14] This sensation, and its parallel in

[12] *Kenyon Review*, 1 (summer 1939), p. 259.
[13] *Short Is the Time: Poems 1936–1943*, New York, Oxford University Press, 1945, p. 5.
[14] A typical comment is that of Ernest Brace on William Gropper's painting, *Air Raid*: ". . . The terror of implacable, blind force, the senseless and indiscriminate destruction of human beings by other human beings too remote, too mechanically indifferent to wonder who or why." (*Magazine of Art*, Vol. 30, August 1937, pp. 467–68. Quoted in Guttmann, p. 182.)

ideological revisions, affected the literary images of the Second
World War. It was a matter of temporary withdrawal from the
slogans that had *almost* been believed in the 1930's, to see what
might be to and with them in the new circumstances.

—[ii]—

World War II raised several questions: what is it like: who
am I that I should be in it; what resources do I have for understanding it; how may I endure its terror? These questions were
at times merely stared at, with no attempt to answer them: in
which case, the artist presented the image of the soldier staring
at his wound, or in implication dying with his victims as an
agent of the assailant but also as a victim of his own subconscious complicity. He could, of course, describe without
elaborate comment the experience of the soldier in a campaign,
and leave it at that. There was an extraordinary sense in this
case of the metaphysical quality residing in violent experience;
it seemed almost as though concentration upon the specifics
of violence yields an abundance of intellectual values that too
much overt discussion of them tends to suppress. The writer
might as well present in elaborate detail a metaphoric journey
through hell and submit at its conclusion a modified psychiatric report of its effects. Writers of the second war did all of
these things, and more. The literature can quite legitimately be
described as the record of sensibilities in a condition of overwhelming violence, and of minds steadying themselves to comprehend "terror's unique enigma."

A passage from John Hersey's novel *The War Lover* (1959)
will serve as well as any to introduce the first of our types, what
I have called the "liberal ideological" novel, in which the questions of responsibility, guilt both active and passive, and moral
definition are raised, though they are seldom satisfactorily answered. "There's too much idiocy at large," says the narrator,
"about how we were disenchanted young men who'd been wised

up by *A Farewell to Arms* and *Soldiers' Pay* and *Three Soldiers*." This reflection refers to a quarrel with the writers of the 1920's who had, according to persons like Van Wyck Brooks, Archibald MacLeish, and Bernard DeVoto, developed and encouraged an *irresponsibility* through being preciously occupied with "the word" in isolation. Since this criticism does penetrate a type of war literature, it is worth raising it momentarily from the oblivion to which it has gratifyingly been consigned. Boman continues:

> We were up to our tallywhackers in illusions, slogans, shibboleths, belief in magic—mostly out of ads. We were ready to die to the last man for Dinah Shore, rare sirloin, a cold beer, and a Caribbean cruise. Maybe we didn't put much stock in the Four Freedoms; that was propaganda. But we really believed in *Time* and the *Post* and *Collier's* and *Life*. . . .[15]

Typically, this statement descends to the unwittingly facetious. The important point to remember about this first kind of war novel is that the intellectual and ideological matter is drawn from the position of the 1930's, mostly liberal in the tradition of American liberal optimism and courage, part-way leftist, and only occasionally Marxist. The point is that the effort to take hold of the war in this way is not conspicuously successful. It was one thing for Irwin Shaw (in his plays, *The Gentle People*, 1939, and *Bury the Dead*, 1936) to scold entrepreneurs of evil and oppression; quite another, for the same "warm, neatly just" position to assume the task of giving World War II a proper and thorough moral perspective.

This is not to say that writers did not try; several of them did, and produced what Joseph Waldmeir at least called the war literature most likely to endure.[16] Mr. Waldmeir's prophecy is

[15] *The War Lover*, New York, Knopf, 1959, p. 225.
[16] "Novelists of Two Wars," *Nation*, 187 (November 1, 1938), pp. 304–307.

of dubious value, but the novels emerging directly from this situation were certainly the most widely read, the most immediately successful. Irwin Shaw's *The Young Lions* (1948), for example, comes directly from the 1930's, where Shaw received his education in the educational proprieties. It is by all odds the most obviously emphatic "liberal" perspective upon the war. The several characteristics of this position are quickly seen and judged here.

Two of these stand out from all of the others: the "crusading spirit," that is, that this is a "must war" against a clearly seen, an obvious enemy; the fear of an indwelling nazism, a self-analytic devil search, in which questions of guilt, complicity, irresponsible sins of neglect and omission, were all examined. For reasons which perhaps do not need explaining, the intellectual (Harvard, "Copey's" classes, little magazines, a novel halfway written when the call to duty sounded, etc.) often assumed the role of auxiliary scapegoat; or part of the plot had to do with his dropping his "phony stance" and learning from blessed simplicity.[17] The Shaw novel focuses upon three character types: the American Jew, Noah Ackerman, who is going

[17] Cf. Allen Tate's poem, "Ode to Our Young Pro-Consuls of the Air," which treats of the liberal introspection with a fine mocking irony. After speaking of Pearl Harbor, "When the Jap beetle hit!" Tate goes on, to present our "brave response":

> It was defeat, or near it!
> Yet all that feeble time
>   Brave Brooks and little MacLeish
>   Had sworn to thresh
> Our flagging spirit
> With literature made Prime!
>
> Cow Creek and bright Bear Wallow,
> Nursing the blague that dulls
>   Spirits grown Eliotic,
>   Now patriotic
> Are: we follow
> *The Irresponsibles!*
>
>> (St's 12–13; in *Poems, 1922–1947*, New York, Scribner's, 1948, pp. 98–99. Reprinted in *Poems*, Tate's latest collection. The last line of stanza 13 refers to a notorious essay by Archibald MacLeish.)

into the war to fight both the Nazi evil and its native American examples; Michael Whitacre, the intellectual who must come a long way before the "meaning" of the war (one assumes that this is its enduring value) will finally be assimilated; and the German Nazi, Christian Diestl, the finest product of Nazi demonology.

In an early passage, Michael Whitacre, in Hollywood when the Japanese strike at Pearl Harbor, thinks of the people he has seen on the day of the attack:

> Are these the people, created in greatness by the work of Jefferson and Franklin, he thought, are these the bitter farmers and craftsmen who came out of the wilderness, furious for liberty and justice, is this the new world of giants sung by Whitman? [18]

Whitacre has a long way to go—the full way of the war itself —before he properly "understands." The culminating scene must inevitably be sheer melodrama, in which the extremes of the three characters are played out as they are bound to be. *This* is what we've fought for, says Noah Ackerman ecstatically: "'The human beings are going to be running the world!'" (680) His moment of exaltation proves to be his last; for Christian Diestl happens along, and his Nazi weapon dispatches Noah. Whereupon, Whitacre, now fully matured, avenges Noah, and carries the sacrificial victim to the camp and deposits him before the feet of the liberal Captain Green:

> . . . Then he picked Noah up, and, carrying him over his shoulder, walked through the growing dusk, without stopping once, back to the camp. And he refused to allow any of the other men in the Company to help him carry the body, because he knew he had to deliver Noah Ackerman, personally, to Captain Green. (689)

[18] *The Young Lions*, New York, Random House, 1948, p. 187. Other references to this edition may be found in the text.

236

This is perhaps an extreme example of the ideological melodrama; at any rate, it is scarcely ever equalled in forced pathos, melodrama, and the direct imposing of conviction upon art. The novel does have characteristic traits: the intellectual who must mature, the external menace or bogey, the signs of inner corruption that resembles the enemy.

One of many types of hero is the intellectual whose peacetime talents are tested against the nervous demands of combat. Anton Myrer's intellectual speaks of "rot and rhetoric." [19] War fiction is rather liberally inhabited by heroes (very much like their authors) who undergo successive humiliations. Reality is barely literate, if at all, and it is very easily upset by cultural displays of artifice. "God, what a speech," Myrer's Newcombe reflects. "Couldn't he say anything—anything at all—without wallowing in a hash of maudlin rhetoric six feet deep" (172). The journey to humility is described in *The Big War*, in Norman Mailer's *The Naked and the Dead*, in Herman Wouk's *Caine Mutiny* (1951), in Irwin Shaw's *The Young Lions*. It is not a pretty sight, and it scarcely helps to raise the level of the art.

Lieutenant Robert Hearn of *The Naked and the Dead* is the best of these suffering minds. His kind of vacillating intellectual good will is opposed on one side by the hard-bitten man of tactics, General Cummings, on the other by a brutal man of force, the professional sergeant Croft. In an effort to note the irony of these clashes of will and intellect, Mailer has Lieutenant Hearn put in charge of a reconnaissance party in the rear of the Japanese lines. Croft and Hearn work in bitter hostility, and in the outcome neither succeeds in impressing his character upon the G.I. Hearn is almost instinctively suspected and mistrusted; his view is both too complex and too naively simple. Croft is preferred because he gives the soldiers an ele-

[19] Anton Myrer, *The Big War*, New York, Appleton, Century, Crofts, 1957. Other references to this edition are in the text.

mental sense of certainty. "Croft they would obey, for Croft satisfied their desire for hatred, encouraged it, was superior to it, and in turn exacted obedience." [20] But he too fails, not from the intensity but from the limitations of his view of man.

The deficiency of Hearn's kind of portrait is that the intellectual substance is too much made up of tags and titles. Culture serves mainly to confuse and to paralyze the will to action. Hearn is interested in Eliot, Rilke, Mann; he had written an honor's thesis on *The Cosmic Urge in Herman Melville*, and was otherwise intellectually occupied in the years before the war. He is not a genuine intellectual, but suffers rather from an anthology neurosis. Yet portraits of this kind are a sign of one important preoccupation in World War II fiction. Especially in its American variant, this hero earnestly attempts to assume responsibility for interpreting the war to the reader. Unfortunately, he is also in some degree its scapegoat; of all war heroes he is liable to be furthest removed from bone-chilling and skull-crushing reality.

The most flagrant example of this superficiality is in Myrer's *The Big War*. Here the contrast between Newcombe and Danny Kantaylis is eventually eliminated, not only by their deaths but even before, in Danny's steady, almost saintly, forbearance and Newcombe's willingness to come more than halfway. In fact, his education is a specious one at best, and in any event his books "understood nothing of him or his estrangement" (48). Not Newcombe's but Myrer's rhetoric is a residue of the self-conscious, romantic, flagellant irony of the modern

[20] *The Naked and the Dead*, New York, Rinehart, 1948, p. 506. Croft is one of those symbols in modern literature of almost pure sadistic force; a study of them might do much to help in answering the question of Satan's disappearance from modern man's thinking. A Croft in a modern novel serves the role of a Svidrigaylov in Dostoevsky; he is the firm line of evil that is lacking in the vacillating and uncertain hero. To do Mailer credit, his war novel is several notches above its companions. There is a stubborn realistic honesty about it, and the war is rarely if ever simply used as backdrop of drama or contention.

intellectual, the *mélange adultère du tout*, the rootless, feckless, witless organ of erudite echoes, from "Empty cisterns and exhausted wells" (139). He is a stranger in a strange land, stranger than most, and a victim not so much of his unsteadiness but of a psychotic tic of articulation.

In the battle scenes of *The Big War*, often brilliantly given, Newcombe overwhelms the sensibility in inundations of "meaning." Every suggestion from books, classroom, study, and workshop floods through the open gates. During saturation bombing, "you have been depersonalized . . . atomized in the immeasurable merciless length and breadth of this void which is your destruction" (234). The war had changed them, "by some force as swift and malevolent as Circe's wand: a race of numbed, exhausted beasts in holes, wolfing mechanically the tasteless contents of green metal tins" (305). The view of death is similarly disposed to rely upon literary tags:

> Ah, but death was everywhere, hovered silently around them. Sacrifice and violence in one fierce embrace. Dulce et decorum. Happy those, who with a glowing faith . . . Jesus. Wretched, wretched. It was not sweet to die. . . . To come to this—a maggot-ridden substance consigned to putrefaction, breeding pestilence in season, out of season . . . (309)

Throughout, he is contrasted with the blessedly simple Danny Kantaylis, a creature of great courage and charm, against whom Newcombe must ultimately measure himself. The result is a purging of his talent and the assumption of a "new humility."

The virtue of this seems to be cathartic; it is a way of ridding the soul of irrelevancies. Newcombe appears at times to be a modified Falstaff, comically fending off danger with words. But the logorrhea is throughout considered at worst an interesting disease, and he dies with a poem (this time his) but recently on his lips:

Know, stranger, all that you confront is strange—
and your own image. (456)

Even in its exaggeration of effects, *The Big War* is an interesting specimen of the almost strenuous effort of the war intellectual to purge his imagination of elements unsuitable to the
stringencies of violence. Throughout, he is contrasted with the
blessedly simple Danny Kantaylis, a creature of great courage
and charm, against whom Newcombe must ultimately measure
himself. The result is a purging of his talent and the assumption
of a "new humility." But the novel fails because of its deadly
earnestness, the sentimental rebellion against egg-head sophistications, the implicit celebration of home and hearthside. The
terror of the war is imperfectly sensed, as though Myer had
wanted to preach about its morally reductive effects.

The men of this war are extraordinarily conscious, even of
what they cannot tolerate intellectually or absolve morally.
When they say the war is absurd, they are by several degrees
superior in sensitivity to Dos Passos' Martin Howe. The worst
effects of this hyper-consciousness are seen in Vance Bour-
jailly's *The End of My Life* (1947), which is not so much a
war novel as it is a series of discussions, Gide cum Fitzgerald,
of the intellectual confusions leading into and persisting
through the war. It is an interesting game of contretemps and
divagation, formalized at one point as the world's champion-
ship intellectual football game, with Heywood Broun as defensive end, Lincoln a good steady halfback and Lenin calling
signals.

Myer's Danny Kantaylis is the sublime example of the un-
tainted primitive, who is all courage and skill, and hates no
man; he is a scarcely mysterious twentieth century avatar of
Cooper's Natty Bumppo.[21] Another type is the ultimate ex-

---

[21] Almost every one of these novels has its "primitive hero": John Horne
Burnes's Max Shulman, for example (*The Gallery*, New York, Harper's,

pression of personal evil. This person is not necessarily American, but American habits of life seem to have encouraged him in his villainy. The Raditzer of Peter Matthiessen's novel is an especially strong example. Always "grifting," seeking out his own advantage, "sharp-eyed and quick-fingered, a sort of human magpie," [22] the novel culminates in a tortured dream. The quiet, long-suffering hero, Charlie Stark, dreams of Raditzer's being pursued by a mob of the victims at Hiroshima:

> . . . a grey skeletal landscape where a hellish mob, tattered and charred, pursued a screeching Raditzer across the smoking ruins. He himself was running with the mob, striving to dissuade them, but he did not run fast enough, and Raditzer was stoned to death and lay there dying. He stood over Raditzer, shouting, He's no guiltier than yourselves. You're all guilty. . . . (136)

Rarely are the moral differences resolved, as they so melodramatically are in *The Young Lions*. Stefan Heym's *The Crusaders* (1948) takes its men the full way before the "good" triumphs. The book is charged by a driving necessity to raise and to answer the question: what are we fighting for. There is something curiously dated about this novel; it seems to have cut a swath through the 1920's, 1930's, and up to the very latest of Churchill's speeches. In this vision of them, the war years are truly "valiant years." The distinguishing feature of *The Crusaders* is not that the fight against evil, both native and foreign born, is brought to a triumphant conclusion, but that at each step of the way a Christ-like scapegoat seems ready to offer himself so that the victory can be achieved. The key

1947), who dies smiling at his enemy: "Himself was ebbing away from himself with a powerful melancholy, with no hope of recall.
. . . So Moe smiled back at the German, and he felt his face dropping toward the floor." (p. 341)
[22] *Raditzer*, New York, Viking, 1961, p. 40. Other references to this edition are in the text.

symbol is the Christ figure (rescued from World War I symbolism) in the graveyard at Isigny:

> The car slowed down, and through a large, jagged gap Yates caught a glimpse of the Christ. He saw the crudely carved ribs and the pain-torn, almost square mouth. The Christ had lost his feet and his right hand and was hanging by his left.[23]

Heym's novel follows the pattern of the others, this time through the entire scope of the war following upon the landings in Normandy. Its American villain is Dondolo, an Italian-American, who thrives on black market sales of army supplies, and brutally beats up anyone who accidentally or courageously gets in his way. He is aided and abetted by the easeful yielding to temptation on the part of his fellow soldiers. The novel is shot through with ironies: that is to say, the good often die, by accident or intent, and the villains thrive. Until, that is, the novel's conclusion. After many misadventures, and the traumatic experience of releasing concentration camp prisoners, a measure of moral order is restored, and it is to be assumed that it will be maintained. The final text is spoken by Yates, one of a few apostles of the Isigny Christ:

> ". . . We have an obligation. When we pull out of here, finally, we want to leave behind a country minus the bastards who forced this war, their power smashed. . . ." (585)

This is a form of functional ideology, a practical measuring of the good against the evil, sustained—despite the trauma of the concentration camp—by the steady conviction that the war, destructive as it is, has a "purpose" and will somehow end "progressively." No such conviction supports Herman Wouk's *The Caine Mutiny* (1951), though all of the other liberal principles are there, in diluted form. Mostly, *The Caine Mutiny*

[23] *The Crusaders*, Boston, Little, Brown, 1948, p. 19. Other references to this edition are in the text.

is concerned with a war as a force contributing to the soldier's maturity: as though, somehow, despite (or because of) the violence and the irrationality, character is inevitably "grafted on" to personality. There is much said about the imperfect (or even "phony") intellectual, who will either be shown up for what he is by the war or will drop his stupid, false sophistication, as having no practical value.

Captain Queeg is somehow vindicated in the end; and even directly after he has lost his case because of the skillful tactics of the Jewish lawyer, Barney Greenwald, his major enemy is mocked and ridiculed by the same attorney. The Germans are killing off the Jews, he says to Tom Keefer, the pseudo-intellectual, part-time novelist, and enemy of the military. They are melting his relatives into soap. And however warped and ludicrous Queeg may be, he is protecting the Jews. In an agony of self-retribution and scorn, Greenwald ends his speech with these words:

> ". . . I defended Steve [Maryk] because I found out the wrong guy was on trial. Only way I could defend him was to sink Queeg for you. I'm sore that I was pushed into that spot, and ashamed of what I did . . . Queeg deserved better at my hands. I owed him a favor, don't you see? He stopped Hermann Goering from washing his fat behind with my mother." [24]

The novel's conclusion is a mixture of patent ironies and *schmaltz*. Keefer, the new captain, does indeed prove himself a coward, a "Lord Jim" as he sadly admits, at the first occasion of violence and danger. Willie Kieth survives the Kamikaze attack (it is the only real case of violent death in the career of the *Caine*) and is ennobled by it; whereupon he determines that he is a changed man and will fill the roles of mature sailor and civilian both. For death (or the sight of it) does to Willie

[24] *The Caine Mutiny*, Garden City, New York, Doubleday, 1951, p. 443.

Kieth what it had done to all his predecessors in a hundred historical novels: it matures him without greying his hair or otherwise touching his charming personality.

—[iii]—

The approaches to violent death are scarcely satisfactorily
portrayed in these novels. For the most part, the essential issues are evaded, or they dissolve in ideological sentimentalities.
The phenomena of intellectual self-consciousness are seen to
immeasurably better advantage in the poetry of the war. Here
the heritage is restrained; sentiments, which in narrative dialogue suffered from the effort to establish legality of cultural
heritage, are curbed by the formal necessities of the verse.
Herbert Read's *A World Within a War* (particularly in the
"Ode" which begins it) considers the war in the light of its
predecessor; rather somberly bitter over the total failure of the
first war to give its participants any light, Read speaks of the
years intervening as showing

> Belief without action
> action without thought
> the blind intervention
> of years without design

He concludes on a sad note, simply given, concerning the illusion now in danger of collapse:

> But we who have put our faith
> in the goodness of man
> and now see man's image debased
> lower than the wolf or the hog— [25]

[25] *A World Within a War*, London, Faber and Faber, 1944, pp. 14, 17.
The final line of Read's poem is "Where can we turn for consolation?"
Since the poem was written after the withdrawal from Dunkirk in 1940,
we may assume that Read's critical activity since then has provided a
partial answer. Of the many volumes, *The Forms of Things Unknown*
(New York, Horizon, 1960) especially suggests a bitter-end struggle of a

Richard Eberhart several times fought the poet's fight to restore meaning to the soldier's. In the spirit of Stevens' "war between the mind and sky," Eberhart spoke, in "War and Poetry," of the war as a "rot of imagery," and went on to suggest the uses of poetry in preserving man from it:

> No eclectic dialect, no feverish impishness
> Should wrest from flesh nor take from us
> The powerful bent; no histrionic extravagance
> Conceal the central impetus.
> All should be calm, massive, and perpend
> The welfare of the inner ecstasy,
> Inviolable voice of universal form.[26]

His best contribution to this reasoning is "Aesthetics After War" (*Undercliff*, 56–62); here the ambiguities of modern violence are examined with an excellent circumspection. Taking the extreme form of the malaise and examining it dispassionately, Eberhart asks a basic question of form: was Hiroshima a superb spectacle or a horrifying calamity?

> Our men testify to awe
> If not to aesthetic charm,
> On seeing man's total malice over Hiroshima,
> That gigantic, surrealistic, picture-mushroom
> And objectification of megalomania. (57)

.   .   .

The extra-human perspective involves one again in the central question of assailant and victim. Physical visibility is limited and would argue an obligation to the victim; instruments, on

---

Jungian archetypal aesthetic conscience against science and its logical positivist cousins. Far from urging, along the lines of C. P. Snow's Book-of-the-Month-Club sermonizing, that humanists learn the laws of thermodynamics, Read offers an eleventh-hour *j'accuse*, scolding scientists and philosophic methodologists for ignoring human values, and suggesting that the artists take over before it is too late.

[26] *Undercliff*, London, Chatto and Windus, 1953, p. 65. Other references to this edition are in the text.

the other hand, immensely extend the distance beyond visibility and suggest a very limited engagement on the part of the soldier:

> So that as semi-automaton all the young gunner
> Has to do is to frame the enemy plane
> In this brilliant circle of light and blaze away. (58)

The difficulty involves one in an examination of the pathos of the assailant. He is now in only a very limited way an arbiter of his own actions; he is a trained servant of precision, and the precision is mathematical, scientific, a hair-line sighting for accuracy.

. . .

> The mystery is whether the object
> Mystifies man,
> Or whether the mysteriousness within man
> Transubstantiates the object;
> Whether the world is finally mysterious,
> Or if the Deity has put a mystery in man. (59)

In every respect, the issue of assailant and victim is most sharply put in the analysis of the airman. There is the double hazard, of narrow specialized training in the use of instruments and of extraordinary distances, steadily increasing, between the agent of violence and his victims. John Horne Burns speaks of the American airmen in Naples, alone, afraid, ill at ease, too young to understand where they are or what they have done to get there.[27] Throughout the poetry, there is a strong, even an obsessive, awareness of this irony. Randall Jarrell speaks (in "Losses") of cities known only from geography textbooks and seen in no greater intimacy of acquaintance from the air. The pathos of the victim mingles with that of the assailant; these bright, fresh, clean, and wholly inadequate personalities act

[27] *The Gallery*, pp. 42, 75.

not from passion but from inhibiting knowledge. Even when the tables of war are turned upon them, the result is annihilation rather than revenge, and the pathos caused by the aviator's ignorance is sustained.

From my mother's sleep I fell into the State,
And I hunched in its belly till my wet fur froze.
Six miles from earth, loosed from its dream of life,
I woke to black flak and the nightmare fighters.
When I died they washed me out of the turret with a hose.[28]

There is no more pathetic image of immaturity than this of the womb, of the mother and the state; man has never escaped, but remains protected and contained, from birth to the moment of annihilation. The distance from air to earth is in itself a sponsor of impersonality; it keeps man far from the rhythms of life and forces him to see the world of objects in reduced perspective. In contrast to the infantryman, who moves slowly along the earth, hugging it and testing its concavities for refuge, the airman gains his safety and protects his power in remote ranges of distance.

> Lethal commuter, he stayed unconcerned.
> His element was air. The landscape was
> Purely impersonal, full of toys and patches,
>   A quilt in which a man might burn a hole.[29]

The situation has its own attendant agonies. The fear of causing pain is itself painful. There is the additional anomaly, that pain can be caused without one's seeing it done, or at best seeing only the smoke of souls rising from the earth's substance in protest. So it is best to avoid scrutinizing the art, if one is to survive the agony:

[28] Jarrell, "The Death of the Ball Turret Gunner," in *Little Friend, Little Friend*, p. 58.
[29] Harry Brown, "Sortie," in *Poems*, London, Secker and Warburg, 1945, p. 26.

Hoist up the bombs carefully into the belly
Of this great monster and do not look too closely
At the work of your hands as you thread the fuse, performing
The set procedure, till the thing is ripe for killing.
Was there not a time when you turned aside to avoid
Crushing a beetle or marring a spider's web?
Well, man grows wiser and older—wickeder also.[30]

Perhaps the most complex analysis of those matters is Wallace Stevens' *Esthétique du Mal*. Written in the late stages of World War II and first published in 1944, this poem comes full force at the problem of evil in a modern setting. Its focus is upon the soldier who tries to understand evil in terms of the aesthetic tradition. But "Pain is human," and in this sense hard for us to accept, a "part of the sublime / From which we shrink. . . ."[31] This absolutely *human* quality of pain, its intimately personal reference, alerts us against it and makes us want to rule it out of our experience. An "over-human god," who makes himself man and relieves us of the burden of suffering, weakens our resolve to bear it and in moments of extreme violence leaves us with no power of adjustment.

Stevens proposes that we restore evil to our aesthetic and moral vision, since efforts to eliminate it have impoverished us.

> The death of Satan was a tragedy
> For the imagination. A capital
> Negation destroyed him in his tenement
> And, with him, many blue phenomena. (319)
>
> . . .

---

[30] Hyam Plutzik, "Bomber Base," in *Aspects of Proteus*, New York, Harper and Row, Publishers, Incorporated, 1949, p. 37. For other poems which speak in much the same way, see Charles E. Butler, *Cut Is the Branch*, p. 60; Eberhart, *Selected Poems*, 1951, pp. 73, 75; John Nerber, *The Spectre Image*, p. 23; Jon Beck Shank, *Poems*, 1945, p. 43; Arnold Stein, *Perilous Balance*, p. 7; and several others in Jarrell's *Little Friend, Little Friend* and *Losses*.

[31] *Collected Poems*, New York, Knopf, 1955, p. 314. Other references to this edition are in the text.

The major necessity is for the metaphor, for the "abstraction blooded" as he puts it in *Notes Toward a Supreme Fiction*. The images of reality (of things as they are, life as it is) unite in the "shaping form," and to remove the imagery of evil from them risks impoverishing the mind; it is impossible to ignore pain, violence, and mortality,

> As if hell, so modified, had disappeared,
> As if pain, no longer satanic mimicry,
> Could be borne, as if we were sure to find our way. (316)

Stevens speaks of the "logical lunatic" who tries to see all life in terms of one narrow segment of it. The "grandeurs of the mind" are often more impressive than either comforting or accurate. The logical lunacy would include both ideological and scientific restrictions of the substance of life. The mechanical extensions of power are also extensions of evil, and, further, take both beyond the limits of human control. The abstracting mind combines with a reckless emotional commitment to the consequences of his reasoning:

. . .

> He would be the lunatic of one idea
> In a world of ideas, who would have all the people
> Live, work, suffer and die in that idea
> In a world of ideas. He would not be aware of the clouds,
> Lighting the martyrs of logic with white fire.
> His extreme of logic would be illogical. (325)

The ultimate resolution for Stevens is to have death, as all human phenomena, a creation of the human imagination. This is the intention of *Esthétique du Mal*: to point up that the imagination can solve the puzzle of violent death by incorporating it into the world of the "essential poem," which is "at the centre of things." [32] That is, the imagination colors the images

[32] "A Primitive Like an Orb," in *Collected Poems*, p. 440.

of death, thus disposes man to them; so that death joins other human experiences at the level of the new reality, the "abstraction blooded." But there is scarcely a suggestion here of permanence, or of an enduring surrogate of immortality. The "mythology of modern death," as he calls it in "The Owl in the Sarcophagus," [33] spells a decisive end to imaginings. The "monsters of elegy" are "death's own supremest images," "Compounded and compounded, life by life" (436). In the sense that the mind and the imagination create the forms, including the ultimate form, which is death, death is willed and shaped as a human idea and form. The responsibility lies with man.

—[iv]—

The responsibility lies with man, for "Pain is human," and it is necessary to make sure of "the most correct catastrophe" (314). So too, the guilt, the aligning and the measurement of moral censure, the "agenbite of inwit," are a primary issue in modern war literature. It was, in most cases, too late to cry bitterly over fate, over Hemingway's "They," [34] or to indulge in the "romantic, naturalistic" poses of the 1920's. In a second major group of war novels, the situation is represented in stark, unrelieved simplicity. The naturalistic often eventually merged with the nihilistic, with whatever variants of neurosis, psychosis, and hysteria the second position encourages. This type of literature emerges from the 1920's style (but often without its immature ironies), from the 1930's repertorial pose (Dos Passos' sense of the self mixed in a social and political bog), and from the general skepticism concerning the absolute virtue of liberal objectives.

At one extreme, we have a number of fictions which report

[33] In *Collected Poems*, p. 435.
[34] "That was what you did. You died. You did not know what it was about. You never had time to learn. They threw you in and told you the rules and the first time they caught you off base they killed you. . . ." *A Farewell to Arms*, p. 350.

the war with a remarkable economy, free of all ideological pressures, but concentrating upon the facts of it, for what they are worth. These reports are almost too barren, but they are nevertheless rich in suggestion. Their intent is best expressed in a momentary pause in the best of them, Harry Brown's A *Walk in the Sun*. The war is a dull business, he says, "the dullest business on earth."

> War is a period of waiting. Each day of it is crammed with the little hesitations of men uncertain of themselves and awed by the ghastly responsibilities—responsibilities of life and death, the responsibilities of gods—that have been thrust into their hands. The soldier waits for food, for clothing, for a letter, for a battle to begin. And often the food never is served, the clothing is never issued, the letter never arrives, and the battle never begins. The soldier learns to wait meekly, hoping that something will happen. And when the period of waiting is at an end the something that does happen isn't what he expected. So in the end he learns to wait and expect nothing. That is patience, God's one great gift to the soldier.[35]

This unpretentious bulletin-summary of the soldier's life supports an equally muted account of the death of a handful of soldiers on a very unimportant mission in the Italian campaign. That they should conduct themselves humanly though bravely, that they should suffer corpses in so routine a way as to appear indifferent to them, does not minimize the situation but rather offers it in depth. There are almost no such portraits in the literature of World War I, most of which forced the issue of shock and horror.[36] Very much like Brown's novel, Lawrence Kahn's *Able One Four* is indisposed to digress but stays narrowly within factual boundaries. The occasion is the progress

[35] New York, Knopf, 1945, p. 34.
[36] The best parallels are in a few of the "chapters," or chapter headings of Hemingway's *In Our Time* (1925), and in Book Three of *A Farewell to Arms*.

of an armored detachment through Germany near the end of the war. As the group proceeds the tension increases, and each incident adds to the prospect of its getting out of hand.

> They had been working just ahead of the gun and one of them must have gotten a direct hit for he was pretty well scattered over an area about ten yards in diameter. The other one was on the ground moaning and holding his guts as they went past him. Spec looked at the dead man disinterestedly, but avoided looking at the wounded. There was nothing they could do, and there were medics behind. Rick stuck his head up to see what this looked like, but he took in the two casualties in one quick glance and pulled back into the turret white as a sheet. Spec hoped he wouldn't be sick all over the place.[37]

Reading this novel after those of Myrer and Shaw, one has the sense of a camera moving widely over the landscape, then coming in to see "what it is all about," in human rather than in almost too aberrantly "meaningful" terms. Peter Bowman's *Beach Red* is also a limited excursion into the intimate details of the war agony. It is more inclined toward a quizzical search for "essences," and it is conceived in the rough line of verse-narrative, but Bowman tries to give a close-up view of the matter at hand. Like *The Naked and the Dead*, this is an account of an island-hopping incident, but there is very little attempt to force the affair into either narrative or intellectual perspectives. On this "barren square foot of a condemned property island," [38] the soldier watches his surroundings narrowly. At the sight of carnage,

You feel ill and fevered and reality has become hallucination, and hallucination is the only thing that has become real. (14)

---

[37] Denver, Alan Swallow, 1952, pp. 50–51.
[38] New York, Random House, 1945, p. 11. Other references to this edition are in the text.

Death is sharply apprehended, and "the simple ease" of civilian death contrasts forcefully with "The agony of living under the strain of battle" (16). The minutiae of violence are given in images that are at times precise, at other times off-center: the tanks, "waddling like slaphappy wrestlers" (19); the flame-throwers, which "inscribe their invitations to hell on ignited sheets" (20). The meaning is contained not in elaborate meditations upon cause but in the intense scrutiny of psychological conditions:

You wonder if there is such a thing as a
physical desire for death, and whether it is just as
strong as the will to live. Isn't there an urge,
a force, a basic compulsion to lead organic matter back
into the inorganic state, and by so doing re-establish a
pattern that was abnormally disturbed by the emergence of life?
(97)

The importance of this kind of writing is that the horror contains its own implication of metapsychological valuation. Contrasting with it, such a novel as Irwin Shaw's *The Young Lions* teases its subject into stammering a message and is never satisfied to allow the scene to speak innately for itself. The overwhelming compulsion of Shaw's class of writer is to invest everything with a shadowy *weltanschauung*, and in consequence his characters perform the double duty of soldiers and commentators. There is more to say about war than that it is hell, but the hell can be seen in terms of its extension of meaning better in the depth and intensity of the experience than in homiletics posted in the middle of war scenes. Colin McDougall's *Execution* follows most of the way taken by Kahn, Brown, and Bowman, but shortly inverts its purpose. A minor vignette of the war (soldiers, sniping from a tower in Italy, conjugate the Latin *amo, amas, amat*) proves, in the confusion of war scenes to have been the one the author wished as the clue to meaning: "He knew man because he *was* man. Today he felt himself to exist at the central suffering core of all humanity.

He was filled with a huge compassion and love and under-standing for every man who had ever lived." [39]

—[v]—

Speaking of the changes in the history of the slaughtering of animals, Siegfried Giedion says that

> What is truly startling in this mass transition from life to death is the complete neutrality of the act. One does not experience, one does not feel; one merely observes. It may be that nerves that we do not control rebel somewhere in the subconscious . . .[40]

We may be reminded of Lieutenant Henry's remark in A Fare-well to Arms, that "the sacrifices were like the stockyards at Chicago if nothing was done with the meat except to bury it." [41] The full impact of the horror of such butchering, as well as an exhaustive exploration of its psychiatric transference to the mind and nerves of man, is found in two novels which supple-ment each other, William Hoffman's The Trumpet Unblown and Glenn Sire's The Deathmakers.[42] Hoffman's selection of the Medical Corps as the war setting brings his hero within direct range of the obscene parallel Giedion indirectly intends. His hero is Shelby of Virginia, a boy trained in the best of the social niceties and manners. He is introduced, at the corps' field station in England, to a group not so much hardened as inflamed by past experience in Italy. In every conceivable way, the men have been brutalized or nervously exacerbated by the daily routine of cutting, hacking, and attending to corporeal

[39] Execution, New York, St. Martin's Press, 1958, pp. 226–27.
[40] Mechanization Takes Command, New York, Oxford University Press, 1948, p. 246.
[41] A Farewell to Arms, p. 191.
[42] See also Pierre Gascar's "The House of Blood," in Beasts and Men (tr. Jean Stewart, Boston, Little, Brown, 1956, pp. 29–56), in which the analogy of butchering and mass killing is developed along quite different but fully as effective lines.

rubbish. The novel's chief representative of force is the corps bully, Blizzard, whose sadism, which plays brutally with the lives of his colleagues, is as close as a psychological state can get to the mentality of a concentration camp official.

After D-day the group goes about its grim business. The ambulances arrive, "disgorging their bloody loads on the ground." Metal drums are put up against the operating tables, "to receive the lopped-off arms and legs. The drums were always overflowing." [43] Shelby lives daily with the most flagrant violations of the decorum he has been accustomed to in his past. He is gradually able to live with death; it no longer upsets him as it initially had, but exposure to carnage corrupts and flays the spirit, as Hemingway's Rinaldi had discovered.

> It became so bad that not even by working himself until he was ready to drop could he escape the mounting compression. Torn bodies and death were crushing him flat, and their force left no tolerance for anything else. Everything was squeezed out but the jagged stumps hanging over the edges of litters and bleeding into the ground, the men who were violent blue from lack of oxygen, and the surgical barrels out of which tumbled arms, legs, and odd bits of intensely colored viscera. (132)

To say that "It was a world with the heroism extracted" (133) is surely inadequate. The world of *The Trumpet Unblown* is an intermediary between those of the battlefield and the concentration camp. While the motive is saving rather than exterminating human lives, the distinction is only infrequently honored in the terrifying confusion of the scene. The shock of transition from Virginia's felicities (everything "back there" suggests an off-white decorum) to the corporeal vulgarities of this scene quite literally destroys Shelby's capacity for judging the body as "The house of the soul."

[43] *The Trumpet Unblown*, New York, Doubleday, 1955, p. 117. Other references to this edition are in the text.

The chaplain lighted a cigarette.

"Shelby, God doesn't make war."

"Then we all ought to be damned for this."

"Without the grace of God we are damned."

"I'll put it another way. Have you been in the morgue recently?"

"No."

"Go take a look and tell me all that meat in there doesn't make any difference."

"With God all things are possible."

"You're wrong. Those things are dead, finally, forever, and absolutely dead." (136) [44]

As they push into Germany, it is their duty also to care for the concentration camp prisoners. There is little distinction between assailant and victor in this case; the human substance released from the camps is too weak to sustain itself on a freedom won too late. "Some of the Italians had stumps for legs and arms, and none had teeth or hair. They were covered with sores and like inferior vermin. They cried with joy but did not live long. They had not eaten for so long that their systems could no longer handle food" (190). For the Medical Corps, moral distinctions are no longer possible. Their power to discriminate has literally been drained from them.

The novel moves further and further into this moral hinterland. In one village along the way, they come upon a barn full of the corpses of concentration camp victims, stacked row upon row. ". . . the Slavs had been made to lie down in layers on the barn floor until they were stacked high as the windows. Then the flame throwers, the upheaval in screams, and a living sea of heaving, crackling flesh" (198). The corps settles down in the middle of Germany, waiting for the word to disband. But the word does not come; Shelby abandons first his sense of

[44] Contrast the harshness of this passage with the implicit tenderness of the priest's conversation with Lieutenant Henry at the field hospital (A Farewell to Arms, pp. 73–78)

duty, then his desire for innocence, finally his capacity to judge in terms of anything beyond the horrors of the slaughter house.

In the end he returns to Virginia, but he can do nothing to restore his prewar moral vision. He has to give up everything because to him the human personality has deteriorated to the vulgarity of torso and stump and inner organs. Suppose he were to say to his parents: "When I look at you and everyone I see your intestines and smell the way you would stink with gangrene and can never forget how pitiful you and I really are or how easily we can be broken into nothing" (299).

The perspective of this novel is deliberately and frighteningly foreshortened. Nowhere in the literature of the second war is the line of vantage so thoroughly destroyed. The assailant is no longer assailant, the victim no longer victim. The incentives to reasonable, decorous forbearance and tolerance disappear. The horror consumes its victim. The novel pushes against the reader's tolerance of fact repeatedly and exhaustingly.

The Trumpet Unblown almost goes the entire distance toward assimilation by horror. There are no protective devices, except to imitate the horror in personal excesses of brutal living. The bully who beats Shelby's face into a pulp in the novel's beginning almost triumphs symbolically over the virtue of a peace-time world. Almost, but not quite. He is himself reduced by the one man of the Corps who survives and remains whole: a cheerful, resourceful entrepreneur, a "bushwhacker," who has spent most of the war exploiting the assorted greeds and weaknesses of his contemporaries. He will return to the States quite untroubled by the experience, and will use his power of assimilating vulgarity to his advantage. To him men had never been more than animals, and he has no compunction whatsoever over the reductio ad absurdum his more sensitive fellows have failed to comprehend.

This is in a very real sense the terminus ad quem of the literature of violence. There is only one vision left—of the total landscape, with right and wrong indistinguishable because experience has obliterated the psychological and moral power of decision. Shelby is as much a victim of the war as if he had spent the years in a concentration camp. His nerves had fed on disaster until they cracked disastrously. In yielding to the holocaust, he himself became a part of the landscape of horror. The final stage in the literature of violence describes the assailant as landscape; it is not only dehumanized, but chaotic. As in the Guernica painting of Picasso, the bodies and sensibilities are twisted, misshapen, and fragmented, and they blend with the contours of the blasted landscape. In such a setting man relies on neither courage nor a sense of the right, but upon a busy (even at times, a frenetic) earnestness to define himself. In his soul are contained both the energy of the assailant and the masochistic receptivity of the victim.

The kind of extreme brutality described in *The Trumpet Unblown* can lead to only two results: either an absolute nihilism, in which no respect is paid humanity that the prospect of pain and death does not negate; or a type of farce, in which the *snafus* in military or naval organization become a patterning of chaos. The first of these is seen in Glenn Sire's novel, *The Deathmakers* (1960); it is surely as meticulously developed as in any war literature.

The American soldiers in *The Deathmakers* move quickly over the German landscape, in a Patton-like mechanical warfare. This means quick exchanges of fire-power, sudden and grotesque deaths, and a progressive brutalizing of the soldiers themselves. Captain Joseph Brandon, point commander, is an intelligent young man who tries desperately to hold on to his sanity but has to meet emergencies and to make crucial decisions with little time for reflection. What chance he does have is spent on the gloomy subject of death-as-annihilation. The relationship of rational planning to induced chaos is persistently and agonizingly evident at every turn of events.

Throughout, Brandon suffers from trying to preserve the distinction between *kill* and *murder*: the first is what you do "with respect and dignity" and according to rules and plans of warfare; but the second—the brutalized, vicious slaying of the enemy—invariably intervenes, as a consequence of the *way* your war is fought:

> . . . You do this terrible thing. You commit this monstrous act. This is it, right here, right now, with you in middle of it, with time running off in seconds that seem like years. This is a part of the craziness of your world.[45]

Death is a return to nothingness. The grotesqueness and the viciousness of modern warfare have driven all thoughts of immortality from his mind; he is left with pure nihilism. This war is a frenzy of death-making and death-wishing:

> . . . At the end of all the planning and organizing, of all the maps and phase lines and bomb lines, was the chaos and the cyclone where men tore their machines and their homes and their bodies apart in the frenzy that had to be, if it ever was to happen at all. . . . (3)

There is almost no protection from the hard, harsh reality of this kind of war; man's body is "small and vulnerable and incredibly delicate" (4). Living in the midst of death, you have a sense of cold terror at the thought of your own death, and it is impossible to think of it with dignity. (5–6)

The Deathmakers is a vision of the ultimate surrender of grace. Brandon can only try to conduct himself with a surface propriety and reasonableness, which do not match anything in the landscape. The book is also an exhaustive catalogue of kinds of dying and annihilation. Caught in a struggle with a German soldier, Brandon has to fight viciously, and at close range: "The thing underneath him twisted and turned and clawed at his face, and then it grew weaker and was quickly still . . ." (16).

[45] New York, Simon and Schuster, 1960, p. 13. Other references to this edition are in the text.

After the encounter, he has to return to killing "Them" at long range:

> They fall down 'way off, holding their bellies and scream-
> ing, and you don't get to know them. That way they're
> not people they're ducks. . . . It's not intimate, that way.
> It's like working an adding machine. It's modern. Scientific.
> Clean. . . . (17)

In order to create *some* kind of form out of these deliberations and actions, Sire provides Brandon with two selves, who
talked to each other, in the manner of Robert Jordan's dialogues
in Hemingway's *For Whom the Bell Tolls*. The result comes
eventually to something like the gruesome and desperate
schizophrenic essays in self-preservation of the concentration
camp. Hemingway's hero debated the "right good reason" for
doing what he is committed to do. There is nothing of the sort
here. Brandon's two selves take up the dialogue of the self
and the soul, with the soul reduced to a matter of preserving
appearances and the external mannerisms of courage.

There is, understandably, much ironic brooding over what
Brandon calls "the harvest of man's wisdom and meaningful-
ness . . ." (23). The truth is that he finds it difficult to distinguish the corpses piled up at Bastogne from those disposed
of in concentration camps. *Haven't* we actually reached the
point where *no* kind of rationalization is even momentarily
extenuating? Occasionally, his reflections resemble those of
Lieutenant Henry in the retreat from Caporetto. But Henry's
anger over the madness always assumed a point of moral
vantage: that is, if this war is mad, there is something that is
sane. Momentarily, Brandon also feels that there is: the love
of his wife, of her for him. But the memory of his parting recedes, and leaves nothing before "the impersonal enormity of
the thing that was tearing the private fragile tissue of their
lives apart . . ." (25).

"They" has been the great impersonal pronoun in this literature. Each use of it has shown a gradual relinquishing of personal identity. "They" are a dreadful naturalistic force in Sire's
novel, ready to subtract "you" from the living, without apology
or explanation. It is a fitting companion thought to that which
tried to sum up the nothingness into which "you" were going.
How honor the occasion? What kind of ceremony can we use
to pay tribute to the "Götterdämmerung of nothingness"? (41)

The Deathmakers is concerned with the great redundant effort to destroy, repeatedly to wipe out everything. As a scientifically calculated and organized operation, the war had a
center of "meaning": that is, if you stayed at your job and
weren't killed first, you progressed toward a goal, which was the
end of the enemy. Ultimately, the experience turned you into
an image of him; so that there was no real distinction between
you and him, except what you could make or prove by being
better (more coldly efficient) than he. Always the center line
of sanity threatened to break down. At the edges hovered insanity, the grotesque, the madness of the war's consequences.

There is, of course, one other possible approach: if this be
madness, why not dismiss it as a grotesque master symbol of
the great Lord Snafu? In other words, isn't it "better to die
laughing"? [46] In all of the humorous novels of the war, there
is a recurrence of themes that, when treated seriously, lead to
the conclusions found in *The Deathmakers*. Perhaps there is a
point at which the madness must be considered laughable, in
the manner of Faulkner's treatment of Flem Snopes in Hell.[47]
Joseph Heller's *Catch-22* (1961) [48] is the most notorious of
this kind of war novel. Here there is almost no reason left, except perhaps in the "hero," Yossarian, a person committed to
preserving himself and his sanity. He is a far cry from the "good

[46] See John Muste, "Better to Die Laughing: The War Novels of Joseph
Heller and John Ashmead," *Critique*, 5 (fall 1962), pp. 16–27.
[47] *The Hamlet*, New York, Random House, 1940.
[48] *Catch-22*, New York, Simon and Schuster, 1961.

soldier Schweik," [49] and yet Schweik is his parallel from an earlier time.

The "central Snafu" is made up of many minor snafus; some of them are deliberate (black markets, petty thieveries and grand larcenies), others are the result of sheer stupidity. In fact, the effect of *Catch-22* is of reason suddenly turned upside-down, or of Yossarian down a rabbit hole into the "other world," where everything comes through in a reverse image. There are so many examples of petty insanity (in the manner of an S. J. Perelman finally gone mad) in the novel that it becomes wearisomely clever. But there is no doubt of Heller's intention, and one may assume its "meaning" in the phrase "better to die laughing." Superintending all of the minor follies and insanities is the master *Catch-22*, which always acts at the last minute to defeat logical expectations or undermine the threat of sanity's return. The basic theme of the novel is that the war is insane, and it is managed by incompetents, but that it is inevitably entangled with calls to "duty" and irrational orders; so that ultimately you must accept the "craziness," while at the same time you took as much advantage as you could of stupidities to preserve yourself and to make life as tolerable as possible.

The reality of the war itself is not ignored. As John Muste has said, "Yossarian's desperation . . . would be merely funny if Heller had not convinced us that the flak is real. . . ." [50] The comedy is intruded upon by reality and pathos. Yossarian's efforts to stay alive (nothing has meaning if you're dead) lead him to a succession of contrivances, to evade regulation procedures, but they also suggest a position with respect to the war; so that from time to time the farce of the war threatens to turn serious. But the imbalance which has set in from the beginning—a kind of nervous tic of giggles and laughs, like a punster stammering—succeeds in holding off the threat of

[49] Jaroslav Hasek, *The Good Soldier Schweik,* tr. Paul Selver, New York, Doubleday, Doran, 1930.
[50] "Better to Die Laughing," p. 25.

meaning. One point, of course, is abundantly made: that the war is mad and stupid and run by idiots, and the best one can do is to stay alive while it is going on. But attempts to penetrate the surface of the war's inanity, or to introduce pathos into a world that would apparently not recognize it, do not succeed.

John Ashmead's *The Mountain and the Feather*[51] is a less explosively "funny" book and more successful in communicating its perspective upon the war. Its hero, Monty Classen, is a translator in the Navy, who moves in and out of Pearl Harbor on several kinds of assignment. He is close to the officer class, and is able to provide a steady, wry commentary on officer types. As in *Catch-22*, there is a steady reminder here of death, of the threat of it, and of the need to come to some personal decision about it. In Ashmead's novel, there is "that strange rich odor which you later come to recognize as the odor of the dead" (46). He is speaking here of the documents sent to Pearl Harbor from Guadalcanal, but the odor persists as a reminder of the kind of war they are after all involved in. Classen occasionally takes part in beach landings, so that he is close to the act of death-making himself. In one case, he notes an efficiently managed cemetery:

> . . . There was a firing squad and taps were blown, and the flag was dipped in salute. There was a bulldozer permanently attached to the cemetery; each day it pushed a deep trench a little further along, and then went back and covered over the newly lowered boxes. When taps blew for CPO Gunner the bulldozer clanked forward, pushing the dirt in front of it. (155).

Throughout this novel, several "leaders of thought" are presented in acts of futile and comical effort to understand and explain what is going on: Professor Begel, the naval historian, from whose "monumental work," *The Battle for Visaya Gulf*,

[51] Boston, Houghton, Mifflin, 1961.

quotations are drawn to head the novel's chapters; the chaplain, whose principal remark was "dignity, dignity," who dies one day in an island invasion, as he is trying to make his way through the three syllables of that strange, inappropriate word; and a variety of officers, who behave in the manner of Heller's idiots, but are somehow given less prominence. In short, Ashmead balances the farce against the pathos of the war; its realities are not smothered by its comical or obscene or outrageous snafus. One may make the same judgment concerning Classen's fate. Invasions are themselves comedies of errors: stupid decisions stubbornly held to because of "face," quick upturns and shifts and changes of fortune, the grotesqueries of desperate strategies and counter-strategies. Meanwhile, Professor Begel sits at his typewriter recording on the spot the "magnificent story" of the "deathless glory."

In the end, Classen, having smelled and seen death, and been within very close reach of it, is himself killed, and he has prepared himself to accept it as a distinct probability. Both *Catch-22* and *The Mountain and the Feather* are concerned with this necessity. Both heroes fight against it, but only Classen comes to some understanding of his fate. The fearful calamity of annihilation without cause is all but impossible to accept. The alternative to accepting it is to make it the accidental end-result of a thousand monstrous idiocies. But these are not the follies of Private Hargrove or Sergeant Bilko: they are mistakes leading to great and real disasters. And they are all the more catastrophic because the instruments involved have an extraordinary power and force. The humor is often strained, and it is difficult to find a balance between it and the realities with which the novels are apparently concerned. There is more of a sense of the existentialist decision in Ashmead's work. The irrationalities of *Catch-22* make almost any decision impossible, or implausible, as the free choice within a continuing and responsible existence.

—[vi]—

In all of these examples of it, the literature of World War II describes several important attitudes toward violence. In one case, the writer (and especially the poet) tries to comprehend the violence, in terms of his vocabularies, to grasp the *metaphor* of the evil; or he allows the bare factuality of violence to speak for itself; or he creates a mythology to account for it; or he tries (and invariably without success) to create from its tensions an ideological melodrama; or, he assumes it to be a kind of madness, to be treated as a farce, the metaphors of which alternate between the trivial and the grotesque; or, finally, he calls it inhuman and intolerable and not at all comprehensible in any customary terms. Throughout, the question of guilt is raised, and with it the responsibility to face and to define death; these matters are often at the surface, or they are inadequately suppressed. The basic problems are to distinguish between assailant and victim, accurately to locate each, and to distribute the onus of guilt between them. These problems are often not solved; they are referred to the essential absurdity at the core of this type of human event.

The meditations on the question of guilt are especially important. The difficulty lies in the qualitative separation of language from event. When the soldier contemplates his wound, he very often thinks of himself as participating in the violence; it is one way of making amends for his being forced to assume the role of assailant. But the wound remains an enigma; the larger statements of "value" are inadequate to explain it; and in any case the soldier's mind is scarcely prepared to equate his role of assailant with his personal hurt and grief. The strength of the guilt feeling varies with the power of the violence of which he is an instrument. Many subtleties remain unexamined. For one thing, there is no time to examine them; also, the rhetoric of public explanation does not suffice. It just is not applicable to the individual case. The soldier wanders in a forest of generalities; they seem uncomfortably familiar to him, yet none of them makes sense at the moment when he meditates upon "terror's unique engima."

8

THE HERO IN ABSENTIA: THE CONCENTRATION CAMP

. . . there is nowhere but here, there are not
two places, there are not two prisons, it's my
parlour, it's a parlour where I wait for nothing,
I don't know where it is, I don't know what it's
like, that's no business of mine, I don't know if
it's big, or if it's small, or if it's closed,
or if it's open, that's right reiterate, that
helps you on . . .
—SAMUEL BECKETT, *The Unnamable*

CLOV: If I don't kill that rat, he'll die.
—BECKETT, *Endgame*

—[i]—

ON ONE OCCASION in Ernst Juenger's anti-Nazi fantasy, *On the
Marble Cliffs*, the narrator and his friend come upon a clearing
in the forest beyond Marina. It is "overgrown with withered
grass"; two large bushes stand out from the landscape, "flecked
with the yellow to be seen on butchers' stalls." As the two men
proceed into the place, they notice strangely neat figurations on
a narrow gable frieze, "which appeared to be formed of brown
spiders"; but, "Suddenly we guessed that it was fashioned of

human hands fastened to the wall. So clearly did we see this that we picked out the little peg driven through the palm of each one."[1] The search culminates in the sight of a dwarf, who is working with a pick and whistling an air.

> Then we heard the wind rocking itself as if in accompaniment among the pines so that the pale skulls on the trees rattled in chorus. Into its lament was mixed the swaying of the hooks and the twitching of the withered hands on the barn wall. The noise was that of wood and bone, like a puppet show in the kingdom of the dead. At the same time there bore down upon the wind a clinging heavy and sweet smell of corruption, which made us shiver to the marrow of our bones. Within us we felt the melody of life touch its darkest and deepest chord. (74)

The withered grass is a reminder of the waste-landscape of the first war; the yellow stains survive the spilling of blood and the butcher's stalls are an image of the war's "stands of brutal death." The landscape becomes a more and more horrifying reminder of "the degradation of human dignity and human freedom" (75). The concentration camp, which this scene visualizes, is the end result of modern violence. Not only does it eliminate all possibility of dignity in dying, but it all but destroys any meaningful relationship between assailant and victim. Simone Weil has said of violence that "The vanquished is a cause of misfortune for the victor as much as the victor is for the vanquished."[2] Death in these circumstances is beyond the reach of analysis; even description becomes difficult, because the succession of brutalities dulls the sensibility, and they may make distinctions meaningless.

This condition threatens to be the most serious of all human

---

[1] (1939). Tr. Stuart Hood, New York, New Directions, 1947, p. 73. Other references to this edition are in the text.
[2] "The 'Iliad,' Poem of Might," p. 39.

disasters. At the center of its terror is the fact, as Albert Camus puts it, that one cannot any longer define death: ". . . the death or torture of a human being can, in our world, be examined with a feeling of indifference, with friendly or experimental interest, or without response . . . [and] the putting to death of a man can be regarded other than with the horror and shame it should excite. . . ." [3] The progress toward this human crisis is marked by a steadily increasing distance between assailant and victim. There is a point beyond which no kind of human emotion is relevant.

At the opposing poles of human sufferance are the emotions of deep concern and indifference. Indifference can mean the absence of passion, or it can (in the form of active and practical contempt) become a powerful, negating passion. An additional element of modern terror is its quantitative extension. Not only does the human sense of responsibility fade as the assailant moves further and further away from his victim; the number of deaths produced, as well as the "efficiency" of production, pushes the event beyond the power of man either to imagine or emotionally to assimilate it. The word *murder* no longer has any meaning in a situation permitting a mass production of corpses. The phenomena of the concentration camp exist beyond the limits of judging life-death relationships. Both individual and the political discourses of evil are not possible on these terms. Hannah Arendt puts the distinction in this way:

> The murderer who kills a man who must die in any event, moves within the familiar realm of life and death, between which there is a necessary relation that is the basis of dialectics, though dialecticians are not always aware of it. The murderer leaves a corpse and does not claim that his victim never existed; he may obscure the traces of his own identity, but he does not efface the memory and grief of those

[3] "The Human Crisis," *Twice a Year*, Nos. 14–15 (fall–winter 1946–47), p. 22.

who loved his victim; he destroys a life, but he does not destroy the very fact of its ever having existed.[4]

The drift away from identity in the condition of modern violence has two apparently antithetic characteristics, extreme congestion and extreme distance. Both produce impersonality. Hundreds of persons crowded into one car or one "block" are no longer hundreds of identifiable persons but a mass of un-differentiated human matter; the "soul" of each one is in this case "trampled by insistent feet" and stretched to the point of anonymity. Extremes of distance from target have the same effect, as I have shown. One might assume that the sense of guilt would remain alive and even be stimulated by proximity; but this is not the case. In the one example, the concentration camp, visibility and physical contact in very close quarters en-courage either a total separation of the self—a split into de-tached observer and observed victim—or perversions of com-munity.[5] But the assailant who is beyond sight of his victims is not therefore saved from guilt. He may come to it, or it to him, many years later; this is true of Claude Eatherly, who com-manded the lead plane over Hiroshima and in 1947 began the long journey to a recognition of guilt.[6]

The first modern literary account of the phenomenon was Dostoevsky's *Memoirs from the House of the Dead*. Compared with reports from World War II, Dostoevsky's is relatively tame. In a letter sent to his brother shortly after his release in February 1854, he speaks of the lack of space, the filth, stench, cold, the indifferent food, and the inadequate care of the ill.

[4] "The Concentration Camps," *Partisan Review*, 15 (July 1948), p. 747.
[5] See Sartre's *Nausea*, where the autodidact describes his prison ex-periences and praises their contribution to "brotherhood," while they had actually developed a latent homosexuality in him. Tr. Lloyd Alexander, New York, New Directions, 1949, pp. 143, 154–55. Originally published in Paris by Gallimard, 1938.
[6] See *Burning Conscience*, New York, Monthly Review Press, 1962.

Add to all this the almost complete impossibility of possessing books, . . . the eternal hostility and brawling around
one, the wrangling, shouting, uproar, din, the being incessantly under guard, never alone, and all this for four years
on end—you might be forgiven for saying it was bad.[7]

Perhaps the best clue to the meaning of Dostoevsky's experience is contained in the words spoken when he was released:

> The fetters fell away. I lifted them up . . . I wanted to
> hold them in my hand and look at them for the last time.
> It seemed amazing now that it was my legs that they had
> been on a moment ago.
> "Well, God be with you, God be with you!" said the
> prisoners, in gruff, abrupt, yet pleased tones.
> Yes, God was with us! Freedom, a new life, resurrection
> from the dead . . . What a glorious moment! (294)

There were several details of the experience that may in the
perspective of a century be called "mitigating." Dostoevsky was
sent to the Siberian prison for specific reasons. He had no difficulty determining the relationship of cause to effect in his consideration of the event. The fact of himself as a person specifically and clearly identifiable in the experience was never denied
or brushed aside or ignored. However miserable and crude the
imprisonment was, he could still write of it in personal terms.[8]
Dostoevsky's record has many minor details which anticipate
the concentration camp of the twentieth century, but its frame
and structure remain within the nineteenth century. It is not
so much a question of his being capable of indignation as that
his indignation proved relevant and effective. Above all, the

[7] (1861–1862). Tr. Jessie Coulson, London, Oxford University Press,
1956, p. xi. Other references to this edition are in the text.
[8] He begins by writing it as a fictional account, but soon his personal
involvement makes him abandon the thin disguise.

idea that "God was with us" marks a radical separation from any even roughly comparable modern experience.[9]

In 1917 E. E. Cummings was detained for four months in a camp at La Ferté Macé, one hundred miles from Paris. In the frame of American experiences of World War I, his was shocking enough. Its major image is given in the title of Cummings' account, *The Enormous Room*. The "enormous room" was a constriction of the world to a limited place, in which were contained prisoners; outside of it were officials. When he was released, the image of the room went with him. The world was an "enormous room," in which dwelt prisoners controlled and tortured by officials. The two forms of person were characterized by the simplest of opposing qualities. The prisoners were "glad," "alive," and kind; the officials were "absent" (that is, they did not really exist, but only gave an impression of existing), "awkward," and "absurd." Cummings describes his first inquisitor in this revealing fashion:

> His face was seedy sallow and long. He had bushy semi-circular eyebrows which drooped so much as to reduce his eyes to mere blinking slits. His cheeks were so furrowed that they leaned inward. He had no nose, properly speak-

[9] The wide separation of Dostoevsky's view from the twentieth century experience is everywhere manifest in his work. Raskolnikov finally discovers salvation in prison from his murderous detachment from and contempt of humanity; Mitya Karamazov chooses Siberia rather than a chance to escape to America (in this case, the values are strangely inverted: America is the equivalent of the concentration camp, while Siberia holds promise of spiritual rescue). The difference lies in Dostoevsky's evangelically earnest belief that God awaits the prisoner and holds out the promise of redemption. The concentration camp experience often proves to be antithetic; not spiritual illumination, but dehumanization is the consequence. In many cases, the prisoner is left cursing or denying God; he is the Nietzschean *manqué*. God is dead for him, but there is no human surrogate. In all fairness, one ought to point to the many accounts of such dedicated sectarians as the Jehovah's Witnesses, who confounded their persecutors by accepting their deaths in firm expectation of an immediate transition to heaven. But even the slightest doubt this side of total religious exaltation usually had disastrous results. The divine was often denied because humanity was not respected.

ing, but a large beak of preposterous widthlessness, which gave his whole face the expression of falling gravely downstairs, and quite obliterated the unimportant chin . . .[10]

There are many visions which identify the situation as a forerunner of the concentration camp, though also distinct from it. Going to the enormous room, the narrator first finds himself in a chapel, gloomy and ominous: "Staring ahead, I gradually disinterred the pale carrion of the darkness—an altar, guarded with the ugliness of unlit candles, on which stood inexorably the efficient implements for eating God" (56). In this chapel on one Sunday, he was to hear a "high old man with a sharp violet face and green hair" say: "You are free, my children, to achieve immortality—Songez, songez donc—L'Eternité est une existence sans durée—Toujours le Paradis, toujours l'Enfer . . ." (143). The entire book is intended as a mockery of the priest's talk of immortality. It is reduced to the here and the now and to "l'Enfer."

In the same spirit, Cummings expatiates upon the matter of time: in this situation, "events can no longer succeed each other: whatever happens, while it may happen in connection with some other perfectly distinct happening, does not happen

---

[10] *The Enormous Room*, New York, Boni and Liveright, 1922. Other references to this edition are in the text. See also Cummings' poem, "i sing of Olaf glad and big" (in *ViVa*, 1931), which celebrates the spirit of man in *duresse oblige*:

. . .

> Our president, being of which
> assertions duly notified
> threw the yellowsonofabitch
> into a dungeon, where he died
>
> Christ (of His mercy infinite)
> i pray to see; and Olaf, too
>
> preponderatingly because
> unless statistics lie he was
> more brave than me: more blond than you.

The typographic arrangements and "rhetorical punctuation" are designed to suggest the close confinement of the prison, the loss of "breathing space."

in a scale of temporal priorities . . ." (99). The enormous room therefore comprehends a constriction of both space and time: the space is inadequate because there are too many people in it, but also because they are kept there with little freedom to choose if they should stay or leave; time comes to a stop altogether, or exists in a state of suspension.

Beyond these limitations, there is a fundamental failure of privacy, a truly serious deprivation. However bravely the inmates endured their lot, they could not ignore this loss of a basic freedom, the privilege of moving from public to private ranges of existence. Nothing could be done to deny the existence and the necessity of functions; urine and excrement intruded, and it was impossible for anyone to remain a private person.

—[ii]—

The threat of nonexistence menaces the inhabitants of the enormous room, as it does any who live without freedom in a limited space. Cummings' experience, however, was only a prelude to the major catastrophe. The concentration camp threatened the very basis of human privilege: freedom of will over the arrangements of space and time, privacy in matters that should in all conscience remain private, some ceremonially dignified attention—however crude—to the circumstance of dying, and assurance that identity is not lost, whether in life or in death. The First World War offered many menacing hints that these dignities would in the future seldom be honored. Ulysses traveled many miles out of his way to assure Elpenor a burial and to put his soul at rest; troops of our wars often had no time to attend to the dead, who remained for days to offend the air and shock the sight. But the most horrifying visions of this loss occur in accounts of concentration camps. Elie Wiesel describes, for example, the journey of prisoners packed one hundred to the open railroad car in bitter cold and snow; the dead were thrown out each morning upon the snow banks, to lie nude and unburied, until the spring should start decomposition.[11]

The very force of modern violence is an affront to dignity; the culminating irrelevance is the scattering of bodies about the landscape. Together with these insults to human dignity there is the gradual process of eliminating specific human qualities, by means of which personal identities are preserved. The concentration camps of World War II were frightening centers of dehumanization. Estimates of the number killed range from eight to twelve millions. Eugen Kogon reports that many of these were used in "scientific experiments," as in those reported of a Doctor Eysele, who "engaged in human vivisection, subsequently killing his victims. . . . He performed operations and amputations without the slightest reason. He never used anesthesia." [12] The phenomena of mass killing defy comparison, Kogon describes the treatment of five hundred Jews at Buchenwald, in 1938. After the ordeal of admissions, they were assigned a place in a blockhouse that had no tables, benches, or bunks. There was one loaf of bread a day for every five Jews, plus a pint of soup per man. Reveille occurred at three a.m., and from seven to five they worked; for many, work continued until eleven at night. There was no medical treatment for bruises. Many of the group died of sheer exhaustion; others committed suicide, and in two months the number was reduced to 350 (162–63).

[11] *Night* (1958), tr. Stella Rodway, New York, Hill and Wang, 1960, pp. 100–101.
[12] *The Theory and Practice of Hell* (1946), tr. Heinz Norden, New York, Farrar, Straus, n.d., p. 139. Other references to this edition are in the text. Bruno Bettelheim quotes letters to and from a business firm, concerning the prices and uses of human bodies, alive or dead:

"In contemplation of experiments with a new soporific drug, we would appreciate your procuring for us a number of women."

"The tests were made. All subjects died. We shall contact you shortly on the subject of a new load."
(*The Informed Heart*, Glencoe, Illinois, Free Press, 1960, p. 248. Quoted from *Time*, November 1947.)

As the war set in and arrests and imprisonments in concentration camps were multiplied, devices for the mass production of corpses were put into effect. Indiscriminate shooting at masses of prisoners was frequent. Thousands of them were transported in cars so crowded that they had no space to move their bodies. One survivor speaks of the carloads arriving at an extermination camp:

> Sometimes there were shipments that held only corpses. I believe these people must have been gassed in the cars, for I never noticed any wounds. The bodies were convulsively intertwined, the skin blue. Curiously enough there were isolated instances of small children, from three to five years old, who survived these shipments. They were deaf and incapable of speech, and their eyes were haunted. We were never able to conceal them for very long. The SS would discover them and put an end to them. There were also shipments that consisted exclusively of children or old people. They would crouch in a clearing for hours, until they were liquidated by machine-gun fire. (170)

Those people who were not scheduled for such wholesale destruction scarcely enjoyed an advantage. The psychological process of the victim's gradual loss of hope, then of fear, and finally of his very interest in himself as a human being is an especially horrifying aspect of Kogon's report. The prisoner usually began by striving desperately for the "favor of admittance," then tried to accommodate himself to the circumstances of habitation. Shortly endurance flagged, and his energy was directed entirely to the conditions of survival. Not infrequently survival itself became a difficult fact to understand; it was reduced to a subhuman persistence of organic function. The stronger-willed developed the power to act the double role of observer and victim—so that they saw themselves in the specters of other bodies falling into and working out of traps; quite without sympathy or concern for others (the distinction between self and others had been obliterated), they crudely seized opportunities for the most rudimentary of protective stratagems.

In the process, the idea of a conscience restraining crudities of selfish gestures was entirely nullified. Sensitivity threatened survival. Pain, grief, other emotional indulgences proper to ordinary experiences of suffering were impermissible luxuries.

> The range of sensations was almost automatically reduced. The mind developed a protective crust, a kind of defensive armor that no longer transmitted every strong stimulus to the sensitive membranes. . . . Men grew hard and many of them had their sensibilities dulled . . . (276–77)

They developed the dispositions of the "concentrationary" if they survived the first succession of shocks and degradations. In the process it was all but inevitable that they would either acquire in modified form some of the characteristics of their torturers, or become an extreme type of victim; they might gleefully torture others or with a sick sense of masochistic pleasure improve upon their status as victims of torture.

In such an atmosphere, the value of principles diminished, and convictions were so eroded by torture that they were forgotten; men became negations of their former selves. The greatest disaster was that cruelty could destroy conviction, in short that it quite effectively replaced persuasion. From being an instrument of principle, violence survived as the arbitrary concern of both assailant and victim. The assailant had been chosen because he had long since lost interest in principle; the victim was reduced to a subhuman level at which it was impossible to discriminate violence from the cause for which it might be used. In other words, the assailant in this situation was pervasive; it was not a person or a mass of people or a machine, but the entire landscape, including those who killed and those who were killed.

Neither personal nor utilitarian motives explained the spectacle. Kogon speaks of a railway line that was laid as a result of incredibly brutal forced exertions of camp labor. It led to no place of consequence and in any case had been completed from such desperate exertions of failing energy that it collapsed before it could be tested. In the end, the experience distorted not only the balances of life but the fact of death itself. Killing was so much the result of whim, and eventually the product of such mechanical efficiency, that death was among the least of the hazards of the experience.

There have been scores of reports of the concentration camp: memoirs or diaries of victims (Wiesel, Wiechert, Viktor E. Frankl, Micheline Maurel, Michel del Castillo, David Rousset, Anne Frank), memoirs of persecutors (the most notorious of which is Rudolph Hoess's *Commandant at Auschwitz*), novels (Wiechert's *Missa Sine Nomine*, André Schwarz-Bart's *The Last of the Just*), and psychological studies. Kogon's book is a combination of the first and the last of these types, and it is terrifyingly thorough. But the most important speculations are those of Erich Kahler (*The Tower and the Abyss*), to which I have already referred several times, and Bruno Bettelheim (*The Informed Heart*). Both of these go beyond the recital of details and provide serious analyses of meaning.

Bettelheim was himself in Dachau and Buchenwald, to which he went from practice as a psychoanalyst in Vienna. One of his first observations is that, in the concentrationary world, psychoanalysis proved quite inadequate to account for the phenomena of extreme situations; the criteria simply did not apply, or very rarely did, to the extreme of "a total adjustment to a new situation where the new environment is permitted to take over, as it were" (39). He was himself a superior example of the person who had recourse to analyzing his situation in order to survive it; analysis was for him a matter of adjustment.

As a result, Bettelheim brought to an unprecedented experience an exceptional intelligence and training in observation. Almost all customary reactions failed to apply, and were in fact extremely dangerous: hatred of the persecutor, resentment, anger, reliance upon familiar standards of the nonprison world. His imperative need was, instead, "to protect my inner self in such a way that, if by any good fortune I should regain liberty, I would be approximately the same person I was when I was deprived of liberty . . ." (126). The most successful device was "detachment," or a separation of the self that observed from the self that suffered. This split of selves ranged from Bettelheim's own deliberate choice to extreme cases of schizophrenic isolation from actuality. Everything that happened contributed to the deterioration of the familiar self; even suicide was considered an act of self-determination, and suicide attempts which failed were punished by flogging. Survival thus depended upon either the wisdom of detachment or the schizoid's retreat before the total victory of environment over self. But even detachment was risky; one could not *noticeably* observe for fear of showing a personal superiority over the situation.

The essential strategy was to know in one's own person the "point of no return," the point "beyond which one would never, under any circumstances, give in to the oppressor, even if it meant risking and losing one's life" (157). To preserve both this minimal self-respect *and* one's own life required above all a "minimal distance from one's own behavior," so that analysis might serve the function of survival. The concentration camp had to be "the reality." The outside could no longer exist; it was risky to refer or compare life inside to a standard brought in from the other world, or to concentrate upon the wish to re-enter it. These necessities frequently became the brutal means of bare survival: prisoners were vicious to one another; son and father fought to the death for mere subsistence; prisoners imitated the SS, or openly courted their favor; decency, humanity, kindness were luxuries brought over from "that other world."

Partly this condition was forced upon prisoners; emotional energy "was continuously being drained because of the vital energy needed for mere survival . . ." (196). The prisoner tried hard "not to be noticed"; he had to take refuge in anonymity, "to be so much a part of the mass, so devoid of individuality, that at no time could he be distinguished from all others" (210). He had therefore to watch himself with a relentless detachment and a freedom from self-pity or moral indignation; in short, he had to "become invisible" if he wished to stay alive. The prisoner's psychological needs canceled temporarily his moral needs, at least those to which he was emotionally committed. "Anonymity meant relative safety, but it also meant giving up one's own personality, though the body walked about for some time, and more safely" (212). Normal aggressive energies were unused, or if they could no longer be withheld, they might well be directed against other prisoners, because to use them against the SS was suicidal. In such circumstances, the victim, who had begun in a state of environmental oppression, sometimes became so alike the assailant in the projection of energies as to make distinctions useless and invalid.

Obviously the ultimate moral causes of concentration camp abuse existed outside of it. Perhaps citizens did not help or encourage the concentration camp, but they often preferred to ignore it or to be cynical about it. The great moral weakness was the desire to think in terms of "business as usual." This feeling was not only indulged before arrest; it persisted outside the camps during the history of the camps and it seemed unaccountably there when American troops opened the gates for the citizens to look in.[13] Bettelheim offers a shrewd insight into the bourgeois luxury of sympathy for Anne Frank.

> There is good reason why the so successful play ends with Anne stating her belief in the good in all men. What is denied is the importance of accepting the gas chambers as real so that never again will they exist . . . Anne Frank died because her parents could not get themselves to be-

---

[13] See Heym, *The Crusaders,* and Hoffman, *The Trumpet Unblown,* for illustrations of this attitude in war fiction.

lieve in Auschwitz. And her story found wide acclaim because for us too, it denies implicity that Auschwitz ever existed. If all men are good, there never was an Auschwitz. (254) [14]

The evil is pervasive; it has viciously positive and harmful negative properties. Within the concentrationary world, it either forced men to surrender the customary and familiar orientations toward obvious, overt, malicious injustice, or it led to suicidal acts of heroism in a setting from which heroism had fled. The crucial test was the walk toward death. Man as a thinking animal had disappeared; motives for trusting in God's ultimate benevolence vanished; the concentration camp experience often took on the appearance of Nietzsche's cry that "God is dead!" without his humanist alternative; to feel self-pity, or self-pride, or "heroism" was a reckless indulgence or a residual fragment of the emotional past. The crucial test of survival, in Bettelheim's view, was, paradoxically, the victim's attitude toward his dying: "That the SS then killed them is of no less import than the fact that they marched themselves into death, choosing to give up a life that was no longer human" (300). In short, he suggests that only a human view of inhumanity can save humanity.

—[iii]—

This was the extreme form of the figure of assailant as landscape. What was its pattern, its design? Outwardly, there was often an appearance of the most orderly of business, of factories

[14] There is a wealth of implication in this motion (the denial, or death, of Satan), from *Buddenbrooks* (1900) and *The Magic Mountain* (1924) to J. P. Sartre's *Les Séquestrés d'Altona* (1960; first performed in Paris, Sept. 23, 1959). In the last, the question of both proximate and ultimate guilt is dramatized and exhaustively examined. The young Franz wants to think that Germany has been destroyed, to ease his conscience in the matter of his complicity. So he cuts himself off, walls himself in, to deny the existence of the outside world. There is a moral guilt involved in the too easy denial of the facts. Sentimentality proposes the goodness of man,

or stockyards. The offices, as David Rousset reports, seem like a fantasy of busyness:

> . . . great light rooms, sharp outlines, prisoner-clerks at ease, correct, with files and numbers, a soothing indifference; in the strict alignment of military ranks, electric clippers denude dumbfounded bodies, one after the other, precisely, implacably, as in a mathematical game . . . sinuous caravans moving down apparently endless narrow corridors; and the discovery of immense spaces . . . And more offices, even more cluttered with impeccable and bustling prisoner-clerks, grey-faced and serious, straight out of the world of Kafka, who politely ask for the name and address of the person to be notified in the event of decease, and write down everything meticulously on little forms prepared in advance.[15]

The bustling clerks are in a sense a nervous prototype of the prisoners themselves. Both are busily moving to the edge of insanity. For the business here attended to is a form of preparing for skeletons; and as the phenomenon of the concentration camp grew more and more monstrous, the surface exertion seemed clearly a neurotic symptom of the wish and drive for death. Kogon describes the elaborate arrangements for mass killing at Buchenwald. Each step of the way was a stage in an elaborate game, the object of which was to make the death itself as much a surprise as possible. Like the prisoners in Orwell's 1984, these moved for a while in a state of false security, before the disaster struck suddenly and efficiently. One of the functionaries stood by with a hose to clean away the blood. There were also killing machines and mobile pickup gas cham-

---

and therefore shuts off the monstrous possibility of such evils as the concentration camps. See American edition, translated by Sylvia and George Leeson, New York, Knopf, 1961.

[15] A World Apart (1946). Tr. Yvonne Moyse and Roger Senhouse, London, Secker and Warburg, 1951, p. 3.

bers. For truly efficient production, at Birkenau there was a gas plant, to which were attached five crematories, each of which had an average capacity of twelve to fifteen hundred persons (*The Theory and Practice of Hell*, 214).

It is almost just to say that the only product this terrifying situation could have is a kind of anti-literature, since its only material is anti-humanity. There is much in Rousset's comment, however, that "the world inhabited by the camp population drew its inspiration from the imagination of Céline and the haunting obsessions of Kafka . . ." (*A World Apart*, 36). Both Céline and Kafka contribute at least to the possibility of assimilating the concentration camp to the literary consciousness. It is true that the absolute factuality of the camps reduces to mere reportage; even reportage breaks down in Kogon's account, and statistics and diagrams become an indispensable means of communication. But there are several matters connected with this fantastic world of the camps that have a bearing upon the modern literature of violence. The first of these is the contempt of man. No man survived the violence of the first war with a contempt greater than Céline's of those who fought it. *Journey to the End of the Night* is a complex record of his resentment of the madness, the vulgarity, and finally the complete futility of mankind. In the earlier visions he provides of the war, he points the way to the primary motivation of the concentrationary state of mind. "The greatest defeat, in anything, is to forget, and above all to forget what it is that has smashed you, and to let yourself be smashed without ever realizing how thoroughly devilish men can be. . . ." [16]

The change is gradual from the patriot's desire to identify himself with a cause to a state of contemptible anonymity, but Céline considers it inevitable. In the years following the war, he describes his hero serving as a doctor, performing services but with the utmost contempt for his patients. This contempt

[16] (1922), tr. John H. P. Marks, New York, New Directions, 1934, pp. 20–21.

of man comes partly from the phenomenon of numbers. The capacity for love, for kindness, even for the most elementary concern, is exhausted as the number of patients grows. All cases look alike, and soon discrimination fades and gives way to indifference.[17] The contempt is not exclusively a denial of human values; it may be an expression of extreme doubt and uncertainty regarding values.

Something of the same process occurs in the history of the victim himself. There are many literary accounts of this threat of deterioration. Despite Bettelheim's assurances, it is by no means absolutely certain that the victim can survive it whole, or that if he does the strain of adjustment will not make his survival almost futile. Ironies abound in the world of the concentration camp. When a prisoner arrives and is "processed" for admittance, deterioration of himself as a person begins. Miss Arendt speaks of "the murder of the moral person in man." This is accomplished by so reducing the man of principle that he can no longer either assume the dignity or comprehend the nature of martyrdom. Martyrdom involves submission for a reason, the idea of humbly offering one's death. But the privilege of dying for a cause can only be destroyed in a situation where the meaning of death seems itself to be negated. A stack of corpses neither appears like nor is a reminder of lives offered in heroic satisfaction of principles. In this sense, man becomes an object of contempt, for the protective devices that prevent his being seen as contemptible—the privacies and amenities of a civilized life—are rudely dismissed. Ernst Wiechert speaks to this question, in the matter of human cleanliness: "A man who has been accustomed to cleanliness all through his life can easily adapt himself to great simplicity and hardship, but not to filth, which degrades the innermost being of a man to a mere physical existence." [18] The process leading to death never abandons this

---

[17] Surgery on a battlefront often produces such a reaction. Cf. Hemingway's *A Farewell to Arms*, William Hoffman's *The Trumpet Unblown*.

[18] *Forest of the Dead*, tr. Ursula Stechow, New York, Greenberg, 1947, p. 17. Other references to this edition are in the text.

initial degradation. Observing a man causelessly dying, Wiechert invokes the most helpless of protesting cries:

> . . . when at the foot of one of the trees or a light pole a man lay dying, half in the other world already, with his face open to the light of dawn, then all this was a picture of the damned, arisen like a specter from hades, or a vision out of Hell, beyond the brush of the greatest painter, beyond the needle of the greatest etcher, because no human phantasy or even the dreams of a genius can measure up to this reality, which has not had its like in centuries, perhaps never. (67)

The same feeling of helpless loss haunts the victim at the point of his death. A correct posture of dying is indispensable to a man's preserving dignity. If the act of dying is unceremoniously abrupt, if both life and death have become impersonal, human dignity is irrevocably violated. The narrator of *The Dark Side of the Moon*, which describes the Russian camps of forced labor, speculates upon the death of her father, who had ended his days in such a camp, separated from his family. She is distressed that he should have died alone, and hopes that when the moment came, he had someone with him, to attend to his last moments: "When I am very optimistic, this is how I see him—a great old carcass of a man with prominent blue eyes and wet cheeks, dying; and yet not quite alone, not quite like a pariah dog." [19]

The most affecting literary image of this crisis of dying is Pierre Gascar's "The Season of the Dead." A group of prisoners is put on burial detail. They rejoice at first, not only because the work is not difficult, but because they consider they are doing a service; they feel the importance of providing the dead with a ceremony, which at least helps to testify to the reality of their having once lived: ". . . we were a team of ghosts returning

[19] Anonymous, *The Dark Side of the Moon*, London, Faber and Faber, 1946, p. 113.

every morning to a green and peaceful place, we were workers in death's garden. . . ." [20] Despite the fact that the dead they bury have been mistreated, perhaps murdered, their attendants hold to the belief that they are assisting in a ritual which will preserve the continuity of life and death.

These convictions are mocked by subsequent events; they stumble upon a mass grave: first one, then several, then many corpses, and the neat and precise pattern in which they had earlier considered the orderly succession of lives and deaths is now irrevocably lost.

> . . . We turned over the earth till we were exhausted in an effort to cover up the bodies. We were practicing our craft of grave-diggers in sudden isolation. And now it had assumed a wildly excessive character; we were grave-diggers possessed by feverish delirium. Night was falling. We had ceased to care who these men were, who had killed them or when; they were irregular troops on the fringe of the army of the dead, they were "partisans" of another sort. . . . (221)

Now the full horror of their role in the concentrationary world dawns upon them. The task is no longer an errand of grace, nor even a service to man; they have become a part of an insane world, from which all propriety and decorum have fled: ". . . hollow-eyed gardeners, sitters in the sun, fanatical weeders, busily working over the dead as over some piece of embroidery" (233).

Camus has said that "Doubtless our life belongs to others and it is proper that we give it to others when that is necessary. But our death belongs to ourselves alone." [21] If it is ours, it follows that we may invest it with what dignity our human values or our religious beliefs offer. It is indispensable to such proprietorship that death be specifically linked to a life of which

---

[20] *Beasts and Men*, tr. Jean Stewart, Boston, Little, Brown, 1956, p. 185. Other references to this edition are in the text.
[21] "The Human Crisis," p. 29.

it is clearly a conclusion.[22] In upsetting the continuity necessary to such a line of human regard, the concentration camp violates the rights of ownership. Camus wishes that we might strive to restore them, and this is of course the all but superhuman task facing us. For the *condition* of the concentration camp remains —the assailant as landscape, with the victim within the landscape itself, indistinguishable from it. The strongest affirmations in recent literature (among them, Camus' *The Plague* and Faulkner's *A Fable*) have maintained the right of human identification in the midst of the horror. Both deliberately assert humanity in isolation from institutional rules for its survival.

Perhaps the present circumstance of violence is so overwhelming that it is impossible for any literature to comprehend it adequately. Most of the literature written since the second war's conclusion seems to have come from a tacit consent to keep the fact of violence away from the center of such a concern. This literature seems written on wager: life is possible if violence does not dispose of it. Rarely do we have any attempt to explore the human situation in terms of what the assailant as landscape requires of it. The experience of the past has seemed to suggest that human lives are difficult to appreciate at the center of this violence, that every turn of events turns the minimal human pretenses and necessities aside, that bodies no longer belong either to the living or to the dead, and finally that mass deaths cease being much more than matters of statistical estimate. The result of any attempt to represent such a world would seem to be a catalogue of contemptuous evidence of man's loss of identity. It is true that literature has never been silenced by calamity; it has not been especially nourished by it either. Catastrophes in the past, however, either have been ignored or have only temporarily been introduced into the margins of literature. The violence of modern wars provides a quite different kind of

[22] These words of Eliot's "Gerontion" are relevant:

> . . . Think at last
> We have not reached conclusion, when I
> stiffen in a rented house. . . .
> (*Complete Poems and Plays*, 22)

catastrophe. When, as Randall Jarrell has said, "The equations metamorphose into use," [23] both equations and use are a consequence of man's willed life, as a seeker of truth and an exploiter of advantage. Wallace Stevens describes the mind as containing "a violence from within that protects us from a violence without"; [24] I presume he means that the imagination can and does meet the full force of reality, and that an act of mind must and should apply to any occasion of external violence, that it must be equal to the occasion.

The strategy of the mind in the circumstance we have described is perhaps not an easy one to contemplate. Stevens has given us many visions of it at work, but in *Owl's Clover* (omitted from his *Collected Poems*) he too suggests that the violence is personal and must remain so if it is to contain "the violence without." Man means the mob, he says,

> . . . And yet
> In an age of concentric mobs would any sphere
> Escape all deformation, much less this,
> This source and patriarch of other spheres,
> This base of every future, vibrant spring,
> The volcano Apostrophe, the sea Behold.[25]

. . .

At the end of *Notes Toward a Supreme Fiction*, Stevens suggests an interrelationship of the two violences, the soldier's war and the poet's. The meaning of the soldier's violence must be absorbed by the poet's energy of imagination.

. . .

The soldier is poor without the poet's lines,

His petty syllabi, the sounds that stick,

[23] "The Emancipators," in *Little Friend, Little Friend*, p. 14.
[24] "The Noble Rider and the Sound of Words" (1948), in *The Necessary Angel*, New York, Knopf, 1951, p. 36.
[25] (1935), *In Opus Posthumous*, ed. S. F. Morse, New York, Knopf, 1957, p. 63.

Inevitably modulating, in the blood.
And war for war, each has its gallant kind.[26]

Surely the violence of the poet's need, to meet the soldier's, is not the same as the delicately balanced sensitivity of Jane Austen's Elizabeth Bennett or even E. M. Forster's image of force in Gerald Dawes or Charles Wilcox. The question is first if a violence of the mind to equal the force of which I speak is at all possible. If it is, is the literature to be only rarely and resignedly descriptive (as most reactions to the concentration camp have been), or will the imagination invent its own subtleties, to meet the demands of these new forms of outer violence? The language of discontent and disaffection in modern literature has thus far been almost entirely drawn from a world of discourse formed before men felt the pressure of modern violence. The literature is therefore either bluntly descriptive (Zola refined, but with no cause to fight) or vacantly and uselessly ironic.

The prospect of a hero wandering the landscape of violence as set forth in these pages, assimilating the violence and yet remaining intact, requires both a comprehension of it and some philosophical and moral devices for preserving the self. One answer is in existentialist literature; but, while Sartre's heroes and Camus' perhaps survive more credibly, or die more intelligibly, than Hemingway's or Faulkner's, they purchase their immunity from the worst effects of the violence by a too deliberate dismissal of prior assumptions. It may be true that if a hero tries to support himself with these assumptions, he evades the arduous necessities of being. Nevertheless, a writer who wants to comprehend the assailant as landscape as we have seen it needs to alter the language of his questioning while he continues to focus his analysis upon both himself and whatever conceptual form his God may have, after both have suffered and survived the most devastating attacks upon their pretenses to being.

Perhaps Kafka has come closest to beginning such a literature, if only because he accepts the irrationality of both the assailant and the victim, and yet provides some semblance of a grammar of action in terms of it.[27] The universe of the concentration camp and the universe outside it both have the character of willed rationality and inevitable irrationality. Kafka's heroes stumble about the rubble of a rational world, and their assertions of identity and purpose are almost always doomed to failure because they do not clearly associate the disorder about them with the disorder in their minds. Either they arrogantly assert their superiority to evil or they debase themselves before it; in either case, the scene is morally linked to what they do with it and are within it. Only Camus and Sartre have moved beyond Kafka, to an analysis of man's personal involvement in evil which bears a resemblance to formulations of the past. But even here the moral assertions are closely allied to self-determination and far from being recognizable formulations of traditional morality.

[26] *Collected Poems,* p. 407.
[27] Cf. Alex Comfort's remark (*Darwin and the Naked Lady,* New York, Braziller, 1962): "Kafka depicting his prison camp, digging his burrow, or trying to get into the castle is relying on his imagination, but today he could equally well be writing documentaries . . ." (p. 95). See also Nathalie Sarraute, *The Ages of Suspicion,* tr. Maria Jolas, New York, Braziller, 1963, pp. 49–50. The remarks originally appeared in *Temps Modernes,* October 1957. They definitely place Kafka as having anticipated the horrors of the concentration camps.

9

KAFKA'S *THE TRIAL:*
THE ASSAILANT AS LANDSCAPE

Where I spat in the harbor the oranges were bobbing
All salted and sodden, with eyes in their rinds;
The sky was all black where the coffee was burning,
And the rust of the freighters had reddened the tide.

But soon all the chimneys were hidden with contracts,
The tankers rode low in the oil-black bay,
The wharves were a maze of the crated bombers,
And they gave me a job and I worked all day.

And the orders are filled; but I float in the harbor,
All tarry and swollen, with gills in my sides,
The sky is all black where the carrier's burning,
And the blood of the transports is red on the tide.
           —RANDALL JARRELL, "The Metamorphoses"

—[i]—

THE OPENING SCENE of Kafka's *The Trial* describes a quite unexpected interruption in the life of its hero. An upstanding,
virtuous, and efficient man, he has reached his thirtieth birthday and is well established as an Assessor at the Bank. This
morning, however, instead of being greeted with good wishes
and his breakfast, he is confronted by a stranger, who announces

his arrest. This introductory shock is of the utmost importance to the impression the novel will ultimately have. It suggests the intrusion of the absurd into a world protected on all sides by familiar assurances and securities. Joseph K. is especially well acquainted with these comforts; his life is dedicated to an almost endless calculation, by means of which he helps to assure that society will function smoothly. The break in routine at first seems a trick, perhaps a birthday joke, which he will surely soon discover and dismiss. The strategy of this opening scene is to give the reader a brief acquaintance with an unfamiliar world. After all, he understands K., sympathizes with him, and is in many ways his double. There are rules, there is the law; people have long known how to take care of unexpected intrusions. It is unreasonable to expect that the disruption is more than temporary.

This is the first of the novel's contributions to Kafka's analysis of modern circumstance. The element of surprise in human relationships may last only so long; it cannot in any case be permitted to alter the design of human security, or that design will change. Surprise is an indispensable element of the fact of violence in modern life. A carefully plotted pattern of expected events has always been needed to sustain a customary existence. A sudden break in the routine challenges the fullest energy of man's power of adjustment. Suddenness is a quality of violence; it is a sign of force breaking through the design established to contain it.[1]

Another oddity of Kafka's opening scene is that the interruption is not a distortion of the setting in which it takes place. It is the same lodging house in which K. has lived for some years. The arrest takes place in the rooms, and the warders are ordinary citizens, and in the community at large there are universal peace and respect for the law.[2] Kafka describes the warders'

[1] See the beginning of Arthur Koestler's *Darkness at Noon*, discussed above, Part One, chapter 2.
[2] *The Trial*, tr. Willa and Edwin Muir; revised by E. M. Butler, New York, Knopf, 1956, p. 7. Other references to this edition are in the text.

appearance with the meticulous care that is one of his trademarks. One of the essentials of modern literature is that it should define and describe the violent disruptions of conventional life in a conventional way.[3] No work of Kafka lacks this precision.[4] This quality of style means that the enormity, the incredible event, in modern life is represented in conventional terms.

Kafka's skill in presenting the scene as precisely recognizable has another important effect. The scene and the personality at its center are in no genuine sense disparate. They possess a reciprocal status. The hero makes the scene possible, the scene reflects the hero's status. This interaction of scene and hero suggests a profound way of explaining the source of modern violence. We are in a very real sense the heirs of the nineteenth century, in that modern attitudes toward force were originally formed then, and the illusions of protective containment of force were gradually established in that time. The only way to understand violence—beyond superficial devices for merely admitting it as a fact of modern life—is to assume it as somehow the result of our willed interference with the balance of force and power in the human economy. We live constantly in a world in which this power is being extended. Many decades ago the instruments used for propelling force first exceeded the strength of man physically to contain or endure it. Almost daily now the means are improved to increase the disparity of force and personality and to lengthen the distance between assailant and victim.

---

[3] At the beginning, Joseph K. is entirely convinced that, "Once order was restored, every trace of these events would be obliterated and things would resume their old course." (24)

[4] Günther Anders says of Kafka's style: ". . . since he draws his strangely remote images . . . with the most scrupulous regard for detail, the result is a discrepancy between extreme unreality and extreme precision. . . ." The problem, as Anders puts it, is to decide "to what extent [Kafka's work] should be read in the indicative, and to what extent in the subjunctive." *Kafka*, tr. A. Steer and A. K. Thorlby, London, Bowes and Bowes, 1960, pp. 17, 53.

The warders who have come to inform Joseph K. of his arrest are persons like him. As K. is to discover much later, they are phases of himself, parts of the intricate conscious and subconscious pattern that is the totality of K. In any scrupulous analysis of K.'s situation, we shall have to say that K. has been interrupted by—K.; that his neatly efficient and rationally ordered life has been interfered with by himself.[5] In the spirit of a half-recognition of this shared impulse, K. takes his stand on a question of protocol, of form: by what right do these men invade his privacy; on whose orders? The warders as well manage the arrest in terms of rules: K. is supposed to stay in his room, he is not allowed to wander about the house, he must wait for the Inspector to arrive.[6] This is to suggest that the rules for order are not vastly different from the rules for disorder. They are both a part of the same man, of his will and of the way he exercises it in society. Manners are flexibly pertinent to each expression of human motive. One of the most persistent challenges to literature in an age of violence is that of accommodating human manners to violent occasions. The grammar of violence is achieved through a realignment of the grammatical terms of peace. In the modern war novel, for example, both the descriptions of violence and the matter of accommodation to it are given within the same range and scope of human intercourse.

I have several times suggested that modern literature of violence may best be seen in terms of the metaphor of the assailant

---

[5] In quite another context, Lionel Trilling, speaking of Freud's conception of the mind, says that "it is based upon the primacy of the will, and that the organization of the internal life is in the form, often fantastically parodic, of a criminal process in which the mind is at once the criminal, the victim, the police, the judge, and the executioner. . . ." "Little Dorrit," *Kenyon Review*, 15 (autumn 1953), p. 581. The inner complicity of which Trilling speaks is what K. persistently refuses to admit, trying again and again to project guilt feelings upon society and the legal system itself.

[6] Politeness is the ironic tone throughout. In the end, K.'s executioners bow ceremonially, and fastidiously attend to protocol.

and his victim.[7] The economy of this relationship may be defined as the distance achieved between the two. It is generally true that the range of psychological resources is best and most clearly employed in violent situations in which the distance between the assailant and the victim is so limited that the two protagonists are within sight of one another. In any violence there is a form of collaboration of the two involved in committing the act. The assailant strikes with force, the victim receives the force. The basic changes in the relationship occur when the distance becomes too great to allow for moral and emotional visibility as an element of the experience. It is only when that visibility is no longer possible that violence can be called "surprising." K. is surprised by his arrest, not because the warders are invisible, but because they are not the real assailants. He finds it all but impossible to adjust to the rules and regulations governing his arrest because he cannot see the source of it or the motive for its having happened. *The Trial* is made up largely of scenes in which K. searches energetically for his assailant. He never knows who he is, and dies without entirely understanding, or accepting, his complicity as victim. This desperate circumstance is repeated in a thousand ways in modern literature. The great energy invested in modern tragedy lies not so much in the carnage which is its established feature as in the uncertainty about causes and motives, the extreme difficulty in determining the victim's relationship to the act of violence.

—[ii]—

K is at liberty in the days following his arrest. The initiative of establishing the reality of his case is left to him. And at first he tries to hold to the idea that the whole thing is after all a hoax, or at worst so flagrant an injustice that he will need only to be firm and honest to have the affair exposed. His new role

[7] See above, Part Two, chapter 3.

of criminal is at first only moderately recognized by the men and women around him. The *idea* of criminality is communicated at first in terms of atmosphere and scene. There are no machines at present at the disposal of an assailant. Since the assailant is not known, to the Court, to K.'s friends, or to K. himself, nothing is specified in the usual sense. The elaborate devices used for criminal detection, with which any reader or viewer of murder mysteries is familiar, do not exist. Instead, the Court and its subordinate functions are found in rooms, located in buildings not unlike K.'s rooming house.

On one Sunday morning K. makes his way to such a house and is surprised that the scene provides no sign of its function as a court building. Once inside, he is again puzzled and annoyed that they should not have given him more definite information; ". . . these people showed a strange negligence or indifference in their treatment of him, he intended to tell them so very positively and clearly" (44–45). This dismay over the absence of conventional signs is closely related to the bewilderment over the accusation itself: who made it, why has it been made, how can he defend himself if he is so vague about its character? ". . . his mind played in retrospect with the saying of the warder Willem that an attraction existed between the Law and guilt, from which it should really follow that the Court of Inquiry must abut on the particular flight of stairs which K. happened to choose" (45). This is his first real insight into the nature of the crime; it is of the very substance of himself, and therefore the course of his discovering what it is follows the line of his will and choice. He is, however, by no means convinced of his guilt, as his speech in the Court attests. Innocent persons are accused of guilt, he tells his audience, "and senseless proceedings are put in motion against them, mostly without effect, it is true, as in my own case" (57).

No great exercise of the imagination is needed to grasp the significance of this remark, made as it is in a crowded room, the atmosphere "fuggy" and unclear, the audience divided in its view of the case.[8] K.'s talk is motivated by a "reasonable" indignation over the violation of his privacy. It stresses once again the role of the irrational in modern literature. The majority of literary reactions to the First World War were primarily expressions of shock, disbelief, extreme anger over the "unreasonableness" of the proceedings. This literature is clear at least on the question of the sources of violence. They are linked closely to the "fuggy" atmosphere created by force employed in the functioning of our economy. But beyond that, and more subtly, the mist, fog, smoke of the scene are of our own making. K. is talking into the dim and dirty atmosphere of his own mind as he strikes out at the unreasonableness of his circumstance. But he speaks as the Bank officer, setting that aspect of himself off from the other selves that may inhabit him. The scene of his protest is thus unreasonable; he finds it difficult both to see into it and to determine what if any part of his audience is sympathetic to him.

Moral tragedy has two major determinants: the matter of the hero's complicity, as assailant or victim, or a fusing of both; the matter of his state of awareness of his complicity. Hemingway's Lieutenant Henry, at first maddened by the irrationality of the Caporetto front, ends by saying that the war did not have anything to do with him. The worst fear haunting the protagonist of *The Waste Land* is that of his involvement as a sacrifice to the necessities the scene describes. Anger and fear are variously interrelated in modern literature, to suggest the deep bewilderment of the modern soul over the question of his precise relation to the criminal circumstance in which he

---

[8] References to fog, "dense air," "reek," thickness of the air, are not infrequent. See also pp. 47, 49, 58, 178, 186, 194. In the third of these, "the reek of the room and the dim light made a whitish dazzle of fog" (58). Later, K. feels momentarily faint, because of the stuffy, heavy atmosphere (83–84). The fact is that contact with the inner resources of his moral sense, without the protective diversions of his position in the Bank and in society is a frightening experience. The contrast of the heavy interior atmosphere with the crisp, fresh air of the outside has a bearing upon K.'s self-analysis in the matter of his guilt.

lives. In his own confident expansion of the possibilities of force, he has pushed assailant and victim further and further apart, until the instruments of violence have acquired such overwhelming force as to make the distinction all but impossible. The scene of the violence becomes the sole remaining evidence of motive and its relation to force; the assailant is the scene itself, and the scene includes the victim. The most extreme of our literary efforts to come to terms with violence begins by describing painstakingly the deterioration of the victim, to the point where he resembles the assailant and is to all intents and purposes indistinguishable from it. This condition is in part revealed by the fact that the modern hero is not distinguishable from his fellows; or, if he is different, it is only in the degree and detail in which he externalizes his inner violence. The hero is a man of inner and outer violence, moving from one to the other according to the disposition of the author toward the scene. Throughout there is a sense of the dim, strange, "fuggy" atmosphere that defines the condition at the same time as it prevents a clear grasp of the meaning of the violence.

The progress of Kafka's hero is in terms of such a metaphoric scene of diffused violence. K. steadfastly refuses to admit the scene as part of himself. He comes back a week later to the Court of Inquiry and, finding it unoccupied, looks about him. He picks up a volume of what he assumes are law books, but finds in it an indecent picture, crudely drawn, of a man and woman sitting naked on a sofa; another bears the title, *How Grete Was Plagued by Her Husband Hans.* Surely, he thinks, the courts must be more corrupt than he had guessed; to give his own case more than the most perfunctory and contemptuous attention would certainly mean contributing to an already bad situation. He turns to a woman in the room and finds her also involved in the corrupted scene. Quite without clearly recognizing the irony of his position, he is shortly engaged in wooing her support for his case, but also in spite of the Magistrate's claims upon her, in terms of the very corruptive influence he has just recently scorned: "And probably there could be no more fitting revenge on the Examining Magistrate and his henchmen than to wrest this woman from them and take her himself" (70). He is at once the outraged victim and the conniving collaborator of the situation. Throughout the progress of the novel, this dual role suggests itself in trivial acts and gestures; K. makes his way toward his death, never fully suspecting the force of his own role in causing it.

The most brilliantly revealing scene in this connection is the episode of the flogging (104–108). The two warders who had first arrested K. have been sentenced to be whipped because of a complaint he has made about their behavior (they had tried to appropriate some of K.'s private belongings). But, K. insists, he hadn't intended to have them whipped; he was "only defending a principle" (105). In any event, he is shocked that the scene should be taking place in the Bank building, and most disturbed that the noise might rouse the attention of the men still there. Here he is directly forced to see that he can be an agent of violence, and the sight disgusts him. In what way is a man involved in the sufferings of others? The disparity of principle and human incident is here eloquently presented. The intricate and complex wavering of principle and chance in our moral life causes incidental and sometimes violent pain to others.[9]

This universal enigma is especially and compellingly evident in the literature which attempts to explore the intricacies of motive in modern violence. How much may we say of the degree of responsibility for great violence done many persons, for destruction on a vast scale? The modern hero often quickly loses sight of the question, or is distracted from it by the impact of violence itself. There is an especially vivid illustration

[9] This point is directly related to civilian responsibility in the matter of the concentration camp and similar tortures. See Bruno Bettelheim, *The Informed Heart* (1960) and J.-P. Sartre's introduction to Henri Alleg's *The Question* (1958).

of the confusion this question leads to in a French novel of the second war, Robert Merle's *Weekend at Dunkirk*.[10] The hero, Maillat, is from the beginning involved in scores of violent scenes; his own friend is quite suddenly, "unreasonably" destroyed, almost before his eyes; he himself narrowly escapes being destroyed on a British ship which has taken a direct hit from a Nazi bomber. When he enters a room in a partially destroyed home, he finds two fellow soldiers engaged in raping a French girl. Outraged by the scene, he kills the two men; as he confesses later, he had "enjoyed" the experience of seeing them cringe before him, "obeying" his power over them. The will, strongly roused by the incident, exerts itself violently shortly thereafter, and he takes the girl himself.

Not only is the will to violence stimulated by the act itself; the force within us is nourished by the exigencies of a violent scene. Kafka's scene merely suggests that the will to violence exists, that it may set off physical action despite the strongest of expressed desires to contain it. Kafka's hero is deeply involved in the flogging scene, and not only because he has initiated the action. His reasons for protesting it are primarily selfish; he does not wish to admit himself capable of such a will; he first tries to bribe the Whipper to let them off; and, when a cry of pain rises from one of the victims, he is distressed, but only because someone might hear the ugly sound. As two clerks of the Bank come up to inquire if anything is wrong, K. turns them aside with the remark, "It was only a dog howling in the courtyard" (108). K. cannot afford to let persons associated with the dignity of his own position know about the tangle of efforts rising from his arrest.

The meaning of this detail expands beyond itself, to the pattern of the novel itself, and beyond that to the phenomenon of the wound. A short story of Kafka's, "A Country Doctor,"

[10] Originally published as *Week-End à Zuydcote* (Paris, Gallimard, 1949), this novel won the Prix Goncourt and was translated by K. Rebillon-Lambley (New York, Knopf, 1951).

contains a series of weird mischances, the worst of which is the sight of an incurable wound. The patient, a young boy, had not at first seemed very ill, only mildly feverish; so that the wound made its appearance shockingly and without discernible cause: "In his right side, near the hip, was an open wound as big as the palm of my hand. Rose-red, in many variations of shade, dark in the hollows, lighter at the edges, softly granulated, with irregular clots of blood, open as a surface mine to the daylight." [11] This is the open wound of the human disposition to pain, and the doctor discovers upon closer examination that it also contains the consuming worms of death.

The meaning of this weirdly shocking detail is not easy to grasp; but it would not be too much to say that the boy had willed the wound, or that—in the light of his relationship to the shock of life—he had welcomed it, at any rate that he was scarcely indifferent to it. In Kafka's story, it is the doctor who suffers the worst calamity; the wounded boy submits to death as in a most revealing way the victim of a self-willed affliction. Once again the strange paradox of the assailant as landscape confronts us. For, as our indifference (as in K.'s thoughtless complaint) involves us morally in the suffering of others, we move with even more force of anger and desire across the landscape of violence, to participate in our undoing. Kafka's novel above all stresses both our journey across this landscape and our unwitting share in its malevolent character.

—[iii]—

This effect persists throughout. K. is gradually brought to a partial awareness of the seriousness of his circumstance, but he does not relinquish the privilege of righteous immunity. There are always extenuations: the corruption of the Court,

[11] In *The Penal Colony: Stories and Short Pieces*, tr. Willa and Edwin Muir, New York, Schocken, 1948, p. 141.

the venality of lesser officials, the protective images of the security his position in the Bank provides, and so forth. At no time is the crime specified; at no time are the officials or minions of the Law made to look like monsters or grotesques. They are common variants of the human condition, of which K. is himself the central image. *The Trial* is in this sense a parable of man's grudging journey to moral awareness. Above all, it stresses the fatal deficiency of common moral safeguards. We are aware of their failure only when, suddenly and without warning, they fail us. One of Kay Boyle's novels, *The Seagull on the Step*,[12] describes a busload of passengers on a routine journey in southern France soon after the end of the second war. Her attention is dispersed throughout the crowded bus and only occasionally focuses upon the driver, who impresses her as the most trustworthy of the tribe. A brake failure at the last plunges the vehicle down a cliff to destruction and death.

This melodramatic instance simply points up an obvious fact which is all but willfully neglected. K.'s concern for his innocence is only gradually moved from the center of his belligerent confidence in conventional rectitude. His uncle arrives from the country, profoundly disturbed over the news of K.s' arrest and even more upset that he should not have more scrupulously attended to his case. On one of his visits to Dr. Huld, the Lawyer whom his uncle has engaged in his behalf, K. finds a commercial traveler, named Block, already there and apparently in constant, eager attendance upon the Advocate's every word. Block is an example of the force of unrelenting piety, the parody of a narrow moralistic self-concern. His submission to the most ludicrous of requirements does not testify to his being in any sense a righteous man, but rather suggests an energetic passivity, almost a ruthless drive toward self-involvement in guilt. While K. holds the Court guilty of a malicious miscarriage of procedure, Block submits to whatever may be with a diligent persistence. His

[12] New York, Knopf, 1955.

action suggests a soldier hurrying from skull to skull, in search of whichever one had once been his head. When K. visits Dr. Huld, it is with the intention of telling him he no longer wishes his services, that he feels he will now go on his own. The contrast of Block and K. describes the range of earnestness in the moral life. It is significant also that Block should consider independent action abhorrent, and that K. should endorse it and follow a course of unavailing private vindication (219).

If only because the demands upon his time have made him weary and listless in his performance as Bank Assessor, K.'s quest of definition shows obvious signs of absorbing his attention more and more.[13] Without relinquishing his firm belief in his innocence, he nevertheless improvises strategies of self-defense. He thinks of sending in a written defense, with explanations interpersed, wherever his actions seem to suggest them (142). But of course this would scarcely be proper, and in any case it would be lost in the clumsy proceedings of the Court.[14] The "busyness" of K.'s mind suggests an active concern with the question of his guilt; and as he becomes absorbed in it, rational procedures seem shunted aside and K.'s "stand" of shocked innocence recedes.

On one occasion he visits a painter, Titorelli, who makes a poor enough living doing portraits of minor officials. The scene of Titorelli's quarters is itself a revealing image of the moral landscape. It is even a poorer neighborhood than that in which K. had encountered the Court of Inquiry for the first time.[15]

> . . . the houses were still darker, the streets filled with sludge oozing about slowly on top of the melting snow.

[13] "The thought of his case never left him now" (142).

[14] It is important to note that the accused needs to push his case, to provide the initiative for it (148–49). This written plea is a gesture of the victim toward his assailant, an attempt to penetrate to the truth or the falsity of the charges against him.

[15] Of course, there are courtrooms everywhere (see p. 205); there would have to be, if the scene and the mind of the hero are considered phases of one search for guilt.

In the tenement where the painter lived only one wing of the great double door stood open, and beneath the other wing, in the masonry near the ground, there was a gaping hole out of which, just as K. approached, issued a disgusting fluid, steaming hot, from which some rats fled into the adjoining canal. (176)

Like many others of Kafka's scenes, this may be taken to suggest a variety of meanings. Surely it is in itself identifiable as a disheartening and disgusting slum, whose chief distinguishing marks most candidly define the body's private functions. As the relationship to space diminishes, the chance of either hiding such functions or breathing good air all but disappears. K. may be said here to have undertaken a journey to the ugliest sector of his own moral world. Within the tenement he encounters three ugly, bold-faced young girls; one of them "nudged him with her elbow and peered up at him knowingly. Neither her youth nor her deformity had saved her from being prematurely debauched" (177). When K. finally finds his way to Titorelli's room, he notes that the air here is even more atrociously hot and foul than that of the courtroom he had visited. The entire scene clearly defines the decor of human evil. It is not an evil of commission, but an evil of disregard, of the impurities which the body's efforts for survival create in an imperfect and vulgarized atmosphere.

In another sense it is an atmosphere of purgation. The foul smell, the darkness, the constriction of space are all elements identifying the character of the body, its emission of impurities in the ordinary course of its progress toward inevitable corruption. K., in entering it, may almost literally be said to be journeying toward death, for the smell of death is about him and the space he occupies is not much larger than the space of a tomb. In such an atmosphere, K. discusses his case with Titorelli. He is unregenerately convinced that the whole affair is an elaborate injustice, but he is also aware that the ways of justice are skillful, subtle, and devious: ". . . And in the end, out of nothing at all, an enormous fabric of guilt will be conjured up" (186). This remark and the scene in which it is made are available to numerous interpretations, but none of them is free of some suggestion of the idea the novel as a whole supports. The intricacies of human justice and intelligence are a composite of many fragmented decisions and their underlying motives. Evil is subtly and slyly intermixed with the good; indeed, the good is scarcely to be defined by itself, since a just impulse can easily react painfully upon a weaker self.

The portrait Titorelli shows K. gives an ambiguous impression of Justice and Victory combined, though a trick of light and shadow also brings out the impression of "a goddess of the Hunt in full cry" (182–84). The passion for "right feeling," for a principled life, might easily be confused in the chance admixture of aggression, so that one portrait reveals all three. The impression should convince the hero that he cannot longer expect surface good will to save him from the crime of which he is accused. One strong impression this scene gives is that the human will is never free of the taint of arrogance or ambition; nor is a human act ever free of the chance of causing pain, however indirectly.[16] Quite aside from the very real service K.'s visit to Titorelli performs, that of describing the "bureaucratic" deviousness of moral defenses, by way of making him more fully aware of the seriousness of his case, the scene is itself the most powerful literary image of the landscape of violence. Here there is no real discrimination between assailant and victim. In submitting to the indignities of this setting, K. is in a real sense examining himself, or seeing the capacity of the self for absorbing the filth of its own making. The most effectively shocking of modern scenes is that in which the disorder

---

[16] Titorelli suggests the possibility " 'that in all the cases known to me there was none in which the accused was really innocent' " (192). If this be true, definite acquittal seems unlikely. It is not his function to define innocence or to draw the line between it and guilt.

of the soul is imaged in a disarray of objects scattered in space. Man's power of calling forth violence, or of enduring within a landscape of its effects, is suggested again and again in modern literature.

More than that, the victim of this violence is himself an initiator of it. K.'s will and soul are here set forth most uncomprisingly. As he discusses the legal possibilities of his case, he remains at the very center of the disorder to which the officials ordering his arrest had originally hoped to call attention. In this very effective way, Kafka shows him growing toward an awareness of his situation at the very time when he is most earnestly exploring the chances of evasion. Effective as this scene is, it has many equals in modern literature: the apartment scene in *The Great Gatsby*, where the potential violence of Tom Buchanan and Myrtle Wilson is imaged in the powerful contraction of pretentious objects crowded into a tiny space; the "Cyclops" episode of Joyce's *Ulysses*, where the violence is an expression of both a belligerent anti-Semitism and a self-indulgence; the shafts leading down into the mines of Zola's *Germinal*, with their human cargo and their constant threat of damage and disaster; the violence of Naphta and Settembrini as they duel for power over Hans Castorp's soul, in Mann's *The Magic Mountain*. In each of these details (and in scores of war episodes) the scene itself reveals a potential complicity of victim in the act of violence. In Kafka's novel the violence is implicit in almost every detail of Titorelli's residence—not the least, in the shameless defiance of the neat and circumspect decorum which K. had at the beginning relied upon to save himself. K. is a partner in the scene; he has himself willed the ugly distortions and constrictions of the reality of which he is now in the center.

As it turns out, the world is a prison to the degree that man wills it to be. In the next to last of the novel's scenes, K. finds himself in the Cathedral, where he is awaiting a visitor whom the Bank has asked him to entertain. The event has been carefully prepared, and is eligible to much easy allegorical interpretation. One can say that K. has come to the Cathedral to hear still another version of his case; or that he is there because of the connivance of the Law officials, who are after all designers of his conscience. Whatever the meaning of the plans, K. is in the dark interior and, waiting for his guest, looks about him. He is curiously drawn to the altar-piece of a small side chapel which appears to contain near its outer edge the picture of a huge armoured knight.

> He was leaning on his sword, which was stuck into the bare ground, bare except for a stray blade of grass or two. He seemed to be watching attentively some event unfolding itself before his eyes . . . (257)

The center of the picture is a conventional enough portrayal of Christ being laid in the tomb, but K.'s attention now aroused, he searches further. His eyes are finally drawn to a small pulpit of plain stone, so small as scarcely to accommodate the preacher whom he now sees for the first time.

The scene is a sharply realistic addition to the parable of K.'s life. Once again he finds himself within a setting that is closely identified with his moral circumstance. The huge armoured knight he had examined so curiously guards the tomb; the small side chapel is the site chosen for his meditation on his "case"—that is to say, on his willed intervention in the affairs of men and his resistance to confession of the guilt. The priest who stands in the pulpit is the prison chaplain, there to discuss his present disposition to the case. Throughout, the lighting is an important part of the decor, as it is elsewhere in the novel. Light seems intended either momentarily to blind K. or, as Heinz Politzer says, "to reveal the depth of the darkness." [17] K.'s relationship to the priest has several ambiguities. First, he thinks of ignoring his act of calling out his

[17] *Franz Kafka: Parable and Paradox*, Ithaca, Cornell University Press, 1962, p. 182.

name. If he should go out of the Cathedral, without turning about, he would still be free. But he does turn, and so commits himself as a person "involved." The communication that follows is half sermon, half dialogue.

In both the telling and the exegesis of the fable, "Before the Law," [18] the moral ambiguities remain unresolved, both of K.'s own position and of that of the Court. "Before the Law stands a doorkeeper, . . ." the priest begins. To him comes a man from the country, seeking admittance to the Law (267). It is a reduced vision of the innocent encountering the intricacies of known, suspected, and unknown moral guilt. The Law may be or is roughly equivalent to the Light, the illumination cast by a central radiance, but again, as elsewhere, there is no light that does anything but prevent seeing or momentarily offer the briefest glimpse of what lies at center.

The fable may also be assumed to suggest the monstrous "bureaucracy" of thought, order, and taste within society. To it all of the persons K. encounters are related; but, as in the case of the doorkeeper, it is doubtful that their association with the Law can help him, and it may (as the priest himself suggests) actually prevent him from seeing himself as he should. Quite aside from the various interpretations given *The Trial* since the end of World War II, there is the overwhelming evidence that K. does not know what he is accused of, is sensitively certain that he is innocent and has been unfairly treated, and holds to the conviction that the matter has been irrational from the beginning and is therefore beyond being taken seriously.

Two statements which the priest makes point up the ambiguity of K.'s circumstance. First, in response to K.'s objection that the doorkeeper before the Law had deceived the man, he says that "The right perception of any matter and a misunderstanding of the same matter do not wholly exclude

---

[18] Pp. 267–76. Cf. "Before the Law," in *Parables*, tr. Willa and Edwin Muir, New York, Schocken, 1947, pp. 45–63.

each other" (271). This is to distinguish between perception (or intuition) and "right reason"; the latter leaves out the emotional qualities of persons, tends to give K. a sense of the "rightness" of his position, and to justify his "using" persons for his own ends. This is an important feature of his guilt; its equivalent can be found in scores of testimonies in modern literature which treat of the moral bureaucracies. The second remark is also addressed to (or opposed to) the assertion of K.'s innocence, or rightness, or sanity in the midst of an irrational muddle. K. maintains a "legalistic" view, for which he has ample justification. He cannot accept either the doorkeeper's remarks or his actions. But the priest says: ". . . it is not necessary to accept everything as true, one must only accept it as necessary" (276). While K. rejects this reading of the fable, because—as he says—"It turns lying into a universal principle" (276), it does strike at the heart of the novel's moral problems.

There is no simple way of interpreting it, no stand which K. can take with impunity, and correspondingly no "right" moral attitude to assume. Kafka's style and dramatic sense are, as elsewhere, extremely precise in detail but ambiguous in meaning. K.'s position, while superficially it may seem to suggest a lonely heroism, is confused by his uncompromising view of his innocence and his being a part of the Bank, whose extravagance of precise and complex organization resembles that of the Law. K. is therefore not a pure martyr to the heroic role of threatened individualism. His defense of himself is throughout handicapped by an unexamined assertion of innocence and by his soiling his own hands in the defective means taken to seek a way out.

Significantly, K. gropes his way out of the darkened Cathedral, unregenerately sure of the justness of his cause, unseeing and unhelped. The lamp he had held during his debate with the priest has long since gone out, and the two are left in the dark. As the "simple story" had lost for him its clarity of outline, so the darkness of the church now depresses him. "The silver image of some saint once glimmered into sight immediately before him, by the sheen of its own silver, and was instantaneously lost in the darkness again" (277). Kafka again and again says "No" to the easy triumph, the surface mannerism indicating virtue. K. is not enlightened, nor forgiven, nor precisely aware of his involvement in evil, as he makes his way out of the darkened Cathedral.

—[iv]—

There is nothing left to do now but send K. to his death. Kafka has conscientiously attended to every conceivable scenic effect, and K.'s soul has been quite exhaustively examined. A year after his arrest on the eve of his thirty-first birthday, two men call at his lodging. Once again their appearance is grotesquely inappropriate to one's expectation of killers on a mission: "In frock-coats, pallid and plump, with top-hats that were apparently irremovable" (279). The circumstances of violence are to the very end the same as those of normality. The men are polite to excess: "Tenth-rate old actors they send for me," K. grumbles. "They want to finish me off cheaply" (280). Still firm in his disbelief, convinced of his innocence, K. walks between and slightly to the front of these grotesquely proper persons, like servants perhaps, doormen or carriage attendants: ". . . the only thing for me to go on doing is to keep my intelligence calm and analytical to the end" (282).

As the walk progresses, K. quickens the pace; and the two executioners, their arms tightly clasped to his, run with him. The death occurs on the outskirts of the town, near an old stone quarry, though there is also "a still completely urban house" nearby. One of the men draws out a long, thin, double-edged butcher's knife, and the two of them pass it to each other across K.'s body. "K. now perceived clearly that he was supposed to seize the knife himself, as it travelled from hand to hand, and plunge it into his own breast" (285). But he does not do so, and the partners collaborate in the death, one of them holding K.'s throat, the other thrusting the knife into his heart.

> With failing eyes K. could still see the two of them, cheek leaning against cheek, immediately before his face immediately before him, cheek leaning against cheek, watching the final act. "Like a dog!" he said; it was as if the shame of it must outlive him. (286)

Just before this act, K. had turned his head to one side and in the direction of the distant dwelling. He saw, or thought he saw, a man reaching outstretched arms to him. Even at this moment of extremity, his hopes were stimulated. Could the man be offering help? Was there still some evidence that might save him? Is it possible that the man was an intermediary, who had the power to call off the execution? But the death does occur, the most ambiguous of conclusions of a baffling case. K. is alert to the end to the shame of his death, to its lack of dignity. It is unworthy of him; it has been committed at the level of an animal cruelly tortured to give sadistic pleasure.

The killing is the final ambiguity which follows correctly from a succession of ambiguous scenes. K. is a superb example of the modern moral hero, whose two great and striking characteristics are that he proclaims his innocence while in the act of willing his guilt, and that as a victim of a scene of violence he conspires with the assailant in the act of his death.[19] There

[19] Jean-Louis Barrault, speaking of his work with André Gide on the dramatization of The Trial, says that in 1937 "Kafka was our temporary comfort . . ." because he helped to explain the modern world. But by 1947, he had become "the true prophet of our times." "The ordinary man who was supposed to be free had less and less freedom in his city: every man was fundamentally guilty. . . ." The Theatre of Jean-Louis Barrault, tr. Joseph Chiari, New York, Hill and Wang, 1961, pp. 123–24. See Maja Goth, Franz Kafka et les lettres françaises, 1928–1955, Paris, José Corti, 1956, especially chapters 4–7.

is no clear separation of the assailant from the victim in this case. The elaborate, scenic meditation of which the novel consists portrays modern man willing his guilt as he asserts principle, most tragically of all perhaps unable or unwilling to discriminate between the satisfactory reason and the ambiguous cause. While men have always fought wars for a cause and have invoked principle in defense of violence, they have not been altogether clearly vindicated in either case. Events culminating in violence lead after their conclusion very quickly to retrospective doubt.

The history of violence in the twentieth century is dominated by examples of ambiguous dying. The worst fate a man can suffer is a death that is undignified, "Like a dog!" as K. had said in pronouncing upon his. But modern violence is especially efficient in producing corpses without and beyond the hope of ceremonial mitigation. The modern man of violence has at his disposal instruments which increase almost incalculably the irrational condition of dying. They are capable of sudden, irrational, calamitous disruptions of the landscape. They are also capable of almost absolute annihilation. These instruments are the creation of man, of his mind and of his genius.[20] They have caused several serious dislocations in the moral balance according to which violence had previously been judged and its responsibility allocated. For one thing, the distance between assailant and victim is now irretrievably lost; there is no certain, discernible, chartable relationship between the two. This means that beyond a certain point the *idea* of an assailant has disappeared.

In the many portrayals of war in modern literature, there is

[20] Günther Anders suggests that Kafka's characters "are prophetically enacting through their grotesque selves and experiences the most ghastly occurrences of our time . . ." (48). And: ". . . although each individual depends for his existence upon being an official employee, no one enjoys the right to see through the role he plays in the bureaucratic whole . . ." (51). The combination of "dislocated function" and bureaucratic busyness explains at least partway the pathos of a society torn by violence whose power has exceeded human intelligence.

a common refrain: that war is inhuman, unreasonable, untenable. But the only literature of violence that can convincingly endure is that which attempts to grasp this fundamental ambiguity: that weapons created by the acts of rational and ingenious men have destroyed the power of the reason either to contemplate or to comprehend the results of their uses. Unless we wish to settle for a kind of historical fiction which merely allows the reader to relive the war experience, some variant of Kafka's approach is surely needed. The overpowering image left at the end of K.'s struggle is of the victim conniving with the assailant in his own destruction. The assailant is no longer a single, identifiable, fingerprinted criminal, whose act can be related to the clear circumstances of a victim's death; the two, in the complex of moral implications described in *The Trial*, are joined in the landscape of violence itself. It is only in this sense that we can understand the paradox of cruelty committed "without cruel intent," or of Eliot's statement that ". . . Unnatural vices / Are fathered by our heroism. Virtues / Are forced upon us by our impudent crimes."

A word of warning in Günther Anders' little book suggests in a number of ways Kafka's relevance and his danger for our time. With apparent prescience, Kafka happened to hit upon a moral issue that has since all but overwhelmed us with its pertinence.

> His work is not of today [Anders says], but of the day before yesterday. He could not have foreseen the historical situation in which it would be made use of. His allusions to the world of terror and conformity, a world of which we now are the contemporary witnesses, were not then allusions to anything which existed. (*Kafka*, 98)

While Anders warns against the opportune use of Kafka as a means of rationalizing moral fatalism in our present behavior, there is no doubt that Kafka's great influence on the literature and thought of the 1950's and 1960's is a part of the effort to find a rhetoric that will explain and adapt to present circumstance the intricate intellectual and moral twisting and turning so exorbitantly undertaken by his characters, and the several images of debasement and humiliation before "authority." These are a beginning in the history of a search for symbolic perspectives upon Nazi Germany and the *esthétique du mal* of literature in terms of modern events. But they *are* only a beginning.

Postwar moralists are bound to find anagogic significance in the ambiguities engendered by Kafka's precise vagueness. The move toward an exact and "proper" rhetoric for the events of the past two decades does not stop with the expropriation of Kafka. The genuine problem is to define the evil without self-indulgence at the expense of a scapegoat. Throughout the literary analysis of violence, there is an uneasy imbalance of Buchenwald and Hiroshima. Literary attempts to define evil in the light of the specific history of Nazism from 1934 to 1945 must unite Kafka's precision with his moral doubt and symbolic disjunctions. The fight to maintain a pattern of literary definition and yet keep within the pace and rhythm of history itself causes many false starts and exorbitant moral gestures (ethical melodrama repeatedly threatens the thrust toward moral precision).[21] The point is Kafka's having (inadvertently perhaps) stated basic issues for twentieth century morality and for literature that is serious enough to break away from formalist securities and to become ethically, historically, and retrospectively significant.

[21] The conflict between the two and its tragic results are no better demonstrated than by an event that took place in Dallas, Texas, on November 22, 1963. A man whose ideological and moral training was at best terribly ambiguous, secured an efficient and precise instrument, by means of which he was able to destroy President John F. Kennedy, who at the time of the shooting was not aware either of his assailant or of himself as victim. Partly this was the result of a series of abstractions, which separated the assailant from President Kennedy. The two were kept apart by an ideological as well as a physical distance (see above, p. 295).

PART THREE

SELF

10

THE TRANSCENDENT SELF

—[i]—

THE CONSEQUENCES of indiscriminate dying are far-reaching for language and literature, and for the modes of sustaining belief in the self. The most significant characteristic of twentieth century thought is that of the self's improvising and experimenting with ways of maintaining self-confidence. We move away from metaphysics and toward forms of epistemology; self-definition becomes a series of improvisational gestures; there is a profound and a poignant distrust of traditional schemes of definition. In his most confident moments of self-assertion, modern man is still in the act of willing his wholeness, his prospects of enduring in time, his dignity and his worth.

The most profoundly charged act of the modern self is an act of the will: it is the "adventure" of choice. The self must choose what he is, what he will be, what he will do by way of assuming a position with respect to his death. The expectation of dying becomes a major issue. As an ultimate boundary situation, one which no one can avoid, it offers additional kinds and degrees of challenge and stimulates new exercises of the will. The choice of dying, of being aware that one is dying, is closely linked to the psychological problem of willing the persistence of self-identity in time.

All speculations concerning the relations of the self to a "higher being," of time to eternity, are hedged by paradox. At best, the nature and condition of immortality are a gamble. The peculiarities of twentieth century meditations on the self are contained in the suggestion that not only immortality but self-continuance are almost wholly responsibilities of the contingent, present, existing self. In the modern philosophical drama, the "I" maneuvers in time, in relational exercises, and with the logic of continuance and the melodrama of survival. As social forms, in the ways in which they are historically described, seem causally linked to the development of destructive powers, the self moves away from their center. Whether boldly (in a drama or melodrama of rebellion) or whimsically or pathetically, the self retreats toward the periphery of well-defined circles, or toward the margin of society. It "goes underground"; or it wanders the surface of the earth in an effort to avoid association with respectable social forms; or it improvises or imagines or conspires to create small areas of humanity in which it can maintain some form of unified existence.

The history of the self in modern literature comprises several rather well-defined situations. In each, the imagination, the moral will, and the speculative power of the ego are *engaged* autonomously; the initiative toward decision and the responsibility of choice are his. The first of these involves the paradoxes of the relationship of creator to creature: these have an almost infinite variety, in accordance with the degree to which the two are seen as separable entities or tend to be fused as single essences. Existentialist man treats the questions of a "supreme being" and of His traditional powers, with the aberrancy of a prodigal son who alternately defies the father and usurps his position as creator. One of the great metaphoric gestures is that of maneuvering the metaphysical properties of the Trinity into areas of secular improvisation: the creator, his divinely created creature, and the "spiritual fire" of grace are each and all given many new forms and roles. In many cases, God, who traditionally speaks in and through thunder and by fiat assertion, is dropped from man's calculations as unmanageable or too remote from the immediate needs of self-adjustment to be tolerated with confidence. Christ, the middle figure of the Trinity, gains immensely in the exchange; and the human imagination is most active in inventing new roles and settings for Him. The devaluation of God the Father is a consequence of the rebellion against *pater familias*; ultimately the revolt against God takes the form of minor discretionary rearrangements of the self as creator of the self, the self as creator of other selves, the self as responsibly engaged in surviving the pressure of other selves.[1]

Closely associated with this *théâtre mélangé* is a series of reflective encounters with the paradoxes of time and eternity. The metaphor of eternity converging upon or resting within a still point of time is a basic challenge. Quite aside from all speculations about creation, the questions are reduced to one: *does* eternity, or *can* it, reside in time? If it does, then movement through time *may* involve the experiencing of eternity, and the religious quality of experience *may* "save the self" from extinction. But even when one is willing to accept this possibility, the general tendency is to make the act of acceptance an act of the will, a "leap" from disbelief to belief.

Generally, the facts do not support this conviction. The modern self is strenuously engaged in analyzing moments of existing, knowing, enduring. The modern philosophical hero is almost invariably a split self: the self who exists and the self who reflects upon his role as an existing being. The engagement of the self with the challenge of endurance (or of continuing in time and space) is a primary literary event. What follows from the initial act of "j'existe" is an almost interminable succession of desperate stratagems whose purpose is to guarantee continuance. They are a *sine qua non* of self-definition;

---

[1] This is especially true in the work of Joyce and of Samuel Beckett. For Joyce, see below, Part Three, chapter 12; for Beckett, see my book, *Samuel Beckett: The Language of Self*, Carbondale, Southern Illinois University Press, 1962. The struggle against the *pater familias* is seen especially as a background of the history of Freud's attempt to diagnose and "cure" psychological illnesses in terms of the family center. The vigorously sententious father is altogether too formidable for many to cope with; he becomes inhumane, or jealousies and hatred prevent his effectiveness.

to define the self is an act which involves one in the burden of successive redefinitions and revaluations. The *qualia* come from immediate sensation, from memory (which is in itself dependent upon sensory experiences that endure by *force majeure*), from a concentration upon image or object, and finally from a symbolic action that is an act of improvisation rather than of belief. One way of putting the issue is that one believes what he has put himself in the way of believing; that is, that he creates the conditions of belief and improvises the means of sustaining them.

It is difficult to prove that all of these exercises in self-assertion are necessary reactions to the violences I have described in Part Two. In many respects, the doubt of eternity, the resistance to the image of God, and the impulse to go the way of self-definition on one's own, are historical phenomena. The differences are more a matter of degree than of kind. It is quite possible to prove a similar stir and activity in the Renaissance, in the seventeenth century, in the nineteenth century. Indeed, most of the language and many of the figurations of twentieth century literary reflection come from the past; but they are less surely relied upon as links to eternity and immortality. The modern literary consciousness, as we shall see, is more liable to going off the deep end, and more inclined to indulge in acts of auto-creation or auto-definition; he is less trustful of the "miraculous conceit" which rescues the self from time and puts him into eternity in that awesome pause between the last minute of "j'existe" and the time of "je suis mort." Finally, more attention is paid the act, or state, of being conscious (the rhetoric of self-analysis has changed, and the "interior monologue" becomes more important); as though that condition in itself contained valid and saving graces of selfness which are substantive, profound, are even testimonies of immortality. We come to the last paradox of modern self-assertion: the effort to make aspects of mortality seem or even validly be guarantors of "immortality." Death is either annihilation or it is the "mother of beauty," the ultimate challenge to the imagination, that it make as much as it can of the threat of impermanence.

—[ii]—

Nothing is so obvious as the change in self-consciousness that has occurred in modern literature. One way of defining this change is to say that our modes of expression have shifted from self-assertion to self-analysis. But this is perhaps too simple; it permits too many exceptions to be a useful generality. A more satisfactory formula is this: the general attitude toward the self has changed from regarding it as substance to analyzing it as *process*. If we extend this latter view, we may allow for the extraordinary range in modern literature of self-analysis: explorations of "streams of consciousness," adaptations of the techniques and styles of analysis to literary expression, and examinations of the moral, experiential, and situational positions of the ego. The principal literary concerns of our century have been the definition of an isolated self, its precise location in both space and time, its relationship to objects and to process. These considerations are at the core of the secular assertions and fears which dominate our literature.

The psychology of William James has had a major role in the history of American culture especially, but also generally in modern intellectual history. James is an interesting example of the Victorian scientist whose researches lead him away from convictions he prefers to hold and land him in an uncomfortable situation, from which he hopes to *will* his escape. In this respect, volition becomes a surrogate agent of belief: the quality, power, and energy of the will, in its projections into possibility, become the means of identifying and measuring the self. More important for modern literature, however, is his having helped in shifting the perspective upon the self:

from the self at center projecting outward, to the self as an inner center, as a focus of analysis, one may almost say a victim of it.

Perhaps we can most clearly appreciate the earlier, Transcendentalist vision of the American self in the design of a circle, the circumference ever widening to include more and more space, and the eye of self at a metaphysical "true center." [2] This image not only testifies to the egocentrism of American valuations; it points to vision as the instrument according to which any and all speculative measurements are made. Other senses were of course useful: Thoreau's extraordinarily sensitive hearing helped him to project Walden Pond into the universe of his choosing. But it was with the eye that the continent was first comprehended; and the geometric designs of its gradual conquest were above all visually comprehensible.

Emerson moved out from epicenter into the imagined universe in terms of a series of concentric circles: "The eye is the first circle; the horizon which it forms is the second." While he warned us never to lose sight of the objects around us, which were grains of cosmos at the disposal of our imagination, he insisted upon the power of the eye to extend the range of its circles:

Our little circles absorb us and occupy us as fully as the heavens; we can minimize as infinitely as maximize, and the only way out of it is (to use a country phrase) to kick the pail over, and accept the horizon instead of the pail, with celestial attractions and influences, instead of worms and mud pies.[3]

[2] This is a central idea of Sherman Paul's excellent study, *Emerson's Angle of Vision*, Cambridge, Mass., Harvard University Press, 1952.
[3] The first quotation is from the Centenary Edition of *The Complete Works of Ralph Waldo Emerson*, Boston, Houghton, Mifflin, 1904, Vol. II, p. 301. The second is from *The Journals of Ralph Waldo Emerson*, edited by Edward Waldo Emerson and Waldo Emerson Forbes. Boston: Houghton, Mifflin, 1909–1914. Vol. X, p. 238. Both are quoted in Paul's *Emerson's Angle of Vision*, p. 75.

The eye ranges outward, as God inward, and shortly the universe is both comprehended by the self, and through a "leap" of the imagination at least, a projection of it. "I become a transparent eyeball; I am doing nothing; I see all; the currents of the Universal Being circulate through me; I am part or parcel of God." [4] In many accesses of egocentric confidence, Emerson pursued the metaphor of the "transparent eyeball," suggesting it as an imaginative means of self-characterization. The self so pictured quite clearly stood at a central point from which it "created" the universe, in the sense of comprehending it actively and significantly shaping it. This exercise of the Transcendental imagination served Emerson at the least as a means of shifting the world view from that of God looking in at man to the more acceptable one of man expansively projecting his energy of vision outward —so that the self and not God is the more active and, so far as the self is concerned, the more creative being.

As Emerson moved through the nineteenth century, his confidence in inner dominion languished, as did that of the majority of his contemporaries. It was all but impossible to stay very long in the century (Emerson lasted until 1882) without yielding a little of that egocentric faith to the importunities of naturalistic "force." The change in Emerson's view is a reflection of a general change in the image-making power of the American. It is to be seen especially in Whitman's celebrations of the ego, which often dissolve into fragmentary accounts of things cut off from their center. Two important facts are at the source of this change: the multiplication of things and the loss of the power of the eye practically to comprehend their range. But in the time of his beginnings there was no sign of hesitation in Emerson's affirmation of the creative and dominating self.

In another corner of Concord's miscrocosmic center, Thoreau

[4] Emerson, *Nature* (1836). In *Ralph Waldo Emerson: Representative Selections*, ed. Frederic I. Carpenter, New York, American Book Company, 1934, p. 13.

aided the affirmation in many ways, not the least prominent
of which was his contribution to the moral definition of the
self. No one of Emerson's circle hesitated to distinguish duty
from conventional manners; Thoreau more than the others
developed the practical minutiae of the distinction. Speaking
at one time against an expressed belief that conformity was
one of "the arts of life," he said that the only real conformity
was that to the dictates of "an inward arbiter, in a measure
independent of Matter, and its relations, Time and Space." [5]
The Transcendentalist ego is clearly a proper agent of God's
presence, within the finitude and particularity of the world.

Thoreau distinguished between the two selves that inhabited
this earth. At the center of Walden Pond is the pure, real self,
from which circles of attention move toward the shore, the
second self. The self entering the world acquires impediments
to its clarity of projective vision. The idea lies at the center
of Thoreau's imaginative use of Walden: at its center lie deep
waters, which grow shallow as we move toward shore; so the
soul, moving away from its center, may find shallows of conformity and custom which block the way to self-realization.

> . . . there is a bar across the entrance of our every cove,
> or particular inclination; each is our harbor for a season, in
> which we are detained and partially land-locked. . . . At
> the advent of each individual into this life, may we not
> suppose that such a bar has risen to the surface some-
> where? [6]

Emerson and Thoreau both felt that the infinite multiplication of doctrine, convention, manners, cautions, of America's
"enervate Origens" were a wearisome barrier to essential self-

[5] In one of Thoreau's college essays, printed in F. B. Sanborn's *The
Life of Henry David Thoreau* (1917) and quoted in Sherman Paul's *The
Shores of America*, Urbana, The University of Illinois Press, 1958, p. 29.

[6] Thoreau, *Walden*, in *The Writings of Henry David Thoreau*, the
Walden Edition, Boston, Houghton, Mifflin, 1906, Vol. II, pp. 321–22.
Quoted in Paul's *The Shores of America*, pp. 344–45.

reliance. The willingness of the American self to strike out morally "on its own" is a keystone of its character. It is expressed in a fascinating variety of ways. Whitman considered it essential to the celebration of self that he hold "Creeds and schools in abeyance" if nature were to speak "without check with original energy." As she reflects upon the necessities of her Puritan tradition Emily Dickinson almost whimsically sorts out Calvinist pressures on the self. One of her many poems addressed to "that Bold Person, God—" demonstrates her right of self-scrutiny:

> "Heavenly Father"—take to thee
> The supreme iniquity
> Fashioned by thy candid Hand
> In a moment contraband—
> Though to trust us—seems to us
> More respectful—"We are Dust"—
> We apologize to thee
> For thine own Duplicity—[7]

One of Tocqueville's central observations about Americans is that the very circumstance of their life allowed them to dismiss precedent and tradition: "In the midst of the continual movement that agitates the democratic community, the tie that unites one generation to another is relaxed or broken; every man there readily loses all trace of the ideas of his fore-

[7] Poem number 1461 of *The Complete Poems of Emily Dickinson*, edited by Thomas H. Johnson, Boston, Little, Brown, 1960, p. 619. Emily Dickinson's attitudes towards death have of course been often noted, perhaps never so acutely as in Thomas Arp's *Dramatic Poses in the Poetry of Emily Dickinson*, an unpublished Stanford University Ph.D. dissertation (April 1962). In her best poems on death, Professor Arp says, Miss Dickinson "neither examines her own death nor limits herself to the vivid description of the death of another but uses the death of a friend and a few details about the moment of dying as the occasion to define her own responses to death and the problems it raises . . ." (p. 66B). There follow examinations of several poems about death, of which numbers 519 and 1100 of the Johnson edited collection are cited.

fathers or takes no care about them." [8] Not only does he forget; in many cases he deliberately discards precedent. The continent invited the act of rejection. Not that history was in itself objectionable, but that it could or should not exercise authority. History was after all the record of human beings moving through space. The self had in this quite new phase of the story come upon an entirely fresh and uncrowded space; it was therefore in the position of a "new chance," a beginning.

This is not to say that American man did not know the difficulty of these freedoms. Nevertheless, there is no denying the impact they had upon him. Perhaps we can state his point of view in this way: the American space existed as an extension of European space but obviously free of its cultural accumulations and its congestions. The experience of the new continent is a challenge to the self as venturesome and reliant spirit. Crudely stated, the confidence of man borrowed strength from the fact of his living now and from the prospect of what he might do in the future.

While the image of a recaptured Eden is immensely useful in this connection, it is important that we commit ourselves to the full implications of Genesis.[9] Assuming that Adam does return *after* the Fall, to re-enact the story, the crucial phase of his new experience has obviously to do with his decisions and acts within the new Eden. The point is that he does *not* have the innocence of the original Adam, but acts and adjusts in terms of the "New World" in post-lapsarian

[8] Alexis de Tocqueville, *Democracy in America* (1835). Tr. by Henry Reeve, revised by Francis Bowen, edited by Phillips Bradley, New York, Knopf, 1953, Vol. II, p. 4.
[9] The idea of a "second Eden" is of course developed in R. W. B. Lewis' *The American Adam* (University of Chicago Press, 1955). Henry Nash Smith's *Virgin Land* (Cambridge, Mass., Harvard University Press, 1950) provides the principal documentation for any analysis of it. See my essay, "Freedom and Conscious Form" (*Virginia Quarterly Review*, Vol. 37, spring 1961, pp. 269–85), where these matters are treated more elaborately than they are here.

fashion. Thoreau and Emerson were aware that the self cannot be guaranteed any automatic success from indulgence in impulses. Fundamental to Emerson's trust in the self is his confidence in its *shaping power*, the intrinsic accuracy of its *making* the forms of experience. These forms are implicitly already there, in nature. Man has but to act in recognition of them, as well as in response to his imaginative comprehension of them as in *himself*.

Genesis, however, involves an experience of self-knowledge which seems more extensive and more particularly self-involved than that. Its major concern is with the self's involvement with evil. The basic metaphor of our moral history, that of original sin, describes the experiencing of evil. In any such fancy as the re-experiencing of Eden, the question whether evil need also be re-experienced has to be asked. But the American experience involved us in a reciprocal activity of self-knowledge; the self made the wrong decisions, or acted upon the wrong impulses; it imposed bad forms upon nature, or left it with no forms at all; there was a woeful lack of discretion, tact, or taste in its use of Edenic opportunities. The real American crisis would therefore seem to have come from an irresponsible naïveté concerning the use made by the self of its opportunities.

It is not that Emerson and Thoreau were naive, but that they did not allow their perceptions of evil to destroy their confidence. More specifically, as Van Wyck Brooks pointed out in 1915, the separations in the American intellectual life allowed for little if any appreciation of what the growing power of science and materialism was doing to the self. Its worst effect was to collapse the beautifully simple, idealistic metaphors of the self at center, creatively projecting its substantive nature, to make sense and reality out of the cosmos. The retreat of the ego, its withdrawal inward, into a state of fear and self-analysis, is a major figure of nineteenth century intellectual history.

—[iii]—

To preserve the self in this situation necessitated first of all an attention to it as process. William James, instead of asserting the self, examined it as a stream of consciousness. In so doing, he radically altered the space-time relationship within it. To explain process requires the assumption of an instant of time moving from another, toward still another. The process is saved from extinction through the positing of a temporal instrument of continuity. Ultimately the examination of process must have both subjective and objective contexts: the I observes the me, or experiences the me in the instant of procedural being. To go beyond the process itself is to suggest a volitional self who directs it and decides as between one option and another what the self will be. Within the will reside the powers of ultimate decision, even the final decision to risk believing what is not proved, or what cannot be proved.

This development meant that the ultimate character of reality was a willed thing, further that reality is what the will decides it to be, in accordance with what the process of experience should become. James therefore put the vital question of the self as a challenge to the will to make of reality what it can: "Each must act as he thinks best; and if he is wrong, so much the worse for him." [10] The results of his analysis of the self pushed James further and further away from science itself, and toward a transcendent affirmation of the self that seems a mixture of exasperation and nostalgia. "These inhibitions, these split-up selves," he wrote his sister, "all these new facts that are gradually coming to light about our organization, these enlargements of the self in trance, etc., are bringing me to turn for light in the direction of all sorts of despised

[10] *The Will to Believe and Other Essays in Popular Philosophy*, New York, Longmans, Green, 1896, p. 31.

spiritualistic and unscientific ideas. Father would find in me today a much more receptive listener—all *that* philosophy has got to be brought in." [11]

James's career of self-analysis forced him away from science and into a modified voluntarism that was not entirely unlike the ideas of his father, at least in its essentials. But the examination of process is more important for the history of the American self than any account of James's frustrations. His description of "streams of consciousness" and his reflections upon "hidden motives" do more than any other nineteenth century speculation toward pointing in the direction of the twentieth. The American self, the space for its maneuvering exhausted, is caught in a naturalistic trap, from which James's assertions of volitional power cannot rescue it. Above all, American versions of the self are significant because of their sense of spaciousness and of the changes of spiritual renewal. These values depended upon a visual recognition of space available infinitely. They were bound to lose their value when the space "closed in."

Henry James had always suggested, and often specified, what lay beyond the process of seeing and experiencing the substance of the world. He insisted that life *needs* forms; without them it is a dreary waste. The spatial substance of America has an important role in James's speculations about forms. It is, after all, an area of opportunity for the human consciousness; for while America has no "ruins" upon which the artist may retrospectively gaze, it affords the widest opportunity for the exercise of the intelligence. The role of the American in the exchange with Europe is indispensably associated with this liberality of choice. At the beginning of his career, on September 20, 1867, James wrote a letter to his

[11] Letter of July 6, 1891, in *The Letters of William James*, edited by his son, Henry James, Boston, The Atlantic Monthly Press, 1920, Vol. I, p. 310.

friend Thomas Sergeant Perry, who was touring Europe; in it he summed up the American "opportunity" and its relationship to Europe's established and traditional frame:

> We have exquisite qualities as a race, and it seems to me that we are ahead of the European races in the fact that more than either of them we can deal freely with forms of civilization not our own, can pick and choose and assimilate and in short (aesthetically, etc.) claim our property wherever we find it. . . . I think it not unlikely that American writers may yet indicate that a vast intellectual fusion and synthesis of the various National tendencies of the world is the condition of more important achievements than any we have seen.[12]

These remarks link James to the central American situation. The American self is free to choose; no premium is put upon his adherence to traditional forms or manners. He may therefore exercise an unimpeded taste in his improvisation of manner. This is not to say that Americans are characteristically without fixed and forbidding scruple. The Protestant, Puritan ethic plays a very large role, for good or ill, in the careers of James's creatures. Yet the central intelligences of his fiction find it to their advantage that they are free, or relatively free, of traditional forms. The international exchange is, in some respects, a parable of the crucial experience any consciousness must undergo. The best of James's Americans are metaphorical figures, seeking the finest opportunities for actualizing their insights.

James's reading of the American consciousness is superbly relevant to the circumstances of its freedom. There is, first of all, a remarkable sense in it of the interplay of spaces: the moral sense is always there, and to the degree that we stub-

---

[12] First printed in Virginia Harlow's *Thomas Sergeant Perry*, Durham, North Carolina, Duke University Press, 1950, pp. 284–85.

bornly adhere to inherited obligations, we are not entirely free. Beyond the settled cautions of his conscious "East" (it was of course also an East of Washington Square and Concord, of his father and of Emerson), there was the West, which appeared to him, as in another sense it appeared to the general run of his contemporaries, to be an open society where vigor and energy are rewarded and the advantages of improvisation remain free. Truly, this society had as yet no established, demonstrable taste; it had only the willingness to withhold judgment, to wait for experience to justify itself. James offers a major distinction, however, between the closed and the open consciousness. It is made in many ways, but primarily in terms of a willed arrangement of objects in space. Buildings and patterns—the external, architectural evidences of realized forms —help to identify the success or failure of conscious life. One is almost always aware in his novels of the intimate and revealing correspondence of mind and things seen, handled, lived in and with. His father's lifelong preoccupation with the basic differences between the "spontaneous" and the "closed" mind is in James's work dramatized as a conflict of a full and sensitive moral life against a closed life, cut off by deficiencies either of the moral sense or of the intelligence.

For Henry James, the American consciousness was freely responsible to do what it could with the forms at its disposal. He was concerned about the pathetic ugliness which was often the result of its freedom, and in *The American Scene* (1907) documented his distress over American failures. But he was scarcely disturbed over the ultimate question of the self: that is, whether it did or should substantially exist. His brother William preferred also to think that qualitative distinctions of consciousness survived the actual processes of conscious experience. He was not sure what he should call them, but he was sure that they must exist. In a passage of the brilliant *Principles of Psychology* he spoke of the core of Self which men insist on preserving from the process itself:

If the stream as a whole is identified with the Self far more than any outward thing, *a certain portion of the stream abstracted from the rest* is so identified in an altogether peculiar degree, and is felt by all men as a sort of innermost centre within the circle, of sanctuary within the citadel, constituted by the subjective life as a whole . . .[13]

Like much of James's prose, this is charged with the kind of metaphor that strives to rescue consciousness from the somberly boring fact of its flatly existing in process. So too his saying that "whatever qualities a man's feeling may possess, or whatever content his thought may include, there is a spiritual something which seems to *go out* to meet these qualities and contents, whilst they seem to *come in* to be received by it" (1, 297). Henry James might have said that this "spiritual something" is no more than the self's receptivity to experience, which qualitatively varies as the vigor and the intelligence of the self changes. But this kind of dialectical difference in approach is explainable solely in terms of Henry's having come to consciousness from the direction of the transcendent self, William's (often reluctantly) from the direction of descriptive psychology. For the one, consciousness was an undeniable privilege, for the other a provable reality; it is the basic distinction between moral assurance and scientific probability.

The perspective upon the self, as between the two Jameses, shifts from scene to process. It is as though Henry had seen all three elements of the formula, *the self sensing the object*, while William wished only to examine the act and the character of the sensing, and hoped perhaps that all three might prove legitimately real in the total experience. At the crucial point of the self's experiencing, it "converses," not outwardly with others or with nature, but inwardly, with itself. In fact, it is difficult to determine that there is a self at all, except in

[13] *The Principles of Psychology*, New York, Holt, 1890, Vol. 1, p. 297. All other references to this edition are in the text.

the resemblance among parts of a stream of consciousness: "There is no other identity than this in the 'stream' of subjective consciousness . . ." (I, 336). James appealed to John Stuart Mill's reference to "the *inexplicable tie* . . . which connects the present consciousness with the past one of which it reminds me . . ." (I, 357). In short, consciousness supports the idea of self only through some linking of present with past. James establishes this limited self as of two elements which are "incessantly present" in experiencing, "an objective person, known by a passing subjective Thought and recognized as continuing in time . . ." (I, 371).

James's detailed analysis of the "stream of consciousness" has several important suggestions for the history of the American self. Belief in the self begins in a dependence upon God's willing both its actual existence and its moral nature. Subsequently, it is reconstituted as a positive and independent being, whose relations with space are its primary *modus vivendi*. The privileges of choice and initiative are its essential definition. Emerson and Thoreau required an ideal self, to which they insisted all may aspire; the "inner me" is spiritually feasible and functionally necessary. The elder Henry James endowed the self with the highest degree of creative consciousness:

> Creation, to allow of any true fellowship or equality between creator and creature, demands that the creature be *himself*,—that is, be *naturally* posited to his own consciousness. And he cannot be thus posited save in so far as the creative love vivifies his essential destitution, organizes it in living form, and by the experience thus engendered in the created bosom lays a basis for any amount of free or spiritual reaction in the creature towards the uncreated good.[14]

[14] Quoted by William James, Introduction to Henry Sr.'s *Literary Remains*. In F. O. Matthiessen, *The James Family*, New York, Knopf, 1947, p. 148. Originally this appeared in *The Secret of Swedenborg* (1869).

The general impression of all three—Emerson, Thoreau, and James, Sr.—is of a creative self whose value comes from its own initiative and is judged in terms of its success in approaching an ideal nature. There is much to suggest in this of an identification of the self with God. The elder James posited an ideal point of identification in which the divine and the human are one, a point reached through mutual endeavor of the creature and his creator. In American intellectual history the decline of this surmise is coincidental with the closing of spatial opportunities. While the elder James needed no space (or could change spaces at will), but only moral and social forms, for the achievement of his "harmonies," the actual physical history of self-promise and self-confidence was a history of spaces seen, exploited, and finally exhausted.

When William James attended to the minutiae of experience as process, it was in the nature almost of an autopsy of the ideal self. The Transcendental self required an infinity, which was supported by the metaphor of an "infinite space." Whitman added to the figure by insisting that variety was in itself a testimony of the infinite, though the time was close when he should be disabused of his confidence. James's conclusions about the "stream" of self can only be defined as the triumph of finitude over infinity:

> Psychology is a natural science, an account of particular finite streams of thought, coexisting and succeeding in time. It is of course conceivable (though far from clearly so) that in the last metaphysical resort all streams of thought may be thought by one universal All-thinker. But in this metaphysical notion there is no profit for psychology; for grant that one Thinker does think in all of us, still what He thinks in me and what in you can never be deduced from the bare idea of Him . . . (*Principles*, I, 367)

In a very real sense, James reasserts the American suspicion of conceptual activity. Reality is grasped as the self perceives it in experience. Belief must submit to the test of experience. I believe because I have experienced the functioning of my belief; or, I believe in order the better to anticipate experience. In any case, the test of belief (and of *any idea* of the self) is that it will be proved in the process of motion from present to future. As Ralph Barton Perry has defined the experience, it is a "feeling" of both actual process and the logical circumstances that hold it conceptually together. "It is the apprehension of the *in-itselfness* of some root character, discriminable from all others, requiring a name of its own, and evoking the comment, 'I see what it is,' from minds possessed of the appropriate sensibilities and directed to the right context." [15]

James transcends process, first by stressing its importance (that is, the strength of the experiencer), then by positing the will of the experiencer as an active projector of experience, finally by relating unprovable absolutes to the conditional needs of the will; so that, in a sense, James triumphs over naturalistic threats to the ego by allowing it to will values and to choose forms of transcendence. He maintains that volitional forces enable the self to bring cosmic reality within the range of personal experiencing. The scientific attitude strives to limit experience, but it is inadequate because "so long as we deal with the cosmic and the general, we deal only with the symbols of reality, but *as soon as we deal with private and personal phenomena as such, we deal with realities in the completest sense of the term. . . .*" [16]

This last quotation most suggestively reveals William James's relationship to modern thought. He discriminates between scientific and personal perceptions, claiming a greater power

[15] *In The Spirit of William James*, New Haven, Conn., Yale University Press, 1938, p. 83.
[16] *The Varieties of Religious Experience*, New York, Longmans, Green, 1902, p. 498.

and a greater "truth" for the latter. This is to suggest that scientific analysis is always more impersonally general than personal motive and will. In any case, modern literary examinations of the self have usually been divided into two kinds: those which describe the human consequences of self-realization in the very limited sense of consciousness and process; and those which reflect contemporary views of the human will. If James will have us accept the self's privilege of choosing its forms of transcendence, literature has given us a very great variety of its willed choices. Not the least important of these is the extremely limited one of ignoring the need of transcendence altogether and concentrating upon the nature of the ego as consciousness and as process.

This stratagem poses the moral issue as an ontological, even an epistemological one; or it leads to an exploration of all literary techniques that are commensurate with a very limited picture of consciousness. James's will-to-believe becomes almost excruciatingly the existentialist crisis of decision and choice. The will is often all but entirely dissociated from tradition; in fact, its energies are spent in the effort to preserve identity, to maintain a continuity of self, and even to guarantee its situational integrity.

—[iv]—

The influence of the Transcendentalists is of course pervasive; it is almost unpatriotic to suggest that it is not. Indeed, listening to Yvor Winters, one might assume that its baneful presence was felt everywhere. In the two senior citizens of modern American poetry, Frost and Sandburg, the nineteenth century self persists and is celebrated whimsically, nostalgically, or pettishly. Frost can remind us, in an inaugural ceremony, of a poem he wrote some nineteen years ago which scolded the Westernizing man for having fled the responsibilities of self, evading in his move through space the need to look inward:

Something we were withholding made us weak
Until we found it was ourselves
We were withholding from our land of living,
And forthwith found salvation in surrender.[17]

William James offers us the spectacle of a man similarly tormented. His sense of the precious transcending power of the self is forever running against his failure to see that *a* self, as substance, actually does exist at all. So the Transcendentalist exercise is now generally left for such occasions as a Presidential inauguration or the celebration of Sandburg's eightieth birthday. In *Principles*, however, James was wholly and honestly committed to setting down the melancholy facts of self as process. He surreptitiously returned substance and will to the self in his private letters and in his Gifford Lectures; and in the little essay on *Immortality* (1898) he even went so far as to insist that the soul (or at any rate an immortal substance) *is* because it *must be*—using much the same kind of rhetorical assertion as E. A. Robinson depends on at the end of *The Man Against the Sky*.[18]

In fact, James's predicament is not uncommonly duplicated in twentieth century literature. The resolution of it, which he suggested only on private and public occasions of some intimacy, was Victorian; but the realization of self as process, or self as non-self, lands everyone in much the same kind of desperately awkward circumstance. Jean-Paul Sartre went so far as to say that "each instance of our conscious life reveals to us a creation *ex nihilo*. Not a new *arrangement*, but a new

[17] "The Gift Outright," in A *Witness Tree*, from *Complete Poems of Robert Frost*. Copyright 1942 by Robert Frost. Reprinted by permission of Holt, Rinehart, and Winston, Inc.

[18] The conjunction of these works is not accidental. Both Robinson and James are forced to argue immortality from the same basis, as a conjecture upon which essential human destinies are based. Both are impelled by the same impulses, that a materialist philosophy does not encourage belief, and that belief is necessary to justify existence. See Robert Stevick, *E. A. Robinson's Principles and Practices of Poetry*, an unpublished Ph.D. dissertation, University of Wisconsin, 1956, pp. 212–13.

existence." [19] No one, not Sartre himself, except Beckett (and he only occasionally) allowed the matter to stand at that. Instead, modern literature, existentialist or not, almost invariably avails itself of the "will to believe," or decide, or act, or destroy, as a way out of the impasse described in *Principles*.

Much recent American literature is "nihilist" in the sense that the informing self (the narrator, the poet, even the man who serves as scapegoat or victim of the poet's anger) is engaged in the expression of an all-consuming, all-negating will. He asserts his mortal identity in the face of the same realization at which James arrived in *Principles*, that the self is at best an instant of consciousness and can be sustained only by a series of questionable decisions and acts. There are no guarantees, and the freedom that so negative a will assumes for itself is at most a "dreadful" freedom that must forcefully be continued from moment to moment.

The history of this vacillation between process and a willed continuance is extremely complex. Literary attitudes alternate between quiet despair and angry volition. Sartre puts the onus of willed decision upon the self at each instant of free and dreadful choice. Beckett's characters are in a constant state of uncertainty about their precise ego-definition and shift uneasily from an assertion of a creating or a "naming power" to a tendency to submit resignedly to nonexistence. Annihilation is the terrifying expectation of either a Sartre or Beckett hero, or it is at any rate the fate one must strive desperately to avoid. In any case, whether Sartre or Beckett or any of their contemporaries, the question of an a priori self-determination has been set aside.

But the decision is not always either calmly or timidly made. The most excruciating example of the dilemma precisely stated by James is Dos Passos' "Camera Eye"; this strangely restricted ego seems through most of the trilogy *USA* timidly victimized

---

[19] *The Transcendence of the Ego*, tr. Forrest Williams and Robert Kirkpatrick, New York, Noonday, 1957, pp. 98–99.

and neurotically inept, but rescues its strength at the end in angry bursts of social and political vigor. The cause of its explosion, the Sacco-Vanzetti executions, is ironically to be found in the deaths of two anarchists, of whose radical individualism the Camera Eye seems the direct antithesis in most of the work. American literature since the end of World War II often presents a much more vigorous self-assertion, though the circumstances are not dissimilar. In the great majority of these works, the bare limits of the Jamesian consciousness are assumed, but they are not often the occasion for ego withdrawal. Instead, the ego cultivates a "violence within" to match and dominate the "violence without." Compared to the ego-projections of Norman Mailer, William Burroughs, and writers of their type, Sartre's characters may appear to exist in a state of ontological anxiety that is debilitating and ridden by rational discretions and fears. All of them share with William James his distrust of metaphysical certainties, but the range of reaction to it is wide and various indeed.

In many respects, recent literature is a violent reaction against the type of philosophical "measurement" of mind and consciousness, of which James's discreet analysis of self as process is a culmination. He breaks away from it himself in an expression of pragmatic voluntarism which allows for a wide range of choice, but he also tries to preserve at least a *feeling* of his father's transcendental self-reliance. The angry protests in modern literature against a steadily narrowing rational philosophy, against "scientism" in its narrower applications (of measuring spaces and instants of consciousness), are an appeal to intuition, to the unexamined (or unmeasured) will, and to a confidence in a voluntaristic self.

Whether justly or not, the violence of World War II and the planning for an infinite expansion of it since are associated with the scientistic philosophies of the post-Cartesian tradition. These are in disrepute. But the basic cleavage between them and early American Transcendentalism is, if anything,

339

even more obvious. The distress shown in recent American writing is ascribable to the fact that neither scientism nor Transcendentalism is acceptable: the one is too inflexible and empty, the other too naive. In any case, both are of the past, formulated in less impossibly violent times, and they do not speak either in encouragement or admonition to the survivors of past violence who live in expectation of a renewal and an acceleration of it.

11

"ECSTATIC TEMPORALITY":
THE SELF IN TIME

. . .

Thou art slave to Fate, Chance, kings, and desperate men,
And doth with poyson, warre, and sicknesse dwell
And poppie, or charmes can make us sleepe as well,
And better than thy stroake; why swell'st thou then?
One short sleepe past, we wake eternally,
And death shall be no more, death, thou shalt die.
—JOHN DONNE, Holy Sonnet x

—[i]—

PERHAPS the most remarkable of all speculative adventures in
the history of man's adjustment to death is his struggle to
understand the paradoxical relationship of time to eternity.
There are several important factors involved. The doctrine of
Incarnation is a crucial exercise of the religious imagination;
it gives substance to what might otherwise have been a mere
speculation; through it, the doctrine is fleshed. Almost equally
significant is the intricate balance of time with eternity at
every stage of man's conscious life. This is closely related to
another imaginative concept: as God's creature, man is in a
substantial and persistent state of creation: as he grows, he is

"being created," or his status as a created being is apparently sustained and strengthened by God's will and grace.

The subtleties of this relationship of creator and creature are no more remarkable than are the rewards accruing to man from his total commitment to it. Essential to his belief is the constant and willing submission to the eternal at each moment of recorded time. The moment is itself within time; it is the only "actually real" substance of a life. But it is also, in terms of its being realized, a physical actualization, a "moment," of eternity. The believer evaluates it for what it reveals of eternity. This reality is treasured for its depth and its clarity of physical substance, but its ultimate value lies in the promise implicit in the major, supervisory illusion of permanence. Man values the momentary experience, though he knows it is impermanent (he is constantly changing; time moves without ceasing); but he cannot appreciate its true value unless he can be sure it is permanent (its value depends upon its surviving the experience of it).

In this schematization of time, there is a close relationship of past, present, and future. In any skeptical view, there is no past and no guaranteed future; there is only a present instant, which is itself uncertain. There is no time, but only sensation. But if time be considered *sub specie aeternitatis*, the Creator serves as a guarantor of continuity. Past thus steadily accumulates; as experience is conceived in terms of generations of experiencing, it becomes "tradition," to which the present serves both as exemplar and result. Future time is conceived in two aspects: it is that toward which the present is moving, but it is also the direction toward eternity, which is in itself a pure future. This close integration of the partitions of time has much to do with temporal rhythms.

The major certitude is not temporal at all, in any mechanical or measurable sense; it is substantially *visual*. To put it in the simplest terms, it is a "felt vision" of recurrent images of spatial variants. Measured time is after all a consequence of the practical will exercised upon the felt and visualized human landscape. Time is a way of notating the condition of created being; or it is the means of providing a reasoned definition of the present locus of an imagined eternity.

Eternity is thus a product of the religious imagination which transcends instants of practical reason. Man "senses" the moment, at which he is a bodily substance inhabiting a space in which there are other objects. He reasons that he exists at this moment in an hour of a day on a calendar, and he measures his relationship to past and future in terms of such knowledge. But he also wills transcendence of that moment. In a sense, his decision to act "tomorrow" is a form of willing continuance and is related to the magnificent conception of eternity which is the finest product of the imagination. The crucial decision in all human activity, however, has to do with his facing the menace of death. That he is mortal is a human hypothesis he may be reluctant to accept as a proven fact; but the evidence is overwhelmingly in favor of its being close to an established one. Despite the strong persuasion the experience of others offers him, he finds mortality a challenge to the imagination. Divinity is a direct result of a resolve not to accept mortality— or, to accept it in the frame of a universal conception that mitigates it.

Since man seems mortal, in the limited, pre-imagined state to which he has often to address himself, he must will the existence of a being not so limited. The strongest and boldest act of the human imagination comprehends a divine being who is also human, or capable of becoming human—even of suffering mortality within the limits of time—but is finally and substantially supra-human. This is the Christian version of an act of religious imagination which has many variants in other religions. The differences among religions are essentially concerned with the minutiae of the relationship of creature to creator, as well as with the schemata of expectations alleged to accrue from the relationship. The vividness of its "literary

343

results"—that is, the terms according to which the universal is realized in particular experience—will depend upon the degree to which man as creature wants to explain evil and its demands upon divine reserves of "forgiveness."

As a human circumstance that impedes the functions of the divine, evil is always closely associated with corruption, which is itself a specific of mortality. In a closed moral system, evil is most frequently defined as a love of temporality, or a lust or an "unreasonable appetite" for its fruits. Since temporality is in itself associated with death—with the move toward death —it is to be assumed that a love of it involves the risk of inviting death, of bringing it closer at the very time when life seems most attractive. Similarly, the most extreme acts of resistance to death are acts of renunciation. The ascetic will turns the emotion of love for temporal advantage into hatred, not only of this advantage but of temporality itself. The ascetic will abstracts itself from the body, in the assumption that the body is impermanent and that what survives it is eternal.

Since time is a reasoned consequence of the realization of death, and since man fears above all the destruction of self, he bases his fundamental trust on a willed transcendence of time, an eternity which will enable him to prevail beyond death. Immortality is purely a matter of risk, an unproved and unverifiable state, a condition he must take on faith, since he cannot as a physical being contained in time actually experience it.[1] The history of the relationship of time and eternity is associated with man's strength of trust, with the power of willed acceptance of what cannot be experienced in time. This condition has its own ambiguities; there are innumerable occasions of doubt, or of the failure of the imagination to sustain what cannot be proved. But the relationship of time and eternity is itself "impractical" and "unreasonable." It bristles with the ambiguities that naturally result from an attempt to

---

[1] Nevertheless, our literature has many scenes which describe man trying to "see his way into it," or man rising from death to report it.

fuse two antithetically disposed conceptions of time. The ambiguities are not resolved "reasonably"; one must believe that time will yield to eternity, that the impermanence of the instant of experience is an illusory gift of eternity, most of all that there *is* an eternity to which time will yield when it must.

The schemata provided by the religious imagination depend for their certainty upon the belief that a creator imagined and willed (*faute de mieux*) will sustain a creature who has willed him, beyond that creature's acknowledged limits. As Georges Poulet says, à propos of the medieval time scheme, "everything rested upon two principles: the continuous creation which established the permanence of the creature and of his substantial activity; and the divine concourse which allowed him to realize himself in time." [2] Conventionally, one maintains that the power of belief in this set of circumstances wavers from time to time, that man is variously persuaded or dissuaded with respect to it. Almost all discussions of the problem of belief assume that the strength of a transcending imagination has been attacked by the reason, and all but destroyed by it. But it is perhaps more proper to say that the reason acts to create distrust of *one form* of imaginative construct, forcing the imagination to create others, or to stimulate an "interest" in forbearance and acceptance. When man is disabused of eternity, he is forced back upon a contemplation of existence without the assurance of a mitigating transcendence. This does not mean that he will remain a disenchanted being; his powers of recuperation are formidable.

Christian history is a remarkable narrative of the hold that one archetypal construction has had upon the human imagination. The strength of belief seems to have been centered mostly upon a complex design of transcendence. This belief weakened, because of the growth of respect for necessary "reasoned" proof,

[2] *Studies in Human Time*, tr. Elliott Coleman, Baltimore, The Johns Hopkins University Press, 1956, p. 7. Originally, *Études sur le temps humain*, Paris, Plon, 1950.

because of the imperfections and ambiguities implicit in a conception that was so bold as to defy comprehension in ordinary terms, and because events of extraordinary and irrational violence could not be persuasively explained by it. As the condition of disbelief was sustained and strengthened, man became a victim of his own limitations, and the persuasive powers of his reason simply exaggerated his distrust in what could not be proved. This is not to say that he was at any time entirely persuaded. The Christian metaphor, since it was all but universally admired and *wanted* (as distinguished from its being available to proof), survived all exertions of the human mind to dispel it. Christian apologists succeeded in assimilating alien doctrines primarily because human time is almost invariably regarded as intolerable without a sustaining myth of transcendence. In other words, death as a limit, as an absolute *terminus ad quem*, is insufferable.

—[ii]—

The experience with which this chapter is concerned can be variously defined: as a loss of belief, as the weakening of the transcending will, as a return to the basic, original challenge that mortality posed to the human imagination. It is, in short, a story of the temporary decline of a willed vision of eternity, as a consequence of which man has had to experiment with forms and kinds of vital temporality. However the situation is explained, or its causes given, several important effects need to be pointed out: the disillusionment with eternity returned the mind and imagination of man to the terrifying problem of his mortality; he was once again forced to speculate upon the possibility of a means of transcendence, since he could not long suffer the thought of mortality in and of itself; he was forced back upon the initial experiencing of the self in time, and was impelled to work in terms of a sensed immediacy of his participation in temporal flow; he became more and more interested

346

in himself *as process*, and he attempted to rescue a value from the fact that he existed in the apparently endlessly repetitive process of becoming something else; he had either to "settle" for instants of conscious experience or to endure the prospect that between one experienced instant and the next nothing could be predicted or confidently expected.

In short, man had consciously to attend to the task of providing from within himself surrogate guarantors of his own continuity. If he could believe in nothing but himself as the experiencer of himself, he had either to solve the problem of his continuance or to risk the menace of his ceasing to continue. This "dreadful responsibility" involved him in related questions: as to the degree and quality of experienced moments; the power of the mind to image these moments; the possibility that they, or some of them, served powerfully as signs of an improvised universality in experience; and the relationship of experience to memory, of time-saturated instants to unconscious reserves of the past. Dominating over the matter of these questions was the all-inclusive one of self-identity. One had to make a substance from an insubstantial flux of sensation in time; which is another way of saying that man had to will transcendence, though he apparently did not need to will either a metaphor or a myth to sustain transcendence in history. He might simply say: I exist in terms of the experience of existing and I will that this experience continue from moment to moment, in which case, the problem of continuity persists from moment to moment, and excites the consciousness into an extraordinarily demanding alertness to the needs of identity.

Let us consider briefly the stratagem of regarding existence as enduring in terms of "a string of images" captured from experience or used to define and recall it. The self is in this case identified as a consciousness that has had, or has had something to do with, moments of articulated experience that are furthermore relied upon as the signs of a continuous self. But each of these images may be "the last one"; nor is it certain that any of them can be definitely associated with the others. The space between one image and the next is a void, which becomes truly terrifying if no trusted guarantor of continuity is available to the imagination. There is "time to kill"; stretches of time intervene between one moment of assured identity and the next, or between one assertion of the ego and a future which might become a present. This is an agonizing and an all but intolerable condition. The self can stake his chances of continued existence upon the recall of images alleged to belong to his past, but he is neither sure of the images nor clear as to the intervening time.

> One says to oneself: "Ten years ago I was there" (Flaubert once wrote to a friend), and one is there and one thinks the same things and the whole interval is forgotten. *Then it appears to you, that interval,* like an immense precipice in which nothingness whirls round.[3]

It is an anguish caused by the doubt of man's sustaining power. Each moment of experience carries its burden of this doubt. For Baudelaire it was an abyss, describing the nothingness that extends beyond the moment of being.

> En haut, en bas, partout, la profondeur, la grève,
> Le silence, l'espace affreux et captivant . . .
> Sur le fond de mes nuits Dieu de son doigt savant
> Dessine un cauchemar multiforme et sans trève.[4]

Not only the greatest vice, but the most anguished experience, is the *ennui* caused by doubt whether of God's will to sustain man in time, or of his own power to maintain a continuous

[3] Quoted in Poulet, *Studies in Human Time,* p. 255.
[4] Above, below, around me, shores descending . . .
  Silence . . . frightful, captivating Space . . .
  At night I watch God's knowing finger trace
  The dark with nightmare, multiform, unending.
—Stanza 2 of "Le Gouffre," *Les Fleurs du mal* (1857). Translations by several persons, edited by Jackson Mathews, Norfolk, Conn., New Directions, 1955, p. 194. This poem translated by the editor.

identity. This doubt comprehends both a failure of active willingness to persist in belief (the sin of "sloth") and a despair of the self's independent will to entertain continuance. It is essentially a metaphysical despair, contained within the deep inner regions of the self, who is partially disabused of the imaginative viability of a God but is also very close (in wanting it) to willing a divinity.

Another surrogate divinity is the popular device of guaranteeing the continuity of the self simply along the lines that the self persists historically, that the history of man is a progress toward perfection. Superficial readings of Darwinist literature encouraged this conviction; and the idea of an evolution toward the perfection of the self became in a real sense a surrogate religion, according to which the ego is not important because at the moment of its "evolution" it is not perfect; it has a value only in terms of what it may become and of what it does to ensure its becoming. This idea has suffered many satirical attacks in modern literature. The fact of death remains an essential point in its review.[5] Death is an alternative to progress; one does not progress because of but in spite of death.

Perhaps the most fervent, and the most pathetic, of these human efforts to solve the problem of continuity, is the self's attempt to assert temporality as in itself containing (in density, depth, intensity) the qualities of a surrogate divinity. This kind of experience, described by one person as a "pure ecstatic temporality," [6] is directly related to the menace of death, which (in the absence of religious guarantees) forces the consciousness to attend the present moment. A belief in immortality serves to regulate the pace of human time; each moment is contained within eternity, and one may say that each physical phenomenon touched by eternity gains a symbolic quality from the exposure to it. Without this guarantee, the moment may be

[5] See above, Part One, chapter 1.
[6] Helmuth Plessner, "On the Relation of Time to Death," in *Man and Time*, tr. Ralph Manheim, New York, Pantheon, 1957, pp. 233–63.

349

asked to serve its own role as metaphysical content and symbol. Hence the growth of a religious attitude toward the object of experience, the suggestion that the object (as well as the language or medium into which it is translated by man) has only to be explored profoundly to reveal a compensatory grace of objective value. There is also some effort to suggest that, in this aspect, the object possesses "eternity in depth," or even some metaphysical power beyond its existence in the flow of apprehended sensory data. Thus, modern criticism frequently suspects a universal magic in a concrete image which is both "thought" and "felt," and even goes so far as to consider the metaphysical "conceit" as an aesthetic strategy designed to wrest universal value from concrete substance.

The history of man's comprehension of self in time can briefly be noted in a quite simple pattern. To begin, the self was assumed to be a substance; that is, it was alleged to exist independently of any specific act of its experiencing. As a substance guaranteed existence beyond human time, it participated in eternity. Even the Cartesian denial of prior assurance of the substantial self had to depend upon the belief in self as *cogito*; since in any analysis of *cogito ergo sum*, *cogito* and *sum* are not causal but interdependent. But the skeptical view dismissed the idea of a prior self-substance and reduced the self to a set of sensations to which certain relations seemed to adhere. In most cases, the end-result of the Humean analysis was to bring the matter of identity down to the self's examining the matter and process of experiencing.

Three major conceptions are involved in the history of the self in time: the idea of the self as containing the power to initiate transcendence (that the self is intrinsically creative and is therefore able to project beyond particulars into universals); the interest in the unconscious as containing both supra-real and sub-real potentiality; and, especially in the light of Bergson's assertions, the analysis of memory, as containing both the substance of a sensed past and, possibly, a truly viable, universal experience. Conspicuously, the first two of these suggest that the self has only to be maneuvered a certain way, to move beyond surface reality toward a transcendent, universal supplemental identity.

In a very real sense, though their incentives and purposes radically differed, Emerson and Rimbaud made comparable assertions concerning the self; "Car Je est un autre," Rimbaud said in his letter to Paul Demeny (May 15, 1871),[7] in a spirit of unconventional defiance and of confidence in the "hidden self" that Emerson could only have admired. The Bergsonian absorption in *durée*, as distinguished from mechanical time, represented still another move toward the isolated self as center and toward the power of the self to find its "eternity" within the process of experiencing. In any of these cases, though they differ extremely from one another, the real challenge is to the self's basic nature, to its power of initiating substance and reality. The range of contradiction, ambiguity, and paradox emerging from these adventures in self-exploration is at least as wide as that implicit in the "controlled paradox" of the religious view of eternity.

—[iii]—

One of the major consequences is the close attention to the object itself, or what can be made of the object through an exercise of the imagination. When the special forms of eternity which govern temporal rhythms cease being useful, the movement from life to death alters noticeably. Experiences are comprehended in depth, independently of the symbolic value a religious imagination may previously have given them. The great emphasis in any initial experience is spatial; time at best can merely indicate the motion and direction of objects in space. Religious symbolism tends to represent objects as serv-

[7] *Oeuvres Complètes*, edited by Rolland de Renéville and Jules Mouquet, Paris, Gallimard, 1951, p. 254.

ants of eternity, physical signs of it. Ultimately the symbolic value dominates altogether; the specificity of objects has almost no importance.

Conversely, the primary emphasis in the literature of a secular world is spatial. It is centered upon the moment of experience and upon what is comprehended in that moment. The literary values of such a point of view are evenly divided between the object itself and the form of its representation. Both acquire symbolic values as their natures are exhaustively explored. Further, there is an urgent sense of the need to avoid any prior metaphysical and sentimental attachments to experience.

Major critics of the twentieth century show an extraordinary scruple in these matters. They wish to detach literary experience from all representational suggestion. The work of art is abstracted from its sentimental inheritance, and the object is subjected to a new kind of technical scrutiny. The motives for this operation are dual; either to recover religious values in experience or to nourish the imagination which has defaulted in its religious objective. This desire to fix the attention upon experience itself is motivated in part by the increase in scientific prestige, but it is not "scientific" in any literal sense. It is a form of discourse that is distinct from both the religious and the scientific. Criticism strives to define and to spell out in detail the character of art as a distinct form of knowledge.

John Crowe Ransom clearly suggests this objective when he says that "the differentia of poetry as discourse is an ontological one. It treats an order of existence, a grade of objectivity, which cannot be treated in scientific discourse." [8] As one of several important statements in modern criticism, this offers a considerable range of speculative insight. In a sense, Ransom's is a critical position directly related to the spatial review of existence. It cautions against both the metaphysical smugness of common-

[8] *The New Criticism*, Norfolk, Conn., New Directions, 1941, p. 281. Other references to this edition are in the text.

352

place religious assertions and the misleading stress upon "efficiency" as an attitude toward modern experience. In another place, where Ransom is especially concerned to define the nature of aesthetic forms, he opposes them to what he calls "economic," or scientific forms:

> The aesthetic forms are a technique of restraint, not of efficiency. They do not butter our bread, and they delay the eating of it. They stand between the individual and his natural object and impose a check upon his action . . .[9]

But this critical position is not so much a defiance as it is a review of metaphysics. Ransom would want us to "get back to essentials," to rediscover what it is precisely that we mean by experience and the exact value inhering in the relation of the observing self to the observed object. Setting aside for the moment the complex variety of approaches in modern criticism, one may say that this is a shared motive for its special directions. Briefly, this criticism suspends prior metaphysical perspectives for the duration of the *first stages* of the critical act. It will begin with the nodus of experience: the self at the moment of its experiencing. This moment is a fusion of relation and process; the one involves its structure, the other its technique. Values are assayed in terms of the differentia of both. In a sense, this act requires a suspension of time; the experience is artificially detached from its suggested associations with history and eternity. But this is only a temporary suspension, and in any case the technique of art, even at the moment of concentrated attention, owes some of its subtlety to the larger circumstances of the artist's world.

In the last chapter of *The New Criticism*, Ransom devises an elaborate scheme of interpretation, which involves our seeing structure, texture, and their very sensitive relationship. *Any* experience may be evaluated in terms of the complex exchange that occurs in a work of art. Ransom describes this exchange in

[9] *The World's Body*, New York, Scribner's, 1938, p. 31.

many ways, as a tension between meaning and technique, or structure and texture; the finished product, a partial resolution of the struggle, reveals the two "at peace" or in a state of highly charged balance.

> The composition of a poem is an operation in which the argument fights to displace the meter, and the meter fights to displace the argument. It would seem that the sacrifices made on both sides would be legible forever in terms of peace, which are the dispositions found in the finished poem, where the critic may analyze them if he thinks it furthers the understanding of poetry. (295)

The balance achieved in the end will most shrewdly and most "truly" describe an experience, the disposition of the experiencer toward it, and the disposition of the poet (who is neither and more than both) toward the complex.

At one extreme of the complex act of modern criticism is the image. We can say that the image is a nexus of experiencing. Though it is related to a "thing," it is not simply or solely a thing. But it is isolated from out of the flow of experiencing, and it has no time values, at least none that figure significantly in the imagist act.[10] In being objectively a record of a momentary experience, it is a mask of the self at that moment. The image is not an object, but is the objective result of the reaction to an experience, and as such it communicates the intensity of that experience.

[10] See Ezra Pound's *Gaudier-Brzeska* (London, John Lane, 1910), pp. 100–103, for his account of an experiencing "the image." It is first a moment in time, but even then the major qualities are spatial. The deliberations which ensue move from a plastic definition of the image to a verbal one; but there is a process of refining, from a thirty-line poem to one half that length, finally to this:

> The apparition of these faces in the crowd:
> Petals, on a wet, black bough.

Presumably, the experience has now been fixed in art, the experience and the image identical. "In a poem of this sort," Pound says, "one is trying to record the precise instant when a thing outward and objective transforms itself, or darts into a thing inward and subjective." (p. 103)

Ezra Pound has defined the image as "that which presents an intellectual and emotional complex in an instant of time." In another place he suggests as one of the absolute minima of poetry that it give a "Direct treatment of the 'thing' whether subjective or objective." Both of these statements are deceptively easy, and in the history of modern poetry they misled the unwary into assuming that the image was purely visual, available to the most forthright of minimal representation. Pound would have us above all avoid pure abstraction, as well as the sentimentally false exploitation of the object. In his effort to redefine the image, and to take the critical responsibility away from the rather less than ideally intelligent sponsorship of Amy Lowell, he replaced the term with another, the "Vortex." In his tribute to *Gaudier-Brzeska,* one of the great documents in the history of the spatial approach to experience, Pound described the new term in this way:

> The image is not an idea. It is a radiant node or cluster; it is what I can, and must perforce, call a VORTEX, from which, and through which, and into which, ideas are constantly rushing . . .[11]

These assertions attend primarily to what is "an experience as object arrested in time." One of the primary motives for so isolating experience was the distrust of popular metaphysics as a means of informing us of the true nature of experience.[12] We begin with Pound's "intellectual and emotional complex," which is "in an instant of time" and therefore timeless. To this arbitrarily fixed point of experience we are asked to address the most exclusive of talents, to apply only the details absolutely necessary, and to do nothing that the initial experience does

[11] *Gaudier-Brzeska,* p. 106.
[12] This concentration upon the isolated moment is also in a sense a reaction against scholarly biography and literary history. The implication, in Pound's case at least, is that if you can isolate the moment in an image or a "vortex" in its purity, you can then write your own history of literature and the other arts. This very complex matter is a part of an "anti-historical" development in criticism.

not ask us to do. On this level, which is simple only in the sense that it requires no elaborate preordained schemata of interpretation, the mind and the emotions function in terms of the medium available to a sensitivity. Pound's general tendency was to move out from this nucleus, to suggest structure as the result of image or vortex working in a state of ever-enlarging areas of tension, but always accessible to a return to what he called the "radiant node or cluster." Ultimately, the poem achieves structure, length, a largeness of reference, even a quality of moral judgment; but it never ceases being what it was originally, an "intellectual and emotional complex in an instant of time."

The most common of all of the functions of generality is that it controls, or helps us to control, the pace and rhythm of experience in time. Significant generality, like the polished, traditionally accepted principles of a religious system, allows us to ignore the center of experience because we already "know" what experience is or means. The peculiarity of much modern criticism is that it insists we discard all props to conventional "knowing" and all stock, easy appeals to sentiment. The effect upon time is to make our awareness of it fitfully selective. We concentrate upon a moment, we move on to another; in any case, we do not use guideposts but come afresh to each moment of analysis. One needs to state the meaning of this tendency of critical thought. It is not merely an attempt to refurbish critical language; nor is it entirely a way toward purifying thought, toward ridding it of the embarrassments of a moldy metaphysics.

A crucial reason is that the established generalities assuring and assuming immortality had lost their persuasive liveliness; they were not "convincing." This is not at all to say that criticism abandoned immortality, only that the techniques of explaining its relation to time were discredited. What had originally been vivid, vital, significant assertions, close to the sources of man's basic concern over the prospects of mortality, had simply become wearisome; they had been taken over in a thousand ways as forms of superficial apologetic. Simple ironies eroded belief. Grotesque distortions of reality, in the war experience especially, were lamely explained away by a form of metaphysics-become-platitude. In this situation the *object* became almost the sole resource of sanity, whether as ironic "object lesson" or as the beginning of a new essay toward metaphysical statement.

There is a clear line of progress from the dismissal of easy generality to the love of complex statement. The popularity of seventeenth century English poets is accounted for in their ability to bring elaborate forms of subtle representation to the problem of defining states of mind. The major attraction of Donne's poetry, for example, is his complex attention to love and death, and to the metaphysical implications of the corruptibility of man. The fact of death in the midst of life, the threat of mortality, makes the irony all the more attractive. Eliot admired Donne's line, "A bracelet of bright hair about the bone," for its "sudden contrast of associations." His admiration grew out of the preoccupation with the struggle for a new and more appropriate language. But the substance which that language should communicate was the grotesque one of "the skull beneath the skin," the "anguish of the marrow / The ague of the skeleton." [13]

The attachment to the "Metaphysicals" grows directly out of the cult of the object, the reductive strategies of modern criticism. The metaphysical conceit is an extension of the technical means of identifying and accurately defining the object. The image in Pound's vision of it is a center of intellectual and emotional energy, but even here the quality of fusion is appreciated in unusual comprehensions of experience. The trope is a step toward liberation from both nonfigurative prose and clichés.

> Figures of speech (Ransom said) twist accidence away from the straight course, as if to intimate astonishing lapses of rationality beneath the surface of discourse, inviting

[13] "Whispers of Immortality," in *Collected Poems and Plays*, pp. 32, 33.

perceptual attention, and weakening the tyranny of science over the senses.[14]

The real challenge to any figurative language is to the freshness, originality, complexity of its having met the circumstance of the experienced "object." Perhaps the furthest extension of this view comes in Ransom's essay, quoted above, in which he moves from "easy figures" to what he calls the "miraculism" of metaphysical poetry:

> Specifically, the miraculism arises when the poet discovers by analogy an identity between objects which is partial, though it should be considerable, and proceeds to an identification which is complete.[15]

The significance of the modern return to the "object" has here advanced spirally, in the manner of Dante's voyage up the Mount of Purgatory. Ransom's defense of "miraculism" is entirely in terms of the interaction of object (that is, experience momentarily fixed) and technique. In the ultimate "metaphysical" expression, the ingenuity of technique compromises with the necessary implications of the object, to lead eventually to a new system of generalities which are both "felt"and "thought." They do not need to be either "felt" or "thought" in time; history is therefore treated loosely as a succession of image and metaphor "clusters," only vaguely associated with milieu.

—[iv]—

The reductive attention to mortal experience can be seen in another and a quite different context. It is defined, imperfectly and whimsically perhaps, in one of Gertrude Stein's critical essays, a lecture she gave to both Cambridge and Oxford University audiences.

[14] "Poetry: A Note in Ontology," in *The World's Body*, p. 133.
[15] *The World's Body*, p. 139.

The only thing that is different from one time to another
is what is seen and what is seen depends upon how everybody is doing everything. . . . Nothing changes from generation to generation except the thing seen and that makes
a composition.[16]

It is significant that the best elaboration of these remarks should
come in her little book on Picasso, who after all provided an
important new instrument of "seeing things" in a modern way:

People really do not change from one generation to another, as far back as we know history people are about the
same as they were, they have had the same needs, the same
desires, the same virtues and the same qualities, the same
defects, indeed nothing changes from one generation to
another except the things seen and the things seen make
that generation, that is to say nothing changes in people
from one generation to another except the way of seeing
and being seen.[17]

One way of suggesting the meaning of these and many other
very similar passages is to say that the texture of the object *and*
the sequence of the saying of what it is change as the attitude
toward experience of a generation of persons change. The
rhythm of living radically alters, expecially, as Miss Stein says,
after an event of major importance.[18] Miss Stein is primarily
interested in capturing the quality of the "thing seen," not only
by analyzing but by reproducing the rhythm of its being seen.
This is an important aspect of the spatial view of experience
forced upon the modern mind by the menace of death. Miss
Stein's is not a time literature but one dominated by a spatial
perspective. She is in a sense limiting her function to that of

[16] *Composition As Explanation*, London, Hogarth Press, 1926, p. 6.
[17] *Picasso*, London, B. T. Batsford, 1938, p. 10. Originally published in
French, Paris, Librairie Floury, 1938.
[18] See *Composition As Explanation:* "And so war may be said to have
advanced a general recognition of the expression of the contemporary
composition by almost thirty years." (p. 26)

capturing the object in a state of process, as William James had earlier suggested the "stream of consciousness" as the condition of the self. But Miss Stein was concerned almost exclusively with methodology. She had no real subject, but only a method; which is to say that (particularly after *Three Lives*, 1909) she could write only about how to write. When she talked about herself, it was in terms of what she had learned and taught about method, or of comparable methods in the other arts. Given these limits, however, she did make a contribution, in the way of suggesting a literary style that held close to the exigencies of immediate experience. A consequence of this concern was that style was for her a distilled essence of experience; it was, to put it in her way, the experiencing of experience, not related particularly to the special qualities of a specific experiencer.

The strongest recommendation one may give the writers who were influenced by her is to say that they considered it indispensable to literary integrity to do justice to the object and to give it in isolation from any and all presupposed manners of defining it. The object exists in a state of mortality at the moment it is caught. Its nuances of line and meaning, slowly, subtly, and minutely change, in the manner of an object which shows the slightest alterations of form and color as the light shining upon it gradually changes. The elaborately careful attention paid it in itself testifies to change, not as time passing but as objective existence altering ever so slightly its particular qualities.

Partly this disposition to experience comes from a failure to understand it beyond the actual limits of experiencing—or, perhaps from a strong unwillingness to characterize it as anything other than what it starkly is. Miss Stein, for all her pretentious "salonisticisme," was essentially a methodologist of war literature. Which is not to say that she understood war (it was, in her experience of it, either a personal anoyance or a personal opportunity), but rather that, perhaps inadvertently, she suggested a

way of seeing things that was very close to the literary requirements of an age of violence. The most important characteristic
of this literature was that ideas were not to adhere to experience; they did not exist, or were condemned out of hand, as
getting in the way of the observer and obstructing his vision.
The consequence was that, in the best of the literature affected
by her discussion of method, the description of experience was
almost entirely a matter of continual improvisation, as the experience moved or "flowed" in the process of changing. This
movement she characteristically described in these terms:

> And after that what changes what changes after that, after
> that what changes and what changes after that and after
> that and what changes and after that and what changes
> after that.[19]

Stylistic values are a fairly clear indication of self-evaluation.
Hemingway's style is after all a direct consequence of an experience with violence, which shocked him out of all love of elaborate rhetoric. The deliberate underplaying of significance, the
avoidance of what he called "spiritual faking," his nominalistic
concern for experiential minima, are all a product of his felt
need to improvise in terms of direct exposure to the "thing
seen" and "what changes after that." The effect is not realistic
in the conventional sense. The "data" of Hemingway's fiction
provide a minimal index of experience, upon which there is very
little ideational elaboration or rhetorical embellishment. This
style may be defined as the exposition of reality without either
ceremonial or philosophical mitigation.[20]

One has to move far beyond the repetitious simplicities of
Gertrude Stein in order to capture the full significance of these
developments in modern literature. We need to assume a state
of sudden and unprecedented violence. An explosion of force
has several consequences: it at first destroys time at the very

---

[19] *Composition As Explanation*, p. 20.
[20] See above, Part Two, chapter 4, "The Moment of Violence."

moment that it alters the space in which it occurs; further, by making death commonplace, it destroys all power to conceptualize the experience of dying, and it allows no time for an appeal to rhetorical forms of alleviation; in a grotesque though absolutely essential way, it forces the attention of the self upon the moment of its experiencing violence. With respect to this last effect, the self becomes an object abnormally conscious of itself (though not in the usual sense "self-conscious") in a spatial relationship with other objects. They are not persons; they are bodies, that is to say, objects suddenly and forcefully propelled into and through space.

There is obviously no time for meditation; in fact, all of the patterns of the self's movement toward death are crushed into a two-dimensional formal instant. It is impossible to *represent* this occasion as it is, since language is designed to qualify experience, and this experience has no time for qualification. The most one can do is to limit rhetoric to the barest of essentials, to concentrate upon nouns, to convert most verbs into participles, and to utilize such connectives as "and," which least subtly interfere with objective instantaneity. This is the ultimate form of objectification. Direct and sudden, the style and form offer the least possible barrier to an immediate apprehension of the thing seen in the moment in which it is seen. In these circumstances, it is almost possible to say that the seer *is* the thing seen, or that he is a part of it, since there is no time for even the simplest spatial distinctions that uphold relational values.

Sudden violence also forces the self either to project its suppressed will or to retreat toward the interior self, in which things are arranged in an order entirely different from that of conscious discipline. One version of this experience is the quick removal from maturity, a retreat to the sensory world of childhood, in which desire and reality are very closely associated. The dream (or the sudden, brief loss of consciousness) becomes so closely identified with consciousness as to become a part of it, perhaps even the dominant part. One may think of this as a move away from imminent death to a time when death was not an intelligible or an expected experience. But mostly it is a surrender of the conscious, disciplined, formal, and conventional strategies of arranging and regulating life. I do not believe that the return to the unconscious is exclusively a result of violent circumstance, but it is surely a form of "inner violence" called upon to meet, to adjust to, and in critical circumstance to replace the outer violence.

Hemingway's Nick Adams sequence comprehends the full range of stratagems used to adjust to violence. Nick is at first pleased to confine himself to the simple ceremonial niceties of outdoor living, and he will not tolerate even the mildest threat to their simplicity. But he comes against, as he will and should, both irrational behavior ("The Battler") and inexplicable violence ("The Killers"). His first response is to shy away from the unfamiliar ("I'm going to get out of this town"), perhaps to return to idyllic simplicity as a refuge from it. But he is, after all, a modern hero (or at least a preliminary exercise in modern heroics), and he must therefore—as the son of Hemingway's imagination—go to the wars. In the war episodes, the early, woodsy wholesomeness gives him a fake start, and the shock of change without transition in his life brings on a surrealistic, "depth" response ("A Way You'll Never Be"). Not only in this Hemingway series but in many contemporary accounts, the problem of the self's maintaining an objective status is proved to be all but unsolvable, at least along either rational or sentimental lines. Surely Nick Adams is a *naïf* of the modern self in this context. He does not invite violence but encounters it, and yields to a surreal reconstitution of self only as a result of a traumatic introduction to violence.

There are many lines of literary expression other than Hemingway's which are concerned to revalue the self in a condition of either willed or unexpected violence. The lines of development from Arthur Rimbaud is one of them; expressionism, at least in some of its aspects, is another. To consider the first, Rimbaud's deliberate cultivation of the irrational had as its original motive the desire to realize the self in an altogether unconventional, surreal mode. He penetrates beneath conscious experience, many levels below the Proustian recapture of memory flow. But he does not pretend to find a universal self, unified by values not grasped by the intelligence. Instead, he greets the unknown, embraces it for what it *cannot* logically or coherently say about the self:

> Le Poète se fait *voyant* par un long, immense et raisonné *dérèglement* de *tous les sens.* Toutes les formes d'amour, de souffrance, de folie; il cherche lui-même, il épuise en lui tous les poisons, pour n'en garder que les quintessences. Ineffable torture où il a besoin de toute la foi, de toute la force surhumaine, où il devient entre tous le grand malade, le grand criminel, le grand maudit,—et le suprême Savant! —Car il arrive à l'*inconnu!* . . .[21]

This cultivation of extreme forms of unconscious reality is not uncommon in modern approaches to the self. The surrealistic exploration of these dimensions is a part, dramatic or philosophical or both, of many postwar adjustments. It is a mistake to refer to them as exclusively spatial improvisations; they are rather imaginative reconstructions of the space which a self inhabits. They are still largely spatial in their literary results, since the object of reordering is to defeat time, to defy death by indulging in a form of unconscious experiencing that discountenances the orderly rhythm of life's move toward death. In a special sense, it is possible to experience death in the very

[21] Letter to Paul Demeny, May 15, 1871: "The poet makes himself a *seer* by a long, immense, and reasoned *derangement* of all of the senses. All forms of love, suffering, madness; he himself seeks and consumes within himself all poisons in order to keep only their quintessences. Unspeakable torture, wherein he needs all constancy, all superhuman strength, wherein he becomes among all the great invalid, the great malefactor; the great outcast,—and the supreme Savant! . . . —For he reaches the *unknown!* . . ." (*Oeuvres Complètes,* p. 254.)

act of defying it; the unconscious is a death state in the sense of its being anterior to consciousness and hostile to it.

Another manipulation of space in the secular reappraisal of self is the expressionistic spatial "performance" of the psyche. However crude this technique often seems to be, its initial aim is to externalize psychic forces, to give the unconscious an actual and maneuverable position. Once again, the literary effort to fix the self in space, and to discuss its psychic values theatrically, is a replacement of time, a triumph of form over mortality. Expressionism, in its simplest forms at least, is a direct representation of the "inner life," a formalized, spatial integration within a fixed, unmoving time of the total self.

Expressionist techniques tend to over-simplify, but they do superficially what Rimbaud's *dérèglement de tous les sens* tries to do in depth: to remove the barrier between the conscious and unconscious areas of the self. The general effect is the trial of many selves, each of them a separate mask, a *persona* briefly figuring the symbolic self and giving way to or alternating with its successor. In the course of expressionist history, several major masks were tried: the Christ figure, who served significantly in the role of the God reduced to common man-scapegoat; the alienated artist, marginally ruminative and self-pitying; the sub-human, bestial figure, reduced to an absolute physical minimum. In American adaptations of expressionism, characters *become* environment, assume the qualities of the world in which they work (*The Adding Machine, The Subway*); or they play out an intricate morality mask, in which selves shift and change for obviously polemical reasons (*The Great God Brown*).

In the literature that exists for the purpose of exploring the self independently of the question of its mortality, spatial arrangements are again and again invoked to modify the concept of the self. The tombs of Poe are like the narrow streets of Baudelaire's Paris, symbolic confinements of the consciousness, in which the space occupied is identified with the consciousness itself. Poe's maneuvering of narrow, box-like, tomb-like forms is an effort to alter the self radically, to make it into a nonself or a nonconscious, depersonalized being. It is as though Poe were trying to answer the question: how does it feel *not* to feel, not to be conscious, not to have any *personal* stake in the circumstances of existence? This is an exposition of the self at the moment of death, or beyond it. The sketch or story of Poe, when it does not simply over-dramatize fears, works in terms of a terrifying calculus, works coolly, logically, and indifferently with self as reduced, denatured substance.[22]

This is an attitude of supreme indifference to the sentimentalities attaching to the self. The view of death is one of calculated curiosity over the experience of death, of the loss of consciousness. Certain literary expressions, in a move toward infinite elaboration of the imagist position, reduce human action to a problem of spatial relationships. The position of an observer (who is a "hero" without any heroic status) is judged and measured in terms of his location in space, with relation to other "objects."

> Let it be first of all by their *presence* that objects and gestures impose themselves (Alain Robbe-Grillet says), and let this presence continue to make itself felt beyond all explanatory theory that might try to enclose it in some system of reference, whether sentimental, sociological, Freudian, or metaphysical.[23]

"Man looks at the world, and the world does not return his glance." Both objects and persons are important *only* in terms of their "being there," their status, positioning, and arrangement in space. Time is not involved, except as spatial relationships show change. In this reductive technique, one notes an ultimate kind of defensive mechanism at work, to prevent the

[22] See below, Part Three, chapter 14.
[23] "A Fresh Start for Fiction," *Evergreen Review*, 1 (1957), p. 102.

invasion of significance, under cover of avoiding the "common fallacies" of man's influencing objects, or reading into them the emotional dispositions he wishes to indulge.

Robbe-Grillet's view of the "anti-novel novel" is noteworthy for its extreme development of the direction away from philosophical and sentimental reflections upon death. The major objective of this writing seems to be to protect the self from the risks of mortality—or, in some cases, to accept those risks and judge experience as enhanced by mortality. In any case, for the most part, writers who have chosen this way have set aside questions of eternity and settled for a condition of the temporal self as experiencer and/or observer in space.

—[v]—

"The World is trying the experiment of attempting to form a civilized but non-Christian mentality," T. S. Eliot said in 1931. "The experiment will fail; but we must be very patient in awaiting its collapse; meanwhile redeeming the time: so that the Faith may be preserved alive through the dark ages before us; to renew and rebuild civilization, and save the World from suicide." [24]

I should like to consider this important statement solely in terms of one phrase: "redeeming the time." Perhaps a discussion of it will throw some light on the initial problem of this chapter: the relationship of time and eternity, and the intricate intellectual play of paradox that derives from it. No modern poet was more sharply aware than Eliot of the horrors of living entirely within time. His early verse portrays a variety of prisoners of time, only dimly aware if at all of a supervening divine necessity. While the metaphors of the poetry are largely concerned to dramatize a condition of unbelief, or a struggle

---

[24] "Thoughts After Lambeth," in *Selected Essays*, New York, Harcourt, Brace, 1950, p. 342.

toward "the higher dream," the complex maze of time patterns provides an important accessory theme.

In the language of the time-eternity interaction, the Eliot *persona* begins in one of two guises: either he suffers confinement within naturalistic time, without knowing more than halfway the cause of his distress; or he serves in the role of a protagonist-victim, aware of his condition and fighting to defend himself against the penalties due it. For the most part, confinement within time keeps him from exercising the transcendent will. Except for occasional half-insights, reluctantly admitted, the consciousness of man cannot break through to an heroic assertion of this will. He has therefore two kinds of recourse: to remain within the polite social pattern of predictable but futile gestures, or to submit to an unenlightened natural routine. Time as measured "with coffee spoons" has for Prufrock only one antithesis: a violent release from time, into a naturalist world in which he may at least escape its tedium.

Eliot defines the world of ordinary time primarily in the light of tedium, boredom, ennui. The early poems suggest only briefly the profound seriousness of this *malaise*, this in terms of the prospect of death before the self has in any way been identified. An important motif is cleverly captured in one of Laforgue's lines, which Eliot knew well: "Je peux mourir demain et je n'ai pas aimé." [25] The danger of "growing old," of allowing time to pass without significant decision, haunts Prufrock and his fellows. Once the Eliot *persona* has been freed of the Laforguian irony, his state of indecision is seen in a more profoundly moral light. The comic pathos of Prufrock's timid retreats from decision changes to a deep sense of moral helplessness; and the tedium of the "Love Song" becomes the ennui of Baudelaire's *fourmillante cité*. In 1930 Eliot said of Baudelaire's review of that condition:

> His *ennui* may of course be explained, as everything can be explained in psychological and pathological terms; but it is

[25] In the poem, "Pour le livre d'amour."

also, from the opposite point of view, a true form of *acedia*, arising from the unsuccessful struggle towards the spiritual life.[26]

And he significantly invokes, at the end of Part One of *The Waste Land*, Baudelaire's own warning about the total involvement in the malaise: "You! hypocrite lecteur!—mon semblable, —mon frère!"

These references underline the enormous importance Eliot ascribed to the moral failure of human time. Consider the image of man caught in a flow of time toward death, his experience entirely deprived of spiritual mitigation. Eliot does not assume with Wallace Stevens that the condition is in any way a challenge to the aesthetic sense, to make of mortality what it will and can; his is almost entirely an ascetic sense, and the imagery of earthly beauty acquires a value only when it is seen from the perspective of eternity. The sensuous appeal of the particulars of this world is sharpened only at the moment that the self must turn from them. It is either a world in which time presses against the consciousness, or one in which man transcends it. Only from the perspective of eternity is he able to reflect upon time with ease. There are no such satisfactions as Stevens describes for the self admitting his mortality:

. . .

Passions of rain, or moods in falling snow;
Grievings in loneliness, or unsubdued
Elations when the forest blooms; gusty
Emotions on wet roads on autumn nights;
All pleasures and all pains, remembering
The bough of summer and the winter branch.
These are the measures destined for her soul.[27]

[26] "Baudelaire," in *Selected Essays*, p. 375.
[27] "Sunday Morning" (1915, 1923), in *Collected Poems*, p. 67, stanza 2.

Nor does the "trapped hero" of Eliot's poems respond to the "dreadful freedom" of an existentialist experience. Self-awareness for Eliot is always awareness of the soul in the light of eternity, communing with it or on the edge of it.

Time is therefore evaluated solely in terms of a felt or ignored relationship to an absolving eternity. The Eliot self is caught in a maze of tedious and depressing quotidia; or he has reached a state of half-awareness and can at least measure his remorse; or he is on the way toward a full awareness of divinity, in which case time provides for him only the physical imagery from which eternity derives its symbolism. This exclusively ascetic point of view is unmistaken throughout; though surely Eliot admits that man must live "in the world," it is only after he has found a proper way of leaving it that he knows how to spend his days. It is a severe, even a dogmatic injunction, to "redeem the time"; in the course of it, Eliot has offered the most elaborate and the most scrupulously detailed analysis of the relationship of time to eternity.

The two long poems of the early 1920's describe two important aspects of this pattern. "Gerontion" (1920) is, among other things, a discourse upon time and history; the loss of spiritual insight is here associated both with the earlier, semi-comic Prufrock incompetence and with the more profound spiritual agonies of *The Waste Land* (1922). It is significant that "Gerontion" begins the volume of *Poems, 1920*, which contains, among other things, sharply ironic reflections upon the decline of Christian discourse; these are always counterpointed by the raw expressions of Sweeney's unenlightened vigor. Sweeney has also a strength of pathos, but it is his undisciplined lust that dominates in this volume.

Gerontion's discourse on history is most rewarding for an analysis of time in Eliot's work. In the midst of a neo-Jacobean rant, there is a brilliant expression of the moral consequences of time set adrift from eternity. Gerontion begins with the question, "After such knowledge, what forgiveness?" The two terms are antithetic, mutually exclusive; the knowledge is purely of time, of the experiencing and the analysis of secular temporal rhythms. The Christian gift, offered and dismissed, is the gift of spiritual insight into the dependency of time upon eternity. The power to transcend time, and to view it from a perspective of transcendence, has been lost; therefore in any genuine sense, there is no "forgiveness," a term that in this context means a sustaining grace. Once this negation is announced, the reflections upon history proceed along the lines dictated by it.

. . .

> History has many cunning passages, contrived corridors
> And issues, deceives with whispering ambitions,
> Guides us by vanities. . . .[28]

Secular history, uninformed by the Christian grace that directs time toward eternity, can seem only a bewildering maze of false starts, self-deceptions, arrogant distortions of value, erratic essays into heroism which prove futile. The imagery and the poses of the early verses are assumed in this generality. The essential figure it inspires is that of a frustrating series of hesitant maneuvers in time (the murder and creation of Prufrock's monologue which invariably end in defeat). The "whispering ambitions" are a secular parody of the worshiper's humble acknowledgment of the Christ, "to be eaten, to be divided, to be drunk / Among whispers; . . ."

In this state of false knowledge, History

> . . . gives when our attention is distracted
> And what she gives, gives with such supple confusions
> That the giving famishes the craving. . . .

The self who struggles toward identity in a world blinded by enlightenment cannot be guided by any certainty. The word "supple" combines with the earlier "cunning" and "contrived,"

[28] "Gerontion" (1920), in *Complete Poems and Plays*, p. 22. Other references to this edition are to be found in the text.

to indicate the nature of the "giving"; it is not truly a giving, for man knows only the circumstances of a secular life. He has, not a "gift," but an *opportunity*, at each stage of his progress. And the nature of the chance is such that it merely incites the will. This is an uncompromising view of all attempts to locate the "gift" within a temporal and secular milieu. The consequences of a false giving—of any reasoned or imagined surrogate eternity—is not resolution, but confusion. Eliot will not settle for the Joycean hero of time, who possesses the great virtues of the commonplace; nor does he believe that man can either become or create his God.

What follows in "Gerontion" is a brief but cogent statement about the consequence of a misguided movement in time. History "Gives too late," in the sense of forcing a decision upon the self who has not been encouraged to belief; so that the gift is "what's thought can be dispensed with / Till the refusal propagates a fear." The virtues are therefore distortions of human strength, violent diversions from spiritual purpose.

. . .

> Neither fear nor courage saves us. Unnatural vices
> Are fathered by our heroism. Virtues
> Are forced upon us by our impudent crimes. (22)

. . .

This statement scarcely needs elaboration. The "unnatural vices" and the "impudent crimes" are a matter of record. The important idea of the lines is that the psychological substance of the ego is distorted tragically in an unrelieved pattern of secular time.

Upon this passage Eliot offers an almost endless commentary in the poems that follow. The introduction of a mythical reference in *The Waste Land* brings the problem of eternity within range of archetypal patterns. But, while *The Waste Land* provides still another variant of Eliot's analysis of time, the central reflection upon all of the ambiguities and paradoxes inhering in the relationship of time to eternity is in the *Four Quartets* (1942). There are important differences from the other poems. The *Quartets* are offered with a minimum of dramatization; Eliot's usual location of moral and intellectual conflicts in *personae* has by this time been left to the plays, which become increasingly the substitute for the monologues of an earlier period. The *Quartets* are therefore explorations of the relationship in all of its intricacy and complication.

A moment of experience is known primarily through the senses; it is physical, and its physicality is indispensable to its symbolic uses on the level of eternity. Eternity and time are interdependent, in this respect at least. Eliot believes that the value of the physical sensation comes only from the mind's having transcended its temporality; but the aspect of eternity of which it becomes the node depends for its immediate comprehensibility upon a recognizable physical value. This is the reverse of Stevens' assertion, that

> Beauty is momentary in the mind—
> The fitful tracing of a portal;
> But in the flesh it is immortal.[29]

There is a concern with doctrinal certainties in Eliot's work that is not present in Stevens'. Even in the early poems, when Eliot is most interested in mocking them, the paradoxes of history and theology play a dominating role. Stevens builds from the richness of pre-doctrinal experience. While he is equally concerned with "last things," he defines them as part of experience, or as growing out of experience, and a reflection upon it. Death is a shadow observed accidentally and inspiring fear, or a procession of objects whose brightness has disappeared, "winding across wide water, without sound" ("Sunday Morning"); or it

[29] "Peter Quince at the Clavier" (1915), in *Collected Poems*, p. 91.

is indicated in images of exceptional, though casual and transient brilliance, which define the suddenness of mortality.

. . .

> Sweet berries ripen in the wilderness;
> And, in the isolation of the sky,
> At evening, casual flocks of pigeons make
> Ambiguous undulations as they sink,
> Downward to darkness, on extended wings.[30]

. . .

Stevens much respects the Christian metaphors, but he sets them within secular limits. The defining power is not intellectual, but rather grows out of known repetitions and resemblances in nature and human life which the imagination seizes and reshapes. The qualities of life that he values are all *this* side of death, though the fact of death—and one's recognition of it —has a primary influence upon the degree and intensity of one's regard for them. Like Ransom, Stevens values the myths and the metaphors of religion, but insists that their "miraculous powers" depend upon the strength of imagination expended in inventing and entertaining them. He would say that experience contains metaphysical properties within itself, and that these properties are brought within perceptual range by the insistently and freshly creative activity of the imagination. The imagination creates, sustains, and evaluates (that is, shapes, forms, judges) reality in the act of experiencing it; the result is an aesthetically and a physically vital continuum, which of course is "immortal" in both the repetitions of experience and the uniqueness of each of its occasions.

This design includes "evil" experiences, for which intensive metaphors must be found. In many of our discourses on morality, the task of fighting evil has often involved "banishing" it, making it unavailable to poetry. Throughout his career, Stevens

[30] "Sunday Monday," in *Collected Poems*, p. 70.

has associated evil with death and violence; both experiences are frightening to anticipate, and the rational strategy is to deny them, or to invent a means of excluding them from consciousness. Stevens wishes them to remain; transcendence is for him an altogether different fact than it is for Eliot, who assumes eternity as a determinant of temporal reality. "The greatest poverty is not to live / In a physical world," Stevens says, "to feel that one's desire / Is too difficult to tell from despair. . . ." Superficially one may say that Eliot comes to a similar view in "Ash-Wednesday." But the *poverty* of the spiritual life does not concern him, but rather its failure to sustain itself on the transcendent level of "the higher dream." Stevens will not dissociate the two; for him the "metaphysicals / Lie sprawling in majors of the August heat, / The rotund emotions, paradise unknown." [31]

Consider first the special values adhering to physical sensation. In any analysis of it, it is discovered to be momentary, but its true accessibility to the mind is in terms of sensory qualities. Sensory effects are therefore an indispensable component of the self in time. But these effects have the compensating disadvantage of impermanence: the full value of an object in nature comes from its having achieved a stage of growth, which in another sense we may call a stage on the way to its death. To utilize the full value of temporality requires the exercise of the imagistic sense, as we have seen. Eliot advances beyond this level in two ways. Time is a discernible event in eternity, he says, but time stops and eternity does not; the *fact* of a moment as an "event" depends upon the existence of a conscious being, who discerns its physical values, but must give them up as he must also surrender physical consciousness itself.

In another way, Eliot suggests that the symbol in eternity corresponds to the image in time. But the symbol is after all founded upon the image. The qualities of eternity are *sensed* in time, but they reside in heaven. Their universality is demon-

[31] "Esthétique du Mal" (1944), in *Collected Poems*, p. 325.

strated in their radiance, their containing without cessation or diminution the values which the sentient being has remarked in passing. This is in a way what Ransom has discussed under the rubric of texture and structure; it is also the substance of Proust's "involuntary memory." But of course the points and the direction of formulation are different in each case. The most one can say of Ransom, Proust, or Stevens is that structure inheres in and is apprehended in texture. Eliot considers that the wavering and the "death" of sensations are a consequence of our having had only a momentary glimpse of what they formally are in the superintendence of eternal being.

Eliot says, in "Burnt Norton," that

> Words move, music moves
> Only in time; but that which is only living
> Can only die. Words, after speech, reach
> Into the silence. Only by the form, the pattern,
> Can words or music reach
> The stillness, as a Chinese jar still
> Moves perpetually in its stillness.[32]

.   .   .

This apparently "Keatsian" affirmation is not what it seems. It is an assertion, not that beauty is self-sufficient, or that it becomes a fixed reminder of its millions of time-drenched particulars, but that the true reality is beyond time and movement, of which the specific instant and the particular motion are suggestions. As suggestions, if they are not merely indulged, if the sentient being does not merely wish them repeated for his pleasure in their imperfection, they may yield a clue to ultimate truth.

The full meaning of Eliot's perception is no more brightly realized than in the garden imagery that begins the *Quartets*. Here we seem to go back almost to a Proustian childhood; but

[32] *Four Quartets*, in *Complete Poems and Plays*, p. 121. Other references to this edition are in the text.

it is really a formal investiture of all the images of beauty, in their childlike simplicity. These are neither necessarily actual memories nor personally realizable experiences. They exist independently of time, but within the scene time "scurries to attention." No more affecting suggestion can be had of the possibilities available to the sentient being in his limited temporal share of eternity. Eliot's lines deliberately exercise the vantage point of eternity playing upon the scene. The scene is itself both there and not there, both "Never and always."

> Into our first world, shall we follow
> The deception of the thrush? Into our first world.

> . . .

Our "first world" is the child's world, but it is also the sentient world seen *sub specie aeternitatis*. It is inhabited by an infinity of possible impressions: voices, shapes, colors, "In the autumn heat, through the vibrant air." But it is also "unheard music," and "the unseen eyebeam crossed." There are two distinct kinds of reality here, fused and separable.

> . . .

> And the pool was filled with water out of sunlight,
> And the lotos rose, quietly, quietly,
> The surface glittered out of the heart of light,
> And they were behind us, reflected in the pool.
> Then a cloud passed, and the pool was empty. (118)

> . . .

The metaphysics of the *Quartets* is supported again and again by this kind of scenic meditation. History alternates with the brief supernal vision. Succession is replaced by eternity, where there is no movement. In history,

> . . .

> Houses rise and fall, crumble, are extended,
> Are removed, destroyed, restored, or in their place

377

Is an open field, or a factory, or a by-pass.
("East Coker," 123)

In each case, the momentary sensation, the impermanent organic thing is prefigured in physical universals.

. . .

Thunder rolled by the rolling stars
Simulates triumphal cars
Deployed in constellated wars (124-25)

. . .

Eliot relies upon several major devices for his presentation of the ambiguities of the temporal scheme. These comprehend an entire range, from image to symbol. The general portrayal of motion, for example, is noted again and again within both temporal and eternal contexts. The imagery shifts from one level of experience to another; the scene becomes another, in the act of being itself. And in its ultimate context, stillness and movement are one.

. . .

We must be still and still moving
Into another intensity
For a further union, a deeper communion.

. . .

("East Coker," 129)

In another sense, the imagery of flow, of the water's movement, indicates the direction of time toward eternity. The river is a practical, time-laden scene; its motion is toward death, and it is a never-ceasing *memento mori*. The sea is that sequence of moments in flux recast in another mold—vast and eternal, old beyond apprehension,

. . .

Older than the time of the chronometers, older
Than time counted by anxious worried women

Lying awake, calculating the future,
Trying to unweave, unwind, unravel
And piece together the past and the future.[33]
("The Dry Salvages," 131)

Time lost—irretrievably lost, in the limited perspective of mortality—is "recaptured" in the sea image of eternity. Eliot has us go beyond the Proustian illumination, to submit to a power beyond ours, but in a profound sense to *see* that power in a moment's illumination. He enlists the aid of the Christian God and the symbol of the Incarnation, to make the transition from experience to eternity supportable.

The distinction of the *Quartets* from the earlier rhetoric of "Gerontion" is one of style as well as meaning. There are many glances at the Gerontion figure here as well—the agony of aging without "conclusion"—but they are assuredly contained within the frame of eternity. Death is here considered in a very different light. The dead are, in one sense, a result of the inexorable movement of time; but unlike the view given them and their history in "Gerontion," they are rescued from the prison of time, from the "cunning passages" of history, and therefore speak "with fire beyond the language of the living."

. . .

Here the intersection of the timeless moment
Is England and nowhere. Never and always.
("Little Gidding," 139)

In the place of prayer which is Little Gidding, the past is "A symbol perfected in death."

The *Four Quartets* rescues the Eliotic self from the paralysis he suffers in "Prufrock" and in the hyacinth garden passage of

[33] Symbolism of the sea offers still another contrast with Stevens, for whom the sea does not enjoy more than a minimal natural existence, unless it be introduced into a formal aesthetic gesture. In this case the creating spirit is not God, but a woman singing on its shore ("The Idea of Order at Key West," 1934), or an acrobat observing its repetitions ("The Woman That Had More Babies Than That," 1939).

The Waste Land. It is an "orthodox" contribution to the modern literature of time. Eliot sees eternity in a much more strictly doctrinal and documentary sense than in the poems leading to and including *The Waste Land.* He has come the long way, from the Laforguian whimsicality of the Pierrot or the ineffectual Hamlet, to the archetypal vision of spiritual desiccation, finally to what may be called a conventional and a traditional meditation upon the true meaning of time. In the course of this meditation, he comments upon all of the illusory ways of adjustment to time. To rely upon the immediate "pleasure" of the moment is of course one of these. Another is the assumption that aging (growth, maturity) is itself a source of "wisdom." The most attractive of all is the search for time past, the Proustian struggle for a universalized present. One is strongly tempted to settle for one of these. But in any case, the decision, whether to live in the past, in a pragmatic future, or in a "timeless present," leads to frustration. The only true recourse would seem to be to submit oneself as a time creature to an eternity divinely guaranteed.

—[vi]—

It is difficult to accept Eliot's schemata, except as they provide an interesting and a curious reflection upon what his contemporary world lacks. His position is forbiddingly ascetic, but more than that it refuses to account for two rather important factors in modern intellectual life: a stubborn disenchantment with the traditional system of apologetics, and a profound and quite unshakable skepticism concerning the Christian tradition. The definitions of human life in time do not lead to the kind of submission Eliot counsels. The "unstilled world" still whirls "About the centre of the silent Word." [34] The measure of doubt, to whatever end in the human emotional economy, is very strong. The major spiritual configurations which are de-

[34] "Ash-Wednesday" (1930), in *Complete Poems and Plays*, p. 65.

signed to keep eternity within the background of time are accepted uneasily if at all. The modern self does not easily or comfortably overcome doubt. Even those modern writers who, like Graham Greene and Robert Lowell, are involved in the intricacies of religious obligation, develop them more fully to define a hell than to suggest a heaven. Of the three parts of Dante's *Divine Comedy*, only the *Inferno* is truly understood by a great majority of moderns. It often seems as though there were no way out of hell; or, as we might say in relation to Pound's *Cantos*, heaven seems to have happened long ago, and only earth and hell are left to the uses of the imagination.

The skepticism concerning certain necessary "submissions" to the paradoxes of faith is not simply a product of the scientific drive toward proof. In fact, it may be said to apply equally to the affirmations of religion and the confident rational structures of modern progress. No more convincing irony is available than the scene, repeated a hundred times in war fiction, of the chaplain wandering fearfully and vainly through a space made desolate by modern force. The scientist and the priest are often equally guileless and blameless; but the war scene offers no comfort to either.[35] The one has posed as an "emancipator" from the extravagances of the other; but neither survives the conflict.

This is perhaps to extend a partial truth almost to the point of distortion. The religious imagination is as active as any other. But it is not alone, is in fact in competition with many others. In this situation, the fact of mortality is not alleviated, though it is abundantly explained. One of the most astonishing characteristics of modern literature is the imaginative extension of temporal limits. Since man lives in time, and eternity is a debatable and unproved hypothesis, the discrete circumstance, the image of boundaries, dominates the literary sense. Not only

---

[35] The two, brought together frequently in the literature of World War II, are vividly seen, in their personal power and in their ultimate inadequacy, in Hemingway's A *Farewell to Arms* (1929).

does criticism search for ontological properties in objects; the primary stock in the literary trade is the examination of the conditions and manners of mortality. What is the "most alive" of all "dead things"? Where in the move toward death can the living consciousness most profitably pause for meditation? If death *is* annihilation, what is the experience of nothing? These questions were, all of them, also asked by Eliot, much earlier in his career, but they are no longer considered by him worthy of discussion (they were never, in any case thought to be terminal questions). They have become overridingly important for the generations that have followed *The Waste Land*.

In these circumstances, time is a datum of experience, but there is of course more than one way of considering what is given. Is it possible that there is a "dynamics" of consciousness, ordinarily neglected both by the practical will and by the religious imagination? Partly, this question can be answered by saying that a moment of consciousness is as "dynamic" as attention to it will make it. But the full pressure of experience often forces consciousness itself to yield, until a "moment" becomes —in its vividness, density, inclusiveness of vision—more than time, in fact in an altogether un-Eliotic sense, "eternal." This assertion forces attention to a distinction that is especially attractive to literature, that between quality and quantity of experience. Again it is a matter of the degree, kind, and quality of attention paid to experience. In any exhaustive appraisal of modern literature, *intensity* will, I am sure, be a major criterion of value. It was used by Pound and Eliot early in the century to signify a degree of communicated tension. In another context, it is used to determine the "authenticity" of experience. More recently, it has become, as a measurement of experience, a means of defining self-identity.

It is, in any case, a signification of force, of arrested attention, of the demand upon the sentient being that he penetrate beneath the surface of his perceptions. The term *intensity*, in its many applications, marks the essential difference between an experience merely noted in passing and one explored and exploited by the experiencer. In modern literature this marks the movement of the ego in time, in search of a conative value to replace or to supplement a cognitive value. This comprehends still another view of the self. The self is process still; that is, it is not substance in the sense of existing independently, before and after the experiencing of itself. It is rather an object existing in a world of other objects, with which it has a complex variety of relationships. Bergson asks us to believe that sentience implies and demands a sentient being, what we would have to call an "embodied self" whose experiences vary both in quality and in the levels of consciousness on which they take place.

But, while the self is not "substantial" in the sense of having a spiritual substance, or a "soul," Bergson would have us accept the idea of a reservoir of memory, from which, in the progress of experienced identities, selves (or experiences of self) are individuated. Bergson identifies the process itself as a "flow," a stream of "pure memory," in which there is continuous creation and free activity, as against the "rock" of necessity, the challenge of action and specific direction. But there is a vast difference in the matter of what is or will be made of this creative flow, as between the mind and the intuition, the intelligence and the creative *élan*. The mind is an agent of the practical will. It selects from among images those which will practically serve immediate necessity. Much is lost that the self may efficiently continue along a carefully determined line. The neglected images are suppressed, pushed back into the memory reserve, and they will return only if the self at one time in the future permits their re-entry into individuated memory.

This review of the experiencing self allows for an entirely different process of self-identification. The quality of experiencer will depend upon the integration achieved between willed, practical necessity and creative memory. The metaphor contained within the term *memory* comprehends, at least in its potentiality for actualization, as wide a range of meaning as the Christian idea of grace. The self is immortalized in terms of its maintaining contact with pure memory. It is a very different form of eternity, however: an intuited eternity, lasting in depth, the moment pushing vertically down into the unconscious and *becoming* permanent by grace of its intensive properties.

It does not, of course, induce the same kind of experience of eternity as is available to the Christian consciousness. In a sense, "immortality" in the Bergsonian context depends upon the intensity of experience in the moment. Beyond the moment, self endures the uncertainty of a being caught between two fragments of experience. So the narrator of Proust's A *la Recherche du temps perdu* (1913–1927) finds himself in the morning, struggling back to consciousness after sleep, resurrected from unconsciousness. The experience of sleeping and waking is for Proust an elaborate and agonizing ritual, involving each time a release from time and space and the struggle back to a renewal of them. The self earns its identity each time. In the process of growth, it establishes a pattern of expectations, attends to familiar signposts of experience, invests energy in one to the neglect of others—in short, assumes a direction in conscious living.

But A *la Recherche* is a formal, aesthetic reconstruction of an experience that has been primarily a search for the means of aesthetic form. The Proustian *moi* consists of a thousand and one experiences, of varying quality, contained erratically in time and engaged in a constant effort properly to make an investment of consciousness. The growing, maturing narrator is both an experiencer and an analyst of experience. In neither case is he certain, whether of the wisdom of his choice or of the prospect of continuance. The struggle for "real existence" is actually a struggle to defeat death-in-time; that is, to discover pure meaning in life processes is to achieve an immortality within the limits of consciousness. Marcel jealously treasures the moments of experience he finds most revelatory, and tries to repeat them, putting off all interferences with their successfully becoming ritualized. The difference between the practical intelligence and the pure consciousness is so complex and so frustrating that he has constantly to alter his evaluation of experiences as he matures. The precise determination of the "I" is an immensely difficult, almost a hopeless task. Proust's work plays brilliantly upon the two kinds of death which are involved in all literature: the death within time and the death which is a failure meaningfully to exist at all. It is obvious that this second is a variant of the "dying fall" of Prufrock's society. Each set of personalities moves beyond Marcel's youth, to become something less of itself than it then was: sometimes a nervous, obsessive distortion of Marcel's earlier naive vision, sometimes an altogether demonic perversion of it.

Insofar as Proust thought of Bergson at all, the criticism of the mechanized intelligence, as obstructing self-identity, is an important part of his social analysis. Briefly, in the last volume of A la Recherche, Proust looks at the war as a violent extension of destructive mechanisms. Here the impressions of society which have been undergoing radical revision throughout are presented as especially malicious. Violence is an external force which threatens the inner intensity of consciousness; and the self is here described as at its lowest level of realization. But these scenes immediately precede the final, maturing vision, which is to transform Marcel into Proust: the "lost sensations" are recaptured and revivified, become illuminated by an intense experiencing of the "involuntary memory." And Marcel begins, at the end of the novel, the act of the imagination of which A la Recherche is, to our attention, the completed product.[36] At the moment of this realization, the narrator

[36] One of the most remarkable characteristics of modern literature is the work of art as *containing* reality as "fiction" (Stevens), memory (Proust), life-cycle (Joyce); to contain time within form is an act of transcendence. In the case of Sartre's Roquentin, the work of art becomes a desperate necessity caused by the fact of existence, and by no means a certain solution to its problems. (*La Nausée*, 1938.)

perceives that in his lifetime he has had many apparently trivial experiences, whose real value had been ignored by him but is now revealed. As the ego shifts and changes, and suffers great pressures upon its powers, the qualities of these experiences have nevertheless been preserved, to be released in a moment of supernal importance. He has momentarily, in a flash of illumination, been carried beyond time and space, *sub specie durationis*.

The significance of this change, and of the resolve that is its consequence, has to do with the problems of time and space we have considered, more particularly with the difficulty of adjusting to a time-saturated world. Marcel himself, and most of his contemporaries, had lived in a prison of time, from which it may almost be said they did not want to be released. Within this time flow, however, there did exist a "pure" time, in which the self of Marcel participates several times in his lifetime, but especially and climactically in the scene at the book's close. From the precise sensory values suddenly apprehended here, he emerges with a belief in form, or better with a trust in the power of the artist to appreciate fully these signs of sentient immortality. They are almost purely texture, a sharply enhanced and individuated sensory consciousness of what Proust calls "le livre intérieur."

—[vii]—

The principal expression of an artist's *raison d'être* that we find in Virginia Woolf's criticism is very close to the "doctrine" suggested by Proust. It is a very familiar passage, from her essay "Modern Fiction"; but it is indispensable to any judgment of her work.

Life is not a series of gig lamps symmetrically arranged [she says, à propos of the "conventionally successful novel"]; but a luminous halo, a semi-transparent envelope surrounding us from the beginning of consciousness to the end. Is it not the task of the novelist to convey this varying, this unknown and uncircumscribed spirit, whatever aberration or complexity it may display, with as little mixture of the alien and external as possible? . . .[37]

There is a weight and pressure of intellectual and physical "properties" to which humanity ordinarily subscribes; but to give an inventory of these is scarcely to reach the center of consciousness. Frequently, as in *Jacob's Room* (1922), a kind of property will help to determine the quality of present character. But this is quite different from the burdensome detailing of externalia which is the stock in trade of Bennett, Wells, Galsworthy. Mrs. Woolf's fictional approach to reality is a fascinating mixture of inheritances. The sight of things largely constitutes the vision, the kind of penetration to reality her characters will have. It is largely an arrangement of objects or of persons in space, and the minutiae of their interrelationships. What a person sees *in* an object (what it represents beyond what it *is*) is a clear index of the degree and quality of his vision. The sound of things is a criterion of time passing. These two major attributes of the personality conflict with each other, as the informing consciousness strives against the passing of time, to achieve whatever can satisfactorily pass for immortality. Death in life is not very different from death as death. In either case, the consciousness becomes bluntly inanimate. Essentially, Mrs. Woolf derives her sense of what is vital and what is dead from Roger Fry's view of the vitality of visual form. This is closely related to a sense of the vitality and discrimination of the observer.

Mrs. Woolf's image of the sensitive observer is placed in constant opposition to death—to physical death itself (her

[37] *The Common Reader*, First Series (1925), New York, Harcourt, Brace, 1948 (published at this time with the Second Series in a single volume), p. 212. Mrs. Woolf is here attempting to summarize what she believes to be Joyce's view.

major characters almost invariably die or come to a vision of death that is close to the experiencing of it) and to the static intellectualizing of dead objects in a "convenient" arrangement of their superficial appearances. Clarissa Dalloway is one of several of her heroines whose basic mission is to transcend death, or the threat of it, in an extension of personal vision. Like Mrs. Woolf's other central personalities, Mrs. Dalloway is disturbed by the thought that she will not precisely reach the answer to the question of self-identity. Barriers have constantly to be removed, not the least of them the very doubt of the self's value. The consciousness is a trembling, weak center of sensitivity, threatened forever by blunt and sudden disasters. "The world wavered and quivered and threatened to burst into flames." The self is also threatened by the brusk message of time, which points the way to age and death, but also represents an alien formality, antithetic to the vision.

She has finally resolved the issue of her role in life when, as the sound of Big Ben "lays down the law" of time, she hears the news of a suicide, a man she does not know but of whose act she has an intuitive and "right" perception. Septimus Smith is a victim of the mechanical time and mechanical order which, in their extreme form have destroyed his friend in war. His "supreme secret" is first that

> trees are alive; next there is no crime; next love, universal love, he muttered, gasping, trembling, painfully drawing out these profound truths which needed, so deep were they, so difficult, an immense effort to speak out, but the world was entirely changed by them for ever.[38]

Mrs. Dalloway is instinctively drawn to the "truth" of Septimus Smith: "A thing there was that mattered; a thing, wreathed about with chatter, defaced, obscured in her own life, let drop every day in corruption, lies, chatter. This he had

---

[38] *Mrs. Dalloway*, New York, Harcourt, Brace, 1925, p. 102. Other references to this edition are in the text.

preserved" (280). His death had been an attempt to communicate as well as a defiance of "proportion" and order. It is a defiance as well of clock, "unit" time, which sounds out throughout the metropolis.

> Shredding and slicing, dividing and subdividing, the clocks of Harley street nibbled at the June day, counselled submission, upheld authority, and pointed out in chorus the supreme advantages of a sense of proportion . . . (154–55)

In *Mrs. Dalloway* the interrelationships of time, self, death are rather simply given. Nevertheless, the vision which its heroine has at its end is by no means unsubtle. She has asked an essential question of herself, and it has been answered by an act of defiant opposition to all of the defeating circumstances of her life. The novel debates these questions: what is a significant experience, and by what means is the human consciousness led to it? The answer puts a refined sensibility against an assortment of blunted and deadened lives. It is by no means clear that the precious vision of life will be preserved. Septimus Smith is after all a victim, a "marginal self," pushed beyond existence by the deadly prescriptions of "order" and "proportion" that his doctors and guides have forced upon him.

To the Lighthouse (1927) goes over a similar ground more successfully. There are clearly outlined objects arranged in space; abstracted from them but formally "assigned" to them are the canvas and the aesthetic sensitivity of Lily Briscoe. Beyond the space in which the Ramsays have disposed their "objects" is the lighthouse, which is an image of "pure experience," in the Proustian sense of a vision arresting time and formally investing it with meaning. It is significant that at the moment the Ramsays finally reach the lighthouse, Lily Briscoe completes her painting. Experience has at last been formally ordered, and the "vision" of objects ideally arranged in space, in a balance of perfect relationships, is achieved. Mrs. Ramsay does not physically survive to see this achievement, but Miss Briscoe sees it for her, and seals it in her work of art.[39] Roger Fry would have said that the two are necessary to each other, that the forms of life and the forms of art eventually come, or should come, to the same end.

More than in *Mrs. Dalloway*, the progress toward a formal "truth" of existence in time is here invested with a fine sense of the nuances of adjustment. Mr. Ramsay's "truth" is fixed and final and needs no attention to actual spatial arrangements. The two truths exist in tenuous imbalance, Mrs. Ramsay's and his: and the career of these two sensibilities in a place inhabited by many others is an admirable dramatic means of defining the actual processes of mind and imagination in time.

Ultimately, in the scene in which we last see her, Mrs. Ramsay surveys the arrangement of persons about the dinner table, marks the flow and quality of the conversation, "feels herself into" the scene as she has arranged it. These are persons in her life, and the arrangement of them is a "composition" not less important than Lily Briscoe's painting.

> Nothing need be said; nothing could be said. There it was, all round them. It partook, she felt, carefully helping Mr. Bankes to a specially tender piece, of eternity; as she had already felt about something different once before that afternoon; there is a coherence in things, a stability; something, she meant, is immune from change, and shines out (she glanced at the window with its ripple of reflected lights) in the face of the flowing, the fleeting, the spectral, like a ruby; so that again tonight she had the feeling she

[39] Miss Briscoe deliberately undervalues her work of art, but it *is* a formal achievement and as such gives experience a permanence it would otherwise not have had. One has the feeling that Mrs. Woolf regards the work of art, as finally achieved, to be a triumph over time: as though, once it has been created, it relieves its creator of the worry over "continuing to exist." This is a romantic view of the aesthetic object, associated with the history of "image worship" in modern criticism.

had had once today, already, of peace, of rest. Of such
moments, she thought, the thing is made that endures.[40]

There is something here, in this passage, that illuminates
the entire novel for us, that is not so evident in Proust. Each
has come to a form of self-definition in his own way: Proust,
in terms of intensity of the sensory datum (plus, of course,
its associations and its formal pattern in the memory); Mrs.
Woolf, primarily in terms of a "willed" or sensitively devised
formal arrangement of personal relationships. But in each case
the self is incomplete if it lacks the perspective of "eternity."
The sense of eternity is given in Proust's involuntary, "pure"
memory; in *To the Lighthouse*, it is the perspective of the
lighthouse, which Mrs. Ramsay sees through the huge window
but which is actually "reached" (achieved, assimilated as in a
plastic scene) after she has died. For her it is also Lily Briscoe's
painting, which is the second form of Mrs. Ramsay's sensed
reality. Both women strive for some relationship between these
masses, in the one a line which completes an aesthetic form,
in the other a perfect balance of human relationships. Miss Briscoe's painting is to Mrs. Ramsay's scene what *A la Recherche*
is to Marcel's illumination: the form to give the seal of permanence to an experience that is vivid and profound, but
still exists in time and is subject to death.

Whatever the variants of effort, the major concern of this
literature is to define the self as it is contained in time and
somehow formally to represent the major spiritual stresses and
strains comprehended in the ambiguous relationship of time
and eternity. Once again the central truth is that man's major
inventiveness is exercised in an effort to overcome the menace
of death. As death is a naturalistic end of human time, we
must explore the dependability of each of three principal
stratagems: to accept human time as it is and in terms of its
irreversible direction toward death; to attempt a metaphysically

[40] *To the Lighthouse*, New York, Harcourt, Brace, 1927, p. 158.

valid exploration of the quality of experience within time; or, in an exercise of the religious imagination, to transcend time and will the existence of eternity, at the risk of enduring the moral and intellectual paradoxes which result.

12

"THE BOOK OF HIMSELF":
JOYCE AND LAWRENCE

—[i]—

IN THE GENERAL EFFORT to review the status and relevance of religious metaphors, their original strength very persuasively remained, but they were looked at in different ways. The seriousness with which the artist as creator was taken, in the critical revision of attitudes toward literature, involved him in the act of creation as a god whose powers and formal ceremonies were similar to those of the original gods; but they were put to very different uses. In imaginative strategies, a wide range of opportunity existed, for one, in the interrelationships seen in the Trinity, especially in the pattern of Father-Son dependence and interaction. Generally, the Father was beyond reach, or too formidable to risk literary characterization. The major religious figure was the Son, specifically Christ as the suffering and dying god. Like no other figure of religious literature, Christ provided a literary source for the representation of certain basic ambiguities in our moral lives. He was divine and human, and in the Incarnation assumed a major role as a reflection of human moral ambition and failure. The crucifixion offered a double challenge: it was both a spectacle of the dying god and, in essence, a testimony of the relationship of divine transcendence to human corruptibility. In the role of literary representative, the human Christ presented a continuous challenge to modern literature. How closely may the divine approach the human without staining its divinity with corruption? [1]

Presumably, "the natural" contains within it the seeds of evil. Man strives for perfection and the terms of achievement vary essentially according to the view he has of immortality. As man and god, Christ mediates between an absolutist hope and a tenuous expectation. In his discussion of the Christ "archetype," C. G. Jung defines it as "the perfect man who is crucified." [2] In the midst of his work on *The Idiot*, Dostoevsky wrote his niece, Sofya Ivanova, that "the chief idea of the novel is to portray the positively good man," and he could find only one "positively good man" in Christian literature.[3] Dostoevsky's portrayal of the Christ figure in his fiction is perhaps the most exhaustive illustration of the literary opportunities that exist in it. Since he was human, he was available to the naturalistic scene of the human tragedy; but, being divine, he served as the main object of self-analysis. Dostoevsky seems to have been both exhilarated and distressed over the paradox of humanity and divinity in a symbolic figure. The Holbein painting in the Basel museum stunned him into a recognition

---

[1] Eliot's metaphor of the "wounded surgeon," for example, appealed to compassionate spirits, to whom the surgeon and Christ were familiarly joined. Through much of the war literature of the century, the surgeon and the chaplain assumed competitive roles, and the treatment of each in any novel depended mostly upon the move toward "nihilism" and away from idealism. Eliot's surgeon, like Sir Thomas Browne's, is the Christ of the stigmata, attending souls who are dying *into* eternity and rebirth:

> The wounded surgeon plies the steel
> That questions the distempered part;
> Beneath the bleeding hands we feel
> The sharp compassion of the healer's art
> Resolving the enigma of the fever chart.
>
> (Stanza 1 of Part IV, East Coker, in
> Complete Poems and Plays, p. 127)

[2] "Aion," in *Collected Works of C. G. Jung*, tr. R. F. C. Hull, New York, Pantheon Books, 1959, Vol. IX, Pt. 2, p. 69.

[3] Quoted and translated from *Pisma*, ed. A. S. Dolinin, Moscow-Leningrad, 1928, Vol. II, No. 292, p. 60, by Ernest J. Simmons, in *Dostoevsky: The Making of a Novelist*, London, John Lehmann, 1950, pp. 166–67.

of the hazards involved in reducing divinity to the accidents and corruptions of man.[4] There is no more affecting vision of the despair which these risks may cause than the concluding one of *The Idiot*, in which we see Prince Myshkin in the same room with a murderer and his victim.

The figure of Christ encourages, as no other does, literary speculation upon man's contact with divinity. It is the crucial center of a moral drama; and in modern literature this drama becomes more and more complex, as Christ is not only separated from the symbolic figure of the Trinity but—as is often the case—forced into the role of an exclusively human figure, the major key to secularization. The analogies of human with divine levels of experience in modern literature are speculations upon man's ability to endure evil and assert good. The idea of Christ as "the perfect man who is crucified" undergoes many variations in our literature. He is not always discernible *as* Christ, and the particulars of his human experience are frequently entirely secular.

The principal areas in which the work of Joyce and Lawrence seems to converge are those in which their rebellion against or dissatisfaction with the Christian myth provokes a revision of it. Seen in terms of each other, in the context of modern literature, they offer almost a full range of speculation upon the fate of the Christian image influenced by a predominantly secularized imagination. For modern literature is above all a literature of metaphoric substitution and revision. The pull of the natural world, the terrible impact of a close-up view of

[4] Dostoevsky's wife reports his first response to the Holbein Christ: "He stood for twenty minutes before the picture without moving. On his agitated face there was the frightened expression I often noticed on it during the first moments of his epileptic fits. He had no fit at the time, but he could never forget the sensation he had experienced in the Basel museum in 1867: the figure of Christ taken from the cross, whose body already showed signs of decomposition, haunted him like a horrible nightmare. . . ." Quoted by David Magarshack, in the Introduction to his translation of *The Idiot*, Harmondsworth, England, Penguin Books, 1955, p. 7.

man, forces these shifts, reductions, and revaluations. Symbols are reduced to the status of dramatic particulars; they are afflicted by the ambiguities of human failure and environmental pressure. Both Joyce and Lawrence are concerned to bring the Trinity within range of personal reinterpretation, and in the course of this very risky event the figure of Christ is especially vulnerable to attack. In an important sense, Christ becomes a "marginal self" as a result; he is a major casualty of the process of human deflation that has been going on for a century and a half. It is natural enough that, in the course of this history, he should be associated with other characteristically marginal personalities. The pathos of this reduction is especially revealed in the line of association with the clown figures of Picasso and Rouault, in the figure of *le poète maudit*, and in literary representations of the passive, commonplace figure of modern literature. The clue to this history is in the physical scars and the lines of human agony of the Holbein Christ, as Dostoevsky saw it in 1867.

—[ii]—

Joyce's version of the marginal self is substantially that of the "voluntary exile." The son rebels against the father, rejects the social and intellectual forms of his world, and in the process undertakes to replace them with forms he regards as more pure and less tainted by the risks of humanity. Specifically, Joyce's father is responsible for the "Dostoevskian squalor," that strange mixture of melodramatic gesture and physical disorder that so often characterizes the crucial scenes of *The Idiot*. Richard Ellmann's descriptions of the family crises of Joyce's youth remind one especially of the Ivolgin world of Saint Petersburgh. The melee must not have disgusted Joyce so much as it exhausted him. His mother above all put to him the challenge of orthodoxy. She tried pathetically to understand the ambiguities of his rebellion, and fought to keep him to the letter of religious observance.[5] Joyce's reaction to this family chaos was properly intellectual. In short, he tried to readjust the religious perspective of his mother by changing it into a secular design, to which he could dedicate himself.

In Joyce's experience, exile became a truly heroic maneuver. He assumed the role of the marginal self, the unorthodox rebel against those scenes of his familiar world to which he could not adjust. Exile is typically an act of secular change. It involves a realignment of the metaphors of obedience and dedication. It also puts an abnormally heavy burden upon the exiled self. The exile is excessively self-conscious. His experiences serve as mirrors, in which he sees himself in a process of change from the familiar to the unknown. In the end, exile frequently intensifies, if not the love of then the interest in the rejected forms. In Joyce's case, the act of rebellion is reviewed again and again, on as many levels of imaginative exercise as a man's ingenuity is capable of finding or inventing. The artist observes with sympathy, severity, and a comic self-depreciation, the portrait of himself as a young Lucifer. He wants to think of himself as a "martyr," a rebel hero, and a suffering victim. But he is always in the act of observing his life as he lived it; essentially Joyce's success is the triumph of the word and the literary form over life. The disorder of life is conquered in the aesthetic forms which the mind of the exile, removed from it, chooses for the act of observing it.

Ellmann has described this process by shrewdly suggesting the self-conscious manner of Joyce's devotion to exile: "Having

---

[5] One of the few attractive scenes in Joyce's early version of the *Portrait*, *Stephen Hero*, shows Stephen attempting to communicate with his mother, who had never suspected that "beauty" could be "anything more than a convention of the drawingroom or a natural antecedent to marriage and married life. . . ." (*Stephen Hero*, eds. Theodore Spencer, John J. Slocum, and Herbert Cahoon, Norfolk, Conn., New Directions, 1955, p. 84.) In the course of their talk, Stephen says: ". . . An artist is not a fellow who dangles a mechanical heaven before the public. The priest does that. The artist affirms out of the fulness of his own life, he creates. . . . Do you understand?" (p. 86)

stomped angrily out of the house, he circled back to peer in the window . . . if he came to terms with absence, it was by bringing Ireland with him, in his memories, and in the persons of his wife, his brother, his sister." [6] Essentially, exile was for Joyce an act of intellectual separation. His escape from the ordinary was to read his way out of it, beyond that to formulate to himself the intellectual terms of readjustment. A favorite line of his was Mallarmé's "Il se promène, lisant au livre de lui-même." [7] Surely the portrait of the young rebel is most affectingly so described; the act of intellectual reformation assumes a slight quality of the dandy, the self-conscious man caught by himself in the act of conspicuous rebellion.

In a genuine sense the intellectual precision which we all admire in Joyce comes from his initial trust in his imagination's power. He must find order where none had seemed to exist. "I want to achieve myself," he wrote to Lady Gregory, as he planned his first trip abroad, "little or great as I may be— for I know that there is no heresy or no philosophy which is so abhorrent to my church as a human being, and accordingly I am going to Paris." [8] Essentially, he "achieved himself" by reformulating the terms of self-achievement. These were primarily a reordering of sensory attachments to the world of familiar objects. In fact, one may say that the true virtues of Joyce's literary exile were revealed in the pressure of clarity, light, depth, and substance he put upon the central objects of

[6] Richard Ellmann, *James Joyce*, New York, Oxford University Press, 1959, p. 302.

[7] A line from Mallarmé's remarks on a performance of *Hamlet*, used in the library scene of *Ulysses*. For its appearance in Mallarmé, see *Oeuvres Complètes*, ed. Henri Mondor and G. Jean-Aubry, Paris, Pléiade Editions, 1951, p. 1564. The full text of the sentence: "Le héros,—tous comparses, il se promène, pas plus, lisant au livre de lui-même, haut et vivant Signe; nie du regard les autres. . . ." It originally appeared in a paragraph in the *Revue Blanche* (July 1896) and was republished in *Divagations*, 1897. The phrase, *"il se promène, lisant au livre de lui-même,"* appears in the American edition of *Ulysses*, New York, Random House, revised, 1961, p. 187.

[8] Letter of November 1902. In *Letters of James Joyce*, edited by Stuart Gilbert, New York, Viking, 1957, p. 53.

his experience. This is so effective that when, in the Circe pages of *Ulysses* he was to write a comic version of Bloomsday, the psychoanalytic functions of the imagination reasserted the qualities of precision that the novel had up to then brilliantly produced. The object for Joyce has not only an objective existence, but serves the dramatic role of urging the claims of human purpose upon character. Defining the epiphany in terms of precise meaning, Joyce has Stephen stress the spiritual (or imaginative) values of precision:

> . . . First we recognize that the object is *one* integral thing, then we recognize that it is an organised composite structure, a *thing* in fact: finally, when the relation of the parts is exquisite, when the parts are adjusted to the special point, we recognise that it is *that* thing which it is. Its soul, its whatness, leaps to us from the vestment of its appearance.[9]

This statement has been quoted to many purposes; I should like here to assume it as a crucial consequence of Joyce's change from a religious to a secular "garden of definitions." It is essentially a nominalistic adventure, a test of religious universals: the object has a value in being "that thing which it is," but the quality of its existence is enhanced and intensified through its being precisely and meaningfully and suggestively related to a clearly seen plan of objects, spatially ordered, biologically (in the sense of humanly) significant, and historically located. Joyce's *quidditas* ranges from the object in space to its precise location in time and, in *Finnegans Wake*, to its career in a world of dream motion through time. This, then, is the responsibility Joyce assumed for himself, and portrayed in the figure of Stephen Dedalus. It involved first a predetermination of the nature of essences, in which religious metaphors change to secular. As a consequence of this change, the commonplace experience became essential, and the *ideas* of sanctity, heroism,

[9] *Stephen Hero*, p. 213.

glory, were invested with commonplace objectivity. In a sense, the "whatness" of a thing, that which it is, is the secular equivalent of the Passion of Christ and the awesome vision of the Last Judgment.

Joyce's role as a hero of secularization comes initially from the dramatic act of exile, from his having angrily slammed the door and then furtively peered in at the window—at himself angrily slamming the door. Setting aside the wearisome details of what is not always an heroic life, one may summarize his act as an intellectual self-examination: a formal reintegration of the objects and the events of a disordered past, into their true character as viewed in an aesthetic act of redefinition. But since Joyce was thus formally reconstituting his life, he might be said to have lived it on two levels, that of living it and that of recreating it.[10] The continuous "research" into the act of living in the present and into its symbolic and historical implications is a form of meditation similar to that of the religious saint, whose speculations are also an exegesis of a crucial text.

Joyce's time sense was encouraged as his exile was prolonged. Europe provided what Dublin had seemed to lack, a sense of the past. Before exile, he was conscious only of immediate situation and abstract moral speculation; he needed also a sense of a progress of time and especially of the rhythms of past and present. These he found in the two apparently antithetic areas of death and life, of antiquity and biology. In 1906 and 1907 he spent some months in Rome as, of all things, a bank clerk, and brought from the experience primarily a sense of the past, of its overbearing and intrusive presence. The sense of the monumental "remains" of Rome forever obstructing a clear view of present things had other effects as well. In short, his experience of the dead led him to an elaborate plan for the thematic representation of recurrence. The securities of recur-

---

[10] This is especially true of his acts of revising *Stephen Hero* (an almost simultaneous record of a life as it is being lived and judged) and of creating *A Portrait of the Artist as a Young Man,* in which an older Joyce looks back upon a symbolic Stephen.

rence were found in the successive biological triumphs of gestation over death—just as he himself thought of the artist as
creating, in the sense of giving birth to, art. In the role of
creator, the artist allows or enables the word to become flesh.
The career of his "artist as a young man" is at least partway
a progress in overcoming the shame of the word "foetus" carved
in a classroom desk. Stephen usurps the role of the indifferent
God-creator, who "remains within or behind or beyond or above
his handiwork, invisible, refined out of existence . . . ," [11] but
his memory is nevertheless haunted by the enigma of death
in the midst of life, and he struggles against the image of a
mother rising from the grave to accuse him. He fights the
threat of death by assuming the role of the aesthetic creator
of life, or by returning to the womb, in images of fertility, an
excessive tribute to the universal triumph of gestation over
mortality. Mrs. Purefoy of *Ulysses* seems a heroine of parturi-
tion to put against all threats of cuckoldry, self-abuse, and
mortality. In Carlylean accents, she pays homage to the act
of biological sustenance:

> By heaven, Theodore Purefoy, thou hast done a doughty
> deed and no botch! Thou art, I vow, the remarkablest
> progenitor barring none in this chaffering allincluding most
> farraginous chronicle. Astounding! In her lay a Godframed
> Godgiven preformed possibility which thou hast fructified
> with thy modicum of man's work . . .[12]

In short, Joyce sought to conquer death by suggesting an
unceasingly successful fertility. In so stressing the virtues of
commonplace biological events, he sought to assert infinity
as a succession of events not only endless but in essence simultaneous. Finnegans die but Finnegans also 'wake. As the
father and mother of *Finnegans Wake* approach death, they

[11] *A Portrait of the Artist as a Young Man*, New York, Compass Books,
1956, p. 215. First edition: New York, B. W. Huebsch, 1916, p. 252.
[12] *Ulysses*, p. 423.

become (wishfully, but also actually) "sonhusband" and "daughterwife," and thus move into another generation, or circle of selfhood. The ordinary differentiae of time and place are further overruled in the dream play of similitude and illogical displacement. Joyce maintained that, while death haunts life—as he saw it doing in the streets of Rome—it is also negated by the successive guarantees of life provided by biological relationships. The most dramatic event of his *Portrait* comes when Stephen's overwhelming vision of a "foul and putrid corpse, . . . a jellylike mass of liquid corruption," given him in the retreat sermon, is eventually dispelled by the sight of a girl standing before him in midstream, "like one whom magic had changed into the likeness of a strange and beautiful seabird."

> She was alone and still, gazing out to sea; and when she felt his presence and the worship of his eyes her eyes turned to him in quiet sufferance of his gaze, without shame or wantonness . . .[13]

"—Heavenly God! cried Stephen's soul, in an outburst of profane joy." And this explosion of relief carries him beyond the fear of mortality, and turns his mind to a secular refinement of the images which religious sanction had thought to impose upon him.

The common image of Stephen is that of Lucifer defying the divine light. In "Circe," he answers his dead mother's prayer for his salvation, by smashing the chandelier with his cane: *"Time's livid final flame leaps and, in the following darkness, ruin of all space, shattered glass and toppling masonry."* [14] He has usurped the position of God, destroyed the light, and assumed the role of creator himself. But in the final *secular economy* of Joyce's creative act, Stephen remains too rigidly fixed in his adolescence in the time and place of his

---

[13] *Portrait*, pp. 120, 171. First edition, pp. 137, 199.
[14] *Ulysses*, p. 583.

creator's own rebellion. The Joyce of 1904 is the young rebel preparing for his exile and dramatizing his revolt. Stephen is therefore an incomplete, an inadequate secular figure, though his mind provides the formula according to which the word may be fleshed, and the flesh verbalized.

The essential figure of secular grace in Joyce's formal economy is Leopold Bloom, and, replacing him (much more in the image of Joyce's father), the H. C. Earwicker of *Finnegans Wake*. Bloom is the true commonplace hero of the victory over death, as Earwicker triumphs over history. This is true because Bloom tolerates and suffers—almost masochistically invites—the petty buffoonery and truculence of Dublin's run-of-the-mill citizens. He is a variant of Stephen, the young man grown out of all impertinence and become a passive victim of man's mortal chicanery. The *Odyssey* parallel is persistently and deliberately reduced to the Dublin commonplace, and the figure of the ordinary Bloom walking the maze of Dublin, offering his curious meditations upon its established character, makes him the most drastically reduced of all modern Christ figures. He is truly the son of man, and in the imaginative economy according to which the Christ figure has gradually become more human than divine, he becomes a symbol of Christian-Judaic virtues fully and errantly humane. In the sense that this god figure is etched and altered by the lines of human suffering and passivity, Bloom becomes the Christ of Rouault, who is at times indistinguishable from his clown; or he is the marginal personality of Hart Crane's "Chaplinesque." [15] In any case, he manifests both the comedy and the pathos of man's downward way from the heights of divine self-confidence

---

[15] See Mary Parr's *James Joyce: The Poetry of Conscience*, Milwaukee, Inland Press, 1961. It is concerned with the "chaplinesque" values of Bloom as hero. S. L. Goldberg (*The Classical Temper*, New York, Barnes and Noble, 1961) has this to say about Bloom as "commonplace Christ": "Bloom is no Ulysses or Christ, yet in truth he is; the modern world manifests itself in any one day, but so does the world in any age, and Bloomsday exhibits as well as the social contours of today the permanent contours of human life. . . ." (p. 209)

to the level of mundane forbearance. It is Bloom who attends
to the vital statistics of funerals and births, and in his homely
way meditates upon the quotidian pathos of Dublin's routine.

In this fanciful suggestion of the Bloomsday world, the full
range of ambiguous relations in the Trinity secularized is conceivable. In the shift from religious to secular imagery, Joyce
becomes the creator, or God the father; Stephen Dedalus, the
aesthetic form of the young Joyce before and after exile, is
both imagined son and imagining father; thus, Joyce, in replacing his real father with the imagined figure of Bloom, becomes the father and the mother of his (Stephen's) father,
and superintends—in "The Oxen of the Sun"—the full process
of biological and literary gestation. This complex of inter-
relatedness is further extended in *Finnegans Wake*, whose title
suggests that the human comedy is both "funferal" and funeral, and whose hero, HCE, is "Here Comes Everybody"
and "Haveth Childers Everywhere."

Though men rise from the dead in the dream logic of the
"Circe" episode, the crucial gesture of defiance in *Ulysses* lies
in Bloom's passively accepting humanity, and in his being
himself ordinarily, complacently, deliberately, even on occasions scatalogically humane. He is a god figure only in the
sense of being supremely, extraordinarily human. He triumphs
over the familiar objects of the human world by suffering
them, and by meditating in the strange rigmarole of his semi-
rational mind upon them—digesting them, as it were, ruminat-
ing and absorbing them. This is very different from Stephen's
defiance of the world, which consists of translating its formal
essences into aesthetic creations and thus having one's will
with them. But one should also note the reserve of irony and
self-criticism Joyce uses in looking upon the immature artist-
creator. This latter is necessary for the creation of an enduring
fiction, but the artifact is always dependent upon the life
which it formalizes.

It is also of some significance that the Bloom-god or Bloom-

Christ should be, in the ordinary sense, a father and the citizen of a community. He is aware of his body as engenderer of other bodies and as a sufferer with them. As the Ulysses of Dublin, he is aware of himself as an exile figure, a Jew born in Dublin, become Catholic husband, but—in the role of a bearer of human ills—a minor prophet and god. The Saviour "was a jew," he says to his tormentors, "and his father was a jew. Your God." And in answer to profane objections, adds, "Well, his uncle was a jew. . . . Your God was a jew. Christ was a jew like me" (*Ulysses*, 342). The episode concludes with Bloom, having suffered his tormentors, ascending to Dublin-heaven:

> . . . And they beheld Him even Him, ben Bloom Elijah, amid clouds of angels ascend to the glory of the brightness at an angle of forty-five degrees over Donohoe's in Little Green Street like a shot off a shovel. (345)

Bloom as a hero is rescued through the act of art from the century's reductive and naturalistic habits. He is the practical and tediously wise Ulysses, as he is the accommodating and forbearing Christ. In the history of the Christ image in modern literature, however, Bloom represents the extreme of its tendency to detach Christ's humanity from the context of his divinity. It is important to see that Bloom suffers the commonplace, participates in it, and, in his ultimate role (as father to the errant Stephen), is the hero of the commonplace. He thus makes a virtue of a multitude of human defects. In his kindly concern over the funeral of Paddy Dignam and the accouchement of Mina Purefoy, his attention spans the full range of human time. He is trivial, ponderous, clumsy, errant, and long-suffering. In his role the romantic ego of Flaubert's novel is dismissed. Like Bovary he is cuckold, but he transcends in his intelligence and humanity the fate dealt Bovary by his author's vindictive and uncompromising hostility.

—[iii]—

Discussing his work on *Ulysses* with Frank Budgen, Joyce once asked him to nominate an "all-round character" for use in literature. When Budgen offered Christ, Joyce demurred:

> "He was a bachelor, . . . and never lived with a woman. Surely living with a woman is one of the most difficult things a man has to do, and he never did it." [16]

In at least this minor particular we may say Joyce and Lawrence were agreed. For though Joyce was particularly interested in such accounts as Ernest Renan's of the life of Jesus which stressed his human biography, it was primarily to nourish his doubt of divinity, which he once insisted was a stronger motive than faith. He wished, in short, to secure his move from the religious to the secular metaphors of his creative life. Joyce was a philosopher only in the sense that his intellect was able to transfer the most intricate formulations from philosophical to other areas of discourse. He was not a polemicist in religious matters, at least not to the extent of wishing to recast the entire range of religious speculation along lines of individual, emotional redefinition. To this latter task, D. H. Lawrence devoted a major share of his career, and with such persistence that many critics were repelled by what consequently appeared to be an excessive maneuvering of ideas into personal channels.

Central to Lawrence's conception and affecting everything he wrote, was the conviction that, as Graham Hough has put it, ". . . the nature of man is of a piece with the nature of the world in general." [17] This simple thesis is immensely complicated in Lawrence's development of it. It involves him not only in a variety of reformulations along psychological and moral lines, but encourages him to revise all of the major

[16] *James Joyce and the Making of Ulysses*, New York, Smith and Haas, 1934, p. 186.
[17] Graham Hough, *The Dark Sun: A Study of D. H. Lawrence*, New York, Macmillan, 1957, p. 222.

religious metaphors associated with Christianity. The central vision is of what he called the "totality of human experience," which was a vital and a vitalistic matter, as complex as the minute and variegated vision of the human personality can make it.

The primary view of human experience is of a struggle, a conflict, between opposites, with the desired aim of a balance, a "polarity," a state of "still tension"—as he puts it in the *Fantasia*, "a vital, *non-ideal* circuit of dynamic relations between individuals." The crucial kind of such human conflict is set up in the sexual act; its physical and emotional conditions are responsible for "a field of intense, polarized magnetic attraction. . . ." [18] The male and female conditions of polarity are in themselves only one variant of the metaphor; both male and female exist in states of tension with the consciously apprehended and the unconsciously felt universe. Men and women are necessarily vitally *together*, but they are also indispensably apart, separable essences whose responsibilities shift from sexual union to asexual, purposive activity. Morality, he says in one of his many definitions, "is that delicate, forever trembling and changing *balance* between me and my circumambient universe, which precedes and accompanies a true relatedness." [19] In the intricate and complex description of man's physical and emotional nature, Lawrence dismissed both extremes of the mind and sensuality, as equally self-destructive. The immense reaches of the "vast original dark out of which Creation issued" are countered by "the Eternal light into which all mortality passes. . . ." [20] Either absolute menaces stability, the state of "still tension" of which he

[18] *Fantasia of the Unconscious* (1922), New York, Albert and Charles Boni, 1930, pp. 113, 148.

[19] "Morality and the Novel," in *Phoenix: The Posthumous Papers of D. H. Lawrence*, edited by Edward D. McDonald, New York, Viking, 1936, p. 528.

[20] "The Crown," in *Reflection on the Death of a Porcupine and Other Essays*, Philadelphia, Centaur, 1925, pp. 10–11. This essay was written in 1915 and appeared in all three issues of John Middleton Murry's review, *The Signature*, October 4–November 1, 1915.

speaks. It is so difficult an achievement, and is so frequently thwarted, that Lawrence's time is all but consumed by the sad task of recording successive "failures of consummation." In each case of failure, or partial failure, the personal tragedy is equated with a social tragedy, and ultimately with the tragedy of Christianity itself. The figure of Christ is too much the creation of the spirit, disembodied and characterless. He is the creature of pure light, and as such serves a role remote from the sources of vital being. There are almost infinite variations upon the damage done by a narrow spirituality upon the vitality of man.

Even before his elopement with Frieda had energized his polemic force, Lawrence spoke out against what he at least dimly sensed were menacing forces impoverishing the human soul. *Sons and Lovers* (1912), as a key novel of Lawrence's autobiographical sense of "place," is rich in suggestions which later became important areas of discourse for him. Without these later accesses of definition, the colliery setting of that novel gave out its own forms of meaning. The pits—black and yet with their slag-heaps of fire—were a kind of hell of industrial perversion; and the father of Lawrence's family is satanically rough, coarse, and vulgar. Actually, Walter Morel, though he is seen in terms of the narrowly refined sensitivities of his wife and son, is an ur-image of dark strength. He suffers here from the squeamishness of polite society and culture, from which Frieda had arrived too late to rescue him. Nevertheless, the difficulty of the son who cannot leave off being also the lover of his mother is manifestly a version of the Laurentian hell; and the mother's will was to undergo many permutations in the novels that followed. Lawrence's portrayal of Mrs. Morel is often bitterly analytic:

> . . . She could not be content with the little [her husband] might be; she would have him the much he ought to be. So, in seeking to make him nobler than he could be, she

destroyed him. She injured and hurt and scarred herself, but she lost none of her worth. She also had the children.[21]

When Paul wishes to escape this world, he naturally moves toward a woman like the one who has dominated it. Miriam Leivers is above all the primary spiritual will of Lawrence's early work. She is disgusted and frightened by the vulgarity and the coarseness of the world around her. Though she knows that love came from God, yet "it caused her shame"; and she conceived of her love of Paul as a "sacrifice," a giving over of the finer and subtler relations because God seemed to want it that way. The agony of this tortured spirit is especially severe when she is with Paul on walks. Then the exigencies of their love come upon her as a sharp pain, felt without an accompanying joy:

> . . . She saw him, slender and firm, as if the setting sun had given him to her. A deep pain took hold of her, and she knew she must love him. . . . (196)

There is something exquisitely wrong in the relationship, something of which Paul is irritatedly aware and yet—given his intimacy with his mother—cannot entirely understand. His love of Miriam is as "a mystic monk to a mystic nun," he tells her on one occasion. "Ours is not an everyday affection . . ." (295). This tenuous imbalance, in all its variants of suspended emotion and unfulfilment, is linked in a way Paul is not to understand except only vaguely, to the other kinds of imbalance—the hideous yet powerful image of the colliery town, the slag heaps and the fitful gleam of the fire in the dark into which his father disappears, especially in the atmosphere of surface decorum and amiability which his mother creates. In the end, he kills his mother, and walks out of the agony of her death, "towards the faintly humming, glowing town, quickly" (491).

[21] *Sons and Lovers* (1912), New York, Harper's, 1951, p. 21. Other references to this edition are in the text.

It is hard to say just how much Paul Morel's predicament is a consequence of the narrowing decorum of the Christian life. Surely it is true that the mother's will serves to turn the benevolence of Christ and the religious setting of worship into an elaborate psychological tangle. It is uppermost in Lawrence's mind as he prepares to right the balance in 1914 and 1915, turns away from the oedipal dilemma of *Sons and Lovers* to his first full strength of personal conviction. ". . . I am a passionately religious man," he writes Edward Garnett in 1914, "and my novels must be written from the depth of my religious experience. . . ." [22] That religious experience had undergone a radical change, a change not unlike the death and rebirth of the spirit and mind. I believe Horace Gregory has accurately explained it, when he says that Lawrence's

> re-entry into his mother's womb, had with it the sensation of entering a pit, and guarding the pit stood his father, the symbol of hate, love, and life in one figure. Over this was now transposed the act of sex itself, the short death, the self-annihilation deep within the body of another. And over this feeling came a feeling of rebirth which was soon converted into a symbol of life. [23]

This description of Lawrence's rebirth contains all of the metaphors of his subsequent career. The darkness of the pit was to become three darknesses: of the industrial hell, of death associated with the re-entry into the womb (the compulsion to do so is one of several wickednesses of which the self-willed woman is capable), and of the darkness of vital power. The grime, soot, coal-dust darkness of his father's skin was in later years to become the symbolic "dark man" at the heart of vital experience. Above all, his father—and the male figure essentially—was a source of ambivalent hate, love, and fear. The

[22] *The Letters of D. H. Lawrence*, edited by Aldous Huxley, New York, Viking, 1936, p. 192, letter of April 22, 1914.
[23] *Pilgrim of the Apocalypse*, New York, Viking, 1933, p. 31.

dread and dreadful setting of the coal mines is set against the fine marks and vitally subtle lines of natural objects; and it is not accidental that Lawrence's characters should find such joy in the study of leaves and flowers. Substantially, the mines which reduce Walter Morel to the sooted and pathetic remnant of his maleness are symbolically to menace all hopes of "tenderness," love, vital struggle, and polarity.

The Rainbow (1915) is probably Lawrence's purest evocation of the vitality of human life, of his deep sense of tradition, and especially of his appreciation of the process of self-definition in each new generation of human creatures. The human story here given in such simplicity of detail, is a portrayal of the successive trials and retrials of the human spirit, achieving partial individuation, or little, or almost none at all. It is a succession of deaths and rebirths, of generations and the struggle against degeneration.

This sense of resurrection, so strong in him in the years following his escape with Frieda, was to be a permanent condition of the Laurentian mythology. Rebirth is here substantially a reconstitution of the human personality, in terms of shifting relationships. The sexual experience is at its core, but it is also a revision as well as a renewal of life. In terms of Lawrence's own symbology, so elaborately given in the essay, *Psychoanalysis and the Unconscious* (1921), it is a shift of the self along the line of polarities, a readjustment and a move away from extremes. Death is in this sense the cessation of a false, a blind, way, succeeded by the assumption of the skin and soul of a new personality. In the sense that the individual represents the world, typifies its being, the accession of a new life is analogous to his revision of the story of Christ's resurrection. In the sense that man and god are in the same condition of polarity, Christ is humanized, and his career on this earth after the entombment is according to the model set for him in Lawrence's own escape from the tomb-womb-pit of the *Sons and Lovers* figuration.

The lives of the Brangwen generations in *The Rainbow* are
a succession of these trial-and-error experiences of resurrection.
Frequently, as in the case of Anna and Will, there is only a
half-discovery of life: Anna is satisfied to bring up children,
though the essential responsibility of life is obviously not met
by introducing other beings to it. Will attempts to humanize
spiritual aspiration, but the cathedral arch is a false consummation, and ultimately he becomes aware of "some limit to
himself, of something unformed in his very being, of some
buds which were not ripe in him, some folded centres of darkness which would never develop and unfold whilst he was
alive in the body." [24] His daughter Ursula begins at this stage
to look forward to an "extra-human Jesus" who will some day
manifest himself. At this point she runs the risk either of
wasting her life in merely waiting for experience or of destroying her promise by forcefully willing its occurrence. Yet there
is little doubt that Lawrence intends her as a chosen soul,
if not in this novel, in the next. She at first makes the mistake
of asserting her will, of attempting to force a consummation
to which her man is not equal.

> . . . The fight, the struggle for consummation was terrible.
> It lasted till it was agony to his soul, till he succumbed,
> till he gave way as if dead . . . (452)

Her education into the Laurentian world does not end here;
The Rainbow is a gallery of distortions and failures. The
lesbian Miss Inger cynically, harshly, but appropriately marries
Ursula's uncle, Tom Brangwen, and their vapid cynicism is
mirrored in the ugly industrial wasteland of Wiggiston.

> The streets were like visions of pure ugliness; a grey-black
> macadamized road, asphalt causeways, held in between a
> flat succession of wall, window, and door. . . . Every-
> thing was amorphous, yet everything repeated itself end-
> lessly. . . . (325)

[24] *The Rainbow* (1915), New York, B. W. Huebsch, 1922, p. 197.
Other references to this edition are in the text.

Lawrence's characters communicate in terms of these correlatives of place. More successfully than in the work of any of his contemporaries, the power of place is identified with the force of mind and personality. In the arrangement of objects in spaces, in the relationships of human with other animal life, the analogy of individual and moral health is maintained. Ursula is especially sensitive to this identity, as she sees again and again the habitations of souls, and fears for her own. *The Rainbow* is obviously only a partial portrayal. The burden of proof is put upon its successor, *Women in Love* (1920). She is left, at the end of *The Rainbow,* with a look of terror and despair in her eyes, and has been entirely disabused of her original wish for the appearance of an "extra-human Christ."

The two pairs of lovers of *Women in Love* are so closely etched in terms of Lawrence's schemata that they sometimes seem unable to act independently of them. There is no doubt, however, that the sources of failure and success are contained within their separate natures. Gerald Crich's arbitrary force of will makes for the most vicious of all modern tragedies. He is seen early in the novel exerting his will over the world he has been designated to manage; but, though he has pleasure in his power, his is an empty life dominated by a death-wish that must inevitably be consummated. He is incapable of love, but expends himself in lust and looks to sex not for fulfilment but for escape from the dread vision of his empty will. Lawrence distinguishes clearly the drive toward death which moves Gerald in its direction and the acceptance of death—as Ursula learns it from Rupert Birkin—as a fulfilment. There is a fusion, in this latter, of the sexual and the natural deaths: "There is no ignominy in death. There is complete ignominy in an unreplenished, mechanised life." [25]

Gerald manifests his will toward death from the beginning. He is the arch villain of the process of which Morel had earlier

[25] *Women in Love*, London, Secker, 1921, p. 201. Other references to this, the first English edition, are in the text.

413

been a misunderstood victim. His fight with the "underground" is an important event in the literary history of underground men.

> . . . He had a fight to fight with Matter, with the earth and the coal it enclosed. This was his sole idea, to turn upon the inanimate matter of the underground, and reduce it to his will. . . . (239)

It is important to see that this exertion of the will as force is an experience of one person. Its consequences for others are seen in the landscape of evil. He creates a wasteland to mirror the desolation in his own soul. In the process he involves the soul of Gudrun Brangwen, who enters with him into a "sort of diabolic freemasonry" (126). Their relationship is an extreme form of the unvital, unspontaneous life of the mind and will, of which there are many petty examples throughout modern literature. They make love under the square arch of the railway bridge, at the same place where "the young colliers stood in the darkness with their sweethearts, in rainy weather."

> And how much more powerful and terrible was his embrace than theirs, how much more concentrated and supreme his love was, than theirs in the same sort! (349)

The entire pattern of Gerald's love of Gudrun, to which she submits in "an ecstasy of subjection," speaks sadly, even with a vicious kind of melancholy, of the total absence of religious joy. They inflict their love upon one another, seeking extremes of sensual gratification. But they are, withal, cold and unsatisfied. Gerald's death, to which he has been moving efficiently and grimly, is attended by the frozen scenery of the Swiss Alps. He goes off to the deep snows on his skis, and is lost. The scene is the final closing in of annihilation, the snow and the cold symbolizing the destruction of vitality in his drive toward self-willed conquest.

Most significant for a final perspective upon Lawrence is the Christ image Gerald sees as he goes to his death.

> It was a half-buried Crucifix, a little Christ under a little sloping hood, at the top of a pole. He sheered away. Somebody was going to murder him. He had a great dread of being murdered. But it was a dread which stood outside him, like his own ghost. (500)

This is a most crucial image in any study of the Christ figure in Lawrence's fiction. In *Twilight in Italy* (1916) Lawrence had suggested God the Father and God the Son as the Dark and the Light respectively, and maintained that the Holy Ghost is the "relation between them." The Father image is the image of the Dark—of the earth's interior, but also of the heart of passion, and the unconscious world of sexual consummation. The Son is His opposite, not negation, but polar antithesis. Jesus is then the light of the spirit, necessary in a hundred ways to the denial of excesses of passion, to preserve a decorum in human relationships. The ultimate experience of living must maintain a balance between them. Lawrence felt that Christianity had over-stressed the spirit and the denial of the flesh. Mrs. Morel's disdain of the Father, her squeamish rejection of the pit, and her educating Paul in the graces of evasion, are equalled in many situations. Gerald's death in the presence of a half-buried crucifix marks not one but two deaths —the death of the abstracted self-will and the death of the spirit. In a sense, his suspicion of murder is correct, particularly in view of Lawrence's insistence upon the analogy of human behavior and social consequence. Dependence upon the neat, tidy, discreet life of the spirit leaves the "good man" unable to combat the force of the will.

The solution—or the alternative—lies with the Ursula of *The Rainbow* as she goes on, to complete her education, in the love of Rupert Birkin.

. . . It was the daughters of men coming back to the sons of God, the strange inhuman sons of God who are in the beginning. (*Women in Love*, 330)

The consummation is a result of conflict. They insult each other's wills, they are afraid that they will give too much and demean themselves, they fight in each other the caricatures of themselves they have seen before. But they do come together; and in their relationship, as Lawrence would wish us to believe, the image of the crucified Christ, half-buried in the snow of the spirit, has been replaced by a "son of God" responsible equally to the flesh and to the spirit.

—[iv]—

The phrase "sons of God," which Ursula uses to describe her pleasure in Birkin, reminds one uncomfortably of the direction taken in Lawrence's work of the next five years (1920–1925). In *Women in Love* his trust in the marriage ideal had been exhausted. He cast about for a proper definition of "political activity," of some literary extension of the male power so devastatingly abused in Gerald Crich's drive toward death, but contained in Birkin's balanced view. The search led him to excesses of banality and querulousness. He tried in these years to give his theory of human relationship an historical and a religious setting. Having thought that the Indians of the Southwest must have merited the attention the Puritan whites disdained to give them, he made several attempts to celebrate their value. *The Plumed Serpent* (1926) is a genuine crisis in Lawrence's review of the Christ image. Throughout, he had concentrated bitterly upon what he saw as a dilution of spiritual energy, to the point that men and women squeamishly withdrew from the challenge of the body and the opportunities of the soul. The destruction of Christian images in *The Plumed Serpent* is a climax of his rejection of this image.

In the novella, "The Woman Who Rode Away," he not only goes the full way in rejecting the Christ image; he stands back, appalled at the consequences of what he has done. This simple but powerful story describes the journey of a white woman, away from the tedium and living death of her accustomed life, toward a savage, primitive simplicity of religious and natural practice. When she arrives in the mountain community, the Indian tribe puts her to death as a sacrificial tribute to their gods. She is put under sedation, and the entire ceremony of her death is a graphic illustration of the horrors of relinquishing what Lawrence had often called the "white, autonomous ego," and submitting to the full implications of the "unconscious dark realm of the blood."

He was unconvinced, not only of the legitimacy of the "leadership" principle, but also of the total replacement of Christianity by primitive forms of worship. There is enough of "Europe" left in the heroine of *The Plumed Serpent* to suggest that Lawrence would not follow the woman "who rode away," to his own death. Instead, he returns to the scene of *The Rainbow* and *Women in Love* and to the relatively simple set of equations he had treated there. *Lady Chatterley's Lover* (1928) contains, if nothing else, one further extension and enforcement of earlier views. The industrial wasteland is there as it was earlier; if anything, it is even more devastatingly a "lost world." This time, however, it is superintended by a man crippled physically as well as emotionally. In fact, all of the characters are reduced in size and scope of personality from their antecedents in *The Rainbow* and *Women in Love*. Clifford Chatterley is, however, an additional thrust at the modern image of hell. His role of the diseased "fisher king" is a parody of Eliot's use of the idea. His paralysis leaves him deprived not only of sexual power but of sensual will, and he behaves like a child going about in a plaything mechanical chair, through which he pettishly exercises control over his universe. The general effect is of grim humor, a mockery of Gerald

Crich's death drive, and a portrayal of the mind driven by the force of mechanical violence to senility before its time.

Perhaps the most convincing difference lies in the word "Tenderness," which was Lawrence's first choice of title for *Lady Chatterley's Lover*. The word marks not only a revision downward of his belief in unconscious force, but also a decided change in the estimation of Christ's role in his view of religion. He had always maintained that Christian motives were too much governed by a negative, denying, withdrawing sense of sacrifice, by the surrender of the self to the neglect of its realization. Miriam Leivers is the first of these sacrificial spirits; and her retreat before the strength of Paul's love was one in a sequence of the vision of Christianity as a denial of life.

Lawrence's own experience—the "death" and "rebirth" in the life with Frieda—led to a series of redefinitions of human experience. He was convinced that one is "reborn" into a vigorous life of both dependence upon the woman and strong, purposeful separation from her. Crucial to this re-establishment of the ego was the act of coition, to which one was not only dedicated but responsible. A resurrection, as he put it in the poetry of 1914–1920, was a rebirth of the body into a new sense of its vital nature. In a sense one may say that Christianity is dying, but man is continuous. He renews himself as a total being. If this view of the Passion of Christ is to lead to a reassertion of Christianity, Christ must similarly be reborn. Lawrence quite definitely rejected the Christian idea of grace; his motive is to discredit Christianity, but to assert its analogical responsibility to the actual circumstances of human relationship.

This is another, a most interesting, and a vital restatement of the secular problem raised in Dostoevsky's fundamental disturbance over the marks of corruption on the Holbein image of Christ at Basel. Lawrence does not tremble, as did Dostoevsky, over the threat that Christ may have after all lost divinity and thus become entirely human. He simply asserts that Christ is that image of human perfection who has died and is now risen.

His crucifixion was essential, as Lawrence reminds us, because the figure of Christ crucified was indispensably linked to the twentieth century experience of violent destruction. The particulars of the gospel must be true according to our inward experience. For the story of Christ is, after all, made of images "of our own experiences, of our own state of mind and soul." [26] So Lawrence would have us deny, not the death of Christ, for this is a plausible image, but his ascent into heaven beyond the reach of his responsibilities as a risen man. The Laurentian wager has it that if Christ remains after resurrection as a man wholly man, man may himself hope for a survival beyond the journey to oblivion. He will trade Christ's mortality for man's immortality.

This is not wholly an acceptance of the great spiritual symbol of Incarnation. The Word will *remain* flesh, and the human flesh will survive the *idea* of its mortality, at least as humanity in exact consonance with the experiencing of its desires. Lawrence is concerned here to protect man against the threat of spirituality and of its consequences in human relations. In all of their revelations of the details of life, the Etruscan tombs which Lawrence visited near the end of his life testified to what he desired as the best transition from life to death; death became in this setting "a pleasant continuation of life, . . . neither an ecstasy of bliss, a heaven, nor a purgatory of torment." [27]

In *The Man Who Died* (1929), the entire experience of Lawrence's relationship to the Christ figure is reviewed. Upon the dark place to which he awakens is put the weight of Lawrence's dark images, from *Sons and Lovers* forward. One thinks of many men consigned to cold death or its symbolic equiva-

[26] "The Risen Lord," in *Assorted Articles*, London, Heinemann, 1930, p. 106.
[27] *Etruscan Places*, New York, Viking, 1932, p. 28.

lent, and of Walter Morel as the father of them all. But the effect is not altogether retrospective. He speaks of the hope of "a pale chink, of the all-disturbing light, prizing open the pure dark." And this provisional expectation is like the slender hope a man, like Lawrence, going toward his death, must have had of the light beyond his own oblivion.

> And yet out of eternity a thread
> separates itself on the blackness,
> a horizontal thread
> that fumes a little with pallor upon the dark.
>
> Is it illusion? or does the pallor fume
> a little higher?
> Ah wait, wait, for there's the dawn,
> the cruel dawn of coming back to life
> out of oblivion.[28]

. . .

In either case, it is a cold awakening; resurrection is a painful experience for the consciousness, and the way to a fullness of life involves the most dreaded of self-renewals. This is of course a major metaphor of the vital decision in any man, to abandon a life proved futile and to assume another. In this sense it reminds us of a decision made by most of the literary heroes of our time. A "journey toward oblivion" is a turning away from the forms of consciousness assumed in life, a re-individuation of the self. For Lawrence, the change involves, in its larger implications, an assumption of vitality on the part of Christianity. The "green world" and the world of the sun of *The Man Who Died* play a role the reverse of Eliot's sensual imagery of "Ash-Wednesday."

His return to the world does not mean that he will resume the old ways. No longer is it the "Word made flesh," but the

[28] "The Ship of Death," in *Selected Poems*, edited by Kenneth Rexroth, New York, New Directions, 1947, pp. 142–43. This poem was revised several times, but not finished. It was published in *Last Poems*, 1932.

flesh resumed and made whole. The human will fights against his desire for solitude, and for the slow growth toward renewed strength. He saw "the strange entanglement of passions and circumstance and compulsion everywhere, but always the dread insomnia of compulsion." He had himself, in the other life, "tried to lay the compulsion of love on all men." [29] His final return to the strength of man is effected through the touch of a woman, who gently removes the cruel pain of the stigmata. In these last scenes, the Christian vision is joined to the Mediterranean myths of Isis and Osiris; indeed, the meeting of Christ and the priestess of Isis makes him appear to be more Osiris than Christ. For here the identity of the god with the "green world" is much closer than in the Christian story.

> Suddenly it dawned on him: I asked them all to serve me with the corpse of their love. And in the end I offered them only the corpse of my love. This is my body—take and eat—my corpse— (137)

The strange fable closes with this implicit contrast, so often suggested in *The Rainbow* and *Women in Love*. It is the theme of *Etruscan Places* as well: the oddly perverse denial of the self, the concealment of the things of this world behind a curtain of words—in short, a debilitating self-denial:

> We, on the contrary, say: In the beginning was the Word! —and deny the physical universe true existence. We exist only in the Word, which is beaten out thin to cover, gild, and hide all things. [30]

—[v]—

There is a basic lesson that we may gain from Lawrence's and Joyce's attempts to define the self: the religious metaphors

[29] *The Man Who Died*, London, Secker, 1931, pp. 71–72. Other references to this edition are in the text. Originally published, as *The Escaped Cock*, by the Black Sun Press, Paris, 1929.
[30] *Etruscan Places*, p. 118.

used to support man's reaction to mortality are revised along the lines of secular definition. In both cases, the self is left to define its own existence. It is in a sense placed solidly in the midst of a human welter, though both Joyce and Lawrence have carefully specified the degrees and kinds of intelligence required for survival. It is curious that these two men, both of whom were at work on major novels during World War I, should have said so little about the specific violences of that occasion. Nevertheless, the war, or the special moral topography characteristic of its setting, had a major effect upon their use of the metaphor of the Incarnation. The work of both Joyce and Lawrence has many moments of quasi-existentialist awareness. In every case the awareness of the self comes both from a sense of guilt (of the "something" that was "missing" from the decorum of the past) and from a feeling of the need of basic change. Stephen Dedalus escapes the hell of the sermon through an awareness of life uncompleted in the flesh; and he must decide if that life will be reformulated on his own initiative. He is reawakened from a religious hell to a secular responsibility; he must himself create the forms of his own immortality.

In the same sense, Lawrence's characters move toward and away from secular realizations. Conspicuously, Ursula Brangwen endures the several hells of self-distortion, having earlier seen her father's ecstasy of pseudo-fulfilment in the cathedral. But, at the last, the tomb of Jesus, and his wounds, are the *terminus a quo* of a fresh essay at self-awareness. It is as though he had heard, with Stevens' woman of "Sunday Morning,"

. . .

A voice that cries, "The tomb in Palestine
Is not the porch of spirits lingering.
It is the grave of Jesus where he lay." [31]

. . .

[31] In *Collected Poems*, p. 70.

Presumably such a resurrection prefaces self-determination. Lawrence decries the compulsive enforcement of doctrinaire Christianity, but he rescues the figure of Christ from what he observes as the rubble of its consequence, and has him return to the world, not to preach or compel but to become aware of existence, to live. Self-realization must be fulfilled in terms of a natural order sustained in "an old chaos of the sun," to which one addresses the vitality of self. In its stark simplicity of statement, *The Man Who Died* generalizes from the complexity of such novels as *The Rainbow*, but it is also more nakedly a metaphor of the responsibility of self-awareness. It is important that we see that here, as in *Ulysses*, the compulsions, the menaces, the empty assertions of the will are all present, and that they persist beyond the hero's decision to endure them. In what appears to be a period of mad assertiveness, Lawrence was almost destroyed by his own urgent desire forcefully to change this world. But, terrified by the ultimate consequences of his polemic, he turned from "The Woman Who Rode Away," toward and beyond the tomb of *The Man Who Died.*

The images of self that survive in Joyce and Lawrence are sustained by intelligence and good will. The virtues of each must endure beyond the menace and the persistence of human brutality and stupidity. In the end result, neither can depend upon a support outside the natural or the human order. Both suffer a figurative crucifixion, Bloom's at the hands of a Hibernian Cyclops. Finally, they are both informed with their authors' conviction that their conduct is exemplary in its virtue as well as in its triviality.

13

EXISTENTIALIST LIVING AND DYING

—[i]—

EXISTENTIALISM begins as an expression of Christian doubt, of the practical value of universals, and of their personal relevance. From the beginning of its history, it has been a very personal philosophy; Christ was not a professor, Kierkegaard said, nor were the Apostles seminar students. Christianity exists not in propositions, but in men.[1] The paradoxes of the self as a time-ridden creature faced with the task of identifying himself with infinity were involved in the protest against the abstracting power of the mind. Kierkegaard preferred to think that these paradoxes were tolerable if man could accept them as beyond his reason but within reach of his faith.

> . . . everyone for himself, in quiet inwardness before God, shall humble himself before what is to be in the strictest sense a Christian, admit candidly before God how it stands with him, so that he might yet accept the grace which is offered to everyone who is imperfect, that is, to everyone. . . .[2]

This advice marks a break from Christianity, not in principle but in institutional observance. Kierkegaard notes it as the highest stage of man's spiritual development: that, setting aside philosophical disquisition, he should consider the prob-

[1] See David E. Roberts, *Existentialism and Religious Belief,* ed. Roger Hazelton, New York, Oxford University Press, 1957, p. 109.
[2] *Training in Christianity,* tr. Walter Lowrie, Princeton University Press, 1944, p. 71.

lem of religious acceptance on a personal basis. It becomes a matter of the self in relation to the universe; in each case, the task of definition involves self-identity and self-relevance: ". . . When the question of truth is raised subjectively, reflection is directed subjectively to the nature of the individual's relationship; if only the mode of this relationship is in the truth, the individual is in the truth even if he should happen to be thus related to what is not true." [3]

Existentialist definitions of the self are concerned with these matters: to determine if the knowledge of universals, or essences, can be verified by the knowing subject; next, to define that subject and the experience of its knowing; finally, to relocate the subject in the character of its relationship to the object. The existentialist self is therefore most clearly seen as in the act of experiencing a world of objects; it follows that, in terms of such a focus of the knowing experience, the doctrinal principles defining it should be re-examined for their experiential values. The major problem, in the Kierkegaardian review of these principles, was to check the position of mortal being with respect to his prospects of immortality. In Kierkegaard's experience and in that of most of his contemporaries the question was associated invariably with the enigma of a mortality from which the self needed to be rescued: since it was difficult for him to be reconciled to sheer mortality, it was necessary to explore what possibilities of transcendence resided in the self. As for that, Kierkegaard maintained that the validity of transcendence rested in a passionate subjective "interest" in immortality. His purpose was not to deny the prospects of immortality, but to make them convincingly, subjectively real and to prevail upon the self to accept the irrationalities of the supra-real.

The self's activity in this case is still fundamentally religious. It is an act of faith that the self will return to Christian-

[3] *Concluding Unscientific Postscript*, tr. David F. Swenson and Walter Lowrie, Princeton University Press, 1941, p. 178.

ity, after having suffered the agony of doubt and temporary rejection. In his *Journal* of 1836, Kierkegaard quotes with approval a passage from Hume's *Enquiry*:

> "So that we may conclude that the *Christian Religion* not only was at first attended by miracles, but even to this day cannot be believed by any reasonable person without one. Mere reason is not sufficient to convince us of its veracity: and whoever is moved by *Faith* to assent to it, is conscious of a continued miracle in his own person, which subverts all the principles of his understanding, and gives him a determination to believe what is most contrary to custom and experience." [4]

Kierkegaard assumes this analysis, in a quite un-Humean sense, to be an accurate statement of the necessary "leap" from skepticism to belief, or from the level of rational understanding to that of the subjective will. He describes three stages on the way to the exercise of such a will. The *aesthetic*, in which he comprehends man's relationship to nature, is inadequate because nature is an insufficient tutor in the self's moral obligations. That is, one may *know* nature without really knowing himself; and there are many "mysteries" in nature which will only confuse a mind with so limited an insight into its laws. Nor can the self remain at the *ethical* stage, in which he assumes a self-sufficient morality, exercising a nonreligious ethical will. His position at this level is bound to require of him an understanding of circumstances beyond his power to explain. In the ethical world, the self is defined morally but not religiously, and the essential problem of its continuity and persistence beyond mortal time is not solved, if indeed it can even be successfully raised.

[4] Quoted in Walter Lowrie, *A Short Life of Kierkegaard*, Princeton University Press, 1942, p. 108. The quotation is not available in the selected *Journals*, edited and translated by Alexander Dru, London, Oxford University Press, 1938. Kierkegaard found the passage in the writings of Georg Hamman, a German writer for whom he had much respect.

The transition from the ethical to the *religious* stage involves the "leap of faith" which Kierkegaard regards as essential to a final resolution of doubt. For, on the level of religious acceptance, man must reconcile the temporal life with the eternal. Each of the self's moments of experience must involve both its temporality and a transcending eternity which resides within it. This is a vision of the progress of self from doubt to a renewal of religious certainty. Within the circumstances of Kierkegaard's affirming it are the essential metaphors linking religious truth to human experience. At the very center of this crisis of the self is the "compromise" suggested in the religious myth of God's possession of both divinity and humanity, of His existing in eternity as well as in each moment of the self's temporal span. This last marks the principal distinction between Kierkegaard and the secular existentialists. Kierkegaard expects the doubting self to return to acceptance, with renewed faith and a passion for believing in an irrational circumstance.

The reconstitution of the human self becomes a "story" of his progress toward recognition of his share in this mystery. Kierkegaard carefully protects his theory from its being a doctoral defense of God's existence: while God may be proved to exist independently of the self's experiencing His existence, the proof is of no real value to a person until he has himself linked his own experience with it. This deeply personal relationship with God is indispensable to Kierkegaard's feeling that the only acceptable religious experience is based upon personal choice. Belief in the Incarnation is an experience of the self, renewable, in possibility at least, in each successive moment. In a sense God renews the truth of the Incarnation at each moment of each self's temporal history, beyond the actual time of Christian history in which the act physically occurred.

The role of the self in Kierkegaard's report of it is primarily that of an experiencer, an "intuiter," of eternal truths. This position requires a constant striving toward acceptance and reconciliation on the level of personal experience. The self is both an infinite spirit and a temporal creature. But it moves slowly toward an acknowledgment of this complex reality. There are many occasions of doubt and of fear. The self is haunted at first by its obvious limitations and by the ever-present prospect of death. These experiences must be overcome, and to overcome them requires a continuous renewal of the act of transcending their temporal causes. Seen in the light of the paradoxes inhering in time's relation to eternity, the act of faith is "incommensurable with the whole of reality." [5] In his discussion of Abraham's decision to sacrifice his son to what must have appeared a whimsical request, Kierkegaard describes it as "absurd" in the sense that the finite self acts on grounds comprehensible only to a nonfinite intuition: "Faith is precisely this paradox, that the individual as the particular is higher than the universal. . . ." Yet faith must consistently lead to such "absurd" acts; the self must decide as though it "understood" what is incomprehensible and—as in Abraham's case—seems cruelly unreal.

> For the movements of faith must constantly be made by virtue of the absurd, yet in such a way, be it observed, that one does not lose the finite but gains it every inch.[6]

The significance of this early nineteenth century version of existentialism comes from its theological bias. It is, indeed, a revision of perspective upon age-old religious problems, but it leads substantially to a ground of re-acceptance. One may seriously question if self-definition is after all "served" when the self's ultimate experience is not fundamentally, though it is surely sensibly, altered. Kierkegaard's major concern was to free the religious experience from its impersonal and abstract prison of intellectual proof, to restore to it an atmosphere of immediacy and to link it with other kinds of self-experiencing. His

[5] See above, Part Three, chapter 11, " 'Ecstatic Temporality': The Self in Time."

[6] *Fear and Trembling,* tr. Walter Lowrie, Princeton University Press, 1941, pp. 44, 82, 51.

effort is of major interest in such a discussion as this—of the self's involvement in mortality—primarily because he was convinced that the essential problem was still one of resolving the contradictions inherent in the temporal self's relationship to eternity. The myth of the Incarnation is removed from the level of impersonal proof and subjected to a test of immediate and continuous acceptability in the self's experience of it. But the self *does* experience it, and he is apparently committed thereafter to a special variant of "the higher truth."

Whatever form existentialism may have taken since the time of Kierkegaard, it is concerned with these universal issues: either with the realignment of perspectives upon them or with the effort to "get along with" a nonreligious, surrogate explanation of experience. All forms of existentialism share basic approaches to these issues. In any case, the self is a starting point; even in the most fervently religious "rescue mission," religious truths are preserved through their submission to the scrutiny of the self, and their validity depends not upon prior assumption but upon the self's absorbing and "tolerating" them, accounting somehow for them. All forms of existentialism also try to explain the critical experience of doubting, which is characterized in many ways but is in *every* case the reaction to a *loss* of certainty. Almost invariably, the fear (dread, anxiety) caused by doubting is a transitional emotion; it immediately precedes decision and action, or alternates with them. In Kierkegaard's case, it occurs frequently but especially at that point in the "ethical stage" when the reason is sensed to be an imperfect instrument of adjustment to truths that transcend its boundaries.

Every existentialist position is also taken in respect to the mortality of man. Death is an experience that *must* be recognized, whether in a revised schema of the self's relationship to eternity or as a terminal event to which the self must attend in its effort to locate experiencing in time. The self either participates in eternity—that is, it somehow proves itself to be immortal—or it anticipates death as terminus; in either case, it is concerned with a universal, the metaphors of which are a major part of the structure of modern life. In his *Philosophie* (1932) Karl Jaspers lists a number of what he calls "boundary situations"; [7] of them, these six are most seriously relevant: situationality; [8] chance and fortune, which upset plans and disrupt the *pace* of experiencing; suffering, or corporeal pain (the loss of myself *without* or before death); struggle and conflict; guilt; and death. These kinds of experience are a measure of our finiteness, as they are the sources of much human action in literature. Each of them is a form of anticipating death; the realization of death, of the fact that I as self will die, though at what time I do not know, invariably and significantly influences the life of the self, however the manner of explaining it may be. As the recognition of human mortality initiates religious feeling, so the challenge of death creates the major division in the history of existentialism.

In one division, the challenge of mortality forces the self to accept what is not "reasonable" (that is, what cannot be explained in rational terms) in order to provide an extension of experience beyond death. The self in this manner of explaining it leaps beyond the temporal limit, to accept (or to "intuit") a means of transcending it. In the second of the principal areas of existentialist thought, we may say that the self anticipates death as an inevitable experience, and in each case a uniquely qualified one, and that it decides and acts, "authentically" or not, in terms of that anticipation. This experience is in either sense an individuating act. The foreknowledge of death uniquely defines the self, as distinguished from the other, if only because one's death is a uniquely individual experience. No one can die my death, nor can I die anyone else's. As a general condition,

---

[7] Cited, from Volume Two, chapter 7 of *Philosophie*, by John Wild in *The Challenge of Existentialism*, Bloomington, Indiana University Press, 1955, pp. 80–82.

[8] That is, the fact that man is "in situation" at every point of his having to choose existence.

mortality is of little use beyond the point of establishing the limits of human possibility; that is, the proposition "all men are mortal" means very little. As a uniquely personal experience, the expectation of death qualifies and differentiates each self, and remains a continuous challenge to it, to make of its life (and of the ego which lives it) what it can and must. This is the major "essence" to which all existentialisms must refer: I exist, that is, in the sense that I am a being that will some time cease to exist.

It is doubtful that, without the puzzle of mortality, existentialism would have developed at all. This boundary situation becomes the center of existentialist truth for a man like Miguel de Unamuno; *The Tragic Sense of Life* (1912) is concerned almost exclusively with it: "For I do not wish to die utterly, and I wish to know whether I am to die or not definitely." [9] The need of the self to survive, to continue beyond death *as constituted in life*, is, in Unamuno's words, the source of all religious beliefs and rituals: "We personalize the All in order to save ourselves from Nothingness . . ." (140). Once again the major theological imperative lies in the belief that God has suffered through Christ, on the wager that if He is human, man may conceivably be immortal: "The soul allows itself to be absorbed in God in order that it may absorb Him, in order that it may acquire consciousness of its own divinity" (228). For Unamuno, reason "laughs at my faith" and therefore endangers its gifts through ridicule. Don Quixote, the symbolic modern hero, had the great moral courage to accept this ridicule.

Unamuno takes manifest advantage of the self's great fear of death; the issue of mortality is often dramatized in marginal retreats from the structures and plans of the reason. Unamuno wants the self to persist, as a sensible and experiencing consciousness (a physical unit conscious of its uniqueness), beyond death on the simple grounds that such a belief in self-survival

[9] *The Tragic Sense of Life*, tr. J. E. Crawford Flitch, London, Macmillan, 1921, p. 33. Other references to this edition are in the text.

is indespensable. The organism having lived, it is absurd that it should die; and since it is absurd, it follows that it will not or should not die. In the story, "St. Emmanuel the Good, Martyr" (1930), the hero, who has lost his belief in immortality, conceals his skepticism from his parish because he knows that they will lose their identity as legitimate, believing, valid selves: the reasonable truth was "perhaps something so unbearable, something so deadly, that simple people could not live with it!" [10] Don Manuel faithfully "lived a lie," so that his people could happily enjoy an illusion. But his friend, the narrator of the tale, hopefully suspects that the illusion may after all prove to be the truth; he and his faithful companion have died, "believing that they did not believe, but that, without believing in their belief, they actually believed, with resignation and in desolation" (212).

This simple story illustrates the central assertion of *The Tragic Sense of Life*; that immortality is essential to the self, and that without a trust in it the self cannot validate its own experience. Death as a terminus, no matter how convincingly it is proved to be that, is an insufferable fact. The moral economy depends on an immortal continuance, not only of a "spirit" or "soul," but of a sensible being, bodied forth in eternity.

—[ii]—

Unamuno's passionate asseverations are an extreme form of the modern effort to deal with the threat of secularism. In a sense, he wishes to secularize eternity (in continuing in all of its factuality the secular character of the self), rather than to immortalize the self. The most important exercises of existentialism were involved with a very different problem: they had, to put it bluntly, to develop a philosophical means of enabling

---

[10] *Abel Sanchez and Other Stories*, tr. Anthony Kerrigan, Chicago, Regnery (Gateway Editions), 1956, p. 192. Other references to th˙ edition are in the text.

us to understand and to tolerate our limited, secular, mortal selves. We do not serve ourselves, they said in effect, if we passionately pursue an illusion of immortality beyond all limits of acceptable belief. The self begins in naked factual existence. It also ends there. Self-awareness is therefore, in its basically limited function, awareness of a self's being aware. The self exists only in terms of so limited a sense of its relation to objects. Its awareness is not a conceptual matter, or at least it is not at the beginning. Reduced to its severest limit, this is all that we can initially say: I exist *in a situation* (that is, I experience or am conscious of a situation) that is factual and "practical," and I consciously attend to it; further, the situation is a choice I have made from all of the possibilities I might have attended to; finally, it exists only at the moment and for the moment at which I have attended to it. Experience is a movement of consciousness from one situation to another, in the course of which the self "creates" experience from nothingness. While the world of objects does not depend upon my attending to them (they exist whether I attend to them or not), so far as they validly exist *for me* they exist as I choose to "create" their existence in my consciousness. I am free to choose what I am and will be (the two times are not far apart), but that freedom is a "dreadful" responsibility, since I *must* choose in order to exist. I *am*, therefore, my "possibilities" of being; I am nothing else, or at any rate I cannot be proved to be anything else, since the proof of myself is the factuality and the temporality of the experienced moment. Once a man asks, "Who am I?" he exposes himself to scores of scientific and philosophical half-truths.

The existence of the self, which is the sole reliable criterion of its viability, is a spatial existence, since the only verifiable time is the moment at which it exists within a situation. Time and space are all but indistinguishable, but a situation is a spatial relation within a "continuous present," or it is a succession of instants, no one of which has any validity until the self's decision actualizes it. The most reliable of all existentialist criteria of the self is its *intentionality*—that is, its projecting from a present situation into a possible one.

The peculiarities of situational existence are such that it is almost impossible to discuss the self as existing in time. Time is a succession of instants, but these instants are of such short duration that they give way to each other continuously. On the other hand, the identity of self is also a matter of a projected wish; it is a "project" in the least elaborate meaning of that term. The self, if it is to be consistently and reliably identified, *is* what it *intends to be*. This futuristic sense of self-identity assumes a "flow" or process of existing, since the self is constantly "intending," or it freely wills its future existence at the moment at which it presently exists. It is obvious that the self is not concerned with its present, since its presentness becomes past even in the present instant. This description of conscious activity assumes absolutely no conceptual or "binding" activity, and this is of course absurd; for the self can "intend" that its experiencing remain fixed, and it will seem to do so. The memory is a condition of the will to repetition. One "goes back to" experience by "intending" to renew it in the present. The existentialist would have man play upon absolutes as a virtuoso performer plays upon variants of established themes. In each variant, the theme is "mine" and it exists because I have created it.

Beyond this we can have no knowledge of time; nor do we have a valid concept of history. History can be reduced to this formula: I am aware of myself as having changed; or, the body to which the self is aware of having attended in the past does not appear the same as that to which I now attend. Phenomenal peculiarities have altered. But time is also a flow of "possibilities," to which the self in projecting (in deciding upon or planning its continued existence) is addressed. The self experiences the "passing" of time in its privilege and responsibility of continuance. Knowing that he has existed, he wills to continue existing, and therefore "cares" about (in the sense of being concerned over) the necessity of continuing. This is a far cry from the time views of Kierkegaard, of Unamuno, of Martin Buber, all of whom assume that at each moment of experience eternity touches time, unites with it, so that the permanence of the experiencing self is guaranteed not only as of his mortal existence but beyond it.

Such secular existentialists as Martin Heidegger and Jean-Paul Sartre do not and cannot accept this description of time; for, they would argue, to seek a "right relationship with Eternity" is at best the exercise of a dependent will. The agent of continuance in time is not God or a transcendent will or an all-powerful being, but the self, or the consciousness. The self not only must freely choose what it will be; it is alone responsible for the fundamental nature of its continuing identity. This responsibility is immediately pertinent, for between one occurrence of "now" and the next there is nothing—or, more properly, "nothingness." The self is continually the creator of the reality of which it is aware. It alone is responsible to that reality; it can make it exist to consciousness. This isolated superiority and privilege is a cause of great anxiety, so intense that most selves prefer to have the decisions made for them—in which case, they abdicate the responsibility to live validly, or "authentically."

The constant attention to self-identity puts an intolerable burden upon most selves. Indeed, the cultural source of existentialism is the growing protest against the depersonalization of man. This calamity to individualism has two sources: the hardening of convention (which provides "rules" as an escape from selfhood); and technological and social forces, which tend to reduce individuals to manipulatable units of unindividuated substance. In either of these cases man suffers domination by the "Other," or the tendency to reduce the individual to a "thing," a commodity, or an "It." The self as an aware and responsible being all but disappears in these circumstances, and it is often quite content not to exist in any valid or authentic sense.

The phenomena of impersonal force are an especial grievance in modern literature. "In becoming a mere function," Jaspers says, "life forfeits its historical particularity to the extreme of a levelling of the various ages of life. . . ." [11] This condition, described in so much modern literature, is the result of two strong tendencies in twentieth century life: the modern intellectual suffered a number of disillusioning experiences with systems of abstract explanation; the most devastating agent of disillusionment is an impersonal condition of social and scientific organization, which makes it next to impossible for the self to remain free. The ultimate consequence of this tendency is the "scientific brutality" of the concentration camp.[12]

The extremes of forced conformity have in recent literature caused similar extremes of nonconformity and eccentricity. Existentialism is above all a willed return to minimal definitions. It is in large part dominated by epistemological answers to ontological questions, and its center of concentration (one almost thinks, from a desperate need to preserve the self) is in the problems of awareness and of the consequences of awareness: one's commitment to one's self, and the responsibility for its continuance. In his writings, Sartre sets aside the question of God's existence and of His relationship to man precisely because religion has in the past been a means of self-escape—and also because God does not verifiably (nor does He meaningfully) exist within the context of the awareness.

—[iii]—

Like William James, Sartre is largely concerned with self as *process*: [13] that is, with the phenomena that exist and persist

[11] Karl Jaspers, *Man in the Modern Age* (1931), tr. Eden and Cedar Paul, London, Routledge and Kegan Paul, p. 49.
[12] See above, Part Two, chapter 8, "The Hero in Absentia."
[13] See above, Part Three, chapter 10, "The Transcendent Self."

in conscious experience. The similarity is not without its interesting suggestions for modern culture, but it can easily be abused. Sartre has his own peculiarities of definition, and the efforts of James to free himself of the limitations of his *Psychology* would certainly not have appealed to him.

In an extreme reading of Sartre, one would have almost to admit that the self exists only to the extent and in the sense that it does *not* substantially exist. That is, there is no ego apart from consciousness, and the ego does not exist *except as* a function of consciousness. This is to attack the idea of a "substantial self" with a vengeance. "The linkage of the ego to its states remains . . . an unintelligible spontaneity," he said in *The Transcendence of the Ego* (1937). "Thus each instant of our conscious life reveals to us a creation *ex nihilo*. Not a new *arrangement*, but a new existence." [14] That is, one is conscious *only* of an object; or, at the most, of being a self which is conscious of an object. These assertions have had two major effects on modern literature. On the one hand, in the work of such writers as Samuel Beckett, Eugene Ionesco, Alain Robbe-Grillet, and Nathalie Sarraute, there has been a strong emphasis upon consciousness as *situation*: the "I" is an observer of states of being, arrangements of objects, conditions of self-other relationship, and it is so defined and limited. There is a hard-core necessity to accept being in a state of almost pure limitation, though Beckett goes beyond epistemology to a kind of metaphysical speculation about the *absence* of Godot and the consequences for his creatures of absolute self-dependence. The second form of Sartre's influence has led to a strong, even at times a frantic, insistence upon the intensity of states of consciousness. It is as though a self that made twice as much noise as another were considered twice as valid. In either of these cases, Sartrean

[14] *The Transcendence of the Ego*, tr. Forrest Williams and Robert Kirkpatrick, New York, Noonday Press, 1957, pp. 80, 98–99. The essay was originally published as "La Transcendance de L'Ego: Esquisse d'une description phénoménologique," in *Recherches Philosophiques*, 6 (1936–1937).

existentialism has seemed admirably suited to a condition of crisis.

The Sartrean ontology is precise and consistent; the intricate and elaborate exposition of it in *L'Être et le néant* (1943) provides a remarkable source of philosophical answers to every phase and nuance of the question of self-awareness. To begin, Sartre offers the metaphor of the *pour-soi* (the for-itself), consciousness, acting upon the *en-soi* (the in-itself), the world of objective existence. The two exist constantly in a state of "readiness to relate," or in steady conflict, since the *en-soi* is indispensable to the consciousness at the same time as it menaces it forever with the threat of nonexistence. The consciousness must steadily "create" reality from the *en-soi*, though it is nothing itself except the creative function. This is a condition of continuous awareness, of a responsibility to remain aware, and of the free activity of choice from among possibilities waiting to be actualized. The *pour-soi* is otherwise an "emptiness," a void; as we have seen, the self is for Sartre *not* an independent being but exists only to be aware, and insofar as it is aware. Since it has no being aside from function and intentionality, it cannot become aware of itself except in the limited sense that awareness of possibilities is an awareness of a self which has them. This rather intricate and odd form of exposition is indispensable to Sartre for two reasons: he does not wish that any a priori substance intervene before the necessity of deliberate experiencing; and he wishes to exhibit experiencing dramatically, as a struggle with "le néant" which threatens human freedom with *néantisation,* or death. There is no question that this elaborate metaphor forces the attention upon the act of experiencing, to the neglect of a subject as a functioning consciousness.

It is hard to determine the character of choice; presumably a choice is legitimate if it is freely made, if it is not made as a result of pressure from the *en-soi*. The self, if it is to remain pure, must creatively and actively choose. One may pretend to choose his existence, though he actually exists *only* in terms of the persuasions or domineering of others. Similarly, one can pretend or "act in terms of" a choice without really *being* a choosing self; this too is an abdication of freedom. Sartre asks us to consider the behavior of a waiter in a café:

> His movement is quick and forward, a little too precise, a little too rapid. He comes toward the patrons with a step a little too quick. He bends forward a little too eagerly; his voice, his eyes express an interest a little too solicitous for the order of the customer . . . All his behavior seems to us a game. He applies himself to chaining his movements as if they were mechanisms, the one regulating the other; his gestures and even his voice seem to be mechanisms . . . he is playing *at being* a waiter in a café . . .[15]

Genuine existence, on the other hand, comes from a desire to fill a lack, to remove an absence. A choice of being is dictated not by what others (in this case, the observers in a café) might want us to be, but what we "sincerely" desire to be. Sartre proposes valuations in types of being, in accordance with the degree to which a state of being is the result of free choice, independent of the pressures of others, who exist in our *en-soi*, but wish to make us totally a part of their "dead matter." The career of the Sartrean self is a continuous struggle against nothingness, against our becoming a dead or deadened self. The consciousness is wholly responsible for its continuation as a free, choosing self, and it likewise has absolute control over both time and the relevance of objects, since the *en-soi* does not exist in time and "is not relevant" until choice makes it so.

Sartre diagrams the progress of the self in time as a succession of "nows" or instants of experience, which are dependent upon the consciousness for both their flow and their character. One of the most important of his assertions has to do with the rela-

[15] *Being and Nothingness*, tr. Hazel Barnes, New York, Philosophical Library, 1956, p. 59.

tion of being to becoming. Strictly one is what one becomes, since the self is never static but is in a condition of projecting into the future. We are, in short, not what we have been (for that is past) but what it is possible for us to become. At any moment, the self has chosen from its "possibles," and the being so chosen is fixed. It is only in the sense that it can be continued, enlarged, changed, enriched, that being is valuable. It is therefore important as a being that is in the process of becoming something else according to a choice freely made from the possibilities that exist in the *en-soi*. For the world is itself dead; it has neither the conceptual independence of the Kantian *noumenon* nor the free aesthetic independence of the Proustian "involuntary memory." It is of no value except as it plays a role in the self's becoming it or a part of it. The world is composed of "thises" and "thats"; the objects within it have no metaphysical binding relation nor a "value" by themselves. Only as they are experienced—that is, chosen by a consciousness existing in time—are they a part of valid subjective being.

Sartre offers us still another complication in this diagram of self. The Other is presumably a self like me; but for me it exists in the *en-soi*, and I attempt to keep it there, for fear that it will force me to relinquish my independence. For Sartre, life is a constant struggle between the self and the Other, in a scale of interrelationships that becomes increasingly intricate as more selves come into relationship with each other.[16] The struggle is simply described as two selves facing each other, each of them trying to reduce the other to the condition of an object under his control.

This discussion of selves in conflict has a special relevance when Sartre explores, or dramatizes, social relationships. The keenly sensitive, aware self is always on guard against being taken in, or brought under control, by the Other. Weak persons

[16] The contrast of this assertion with G. E. Moore's discussions of "The Good" in *Principia Ethica* marks one of the major differences between nineteenth and twentieth century views of the self. See above, Part One, chapter 1, "Violence and Decorum."

who do not care for the burden of the self's "dreadful freedom" submit easily to the Other's domination, and they prefer it that way. But the struggle for power over Others may also lead to loss of the self. Sartre illustrates this danger in the figure of Aegisthus (*The Flies*), who has forced an image upon his people and now is trapped himself by that image:

> "Since I came to the throne, all I said, all my acts, have been aimed at building up an image of myself. I wish each of my subjects to keep that image in the foreground of his mind, and to feel, even when alone, that my eyes are on him, that my eyes are on him, severely judging his most private thoughts. But I have been trapped in my own net. I have come to see myself only as they see me. I peer into the dark pit of their souls, and there, deep down, I see the image that I have built up. I shudder, but I cannot take my eyes off it. Almighty Zeus, who am I? Am I anything more than the dread that others have of me?" [17]

Orestes, however, has scrupulously resisted the temptation either to create a false image of himself or to yield to one made by an Other. His triumph is a victory of the self over the temptation to become a Being-for-the-Others.

> ". . . Outside nature, against nature, without excuse, beyond remedy, except what remedy I find within myself. But I shall not return under your law; I am doomed to have no other law but mine . . . For I, Zeus, am a man, and every man must find out his own way. Nature abhors man, and you too, god of gods, abhor mankind." (159; 101)

The relationship of self to body poses special problems. In a minimal sense, the body is Other to the self, since it is in the world. Yet it is also part of the self, and the self considers it in a special kind of introspective evaluation. The mirror image

[17] *The Flies* (1943), tr. Stuart Gilbert, in *No Exit and The Flies*, New York, Knopf, 1947, p. 134. Other references to this edition are in the text. References to the French version of either play are given also in the text (in *Théâtre*, Paris, Gallimard, 1947, this passage, pp. 77–78).

in Sartre's plays and stories often illustrates this subtle problem of ego relationship to body. Roquentin, the narrator of *La Nausée* (1938), sometimes uses the mirror as a gauge of his progress toward awareness. The discovery of the body is often a crucial event; the eye of the self approaches the body as though it were an alien ego, an Other, striving for domination of the self—as indeed it is on many occasions. The mirror sometimes offers the risk of self-deception. To give in to the body superficially is a form of denying responsibilities to the self. So Estelle, the nymphomaniac of *No Exit* (1944), has in her lifetime depended upon the mirror to reassure her in her self-deception. But in the hell of Sartre's introspective cosmos there are no mirrors, except as these may be provided by Others in conflict with the self.

No Exit is an especially brilliant adaptation of the problem of the Other in literature. The three persons, Estelle, Inez, and Garcin, who are confined in a room in hell, work upon and against each other in such a way as to define the special aberration of each.

> Garcin: Inez, they've laid their snare damned cunningly—like a cobweb. If you make any movement, if you raise your hand to fan yourself, Estelle and I feel a little tug. Alone, none of us can save himself or herself; we're linked together inextricably . . . (38; 147–48)

The exchange between Inez and Estelle is especially revealing of the defections of each. Inez proposes to be Estelle's mirror, so that she may reassure herself of her charm:

> Estelle: But how can I rely upon your taste? Is it the same as *my* taste? Oh, how sickening it all is, enough to drive me crazy!

> Inez: I *have* your taste, my dear, because I like you so much. No, straight. Now smile. I'm not so ugly, either. Am I not nicer than your glass?

Estelle: Oh, I don't know. You scare me rather. My reflection in the glass never did that; of course, I know it so well. Like something I had tamed . . . (27; 137–38)

The play brilliantly illustrates several crucial Sartrean ideas. Since the three characters have died, they have ceased enjoying the privilege of projecting themselves into the future, the right to "save themselves" from what they have so far made of themselves. Each has discovered his weakness in acts of self-deception; of the three, only Inez comes close to seeing herself for what she is. Estelle and Inez thwart Garcin; Inez effectively disposes of Garcin's last attempt to assert himself as something he is not and cannot be; the cowardice of Garcin and the self-love of Estelle cancel out each other. In the end, there is "no exit." Though the door unaccountably opens, yielding to Garcin's pressure, he does not leave because he cannot. He is irrevocably a coward; the cowardice which was his state at the moment of his death stamps the image of him forever. Hell is —"other people."

Garcin: I died too soon. I wasn't allowed time to—to do my deeds.

Inez: One always dies too soon—or too late. And yet one's whole life is complete at that moment, with a line drawn neatly under it, ready for the summing up. You are—your life, and nothing else. (58; 165)

Each of the three dead spirits of No Exit has struggled against the other's image of him; but they have also refused to come to terms with themselves, have preferred to hide in the self-deceptive images each has created to protect himself. The genuine Sartrean hero performs a more difficult task, exercises his freedom to discover the world and to "choose himself" in the world. The act of choice is a continuous one. The self cannot not choose; at the moment of his not choosing, or not choosing freely and independently, he becomes a part of the

443

en-soi, whether as an inert part of its "massive being" or as an object of the Other.

The discovery of the self is a "tragic experience" in the Sartrean version of human tragedy. It involves a continual coming-to-terms with the *en-soi*, fighting to control it and to avoid being taken over by it. Sartre's first novel, *La Nausée* (1938), is a remarkable literary translation of the experience, a very successful exercise in the direct application of philosophical ideas. The narrator Roquentin significantly records his experiences in a journal. The entries give the illusion of a "continuous present" moving steadily into an accessible future. He first reveals himself as a student-historian, working "in the past" in the hope that he will reconstruct that past. But it is all but impossible to recapture it; and in any case, in Sartre's analysis, a preoccupation with the past (especially with the past of others) is at best a futile pastime. The present continuously intervenes: the basic struggle in Roquentin is to move through successive "nows," to assure himself a continuous identity. He does so at first by borrowing the identities of others: that of the Marquis de Rollebon, whose biography he wishes to write; that of his landlady, whose body he occasionally exploits; those of the townspeople of Bouville. But one notes a steady increase of concern, fear, dread, as Roquentin moves toward the movement of full awareness. Reality is in one sense the *en-soi*, but the crucial experience of reality is that of the *pour-soi* within it and struggling to maintain dominance of it.

Most important are Sartre's descriptions of awareness. Here the actual meaning of existence is given, far more successfully than in his philosophical works. The experience is reported several times. In each case, several major points are made: the *en-soi* is precisely given as revealed to Roquentin; the "I" who feels the *en-soi* remains apart from, yet within it; the I "continues," is the agent of its continuance; and Roquentin feels both dread and excitement over the experience. It is necessary to see Sartre's attempt to present the scene in a "living present," since the matter of time is indispensable to the reality itself.

. . . Existence, liberated, detached, floods over me. I exist. I exist. It's sweet, so sweet, so slow. And light; you'd think it floated all by itself. It stirs. It brushes by me, melts and vanishes. Gently, gently. There is bubbling water in my mouth. I swallow. It slides down my throat, it caresses me—and now it comes up again into my mouth. For ever I shall have a little pool of whitish water in my mouth— lying low—grazing my tongue. And this pool is still me. And the tongue. And the throat is me.[18]

This is the *physical* experience of existing; the narrator's words define the self's *being-in-awareness*. Beyond this there is the exercise of creative choice, the self choosing to exist, "making" its existence:

. . . I *am the one* who pulls myself from the nothingness to which I aspire: the hatred, the disgust of existing, there are as many ways to *make* myself exist, to thrust myself into existence. Thoughts are born at the back of me like sudden giddiness. I feel them being born behind my head . . . if I yield, they're going to come round in front of me, between my eyes—and I always yield, the thought grows and grows and there it is immense, filling me completely and renewing my existence. (136; 129)

The experience of the *en-soi*, and of the consciousness in control of it, brings up again the question of the role of time in experience. One is not always aware of time passing; Sartre's heroes often only intuit the instant. But his major insistence upon the future is presented with an especial clarity in *La Nausée*, not only in the style itself and the tense forms of representation but also in Roquentin's view of the future as "an adventure." It is an adventure in the same sense as it is a responsibility. Time is irreversible; one cannot remake the past, one can only make what one chooses of the future. The past

[18] *Nausea*, tr. Lloyd Warner, Norfolk, Conn., New Directions, 1949, p. 134; French version, Paris, Gallimard, 1938, p. 127. Other references to both editions are in the text.

serves to fix the self, to lock it in. Eventually, of course, in death the past becomes all that there is; the self *becomes* the past, as Garcin of *No Exit* had eventually to discover for himself. But within life, the self has an ever-renewing opportunity to make what he chooses of himself.

> . . . I think this is what happens: you suddenly feel that time is passing, that each instant leads to another, this one to another one, and so on; that each instant is annihilated, and that it isn't worth while to hold it back, etc., etc. And then you attribute this property to events which appear to you *in* the instants; what belongs to the form you carry over to the content . . . (79; 77–78)

This is the "adventure": [19] that you *see* yourself (or feel, sense, become personally involved in the act of) existing, growing in terms of instants of experience, in the course of which you exercise the privilege and freedom of choosing what you will be.

This adventure with time has a special relevance in the matter of Sartre's discussions of death. The existentialist death is an absurd, unpredictable, uncontrollable block to life. This does not mean that the self does nothing about it. His awareness of its possibility is one of the major forces governing his choice. Sartre strongly emphasizes the nature of the *self-image*. The existing being is extraordinarily aware of what he is at the moment of his being it, but he is also concerned over the future career of that image. Garcin says that hell is "other people." In large part, immortality is also "other people." In death, the self as *pour-soi* ceases to exist, becomes *en-soi*, that is, dead matter. But the image of self is, except in rare cases, communicated to others. Aegisthus of Sartre's version of the Oresteiad will always be what he has forced the others to see him as being; he will

---

[19] Generally, Sartre distinguishes between this kind of experience and the forced dramatizing of events. In the midst of a fraudulent "adventure" (such as those seen in Roquentin's photographs), a valid experiencing of existence is possible, but the latter cannot be posed.

be that also to Orestes, who sees through his motive, though Orestes examines the Aegisthus image speculatively and critically. The historical character of the self-image is a difficult thing to maintain, as it is difficult in its nonhistorical phase to achieve. The genuine self-image survives both the detraction of others and the temptations of self-deception.

As life is a continual process, death is a fixation of the image created in the experiencing of process. It is a sudden, "absurd" halting of process, as a result of which the self *becomes the past*; for the first time it is what it has been. But the past is also *en-soi* when it is no longer controlled by the consciousness. It is therefore "fair game" for other, living consciousnesses, who may have special expedient reasons for making it something else. This is Sartre's shrewdest criticism of the Orwellian type of state or group control over history in process. Sartre assumes that the self-in-process is the concern of that self, but beyond that it becomes a necessary obligation to preserve the image (whether good or bad) of others. Immortality is apparently the persistence in time beyond death of a self-image created before death but now at the disposal of others. This aspect of Sartrean ethics is clearly illustrated in the play, *Dirty Hands* (1948), which presents a curiously ambiguous image of fame in its relation to party politics. Hugo, who has killed the Party leader Hoederer, is now asked to renounce his act for Party reasons. The Party has now come around to Hoederer's point of view, so they wish Hugo to detach himself from his "reasons" for the murder. He becomes the custodian of Hoederer's image, and he has therefore not only to analyze his murder of him but to consider the consequences of the interpretation now required of him.

. . . Listen: I don't know why I killed Hoederer, but I know why it was right to kill him: because his policy was wrong, because he lied to the rank and file and jeopardized the life of the party. If I had had the courage to shoot

447

when I was alone with him in his office, he would be dead for these reasons and I could think of myself without shame. But I am ashamed because I killed him—afterwards. And now you want me to dishonor myself even more and to agree that I killed him for nothing. . . .[20]

The question of the preservation of the self-image "in trust" is especially significant in a world accustomed to killing and death on a grand scale. Everything in Sartre's philosophical works testifies to the absolute value of self-choice. The erosive influence of a depersonalized world of "others," in wars, in concentration camps, in organizational maneuvers of one kind and another, is a major threat to the chances of preserving self-identity. They are all aspects of self-abnegation; the act of imposing an image of the self upon others is as serious a crime against the self as any flight from the self into one or another kind of protection. In killing Hoederer for personal reasons, Hugo has most clearly stamped the images of both victim and assailant. The Party wishes to maneuver the act for an impersonal motive, to kill the self that was and to make it another self. Modern literature abounds in illustrations of this kind of depersonalizing strategy. A crucial feature of the existentialist view of death (for Sartre, as for Heidegger and Jaspers) is that in each case it is a unique event: I will die, and it is the act that *only* I can perform. Death remains an absurdity in this view of it, because it is beyond personal choice (suicide is not countenanced in any situation), and because it defeats the self's free selection of future possibilities of being. In many places of his work, Sartre analyzes the problem of the self's living in terms of its dying. There are many occasions in the violence of the modern scene when the personal awareness of death becomes inoperative. In *L'Être et le néant*, he briefly but shrewdly analyzes the error in "waiting for death."

[20] Tr. Lionel Abel, in *Three Plays*, New York, Knopf, 1949, p. 151; French version, "Les Mains Sales," Paris, Gallimard, 1948, p. 258.

. . . This is because there is a considerable difference in *quality* between death at the limit of old age and sudden death which annihilates us at the prime of life or in youth . . . Sudden death is undetermined and by definition can not be waited for at any date; it always, in fact, includes the possibility that we shall die in surprise before the awaited date and consequently that our waiting may be, *qua waiting*, a deception or that we shall survive beyond this date: in this latter case since we were only this waiting, we shall outlive ourselves. (536)

Several observations need to be made about this passage. It is a mistake, a "deception," to assume that one may set the date of one's death; so that death in this view of it is a part of the self's freedom, even though it is also the terminal point of its exercise. The self must live in free but uncertain expectation of death, but to plan for it (whether in suicide or in false martyrdom or in terms of a conventional set of ceremonial expectations) is a form of self-deception. The self cannot *control* the occasion of its death, but it can *maintain* the atmosphere of uncertainty in which death is anticipated. In another sense, however, since death is a "privilege" (its unique applicability to the self is so, at any rate), arbitrary control by others over the death of the self is a true form of evil. The history of depersonalization in modern life comprehends an almost incredible range of brutal and arbitrary control over the self's balance of choice within life and in terms of death. The concentration camp is in a sense the final symbolic circumstance of this development. Other forms of distortion are also criminally possible. The most notorious of these is the arbitrary imposition of organizational living upon the self. The self in this case collaborates in its own destruction, gives in to persuasions when it should resist them. Frequently, as in the case of the anti-Semite, the exercise of prejudice is a serious example of *mau-*

449

vaise foi. The anti-Semite is a man who is afraid, not of Jews but of himself; he chooses a *type* of person he will be.[21]

The implications of a death (or of the threat of it), imposed by an organization of others, acts in the manner of a sudden deprivation. The major image of this organizational imposition is the wall. The wall serves to define the character of any death in the existentialist view: it is as such to be distinguished from the images of the doorway leading to a rose garden (Eliot's *Family Reunion*) and the numerous journey images, all of which suggest death as a stage in the soul's progress toward and in eternity. The wall, on the other hand, cuts off all prospect, primarily because it defeats future expectations. There is no future beyond it. The many adaptations of this imagery in Dostoevsky and in Russian literature following him are in a real sense portrayals of existentialist or semi-existentialist dilemmas. In Sartre's story, "The Wall," the Spanish Loyalist soldier, Ibbieta, condemned to die within a few hours, loses all interest in his "futures" because the wall of his death blocks them off. Sartre offers a compelling analysis of his reactions to the knowledge:

> At that moment I felt that I had my whole life in front of me and I thought, "It's a damned lie." It was worth nothing because it was finished . . .

> [As for his love affair with Concha] When she looked at me something passed from her to me. But I knew it was over: if she looked at me *now* the look would stay in her eyes, it wouldn't reach me. I was alone.

> . . . Naturally I couldn't think clearly about my death but I saw it everywhere, on things, in the way things fell back and kept their distance, discreetly, as people who speak quietly at the bedside of a dying man. . . .[22]

[21] See *Anti-Semite and Jew*, tr. G. J. Becker, New York, Schocken, 1948. This is essentially the argument James Baldwin uses, with respect to the problem of Negro-White relationships. See *The Fire Next Time*, New York, Dial, 1963.

[22] In *Intimacy and Other Stories*, tr. Lloyd Alexander, Norfolk, Conn.,

In the end, Ibbieta is ironically "rescued" from death by the wildest of mad coincidences, but his view of death has not appreciably changed. He has, in the sublest applications of Sartrean valuation, been guilty of "bad faith," in *expecting* his death and depriving it of its role as a "boundary," or as an agent of sudden destruction of human choice. But Sartre is primarily interested in exploring the conflict between the "adventure" of the self (as Roquentin had called it) and the arbitrary imposition of limits encouraged by the scientific "otherness" of the modern world. The hatefulness of this latter is no more powerfully represented than in the figure of the Belgian doctor, who has been permitted to "study" the reactions and behavior of the condemned ones, who records his observations in a little notebook.

> But that swine of a Belgian hadn't missed a thing; he had seen the drops rolling down my cheeks and thought: this is the manifestation of an almost pathological state of terror; and he had felt normal and proud of being alive because he was cold. I wanted to stand up and smash his face but no sooner had I made the slightest gesture than my rage and shame were wiped out; I fell back on the bench with indifference. (17; 19)

"The Wall" provides a continuation of the several major settings used to describe death in modern literature. There is no doubt that the appearance of an enclosed, poorly lighted, filthy space (the cell, a basement room, the narrow corridors of a prison or jail, the exercise yard of a prison) provides a special kind of setting for the discussion of death along the lines of all variants of naturalistic contemplation. It is not only that these scenes are almost invariably associated with the death sentence; they are also as far removed from the prospects of life

New Directions, 1948, pp. 25, 27; French version, *Le Mur*, Paris, Gallimard, 1939, pp. 25, 26–27. Other references to both editions are in the text.

as almost any can be (except perhaps the "premature burial" or "pit" scenes of Poe's tales). They are, in short, a transition to the tomb. Their psychological effects upon the condemned man are in almost every case clearly those of the Sartrean self blocked suddenly—or all but suddenly—from the "adventure" of its experience.

Dostoevsky's undergroundling of course flaunts his gloomy setting, but even he expatiates upon his "wall" and allies it with the wall of the Crystal Palace, the architectural masterpiece of organizational "wall" strategy. In the fiction of World War I the caves, trenches, the "contrived corridors" of history, are emphasized. Sartre's Ibbieta sees the wall in a double sense: it is the barrier to the self, and, cutting him off from the future, throws his entire life into the past (in short, makes him indifferent to it); but it is also the scene of arbitrary death imposed from the outside, and it is in this sense a violation of the existentialist conception of death as absurd within the individual's manageable view of absurdity. In a very important sense, an imposed death is a form of "suicide forced upon the self by the other." Sartre defined suicide as an absurdity "which causes my life to be submerged in the absurd." [23] The death which is an expedient of the other is neither a *crime passionnel* nor in any other sense a motivated death, except in the remote sense of an ideology's forcing men to employ a practical stratagem. Such a death produces what a character in *The Victors* calls "unjustified corpses."

> Henri: We shall die because we have been given an idiotic assignment and because we executed it badly. Our death serves no one. The cause didn't need to have this village attacked. It didn't need it because the project was impossible. A cause never gives orders; it never says anything. It is we who have to determine what it needs . . .[24]

[23] *Being and Nothingness*, p. 540.
[24] In *Three Plays*, tr. Lionel Abel, p. 213; French version, *Morts Sans Sepultures* (1946), in *Théâtre*, p. 187.

14

CONCLUSION: THE WHEEL OF SELF

—[i]—

As it is the most satisfactory means of defining the outer limits of modern selfhood, existentialism is perhaps the clearest form of contemplation upon modern death. Since its area of concentration is the self, its decisions and choices, one recognizes in its literature images of the self of the greatest intensity. In its most remarkable works of literature, it also reveals the consequences, for a modern form of "meditation," of a self-analysis independent of prior securities or advantages. The important fact of existentialist living and dying is that each is given in naturalistic and psychological depth; and style, in the best works at least, is within and a part of the process of self-awareness.

This is the primary direction of modern literature—to present in terms of a succession of instantaneous experiences, encounters of the self with objects, the full nature of the self and of its situational dilemma. This is far different from the "I" saturated perspective of the autobiographical novel. If anything resembles it, it is the tone of the narrator in the most lucidly "free" passages of Jake Barnes's progress (Hemingway's *The Sun Also Rises*). Here, at its best, the novel holds to situational minima; and the deceptive simplicity of the language brings the reader very close to the experienced moment. Barnes is of all pre-Sartrean heroes *l'homme engagé*. He is also an example, on the simplest level, of Camus' *L'Homme révolté*. At any rate, circumstances require that he live in the present; and, while the future is far more limited than that of the average Sartrean self, it is nevertheless there in his consciousness, and he is actively engaged at every moment in choosing from among the "possibles" within it.

In *The Gay Science*, Nietzsche offers his famous parable of the madman's prophecy. A madman, seeking God, is mocked by those who do not believe in him, goaded into a violent attack upon his complacent neighbors: ". . . God is dead. God remains dead. And we have killed him."

> ". . . Are we not plunging continually? Backward, sideward, forward, in all directions? Is there any up or down left? Are we not straying as through an infinite nothing? Do we not feel the breath of empty space? Has it not become colder? Is not night and more night coming on all the while? . . ." [1]

There will be wars, Nietzsche said in *Ecce Homo*, such as never have happened on earth. It is with the "death of God" in this sense that most modern literature is concerned: not so much with the denial of a metaphysical assertion as with the dismissal of certain values and restraints a belief in God had earlier sustained.

Albert Camus is centrally involved in this metaphor. The world he describes in his novels and plays is a world of prisons, of cities under quarantine, of a "state of siege." It is a world suffering from the calamity of brutal imposition and control, of "planned death," of darkness and tombs which signify nothing if not the hopeless absence of essential qualities of human life. It is, in short, the world of Nietzsche's madman. Camus protested in several strong pieces against the concentration camp mentality and against capital punishment, as two instruments of the denial of the self's independent "privilege" of dying. While the indictment is not philosophically sharp, it is

[1] (1882) In *The Portable Nietzsche*, translated and edited by Walter Kaufmann, New York, Viking, 1954, p. 95.

aesthetically shrewd. Camus' heroes are not so articulate as Sartre's, for they do not *know* their "situationality" so precisely; but they do exist in a convincingly real state of doubt, resentment, and "revolt" in respect to their situations.

The basic definition of the Camus hero, as of Sartre's, involves his being independent of absolute certainties. He is mortal in the most precise meaning of the term. There is no God in his life, though there may be "verities" which (like those of early Faulkner novels) are not precisely seen or phrased. Camus has tried to make his fictional hero live within the rhythms and pace of the experienced moment, without benefit either of supporting metaphors or generalized absolutes. In fact, the major atmosphere of his world is comprehended in the Mediterranean sky, sun, and air on the one hand, and the enclosed spaces of prisons, besieged cities on the other. Only in *The Fall* (1956) do we have a setting used as metaphor that extends far beyond situational requirements. The city of Amsterdam of Jean-Baptiste Clamence ("vox clamans") is a projection of his hero's religious meditation, an inferno of the self's confession and suffering. It is also suggested that Jean-Baptiste heralds the return of God; though Camus himself died before he could raise God from the dead.

In his other works, however, Camus assumes mortality as a necessary support of his analysis of self.

> If I obstinately reject all the "hereafters" of the world, he said in *Noces* (1939), it is because I am also not prepared to renounce my immediate riches. I do not choose to believe that death opens on to another life. For me it is a closed door . . . Everything that is suggested to me is an attempt to take from man the burden of his own life.[2]

The dramatic situations of his novels and plays are dominated by the antagonism between man's love of life and the inevita-

[2] *Noces* (1939), Paris, Gallimard, 1950, p. 34. Translated by John Cruickshank, in his *Albert Camus*, London, Oxford University Press, 1959, p. 35.

bility of his death. Those who attempt to mitigate their sense of mortality by access to some form of promised immortality are (as they were for Nietzsche) blocking the way to a full recognition of necessity. Camus would certainly stop short of the exercise of faith recommended by Kierkegaard as a means of resolving the irrationality of experience. The encounter with the absurd, he says, must remain pure and without alleviation.

> It happens that the stage sets collapse. Rising, streetcar, four hours in the office or the factory, meal, streetcar, four hours of work, meal, sleep and Monday Tuesday Wednesday Thursday Friday and Saturday according to the same rhythm—this path is easily followed most of the time. But one day the "why" arises and everything begins in that weariness tinged with amazement. . . . Weariness comes at the end of the acts of a mechanical life, but at the same time it inaugurates the impulse of consciousness . . .[3]

The sudden interruption of these rhythms assaults the mind; it "inaugurates the consciousness." The consequence is "suicide or recovery." Suicide is a willed submission to the absurd. Recovery, on the other hand, is "revolt." Camus' analysis of revolt is both intricate and unusual. The rebel has many choices of stratagem. He may multiply experiences, on the assumption that more of what is valuable in life is a good thing. He may try to turn revolt into political channels, to impose his form of adjustment to the absurd upon others. He may deceive and cheat, both himself and others. But in its most satisfactory form, revolt is "acceptance": that is, man is engaged in a minute-by-minute struggle with the absurd; he accepts his role, but he also defends it from the attempts of others to frame the acceptance of it. While there is none of the frenetic obsession with the "tragedy of nihilation" that one finds in Sartre, there

[3] Tr. Justin O'Brien, in *The Myth of Sisyphus and Other Essays*, New York, Knopf, 1955, pp. 12–13; French edition, Paris, Gallimard, 1942, p. 27.

is a steady awareness of the disparity between an intense love of life (a "Mediterranean" ecstasy) and the realization that the world is basically irrational and absurd. This explains the style of the early Camus, which only superficially resembles Hemingway's. It is so crisply "cut off" from even the simplest kinds of embellishment and complexity as to suggest a living within the sensory minutiae of reality.

Revolt in its purest form is a form of commitment to reality, a living and deciding within it. It is an acknowledgment of role, task, function, a willingness to endure without false supports or illusions. It is also the *opportunity* to live. The Camus hero fights against those who will try to impose manners upon him, or who threaten him with death if he does not live conventionally. The mathematical extension of this imposition leads to wars, the concentration camp, state controls over one's death. Camus acknowledges the absurdity of the world and insists upon it. Yet there are hints of a Kantian moral imperative as well. The reasons for one's assuming his single role in an absurd world suggest at times (and especially in *The Plague*, 1947) a "noumenal certainty" of which he is only dimly but must be at least minimally aware. Nevertheless, the basic assumptions of Camus' work are these: man recognizes the world as absurd and dismisses the solutions of both philosophical (the "leap of faith") and physical suicide; he is called upon therefore to live with passionate intensity, for the very humanistic reason that the duration of life is uncertain; he resists attempts either to support tolerance of death or to escape its consequences; he "fulfills his role" despite all rational suggestions that it is absurd to do so. He does all of these things "if he is permitted": that is, if the individual is not totally lost in the state, or his life is not arbitrarily destroyed by it.

Despite the strong suggestion of resemblance to Sartre at the beginning of his career (they applauded each other's work at first), there is a gradual move in Camus toward a definition of standards which presumably are essences antedating individual existence. For one thing, he speaks of those elements in man which must always be defended, and suggests some abstract values which have an emotional power independent of a self's specifically experiencing them in situation. For this reason, *The Plague* comes very close to abandoning its function as a situational metaphor and becoming an easily manipulable myth. This does not suggest that Camus is giving in to a mythical control of secular existence. The standards are still secular, in the sense that Faulkner's "verities" are naturalistically grounded. Nor are they doctrinally specific; they are merely "humanistic guide-posts." Such beliefs as that in the "worth of man" suggest Faulkner's iterated conviction that "man will endure, and prevail." Since human worth identifies man with humanity, it follows that he is a part of something larger than the individual self, and that he will normally act to deserve his share in the whole. Beyond this there is a responsibility to the whole: the *révolté* will not confine himself merely to adjusting to an absurd world, but will instead attest to the "solidarity" of men: "Je me révolte, donc nous sommes."

Camus' rebel has advanced far beyond the "absurd hero." Meursault of *The Stranger* as a hero is much too simple for Camus' later taste. His awareness of the absurdity of his world begins with the momentary hallucination which leads to the Arab's death. But he himself dies, not as a murderer but as an "absurd man" who fights desperately against those who will "arrange" his life. The hero of *The Plague*, Dr. Rieux, retains some line of connection with the absurd man, noticeably with the mythical Sisyphus; but his *esprit* is as different from Meursault's as their conditions suggest. Rieux rebels by "doing his task" in spite of all discouragement. He is furthermore conscious of his "doing a good," though he does not call it that specifically. It is "good" that men should live, and it is therefore good that Rieux should use his skill to save as many lives as he can. Further, it is "good" that men should discover community in suffering, though Rieux steadfastly refuses the allegorical, religious interpretation offered by Father Paneloux.

Rebellion becomes a more and more selective and "considered" state, as Camus moves away from the situational literature of *The Stranger* and *The Myth of Sisyphus*. There are "good" and "bad" rebels, as Camus analyzes the history of revolt. The violent assertion of difference which he associates with dadaists and surrealists is a waste of energy.

> . . . these frenetics wanted "any kind of revolution," no matter what as long as it rescued them from the world of shopkeepers and compromise in which they were forced to live.[4]

Without at least noticeably accepting his religious conservatism, Camus also admired Dostoevsky's analysis of the "madmen of revolt." The too lucid reasonableness of Ivan Karamazov's arguments for the death of God leads eventually to his permitting his father's murder and to his own madness—a dénouement of which Camus, as did Nietzsche, thoroughly approved. Perhaps the most remarkable conjunction of the three minds comes in their attitudes toward the Christ figure. *The Idiot*, Nietzsche's favorite of Dostoevsky's novels, proved at least in this reading of it that the suffering of Christ is at the most a suffering from evil rather than a struggle to conquer it. Camus' analysis of the Christ figure follows along the same lines: Christ, separated from his divinity, becomes a scapegoat of God, and his death is made to appear a justification for the rejection of God. But this is to use Christianity to an evil end. Camus would prefer that the religious myth be set aside, that therefore the moral strength of man be tested in human terms. He says further that the death of Christ was a primary default of his humanity. There are some interesting lines of agreement

[4] Tr. Anthony Bower, New York, Knopf, 1957, revised translation, p. 94; French version, *L'Homme révolté*, Paris, Gallimard, 1951, p. 122.

among Dostoevsky, Nietzsche, Camus, and D. H. Lawrence, however wide apart they are otherwise.

The true rebel of Camus is a modification of Sisyphus. He is a secular being first of all. He is also a conscious self—though his selfness is more and more fully separated from circumstance and occasion, as Camus moves away from situation to definition in his writings. It is perhaps significant that two of his greatest interests in his last years were Dostoevsky's *The Brothers Karamazov* and Faulkner's *Requiem for a Nun;* he adapted the latter to the French stage. In each case, the "message" extracted concerns a secular formulation of Christian principles. Dimitri Karamazov and Nancy Mannigoe may both be considered secular saints. He said in *Les Nouvelles littéraires* for May 10, 1951, that

> When I analyzed the feeling of the absurd in *Le Mythe de Sisyphe* I was in search of a method, not a doctrine. I was exercising methodical doubt. I was seeking to make that "clean sweep" which preceded constructive effort.[5]

The "constructive effort" involved, in effect, rescuing the absurd man from his absurdity, or at least suggesting a framework of sane principle in terms of which he might endure it. In *The Rebel,* Camus contrasts the dark strength of the North with the penetrating reality of the Mediterranean world. Indeed, the North African scene, which is spatially impressive and atmospherically "pure" and is furthermore almost always bathed in sunshine, suggests a physical maturing that is not possible in darkened, constricted, and enclosed environments. The sun becomes a metaphysical symbol for Camus, in the absence of an accepted religious myth. But it is arbitrary and vague; and efforts to translate its influence into literary "values," as in the novels of Paul Bowles, have not been conspicuously successful. There is more than a hint in Camus' use of it of the superficial

[5] Quoted in John Cruickshank, *Albert Camus,* London, Oxford University Press, 1959, p. 92.

antagonism between civilization and nature. Meursault rejects an offer to go to Paris; he prefers "nature" and the sun, but at least Camus has the honesty to admit the sun's treachery which has scarcely in Meursault's case contributed to "maturity." Bowles tries to make a major, climactic symbolism of the same setting, but the net result is the death of Port Moresby and Kit's violent education in pre-Freudian sexual ceremonies (*The Sheltering Sky*, 1949). And it seems that the behavior of Nelson Dyar of *Let It Come Down!* (1952) in the same setting leads not to maturity but to an early (perhaps the earliest) version of "hipster" nihilism.

Camus took another route, away from Sartre; his analysis of the self lost the purity and precision of attention it received in Sartre's works. He had begun by representing brilliantly and meticulously the world of the absurd; in the end he moved toward a symbolic maneuvering about the complex landscape of human sin. Clamence of *The Fall* is no longer identifiable as a rebel; he is in constant danger of offering an extravagant and sentimental "mea maxima culpa." This not only makes a sinner of him; it removes the absurd world from the level of Meursault's sensory realism altogether.

—[ii]—

One important trait of contemporary literature follows closely the lines of Sartre's diagnostic analysis of the self in relation to reality. This is not necessarily a tribute to Sartre's influence; it is altogether probable that some of it (though not much) is written in total ignorance of Sartre. But the range and scope of the self-as-narrator and the self-as-character of recent literature are most assuredly seen in terms of a basic relational metaphor, not impossibly remote from that Sartre used in *L'Être et le néant*. Consider for a moment the self in relation to matter, in its purest sense, or the *pour-soi* "engaging" the *en-soi*. The primary literary document of that situation is still *La Nausée*, but a number of writers come within reach of it. The fictional situation, for example, is a commentary upon, even a calculated measurement of, these two aspects of basic experience.

To think of one modification of this relationship, the self varies in degree and strength of awareness. The instrumentality leading to the self's status with respect to objective reality is variously strong or weak. Even such simple matters as identifying temporal and spatial areas in which the self functions may fundamentally affect the basic character of a narration, and particularly its "point of view," which in this case must depend upon the self's resources as narrator. Secondly, there is the matter of the *intensity* of the self's response to the challenge of a structured continuance; to put it in Sartrean terms, the degree of emotional power expressed in the response of the *pour-soi* to the *en-soi*, and to the threat within the latter of making the self a "being-for-others."

It is possible to imagine that the "dread of nothingness" so prominent in Sartre's vision may change to a vehement resentment against the agents within the world of otherness and their power to extinguish the self's distinctness. A third way of ranging out from the Sartrean metaphoric center is to consider the power of configuration within the self. Presumably this power does not exist in the self as Sartre saw it, or it exists in a very limited form. But the *way of seeing*, or sensing, the *en-soi* is in some significant way *formal*; that is, the self formalizes its experience in the act of deciding what it shall be. This point of departure will elaborate upon an already strong spatial sense in Sartre, for whom time is largely a manipulation or a projection into "moments of consecutive space." The final possibility would begin to comprehend in an orderly fashion the scope of "tendentiousness" in the modern novel. Literary existentialism is, after all, largely a phenomenon of the years following World War II. One characteristic of these years is the tendency of novelists to be dogmatic spokesmen, "preachers" in a sense. This tendency is in part a result of their having lost, as a reliable

aid, any pre-existing systematic form of philosophical explanation. So the characters of these novels are sometimes spokesmen, or on their way to becoming spokesmen, of some philosophical position, or a combination of them.

To illustrate these matters, I should say that to the first of
these classes belong the novels of Samuel Beckett, Alain Robbe-
Grillet, and Nathalie Sarraute. The second offers a wide range
of possibilities, but the resistance to control by the "other" is
a major characteristic in much modern literature. Certain so-
called "hipster" and "beatnik" literature perhaps crudely but
vividly illustrates the point. As for the third of these, the formal
aspects in which the self attempts to contain experience are a
substantial part of much fiction and drama that often has an
expressionistic quality. The final class comprehends the work
of Norman Mailer, Nelson Algren, and Saul Bellow, though
there are many others whose attempts to define the contemporary self lead them into a variety of moral and philosophical
discourses.

A conspicuous feature of the Beckett hero is the limitation
of his ordering sense. For him the essential problem is not so
much to live meaningfully as to live at all. Beckett has deliberately reduced the intellectual power of his characters to a level
below minimum strength. This does not mean that they are
unintelligent, or incapable of intellection. They are often very
profound creatures, but they are profound in a rudimentary
sense. They calculate truths, moral and ontological, in a limited
geometrical estimation of their spatial positioning with respect
to other objects. Indeed, they are mostly concerned to establish
the most elementary facts and lines of existence: the location
of the I, its distance from the others, its sensory relations and
its obligations to them, the meaning of light, shades, forms, and
a simple estimate of time passing. All of these elementary maneuvers are in a real sense calculations of existence. They attempt to answer the question, not why do I exist but do I exist
at all; that is, is there a recognizable set of spatial and temporal

co-ordinates which, by means of certain calculations, I can use to arrive at the fact of my existing? The Beckett hero invites existence, but he is puzzled and frightened by it because he cannot be sure that he has established the fact of it and is not at all certain that whatever facts he has will remain creditably factual beyond the discrete moment of his having had them.

In some of Beckett's contemporaries, the fictional values are largely derived from the narrator's positioning with respect to scenic arrangements. These often come remarkably close to the basic metaphor of *L'Être et le néant*. They are not overtly novels of ideas, but novels of space which in their arrangements report human disposition. Sartre speaks, in his preface to her *Portrait of a Man Unknown* (1958), of Nathalie Sarraute's "protoplasmic vision of our interior universe . . . Her vocabulary is incomparably rich in suggesting the slow centrifugal creeping of these viscous, live solutions. . . ." [6] The narrator's growth toward knowledge of her "they" world is revealed in terms of the quality of a very vivid subreal environment to which she is sensitive. She calculates and measures the distribution of auras, subtle emanations of sense; these "viscous" realities are quite significantly evocative, not only of their protective evasions and concealments, but also of her sensitive reactions to the world of other persons. The principal clash of personalities in the novel is between an arrogant and harsh father and his long-suffering daughter. The father is consumed by his consciousness of age and his fear of death:

He recognized it, the taste and very color of fear; we both recognized it, the same taste and color as in those wan little garden plots with their clipped box shrubs. . . . No, this time it was a slightly sulphurous odor, the dingy grayness of the railroad station and its platform . . . (122–23; 126–27)

[6] Tr. Maria Jolas, New York, Braziller, 1958, p. xii; French version, *Portrait d'un inconnu*, Paris, Gallimard, 1956, p. 11. Other references to these editions are in the text.

This sensible expression of fear (an example of what is done throughout the novel) communicates—in a sense, "subterraneously"—the essential progress of the self toward death, overwhelmed as he is by frustrations, evasions, and fears.

> There it is, implanted in the heart of our distress, a solid corpuscle, piercing and hard, around which the pain spreads; there it is . . . an image of our own death, our own life. . . . an appallingly clear image, in which the lights and shadows are accentuated and heightened, as on a photograph reduced in size . . . (121; 124–25)

Throughout, the characters of Sarraute's novels protect themselves from the glances and appraisals of others, yielding only small bits of information and these grudgingly, as it were by accident or oversight. They live as if in a "quilted casket, silky and warm, in which they betake themselves from one end of the world to the other . . ." (151; 157).

Not the least of the strategies of these novels is their experimenting with narrative point of view. The object is to preserve as much as possible an absolute condition of non-involvement and to reduce the emotional pressure upon the materials to a minimum. Not only is the point of view of Robbe-Grillet's *The Voyeur* (1955) factually restrained; the scene itself is at least partly in memory. He cannot be said to dispose himself in any specially defined way toward what he is narrating, and in fact we do not know to what extent and in what precise way he is actually involved. An even more meticulous sparseness is to be noted in the narration of Robbe-Grillet's *Jealousy* (1957), though here there is no doubt as to the emotional disposition of the narrator, his "engagement."

He presents the circumstances almost entirely in terms of scene. He is present *in* the scene, but he is a "je néant"— that is, a present observer who does not in any overt way impose beyond his task of moving objects and persons in space. Yet the impact and the force of his disposition toward them are never really in doubt. And Robbe-Grillet assures a maximum exposition of the tension through a skillful shifting of the narrative ground. The hand closes over a napkin ring in a certain way; the image of A— brushing her hair recurs, breaks through a chronology that is unsteady at best, as the growing intensity of the husband's emotion requires its dispersal. The stain left by a centipede the cuckolding lover has smashed against the wall remains, reappears, is analyzed minutely in terms of every nuance of emotional association.

One may ask, to what end are these techniques used? Of what advantage are they? Robbe-Grillet has himself expatiated upon the virtues of his form of extreme objectivity, claiming for it a precision that even Sartre and Camus failed to achieve. His novels, as Sarraute's, are in some small ways refinements upon the basic methodology of existentialist representation. The "I" of *The Stranger*, the Journals of Roquentin, of *Nausea*, and of Rieux in *The Plague* are all methods designed to locate experience in a consciousness existing in what is at best a minimal time span. While we are aware that time passes, we are more inclined to stay fixed within each fragment of the "now," scarcely aware (except as the Journal is dated) of a temporal progress. These characteristics suggest the removal of an auctorial "management" or exploitation of narrative substance to its most remote point.

It is the antithesis of Thomas Mann's graciously ironic indulgence of his characters' frailties and aspirations; it is surely antipolar to Wolfe's ego-saturated hero. Its aim is to present a *fait pur* to an unobstructed sensibility. These characteristics substantiate in a peculiar and in some respects a terrifying way one of the important features of the literature of the 1950's: the withdrawal (the "néantisation") of the self from the center of violence, this even when the self is proved to be at the very center of it, whether as assailant or victim or both. Not "This is how I felt about what happened to me," nor even "This is my report of what took place," but "These objects and these persons have had these spatial and sub-spatial relations with one another, and, as they occurred to me they changed, however slightly, and caused some rearrangement of the way I viewed them." Part of the emotional impact— perhaps a large part of it—caused by these arrangements comes from a certain scrupulousness on the part of the narrator with respect to avoiding commitment of himself emotionally to the occasion.[7]

One may suggest that at times the novel suffers from a "detachment in excess of the occasion." But there is reason to feel that this disposition toward experience is not invalidly a consequence of depersonalization; in roughly the same world, certain concentration camp inmates, observed in Eugen Kogon's *Theory and Practice of Hell* (1950), accommodated themselves to an insufferable violence by withdrawing from themselves and coldly observing themselves as victims of it. The discretion of this fiction is designed to suggest an intensity of experience by shielding the self from it through methodological subterfuge. This proves to be only an apparent substerfuge, however; and the full impact of a feeling would appear at times to have come from a designed withdrawal, or "absence" from it. While the effects are very different, one is reminded at times of the obsessive ratiocination of the narrator in one of Poe's stories, who prepares safeguards against a premature burial, or works out exhaustive analyses of the behavior of apes, or scrupulously attends to the task of walling in a victim. There is much terror in all of this, but it is attended to in a decorously restrained manner; it is a rational explanation of irrational acts. Baudelaire's narrator fled in terror from "les sept vieillards," "du

---

[7] Perhaps the best discussion of the subject at present is Laurent Le Sage, *The French New Novel*, Pennsylvania State University Press, 1962. See also *Midnight Novelists and Others*, issue 24 of *Yale French Studies* (summer 1959), and Germaine Brée's contribution to the second session of the Conference in the Study of Twentieth-Century Literature, Michigan State University, 1962, pp. 59–64, 74–82. For a good study of Robbe-Grillet, see Ben Stoltzfus, *Alain Robbe-Grillet and the New French Novel*, Southern Illinois University Press, 1964.

même enfer venus"; Poe might conceivably have plotted their course and traced their origins in the narrator's diseased mind. This coolly protective, or protectively cool, disposition to the pressures of terror upon the modern mind is one of the most revealing insights into its manners of adjusting to violence.

—[iii]—

On one of the several sea journeys of Poe's *The Narrative of A. Gordon Pym* (1837), Pym hides out in an iron-bound box, nearly four feet high and six feet long. In this tomb-like enclosure he suffers the most extreme of tortures for eleven long days and nights. To all intents and purposes, this adventure is a "premature burial." It is one of a series of simulated deaths, the journey of the self to the edge of conciousness, and beyond. Pym's journey is, as Edward Davidson puts it, "a study in the depersonalization of the self." [8]

In one view of them, Poe's stories may be seen as extensive researches in human consciousness. Both the logical mind and the imagination explore the nature of reality as the self comprehends it; but, beyond that, he pushes into the boundary areas where the consciousness apparently leaves off, giving up its privileges of the senses, and moves into a supersensory area that is abstract and without perceptible content. As Pym's narrative concludes, it disintegrates into brief notes, pencil memoranda of what has happened.

> March 22nd.—The darkness had materially increased, relieved only by the glare of the water thrown back from the white curtain before us. Many gigantic and pallidly white birds flew continuously now from beyond the veil, and their scream was the eternal *Tekeli li!* as they retreated

[8] Edward Davidson, *Poe: A Critical Study*, Cambridge, Harvard University Press, 1957, p. 176.

from our vision . . . And now we rushed into the embraces of the cataract, where a chasm threw itself open to receive us. But there arose in our pathway a shrouded human figure, very far larger in its proportions than any dweller among men. And the hue of the skin of the figure was of the perfect whiteness of the snow.[9]

The *Narrative* is an almost perfect representation of a journey taken again and again in modern literature, away from factual reality to its subsumed intellectual structure. Poe is saying, here and in many other places, that the mind's habits are both linked to and a degeneration of some basic metaphysical unity. He wishes to go all the way, to determine what that unity may be, how much of it the conscious self can perceive, and in what respects it is geometrically pure and timeless. Again and again, the journey of the self leads to its destruction. At a certain point the consciousness is abandoned for a "pure mind" that sees and contemplates only essences. The chaos of the perceived world both deceives and frightens. Poe's characters fear death, but they are immensely curious as well about what lies beyond and behind it. He therefore proposes a transitional consciousness, which is sentient in a very limited way, but sufficiently so to identify abstract figures with elementary data.

Monos, one of those who have "crossed the border," has experienced death as "a breathless and motionless torpor; and this was termed *Death* by those who stood around me."

> . . . My condition did not deprive me of sentience. It appeared to me not greatly dissimilar to the extreme quiescence of him, who, having slumbered long and profoundly, lying motionless and fully prostrate in a midsummer noon, begins to steal slowly back into conscious-

[9] *The Collected Works of Edgar Allan Poe*, Fordham edition, New York, Armstrong, 1900, Vol. 3, pp. 533–34.

ness, through the mere sufficiency of his sleep, and without being awakened by external disturbances.[10]

With the aid of this "sixth sense" (a consciousness reduced to a minimum sentience but possessing an alert sensitivity to forms), Monos attends to both sides of the boundary. The figures who prepared him for his tomb affected him as *forms*: "but upon passing to my side their images impressed me with the idea of shrieks, groans, and other dismal expressions of terror, of horror, of woe . . ." (IV, 279). Beyond, on the "other side," is "the temporal Eternity" (IV, 281); it is a fusion, a unity, of the most remote outlines of reality, the substructure from which human reality had progressed in its sentient existence. It is a "nothingness" in being available to no devices of perception, but it is an "All" in being the primitive source of all being.

> For *that* which *was not*—for that which had no form—for that which had no thought—for that which had no sentience—for that which was soulless, yet of which matter formed no portion—for all this nothingness, yet for all this immortality, the grave was still a home, and the corrosive hours, co-mates. (IV, 283)

The form of exploration of which the "Colloquy" is a rich example assumes an almost dogmatic secularism. There is no god in this cosmos, though the mind—each mind—is its own god, and has presumably some link, to both the cosmic and the moral origins of man. What is most striking about this kind of exploration is the process of depersonalization assumed in it. It involves release from the body, and a rearrangement of the consciousness, which gradually happens through successive stages of decay. Decay is in itself a form of purification. Beyond all this, the human self assumes a double nature; it is both sentient and nonsentient. It appropriates to its powers

[10] "The Colloquy of Monos and Una," in *Collected Works*, Vol. 4, p. 277.

of apprehension both what is and what is not. Decay of corporeal or erodable matter, fissures enlarging in the human landscape, are signs of the cosmic shift from ostensible chaos to enduring form. The "what is not" is the substance behind "what is," and the two change places as the permanent residue of the ordinary self survives its death. Death is a release from the temporal and corporeal into the supersensual real.

The move is from the decaying real to the pure unreal. As the self is released from its body, it *becomes* the place in which the body has been laid. Pym's "iron-bound box," the coffins and tombs of prematurely buried selves, the walled-in spaces built by some of Poe's characters to enclose an enemy: these are all testimonies of spatial surrogates of corporeal being. The tomb is the *form* left of the self when the body dies. The space reserved for A. Gordon Pym in the hold of the *Grampus* is once again instructive.

> [My companion] brought me, at length, after creeping and winding through innumerable narrow passages, to an iron-bound box, such as is used sometimes for packing fine earthenware. It was nearly four feet high, and full six long, but very narrow . . .
>
> A mattress from one of the cabin berths covered the whole of its bottom, and it contained almost every article of mere comfort which could be crowded into so small a space, allowing me, at the same time, sufficient room for my accommodation, either in a sitting position or lying at full length . . .[11]

These ingenious stowaway quarters are even at the beginning both a miniature condensation of the world's properties and an abstraction from them. Pym's consciousness moves, slowly and in uncertain stages, from the "comforts" of his concealment to a condition of semi-stupor. He records the stages of his move from the world and toward the loss of it, with a

[11] *Collected Works*, Vol. 3, pp. 295–96.

meticulous and even an obsessive care. This is but one of Pym's adventures. He escapes from his hiding place, goes on to other adventures. But they are not dissimilar. The earth accommodates spatially to the same motion away from specifics, toward residual forms.

Two major characteristics stand out from Poe's notation of the soul's progress: the formal adaptations of the physical spaces occupied by the body; the minutely conscientious attention of Poe's heroes to their progress away from corporeal substance and toward incorporeal form. These have a bearing for many of the physical signs of modern violence. The landscape of that violence is given hundreds of times in modern literature. It is an experience in spatial reduction repeated over and over, designed to describe the journey of man away from the screaming confusion of the immediate world toward the formal simplicities that antedate that world—and postdate it as well, in the sense of their being there at the time of death. Much modern war literature offers a clutter of bodies and fragments of bodies as a grimly realistic reminder of the horror. But these are for the most part realistic contrivances. The genuine report of modern terror is a report of shock, the release of the consciousness from its customary sentient obligations, its descent into forms large and long enough to accommodate the formal outlines, but "very narrow."

This literature is largely journal, diary, autobiographical research into an experience recently past. The writer reports the particulars of a traumatic journey. Like Monos, he has been in the grave; like other Poe figures, he has returned. The circumstances of the shock are abundantly reported in the fiction. They are relevant here for what they offer us to support the suggestion that Poe anticipated many of them. The land is changed into trenches, holes, caves, huts, to "accommodate" the body, or to keep it out of range of the violence. Within these small spaces scooped out of the terrain of the "big war," the consciousness retreats to its furthest limits. There is little rhetorical mitigation of the terror. The mind attends conscientiously to the circumstances of its trauma. It meditates upon death as life shrieks beyond it.

This is but one of the settings of violence. The concentration camp lends itself even more successfully to the suggestion of Poe's antecedence. Here the body noticeably decays, becomes unfleshed; the mind splits into a half-living agent of survival and a detached observer of itself. In the end, survival depends on what Poe called this "sixth sense," so removed from the sentient being as to be able to regard it objectively, to note its position and its prospects. As the mind dissociates itself from the receding body, it grows toward becoming a pure consciousness. It is conscious more and more of less and less, until, at the climactic moment, it passes beyond the border of life into Poe's transitional state.

Poe would have had a wealth of opportunity for his studies of this state in the concentration camp. He would not have been shocked at the brutality, having early in his life assumed it. His moral judgment accepted no easy distinguishing line between good and evil. The capacity to do either or both is man's from the beginning. Just why he chooses to do what he does is beyond discerning. He apparently *needs* to do evil, or is driven by the "imp of perversity" to act "for the reason that he should not." Man is "morally bound," or inclined, to effect his own degradation. It is only when he crosses the line—in response to a violent expression of ultimate evil—to a state of semi-consciousness, in a condition of extreme crisis, that he comes near to the ultimate source of his being. At that point, the clamor of the world loses its precise, definable quality; voices becomes shrieks and screams; and he himself slowly descends to a formal outline of his corporeality.

—[iv]—

The pertinence of this view for a study of the modern self is surely obvious. Poe's "moral anarchism" is relevant, as is the suggestion that justice and laws are the produce of the human mind without really being linked to any superhuman cause. This is a position almost invariably taken in forms of modern existentialism. However often writers attempt to suggest "verities" which will "endure," their principal view is that the laws governing human action are neither necessarily related to an eternal arbiter or judge nor deterministically linked to observable physical laws of matter. The universe is in this view of it a mechanism, the self apparently one as well; but the self acts erratically and can find no sure means of preserving a balance between individual freedom and absolute justice. The self is "erratic"; it has apparently lost—or perhaps it has never had—a clear moral direction.

This situation leads to a measurable increase of mechanical force, beyond the ability of the self to contain it or to act significantly in relation to it. Since this situation is brought about largely through the manipulation of abstract laws which have only a general relevance to the self's condition, it is natural enough that a variety of intellectual efforts should be made to recover the self, to put it at the decisive center of moral responsibility. The consequences of the history of force, in the two world wars, were such that reactions to them were similarly violent, though violently and radically opposed to the mechanisms of force.

"The society in which we live," Kenneth Rexroth said, "is destroying the person and the communion of persons." [12] The alternative is to move out of all of the Poesque situations that it has been our lot to endure in the past two decades and to start anew, to act along totally different lines, to express ourselves differently. This decision does not guarantee either security or balance; nor is it at all clear that we are not going to be as perversely aberrant as Poe assumes we have always been. It merely *seems* that there is no feasible alternative to the reconstitution of the self that is implicit in Rexroth's remarks.

[12] *The Bird in the Bush*, New York, New Directions, 1959, p. 84. Other references to this edition are in the text.

Existentialism was born and bred of the chaos we have experienced; it therefore seems a natural enough beginning of re-examination.

All modern literature of consequence to Rexroth's generation is bound to a recognition of death and an affirmation of life. The two are closely linked. Death is a locus of the self's renewal. The conventional reaction is to pretend it is not going to happen. But the existentialist position, and all of its variants, begins with a recognition of the "trapped self," who must acknowledge death and assert life.

> All men have to die, and one would think a sane man would want to take that fact into account, at least a little. But our whole civilization is a conspiracy to pretend that it isn't going to happen—and this is an age when death has become more horrible, more senseless, less at the will of the individual than ever before. (201–202)

The condition which Rexroth has so vigorously described is the present form of American retrospection. Its terms are the result of a violent explosion of incomprehensible force which has, among other things, destroyed our faith in ideological systems. The war of the 1940's destroyed not only Marx and the ideological confidence of the 1930's but also all trust in systematic procedures. This event has had a curious result, not unlike the dread of annihilation experienced by the Sartrean self. Norman Podhoretz has suggested that our present loss of values "seems to be taking the form of a recognition that in losing our taste for ideology we have also lost our capacity for passion." [13] This does not mean that we are not angry, but rather that we do not have anything specifically to be angry about.

Indeed, one of the most powerful of all human desires is for an intense experience, an experience that has some "point,"

[13] "The New Nihilism and the Novel," *Partisan Review*, 25 (fall 1959), p. 580.

some direction, but is also not associated with an ideological purpose, since all ideologies are in disrepute. The situation has the result of forcing the self into an expression of passionate feeling in the hope that passion is intrinsically a value. It also encourages experimenting with passion, making the exercise of passion a profound test of the personality, exploring the conditions which seem to allow the passion its fullest expression. In a sense, these explorations of the self are conducted in the spirit of one who hopes either to accept passion as a surrogate of conviction or to expect that it will once again lead to conviction. But since conviction assumes an end and this end should be a "positive something" beyond the energy of passion, it is difficult to accept the validity of such a hope.

The case of Norman Mailer is instructive. The "Myself" he "advertises" in his book of 1959 (*Advertisements for Myself*) is an especially representative one. Mailer was first educated in several superficial ideological and intellectual types of discourse. Whatever there was of a Marxist conviction in his view at the beginning was qualified, both by the more obvious "metaphysical ambiguities" in critical fashion and by the dead-end naturalism of Dos Passos and Farrell. Mailer's war novel, *The Naked and the Dead* (1948), reflects these elements in balance. The intellectual Lieutenant Hearn has had all of them in some measure. The style and structure of the novel reveal them in an extremely interesting way, but the novel goes beyond them, pointing to the world the survivors among his characters must re-enter. It is an interesting point of departure for a look at the literature following World War II. We can discuss the direction taken by *The Naked and the Dead* in terms of three quotations, none of them from it but all quite relevant. The first is from Dos Passos' *1919*, the second novel of his *USA* trilogy,

Joe laid out a couple of frogs and was backing off towards the door, when he saw in the mirror that a big guy in a blouse was bringing down a bottle on his head held with both hands. He tried to swing but he didn't have time. The bottle crashed his skull and he was out.[14]

What strikes one immediately about this quite representative passage is its *automatic* quality. Like most of *USA*, it describes death as a fact in an inventory of facts, or a journalist's account of *faits divers*. The deliberate suppression of emotional values is a necessary 1930's tone; emotion came not from situations but from one's devotion to or puzzling over their ideological meaning.

The second quotation is Sartre's comment upon the first:

> We are inside with him, until the shock of the bottle on his skull. Then immediately, we find ourselves outside with the chorus, part of the collective memory, ". . . and he was out." Nothing gives you a clearer feeling of annihilation. And from then on, each page we turn, each page that tells of other minds and of a world going on without Joe, is like a spadeful of earth over our bodies. But it is a behind-the-looking-glass death; all we really get is the fine *appearance* of nothingness. True nothingness can neither be felt or thought. Neither you nor I, nor anyone after us, will ever have anything to say about our real deaths.[15]

Both this criticism and the passage it comments upon are directly related to Mailer's beginning, specifically to his war book. The lives of his soldiers are given in a contrived, "time-machine" assimilative style, which pushes ahead impersonally, through accumulations of fact. Emotional values are held to an absolute minimum. As in the narrative of the novel's present, there is no basis for stress upon the reader. Sartre introduces an additional feature, a statement about Dos Passos

[14] New York, Harcourt, Brace, 1932, p. 238.
[15] (1938), in *Literary and Philosophical Essays*, tr. Annette Michelson, London, Rider and Co., 1955, p. 96. Original in *Situations I*, Paris, Gallimard, 1947, p. 24.

that penetrates to a fact of enormous significance in much war fiction: that the experience of death is exclusively the privilege of the self who dies. Those who survive it, who may have deserved it, have a "clear feeling of annihilation," but they know about it only through a trick of reportage. Mailer's soldiers observe annihilation, fear it, and expect it; but none of them, except in the most superficial sense, has anything to say about their "real deaths."

The third passage is from the opening statement of Mailer's *Advertisements for Myself*. It is an appeal to passion as against impersonal annihilation, an expression of "rage at the cowardice of our time which has ground down all of us into the mediocre compromises of what had once been our light-filled passion to stand erect and be original."

> . . . So, yes, it may be time to say that the Republic is in real peril, and we are the cowards who must defend courage, sex, consciousness, the beauty of the body, the search for love, and the capture of what may be, after all, an heroic destiny.[16]

It is all here: the rage at the state of "The Republic," the retreat from the shock of annihilation, the recourse to "nihilism," the dependence upon minimal physical verities, which are not attached to a cause or a principle since these seem to have become inoperative. Courage, sex, consciousness, the beauty of the body, the search for love: these are minimal necessities of a passionate life, but they are not identified with any specific form of justification or objective. They are simply, nakedly there, to be rescued from annihilation, to be revalued without recourse to ideological strategy. The second and third of Mailer's novels have writers (of sorts) as their heroes; but the actual writer-hero is a man who finds it very difficult to write about anything except the difficulty itself. Hence the "heroic destiny" of the above passage is the only one of the values which is conditionally offered. Mailer is reduced to the

[16] New York, Putman's, 1959, pp. 23–24.

task of describing passion without a context, or at best within a context that is entirely misunderstood.

When Mailer becomes "philosophical," as he must, it is in terms of an unphilosophical situation: nondidactic, self-defensive, expansively hopeful, and frustratingly, repetitiously sentimental, or passionate. The dynamics of "courage, sex, consciousness, the beauty of the body" are all a part of a self-consuming passion; vigor seems to contain its own philosophical reward. The self is preserved through its relocation at "the center of the Universe." And, in that world of moral anarchy which Poe so elaborately defined in *Eureka* (1848), virtue may be judged as a strength of passion, the deed itself notwithstanding.

All of this is a consequence of the self's trying to recover from a devastating blow. When Mailer refers to the "Hipster" as the American existentialist, he seems to be making a basic distinction. He elaborately enumerates the existentialist circumstance peculiar to this version of him:

> It is on this bleak scene that a phenomenon has appeared: the American existentialist—the hipster, the man who knows that if our collective condition is to live with instant death by atomic war, relatively quick death by the State as *l'univers concentrationnaire*, or with a slow death by conformity with every creative and rebellious instinct stifled (at what damage to the mind and the heart and the liver and the nerves no research foundation for cancer will discover in a hurry), if the fate of twentieth-century man is to live with death from adolescence to premature, senescence, why then the only life-giving answer is to accept the terms of death, to live with death as immediate danger, to divorce oneself from society, to exist without roots, to set out on that uncharted journey into the rebellious imperatives of the self. . . .[17]

[17] "The White Negro," *Dissent*, summer 1957. Reprinted in *Advertisements for Myself*, p. 339. Other references to the printing in *Advertisements* are in the text.

This is a truly remarkable manifesto, of the thoroughly displaced ego. We should note its rhetoric, which echoes the twenties but lacks their levity, suggests the thirties but without doctrinal roots, and is above all a crystallization of a special type of uncompromising rebellion. It is a postwar, post-shock rebellion, which assumes that the annihilation of all values has already taken place. The unreality which Poe described so rationally has become the reality. The "imperatives of the self" are assumed in the face of a total absence of all feasible imperatives of an earlier kind. Finally, the stand is taken with respect both to death *and* to nothingness. The hipster not only accepts the negation of his own death; he will use the threat of death as a basic stimulant of his own passion; he will encourage death and violence, will both "murder and create."

Consider the nature of this hipster existentialist. He is a man of "go" and "swing," who will "make it" and is "with it." He does not wait for Godot, but is on the way to slitting his throat in a back alley.

> . . . In motion a man has a chance, his body is warm, his instincts are quick, and when the crisis comes, whether of love or violence, he can make it, he can win, he can release a little more energy for himself since he hates himself a little less, he can make a little better nervous system, make it a little more possible to go again, to go faster next time and so make more and thus find more people with whom he can swing. . . . (350)

These are the "dynamics" of passion, the rules for preserving action for its own sake. It is a condition of "grace," which in this most secular of all unenlightened worlds means depth of feeling, the sense of passionate self-confidence, the crucial belief in an inner and a muscular rhythm of violence sufficient to smash through a terrifying emptiness into a meaningful experience of action. To "be with it" means that you will be that much nearer to "that God which every hipster believes is located in the senses of his body, that trapped, mutilated, and nonetheless megalomaniacal God who is It, who is energy, life, sex . . . not the God of the churches but the unachievable whisper of mystery within the sex, the paradise of limitless energy and perception just beyond the next wave of the next orgasm" (351).

The ground of Mailer's assertion, as well as its tone, has changed, from an ideational ordering of fact to a situational "integrity." This is not so much a matter of "facing facts" as of "making them," of charging them with energy, of proving oneself in terms of the intensity of one's reaction. The two strongest expressions of this energy are murder and sex. Both involve a violent expression of the self in its relation to the other. Murder in the hipster context means an intense expression of hipster violence, to put against the toneless, spiritless, "efficient" violence which Mailer's favorite hero, Sergius O'Shaughnessy, remembers from his napalm raids over Japan. Sex is creation only in the sense of the vigor of the sexual act. The sex act is a means of making contact with the sex partner, establishing a center of physical strength, and thus justifying the self in defiance of death.

> . . . There was nothing very fleshy about the way she made love, no sense of the skin, nor smell, nor touch, just anger, anger at her being there, and another anger which was good for my own, that rage to achieve . . . just what, one cannot say . . . (489)

Mailer came from his war novel all but convinced that the war had destroyed his reliance on external assurances of truth and order. Nevertheless, he gave the world of the 1930's its "second chance." What follows is a test of ideology against passion. Michael Lovett, the hero of *Barbary Shore* (1951), breaks entirely from the past; he even has difficulty remembering any of it. He is left with his ambition to write a long book about the world as a huge sanitorium, or prison, and about the people confined within it. He does not succeed in writing the book, but the institution is there, in the rooming house he inhabits with an assortment of other postwar derelicts. His room is narrow, poorly lighted, disorderly, and dull: the window faces a wall. The door leads out into a hall, which connects with other halls and other rooms. Within this frame the shreds of ideological hope are once more and finally examined, and rejected.

The world, says one of Lovett's fellow-roomers, is now living in terms of the amoral standards of the concentration camp:

> "Listen to me. We never understood anything. There is a world, and this is what it is like: It is a tremendous prison, and sometimes the walls are opened and sometimes they are closed, but as time goes on they have to be closed more and more."

She goes on, to describe the life of the concentration camp: the guards "nerving" themselves with drink, offering the victims a false chance of survival, seeing them fall upon one another viciously and sadly, finally going to an undignified death as subhumans being swept out of the way.

> ". . . If there had been one who said, 'Let us die with dignity,' but they went choking into the gas with the blood of a friend in their mouth.
>
> . . . Do you understand? There are no solutions, there are only exceptions, and therefore we are without good and evil." [18]

As in all of Mailer's works, his characters suffer threats to their dignity and the danger affects their power to feel and give of themselves. The real challenge is in the sex act: to prove that one is not sterile and can assert himself is to defy the dehumanization of the "real world." O'Shaughnessy of *Deer*

[18] *Barbary Shore*, New York, Rinehart, 1951, pp. 212–13.

Park (1955) cannot enjoy sex, because of his war memory, of burning flesh. The reconstitution of the self awaits a deliberate change of heart; since neither Lovett nor O'Shaughnessy finds the situation that can lead to one, Mailer is left to observe the perversions of "the deer park." He is saying here that anyone will be sexually and physically—and, by implication, morally— as strong and healthy as the *milieu* permits. O'Shaughnessy turns away from the farcically perverse and dishonest world of Hollywood, and heads toward Manhattan and Greenwich Village. He is finished with the postwar world and will apparently attempt to reassert himself, through sex and violence, to find out if he can recapture his courage and "what may be, after all, an heroic destiny."

The world of these novels is heavy with intellectual pretense; yet the mood is honestly inspired. Criticism of the conventional life has a curious history in modern fiction. In the 1920's it was satirized for being dull and ludicrous. In the 1930's it was abused for being economically privileged and morally corruptible. The second war, as the first, served as proof of the ineffectiveness of its moral standards, which seemed destroyed in the general holocaust. The range of attitudes went from disdain to envy to contempt and anger. There were alternative ways of life. The *Bottom Dogs* journey novel of the 1930's described the drift of the economically underprivileged over the face of the land. Steinbeck's *The Grapes of Wrath* (1939) fought the class in power in the name of Emerson, Jefferson, and a homespun democratic faith. Many contemporary novels failed to express so strong a conviction. There is a development from *Bottom Dogs* to the Skid Row novel of manners, to the celebration of the man on the move or existing on the edges of privilege. The novel of the 1950's is far more preoccupied with the marginal self than any other. It has had two sources: the economic beatniks of the 1930's, and those who freely chose to stay "on the margin" after World War II.

Much of this is scarcely above the bohemianism of the

1920's. True marginality is not a pose, but a way of life, as well as the criticism of an alien way of life. The existentialist analysis of the self did not lead directly to first-rate American literature. But the existentialist manner, or what seemed to pass for it, is pervasive in recent American writing. The rare example of the comedy version of existentialist criticism, so brilliantly manifested in Beckett's *Waiting for Godot*, was successfully given also in Ralph Ellison's novel, *Invisible Man* (1952). Ellison's hero is a victim of many social accidents, but his worst disaster is the comical one of his earnest, un-witting desire to *be* what he is "supposed" or alleged to be. Having put on and cast off one after another of the selves the white world demands of him, he finally stumbles upon a proper and a successful disguise: invisibility. Since to be black in a white man's world is a condition demanding exhausting shifts and changes of manner, it is best that he become in-visible. The culminating irony is that he has been invisible all along, that he has never become himself at all. Again and again suggestions of his Negro selfhood come to him, fitfully and furtively, and he is at times at the edge of recognizing them. But the urge to "succeed," to win white friends and influence black people, gets in his way. *Invisible Man* is a re-markable comedy of the pitfalls of what Sartre called *mauvaise foi*.

—[v]—

Much of the literature since 1945 describes a self entirely cut off from a heroic center; he is a hero without cause, a man without meaningful relation, a truly marginal figure. He is represented in several ranges of hopeless passivity or angry, passionate, "essential" action. In *The White Negro*, Norman Mailer defines the polarities as hipster and beatnik, though these scarcely begin to suggest the variations of pathologic independence found in our recent literature. The activist

hipster has as many gradations of self-projection as the beat
has strategies of withdrawal.

Not usually regarded as belonging to these occasions of self-
analysis are the postwar Judaic examinations of conscience
and identity: the heroes of Bernard Malamud, Philip Roth,
Mailer, and many others testify to a new and a quite different
Jewish sensibility in postwar literature. The novel of Jewish
manners is a major phenomenon of post World War II.[19]
Saul Bellow's heroes are given to agonizing analyses of conscience: in *Henderson* (1959), comically anxious; in *The
Victim* (1947), earnestly disturbed over the specifics of guilt.
In *Seize the Day* (1956) the desire for self-identity results in
a mixture of comedy and pathos. The hero is a hard-luck guy,
a man of many mistakes, who rushes about madly from one
mistake to another and nervously and compulsively destroys
all basis of self-esteem.

> Ass! Idiot! Wild Boar! Dumb mule! Slave! Lousy, wal-
> lowing hippopotamus! Wilhelm called himself as his bend-
> ing legs carried him from the dining room. His pride! His
> inflamed feelings! His begging and feebleness! And trading
> insults with his poor old father—and spreading confusion
> over everything. Oh, how poor, contemptible, and ridicu-
> lous he was! . . .[20]

In the end, after an exhausting and a disastrous day, he blun-
ders into a funeral parlor, begins to sob bitterly for death, the
guilt of the death wish, and for the death of himself as a self-
respecting human being.

The extreme forms of marginal selfhood are often a vicious
criticism of the center. The notorious *Howl* of Allen Ginsberg
turns to its account the semi-affirmative line of Walt Whitman,
to protect the decline of the American promise Whitman had
once celebrated:

[19] See Appendix 1 of the third American edition of my book, *The Modern
Novel in America*, Chicago, Regnery, 1964.

[20] New York, Viking, 1956, p. 55.

I saw the best minds of my generation
　　destroyed by madness, starving
　　hysterical naked,
dragging themselves through
　　the negro streets at dawn
　　looking for an angry fix,
angelheaded hipsters burning for the ancient heavenly
　　connection to the starry dynamo in
　　the machinery of night [21]

. . .

There is a dual motive for much of the literature in the beatnik name: to defy the convention and thus criticize its pundits and standard-bearers; and to explore the widest range of difference from the rational, the logical practices of the mind. These objectives are in the tradition of Rimbaud, and the results are occasionally Rimbaldian in tone and effect:

Je m'habituai à l'hallucination simple: je voyais très franchement une mosquée à la place d'une usine, une école de tambours faite par des anges, des calèches sur les routes du ciel, un salon au fond d'un lac; les monstres, les mystères; un titre de vaudeville dressait des épouvantes devant moi.[22]

The "hallucinations" of William Burroughs (*Naked Lunch*, 1959) are less plain; or, rather, they are more violently direct and hostile. Compared with them, Jack Kerouac's literary wanderings in the subterranean world are almost lyrical affirmations. Here, for example, are the mystic vibrations of bop ecstasy, as Kerouac sees them:

[21] San Francisco, City Lights, 1956, p. 9.
[22] "I accustomed myself to plain hallucination: I saw quite plainly a mosque where a factory stood, a group of drums played by angels, open carriages on the sky's boulevards, a drawing-room at the bottom of a lake; monsters, mysteries; the title of a vaudeville song raised horrors before me."—Tr. Delmore Schwartz, from "Deliriums, II: Alchemy of the Word," in *A Season in Hell*, Norfolk, Conn, New Directions, 1939, pp. 66–67.

486

... and she stood in drowsy sun suddenly listening to bop as if for the first time as it poured out, the intention of the musicians and of the horns and instruments suddenly a mystical unity expressing itself in waves like sinister and again electricity but screaming with palpable aliveness the direct *word* from the vibration . . .[23]

Burroughs presents a world created by an addict's mind, a "fix world," as angry as Ginsberg described it and as violently distorted as the full pressure of a state of intense hatred can make it. *Naked Lunch* is based upon the assumption of an "ecstasy of the hallucinated word"; the word is the Logos brought down, not to earth but to unconscious caverns beneath its surface. The real attack is directed against the superego, a violent effort to turn the Freudian world upside down.

The Word is divided into units which be all in one piece and should be so taken, but the pieces can be had in any order being tied up back and forth in and out fore and aft like an innaresting sex arrangement. . . .[24]

The word can be rearranged as you wish, but, "Gentle Reader," it will also "leap on you like a leopard man with iron claws, it will cut off fingers and toes like a land crab, it will hang you catching your jissom like a scrutable dog . . ." (230). The destructive anger of the word is seen at work here especially upon the death of the American promise. The bars

---

[23] *The Subterraneans*, New York, Grove, 1958, p. 34.

[24] *Naked Lunch*, New York, Grove, 1962, p. 229. Other references to this edition are in the text. Ten episodes from *Naked Lunch* were published in *Big Table*, No. 1 (spring 1959), pp. 79–137. Of great importance is the statement from Lionel Abel's review of Burrough's novel: *Naked Lunch* is like two kinds of film, Abel says: ". . . it is rather like those pornographic films that give dispirited people a dull pleasure. It is also like . . . the documentaries, shown after the war, of Nazi concentration camp atrocities. . . . His scenes of linked, unlovely bodies bitten, beaten, and mangled, bodies in the process of destroying other bodies and of being destroyed by them, with sex, of some horrible form, going on all the while. . . ." See *Partisan Review*, 30 (spring 1963), p. 109.

of East Saint Louis turn toward what was once the frontier but is now a line of Skid Rows and desert lands.

> . . . Illinois and Missouri, miasma of mound-building peoples, groveling worship of the Food Source, cruel and ugly festivals, dead-end horror of the Centipede God reaches from Moundville to the lunar deserts of coastal Peru.
>
> . . .
>
> And always cops: smooth college-trained state cops, practiced, apologetic patter, electronic eyes weigh your car and luggage, clothes and face; snarling big city dicks, soft-spoken country sheriffs with something black and menacing in old eyes color of a faded grey flannel shirt . . . (11–12)

To offset these, to get relief "from the whole life process," there is the fix, which throws the order of things into a new perspective, furthermore sharpens the taste for rebellion. This is a revolutionary based entirely on contempt and black bile, truly a grudge fight, the urge to dirty the white short and to toss the oil portrait into the ashcan. "Rock and Roll adolescent hoodlums storm the streets of all the nations," in this bop commune. "They rush into the Louvre and throw acid in Mona Lisa's face. They open zoos, insane asylums, prisons, burst water mains with air hammers, chop the floor out of passenger plane lavatories, shoot out lighthouses . . ." (44) and much more. Burroughs' exploration of the American self is consistently hostile, contemptuous, forcefully hateful. He is neither searching for a range of experience to replace the one blasted by the war, nor investigating the boundaries of consciousness in death. His is entirely a destructive expression, without joy in destruction or anxiety over the search for an alternative. Here there is no desire to defend Mailer's "verities": courage, sex, consciousness, the beauty of the body, the search for love.

—[vi]—

It is a far cry from Emerson's version of an ever-expanding horizon opening to the sight, or from the dread of nothingness experienced by Kierkegaard at the moment of skepticism of God and eternity. The self is no longer recognizable in it. Yet Burroughs' visions of the "revolt of the id" are an end-result of the insistent urge to re-examine the self in its relation to the world it is forced to inhabit. In this case the world inspires sheer hatred, an absolute refusal to temporize; but it is a willing and willed self, not inert or "determined" or prefabricated in any way.

The essential reactions of the self to the phenomena of modern death have been resourcefully and vigorously assertive. In every case they have at least begun with a rejection of all extra-experiential assurances of immortality, preferring to recapture, on individual terms, the rapprochement with eternity. The crucial event in existentialist revisionism is the attempt to establish a perspective of self "on its own"; that is, to meet experience in an improvisatory manner, and to go on from the declaration of Sartre's Roquentin, "I exist," to a gradual improvisation of needed continuity.

The first necessity posed by this rejection of doctrinal religious sustenance is that of adjusting to the world's absurdity, made all the more uncertain and hazardous by the prospect of annihilation. In some literature (Moravia's A Woman of Rome, 1949, for example), the recognition leads merely to cynicism or to mock-heroic efforts to assert vitality. The more widely accepted practice is to show the "absurd man" living very close to the grounds of absurdity, creatively adapting an irrational circumstance to the necessities of self-continuance.

A survey of twentieth century variants of self-definition must begin with the Sartrean ego as the minimal center of existence. In its limitation, it cannot speculatively project into essences;

nor can it morally consider itself as a sounding board of God's will. At least three principal lines of descent in the modern view of the self come to mind: the line of Sartre's influence, that of Camus' mediation of the absurd, and that of religious-secular meditation starting from Dostoevsky's *Notes from Underground* and his *The Idiot*. In the case of the first, we have the most precise, the most dispassionate, the most severely geometrical and spatial representations. It is the literature of existentialist manners, as circumspect in its own way as the manners of Jane Austen's world. The observations of Nathalie Sarraute, Alain Robbe-Grillet, and Michel Butor are colloquies, arrangements, measurements of the self's adventures and its self-deceptions. Not one of them is like Sartre's *Nausea*, which has a sense of the dramatic, an inheritance from more traditionally romantic literature. Roquentin is a romantic in the manner of Julien Sorel, but without Stendhal's historical setting.

Camus' progress from the absurd to a mitigable situation eventually leads to the suggestion of revolt as a mixture of forbearance and integrity. As the world becomes more savage, the hero becomes less so, until his great virtue appears to be his recognition of the contradictions of the world, his holding to a line of self-respecting function, his sense both of hidden verities and of obvious moral polarities. His is the "humanist self," if that phrase means anything; more precisely, perhaps, the "secular hero." As such, he belongs in the tradition of Malraux's Kyo and of the heroes of *L'Espoir*: of Silone's Don Paolo Spada (Pietro Spina) and of the dedicated hero of *The Secret of Luca*, who abandons his career for the sake of rescuing a man on grounds of absolute devotion to integrity; finally of Faulkner's "knights of the verities," who spend their lives tolerating men's follies, helping occasionally to commit them, but fundamentally testifying to an assumed hard core of human reliability and endurance. What we may rescue from the turgid involutions of *A Fable* seems to say of the Christ story substantially what Camus has said of it in *The Rebel:* that Christ's suffering and death ought to testify, not to a denial of Christian values, but to the need to consider them as secular, man-made values and an indispensable support of humanist self-confidence. This attempt to show Camus in the light of his proper associations brings him far beyond the Sartrean existentialist minima, to the point that any suggestion of resemblance is trivial and may even be quite impossible to support.

The line of descent from Dostoevsky actually has two major divisions: the introspective and speculative, on the one hand; and the apocalyptic, holistic, on the other. Whatever there is of irrational meditation in the underground man and in his successors belongs to the first. It declines toward the minutiae of inner debate in Kafka regarding moral status, and toward the exhaustive and feverishly conscientious measuring and surveying of self-relation in Beckett. The other line brings us within the tradition of Rimbaud and the surrealists, an effort to reconstitute the self by means of "un long, immense et raisonné dérèglement de tous les sens." Since much of the literature which appears in this tradition is invested with a passion of expression quite alien to Rimbaud's "raisonné dérèglement," one will have to say that it is not so much Rimbaldian as Laurentian: that is, that it places the value of self-survival upon an intensity of passionate experience, a thoroughly secularized evangelicalism, the religious energies going into the effort to achieve secular consummations. The persons whom Henry Miller admires, for example, are strangers to convention primarily in exercising passion more vigorously than conventional decorum allows. They, and Miller himself, protect the individual against depersonalizing influences by asserting him beyond and beneath conventional strategy and "good reason." Though Lawrence would have thought him a fool, Jack Kerouac is essentially a Laurentian as well; he has acquired excess baggage, it is true, and his spiritual maladroitness is a weakness Lawrence might have deplored, but he has and tries to communicate ecstasies of passion that can only be said to belong somewhere in an area inhabited both by Lawrence and the *Bottom Dogs* world of the 1930's he so reluctantly approved.

To return for one final time to the Sartrean ego-center: there is no doubt that Sartre put a minimal value upon its power to react to the world of the *en-soi*; the "tragic finale" of Sartre's ontology comes mostly from the pressure put upon the self by the non-self: that is to say, the other, groups of the other, and pressures upon the self to abnegate its dreadful responsibility. In its minimally literal sense, Sartre's *pour-soi* can be possessed of no real passion save that of fear of its own threat of annihilation. Otherwise, its approach to the opportunities for passion are cut down into small, analysable instants of observation and decision. "Only the French," said one of the coolest of American existentialist cats, "alienated beyond alienation from their unconscious could welcome an existential philosophy without ever feeling it at all. . . ." [25] In effect, Sartre's analysis of the self is engaged primarily with his consciousness; the source of this is not a French disdain of the unconscious, but a German (Heidegger's) passion for epistemological certitudes and finitudes. Beyond the discrete limits of the insubstantial, experience-burdened self, passion has to be intuited, strengthened through glandular hypotherapy, and nourished steadily by provocations offered by the static world of the other.

The hipster attacks upon these limits of self-analysis are also directed against Freudian discretions. Both psychoanalysis and phenomenology are rationalistic disciplines. Passionate depths of experience are not achieved through scrupulous attention to the ego's standing guard over the id's drives. To paraphrase a famous Freudian assertion, the hipster would have said,

[25] Norman Mailer, "The White Negro," in *Advertisements for Myself*, p. 341.

CONCLUSION

"Where superego was, there shall id be." This is in line with, though it is a considerable elaboration upon, Lawrence's engagements with Freud over the position and function of the unconscious, his efforts to rescue the id from the severely cautious and avuncular indictment of its evil and undisciplined drive for pleasure. The issue is clearly drawn, and not without some savage hostility. Freud, in the image they have of him, strikes the hipster existentialists as a guardian of conservative familial and social impositions upon passion. Passion is indispensably linked with an intensity of experience which is necessary to the new "counter-affirmation" of the personal value against impersonal constrictions.

The vicissitudes of modern self-projection describe some such curve of variants as these. One characteristic subtends all divisions and qualifications of the existentialist self. Wherever it is located: in conscious process, in the unconscious, in the experience of temporary loss of a transcending faith, the self is in this view of it the beginning, the source, and the responsible center of all revaluations of life and of the death that superintends and haunts it.

INDEX

498